Mel Bay Presents the Merle Travis GUITAR STYLE

by Tommy Flint

CD CONTENTS

1. Introduction (Explanation of Style) [2:11]
2. The Travis Rhythm in Tablature [:16]
3. Adding the Melody [:33]
4. Take It Away [:29]
5. Go Tell Aunt Rhody [:31]
6. Travis Licks in Syncopation — Lick #1 [:20]
7. Travis Licks in Syncopation — Lick #2 [:16]
8. Travis Licks in Syncopation — Lick #3 [:18]
9. Maggie [:59]
10. Going Down the Road Feeling Bad [:50]
11. The Guitar Blues [:49]
12. The Three Finger Roll [:30]
13. My Old Kentucky Home [1:23]
14. Bicycle Built for Two [1:50]
15. Instruction [:20]
16. Saturday's Song [1:09]
17. Kelly's Blues [1:02]
18. Drakesboro Coal Drag [:49]
19. Honeysuckle Sweet [:54]
20. Green River Blues [1:11]
21. My Memory of Merle [:45]
22. Walkin' in Beech Creek [:46]
23. Pickin' Like Amos [:51]
24. Bluebell #1 [1:55]
25. Bluebell #2 [2:24]
26. Bugle Call Rag [2:54]
27. Cuddle Up A Little Closer [2:53]
28. I'm Thinking Tonight of My Blue Eyes [1:22]
29. Way Down Yonder in New Orleans [2:30]
30. Bar B Q Rag [2:04]
31. You Tell Me Your Dreams, I'll Tell You Mine [2:18]
32. Memphis Blues [3:06]
33. Merle's Buck Dance [1:57]
34. Dance of the Goldenrod (Instrumental Version) [2:03]
35. Dance of the Goldenrod (Vocal Version) [2:52]

CONTENTS

FOREWORD

It is an undisputed fact that the Merle Travis style of guitar playing is the most copied guitar style in the world today. Techniques from this style are used constantly in every form of music from blues to folk and onward from jazz to rock.

The style was born in the rural coal mining area around Muhlenberg county Kentucky. As it began to go through its metamorphosis, the youthful Merle Travis eventually took it to the road, radio, and on to the recording studios of Hollywood. This is where the world started to hear this new and exciting sound. Over the years it has gone through a number of incarnations, but many believe that the original "'Travis style" is by far the most exciting. What made Merle Travis so different? Was it his special array of chords, many of which were totally unique, or was it that ever present "driving thumb" that Travis possessed? The best way to find the answer to something is by going directly to the source and asking questions. With this in mind, let's look into another young guitarist from Muhlenberg county.

In the late 40's and into the early 50's, one young aspiring guitar player who was inspired heavily by their "hometown star" was Tommy Flint. He had heard his mother talk of Travis and he listened to his music intensely. He also spent countless hours at Mose Rager's barber shop where guitar music and stories of Merle Travis flowed as freely as the hair tonic. Tommy finally met Merle in 1952 and their association began.

Tommy spent the next twenty years of his life refining his guitar playing skills and taking it to the stages of everything from clubs to the Grand Ole Opry, and playing behind everyone from Roger Miller to Sonny and Cher. In the early 70's he began writing instructional guitar books for Mel Bay publications. This is when he got the idea to write an instructional book on the "Travis style." He contacted his friend, Merle Travis, and they began. In the original book, Travis wrote all the chord diagrams, used his hands for pictures and explained his techniques as Flint put them in order and print. To my knowledge, this was the only instructional book Merle ever authorized and signed a contract on. Now, some twenty years later, this great teaching aide has been resurrected with more explanations, songs, techniques, stories and personal family photographs.

Worldwide, the "Travis style" is more popular now than ever before and the quest for knowledge regarding how to do it, is even greater. All you need to play my father's style is a guitar and inspiration. The lessons are on the following pages.

Happy Pickin",

Thom Bresh

I could not have completed this book without the help of Merle Travis' children, Pat Travis-Eatherly, Thom Bresh, Merlene Travis and Cindy Travis. Thank you very much!

Tommy Flint

BIOGRAPHY

Merle Travis was one of the greatest and most influential guitarists the world has ever known and is a very important figure in the history of American music.

The name Merle Travis, his songs and guitar style (thumbstyle), are well known and emulated throughout much of the world. The "Travis style" can be heard from Finland to the British Isles and France to South Africa.

His music is timeless, it transcends generations, styles and fads. It encompasses many types of music from hillbilly, western and folk to pop standards, jazz, dixieland, boogie-woogie, cajun, honky tonk and country.

Travis was a prolific songwriter and his songs are still being recorded by many of today's young artists and brightest stars. "Smoke, Smoke, Smoke That Cigarette" written for Tex Williams was the first million seller for the new (at that time) Capitol Records company. His "Sixteen Tons" which was recorded by "Tennessee" Ernie Ford was the first record to sell a million copies in thirty days.

Merle was a pioneer in the truest sense of the word. He was an extremely creative musician, an inventor, a designer, an innovator, a trail blazer, ahead of his time in many ways. He was one of the first to use the electric guitar. He designed the first thin, solid body guitar with all the keys on one side, which P.A. Bigsby built for him. This was the forerunner of the Fender guitar. It was in no way like Les Paul's "log," which was basically a four by four piece of wood with pickups and a neck, with guitar sides attached to the block of wood. This famous Bigsby guitar is in the Country Music Hall of Fame Museum in Nashville, alongside the well known Gibson, Super 400 that has Travis' name inlaid in the fingerboard.

Merle also designed the vibrato that Bigsby also built for him, which became the famous Bigsby vibrato. Travis' son, Thom Bresh has this first Bigsby vibrato ever built, on which Mr. Bigsby used a valve spring from a Harley Davidson motorcycle. It's on a Super 400 guitar that Travis gave Bresh several years ago.

Merle was in at least thirty-six western movies with Charles Starett, Smiley Burnette, and various other actors. He performed in the award winning film "From Here To Eternity" with Burt Lancaster, Deborah Kerr, Montgomery Cliff, Donna Reed, Frank Sinatra, and Ernest Borgnine.

The name Merle Travis is in the Country Music Hall of Fame, the Songwriters Hall of Fame and the Gibson Guitar Hall of Fame. His name and songs are in the Smithsonian Institution, where he performed several years ago.

Merle Travis was many things — guitarist, singer, songwriter, cartoonist, designer, composer, writer, raconteur and historian of sorts. Most of all, he was a wonderful human being, who gave hours, months, and years of happiness to many, many people.

THE TRAVIS STYLES

I was always fascinated by a photo of Travis playing his Gibson L-10 guitar, fitted with a DeArmond pickup, that hung on the wall in Mose Rager's barbershop. Merle had autographed it and written, "No matter how great my success, I owe it all to you, old pal, for showing me all I know about a guitar." Travis said he learned to play the guitar by following Mose and Ike Everly around and watching and listening to them and memorizing the chords they used.

He had learned from them but he did not sound like them. Merle developed his own style. Each man had his own distinct touch, feel and sound. The styles of Rager and Travis were similar, but different. They fingered chords differently (although both used their thumbs) and sometimes used different chords in the same tune.

Mose frequently used barre chords. The first chord I saw him play was a B♭6 barre chord in the sixth position when he played "Tiger Rag." Merle almost never used barre chords, although I have seen photos of him making barres when he was a young man.

When Mose played rhythm and lead simultaneously, he often picked the ⑥th and ⑤th strings together with his thumb on all four beats. Merle did this sometimes on certain tunes, such as parts of "Memphis Blues," but more often he picked the ⑥th, or ⑤th string with his thumb on the first and third beats and then again, using his thumb, in one stroke, brushed over the ④th, ③rd and sometimes the ②nd strings, on the second and fourth beats.

While his thumb played the bass notes and rhythm, as described, his index finger played a (usually) syncopated melody and improvised on the ①st, ②nd and ③rd strings. He occasionally played a melody note on the ④th string with his finger.

He used the index finger most of the time, however, he did sometimes use the middle finger. We were talking backstage once when he mentioned that he had a nick in his middle fingernail. He said, "I guess the Good Lord just doesn't want me to play 'Blue Smoke' anymore, my fingernail just won't grow out right."

When we were writing the original Travis Style book, he told me that he sometimes did a thumb and three finger roll, p, i, m, a, on the bass, ③rd, ②nd and ①st strings. I never saw him use this in a solo.

Contrary to what has been written in some articles and sometimes taught in Travis Style workshops, Merle did sometimes use alternate bass notes. "Cannonball Rag" is a good example. He usually began with the E7 chord in the fifth position. He depressed the ⑥th string at the seventh fret (B) with his thumb and played the bass note. Then, after the rhythm stroke, he raised his thumb and picked the ⑥th string open (E). He changed to the A chord in the fifth position with his thumb on the ⑥th string, fifth fret (A). He then played the rhythm and raised his thumb and picked the ⑥th string open (E).

When he sang with only his guitar for accompaniment, he very often used moving bass lines. It was much like a bass player playing a walking bass line along with a sock rhythm guitarist. Or, like a bass and snare drum.

When Travis played the melody, bass and rhythm simultaneously, he muffled the bass strings by resting the heel of his hand on them near the bridge. This creates more drive, more punch, much like a snare drum. Sometimes the ④th and ③rd strings were muffled on the rhythm beats. While the index finger was playing melody, the other three fingers rested on the pick guard.

When Merle played two or three parts simultaneously, the parts were distinct and clearly separated. It sounded like two guitars playing a duet. This could be heard more clearly on the L-10 with the DeArmond pickup or the D-28 that he used on some transcriptions and recordings in the 1940's. It was easy to hear on the Bigsby also.

He sometimes played two or three string harmony using thirds, sixths, and tenth intervals. This can be clearly heard on the "Strictly Guitar" and "The Merle Travis Guitar" albums. When he played single string melody, he usually plucked the string in the area between the thirteenth and eighteenth frets. Merle seldom played anything the same way twice. He improvised much of the time, using substitute chords, different licks and sometimes completely different ideas. So consequently, his music was fresh and alive.

Travis' music was not academic, but authentic, natural and spontaneous. It just happened. When he played his guitar, his soul just poured out through his fingers. When he felt great, he played great; he was awesome. When he was tired, depressed or sick, he played only slightly less great. His feelings were always in the music.

Travis' sound changed over the years as he changed instruments and came in contact with more musicians and styles. This is a natural process that occurs in everyone's life.

The great Travis sound has never been duplicated, which is as it should be. I feel that music, just like speech, is communication and comes from the heart. However, there are some great pickers around such as Eddie Pennington, Bob Saxton and Tom Owens who can sound very much like Merle.

Travis' son, Thom Bresh, when he wishes to, can play more like Merle than anyone I have heard. He has the soul. He does an impression of his father that sounds exactly as he did in his later years. The only time he does Travis songs and plays like him is during a short portion of his show which is a tribute to his father. Bresh is his own man, very creative and very original. He is an awesome talent in his own right. A guitarist, singer, songwriter, record producer, impressionist, communicator and one of the world's greatest entertainers.

The Next Generation.

CONVERSATIONS, OBSERVATIONS AND INSIGHTS

From an early age, I heard my mother, who was a guitarist, talk about Merle Travis and his mentor Mose Rager. She told me that before I was born, Mose and another guitar player, George Mauzey would visit her and dad and stay all day and play her guitar, because neither man owned a guitar at that time. She said they would stay for supper and she usually served pinto beans, corn bread and green onions, so I'm sure Mose and George enjoyed the food as much as mom and dad enjoyed the music.

She recalled hearing Travis on a radio show that was broadcast from a showboat that traveled the Ohio river, stopping at different cities to broadcast the performances. She said he was billed as, "The man with a thousand fingers."

Sometime when I was very young, she had sold or given her guitar away, so her reflections and accounts of these things never meant a great deal to me until some years later, when I became interested in the guitar.

When I was around thirteen years old, my father bought a little Wurlitzer guitar from the local barber. I had learned a few chords and could pick out some single string melodies, when one day I turned the radio on and heard this wonderful guitar music. When the music ended, the announcer said, "That was Merle Travis and his guitar." I couldn't believe it was one guitar, it sounded like at least like two or three. I was hooked! I fell in love with the guitar. The most important thing in my young life, as far as I was concerned at that time, was playing the guitar and learning more about it.

Every day and night I would listen to the radio in hopes of hearing Merle Travis. I learned that Mose Rager now lived in Drakesboro, so I went there to see him. I saw the style that Travis had learned from him, playing the bass and rhythm with his thumb, while simultaneously playing the melody and improvising with his index finger. I asked him to tell me about Travis, what he was like, what songs did he play, what kind of guitar, or anything he could tell me.

Travis became my boyhood hero, I idolized him. He became a very important influence in my life. I was delighted to learn from my Grandmother Travis that Merle and I were second cousins. She told me, "We used to visit Uncle Rob and his family when they lived in Rosewood. Merle has a sister Vada and two brothers Melvin and Taylor.

I heard on the radio that Merle would be a guest on the Grand Ole Opry so I talked a friend into driving me to Nashville. We went to the stage door of the Ryman Auditorium which was across the alley from the back door of Tootsie's Orchid Lounge. Getting in was no problem because the guard hadn't arrived yet. I walked in and saw Chet Atkins, Merle and his brother John Melvin. I had met Chet a year or two earlier so, when he saw me he said, "Hey, come in here, I want you to meet somebody," and introduced me to Travis. I was not disappointed, he was very kind to this aspiring, teenage guitarist. He gave me a photo which he had autographed and had written, "To my kinfolk, ol' Tom."

When I bragged on his guitar playing, he said, "Oh no, the world's greatest is standing in there," as he pointed to Chet who was holding his guitar in the dressing room.

I remember that he used some quaint expressions. When he plugged his guitar into a little practice amp to tune, he strummed a chord and said, "That sounds like pouring walnuts in a tub." When he mentioned that he had played Oswego, Kansas the night before, someone asked him where it was located in Kansas. He said, "Everybody knows where Oswego is."

I had recently seen his photo in a magazine in which he was playing his Bigsby guitar, so I was surprised to see he was now playing a Super 400. At that time, I couldn't imagine anyone owning more than one guitar, so I said, "Merle, I thought you had a Bigsby guitar." He answered, "Oh I do, but I have this one too."

When I was a teenager, I seemed to have a photographic memory about guitars, guitar players and especially Merle Travis. I even remember that Travis was wearing grey pants, a white shirt, a green tie, and fancy western boots. That was before he changed into a fancy, blue, Nudie suit to go on stage.

After that first meeting, I always tried to get with Merle anytime we were in the same part of the country. Each time, I learned a new lick, an unusual chord, or enjoyed some great stories.

I later learned that I was not the only one who idolized Travis. He was an impressive figure, six feet tall with shiny, coal black hair, large white teeth and he seemed to always smile while talking with someone. He seemed to have an aura, or magnetism about him that attracted people. When he entered a roomful of people at a party, or such, everyone seemed to know it almost immediately. They stopped talking and looked toward him, or began gravitating toward him. Everyone wanted to talk with him or shake his hand.

Travis had an outgoing personality. He truly loved people. He saw the good things in people and he never hesitated in pointing that out to them. People enjoyed being with him because they felt better about themselves. They felt worthwhile.

It seemed to me that he could fit in and feel at ease anywhere, from the company house homes of his miner friends, to the governor's mansion, the White House and palaces of kings and queens. You can imagine my amazement when I learned that Travis suffered from stage fright. He sometimes felt sick before going on stage. However, that was not apparent to the audience. He was the complete entertainer. Once when announcing his song "Paradise," (That Spells Kentucky, But It Means Paradise) to the audience he said, "This is not much of a song, but it's easier than spelling Massachusetts."

Also, when Merle and his wife Dorothy were guests of the president and first lady, Trav's large Zuni thunderbird bolo tie was somehow removed from his gear and he never saw it again.

Merle told another interesting story of when he and Dorothy were at the Governor's Banquet in Kentucky, the same year Henry Kissinger was there. The governor asked Travis if he could help him in any way, or do anything for him. Merle said, "My brother John has always wished he could be a Kentucky Colonel, but thinks that will never happen." It wasn't long until John received the colonel commission and he was elated.

Travis was quite a raconteur and I never grew tired of his stories of Hollywood, the early days of television and Capitol Records, the road and guitar players we both knew in Kentucky.

One story I found quite interesting was about the filming of the Walt Disney movie "Melody Time" in which the Sons Of The Pioneers sang about the legendary Pecos Bill. The director called Merle and asked him to bring his guitar to the studio and put some music on the sound track. When he got to the studio the director said, "There's a scene where a tornado is crossing the plains and I want you to play something like a tornado." Trav said, "I didn't know how to play like a tornado. I just played some chords lightening fast, in a minor key." It was strictly improvised on the spur of the moment, and there was only one take. He gave an example of something like he did.

Some of the short pieces on the "Walking the Strings" album were also improvised. They were recorded to be used for station breaks for radio stations. The A&R person would tell Travis to play for thirty seconds or forty-five seconds. Merle had no idea what would come out until he began playing.

I couldn't remember the title, "Melody Time" until I called Dale Warren who is trail boss of the Sons Of The Pioneers to refresh my memory. He told me an interesting story about how Merle recorded the version of "I'll See You In My Dreams" that came out on a single in the early fifties, the one that received so much air play. Dale said, "In the studio I sat on the floor, right in front of Merle while he played and I moved the vibrato handle just enough to give the amount of vibrato he wanted."

Speaking of movies brings to mind the story of how Travis was hired to play the part of Sal Anderson in the film "From Here To Eternity." His manager at the time, Bobbie Bennett, told him she had arranged for an interview with Mr. Cohen, owner of Columbia Studios. The next day Merle went with director Fred Zimmerman to Mr. Cohen's office where he was getting a shave. Cohen said, "Fred, do you think he would be good for the part?" Fred answered in the affirmative. Cohen said, "Okay, he's got it. Now get him out of here. Get him out of here." Merle thought it was funny. Travis used his Martin-body Bigsby-neck guitar when he sang "Re-Enlistment Blues" in the movie, so he had to remove his name from the pick guard. I don't believe it was ever replaced.

There is another story of Merle playing the guitar for Tex Ritter when Ritter sang "High Noon" on the sound track from the movie of the same title, which starred Gary Cooper and Grace Kelly. He accompanied Tex on the theme song by tapping the strings with a pencil, instead of picking them. (I had learned how to do this from my mother many years ago, but had forgotten all about it until Merle told this story.)

Travis thought very highly of Tex Ritter and enjoyed touring with him and playing concerts together. One story is of when they were on the same bill at a Houston nightclub. They had a very nice crowd that night and after packing up the instruments, went to the office to get paid. The owner, who Merle said reminded him of an old time mobster, said the crowd had been small and he couldn't pay them the fee they had agreed on. Tex was very good at estimating the size of crowds and knew this was not true. The conversation became heated and Tex gave him a "cussin' out" or "Texas tongue lashing." Merle said he almost froze when the guy reached inside his coat toward his breast pocket.

Travis said "I thought for sure he was reaching for a gun, but instead he pulled out a wad of money and paid us the full amount of the contract." That man was JACK RUBY.

While on the subject of altercations, fisticuffs and such, this story was told by a fellow who was in the same band as Travis in the early days. They were playing for a dance, and a young lady who was on the dance floor with her boyfriend or husband, kept flirting with Travis when they danced near the stage. Merle may have reciprocated, but whatever the case may have been, the fellow was thoroughly agitated by the end of the night. While the musicians were packing up, this guy walked up to the stage and invited Merle to step outside and fight. Travis tried to calm him, but he insisted on fighting. The band member noticed that while Merle was talking and smiling, trying to soothe the guy, he was also wrapping his handkerchief around his hand. Suddenly, with one blow, he flattened the angry guy. End of altercation.

Travis was in several short films, Snader Telescriptions and R.C.M. Soundies in the 1940's and early days of television. Once I picked up a couple of booklets published by the Gibson Guitar Company, that contained photos of Gibson Hall of Fame members. A very young Merle Travis playing his L-10 was on the cover and inside was another photo of him with an all woman band.

That weekend he was appearing at Bill Monroe's country music park in Bean Blossom, Indiana, so I took one of the booklets to give to him. He began telling me when and where the photo was made, etc. One lady was Carolina Cotton, who sang with him on the Soundie. The other women were not actually playing, or were not recorded. He said the music on the sound track (other than himself) was by Joaquin Murphy and members of Spade Cooley's band.

I think it must have been 1983 (the last time I saw Travis) that I was at the Ozark Folk Center in Mountain View, Arkansas for the "Tribute to Merle Travis" weekend. Merle and Dorothy were going to the small auditorium to watch a private showing of some western movies featuring some of their friends, as well as Travis himself. They invited me to go with them and it turned out to be a great afternoon. Merle would say to the projectionist, "Will you run that back just a little?" Then he would tell us how the scene was set up, how the actor did the part and all the details.

They showed Travis and his former wife, the lovely Judy Hayden, singing "Too Much Sugar For A Dime." He was playing a Bigsby guitar that looked to be a hollow body, about the size of a Gibson ES-175. I mentioned that I had not seen that guitar before. He said it belonged to Hank Garland and he had used it for that song. I have no idea why. I have not seen that guitar again or another one like it.

Merle was quite adept at sound effects, using only his voice and mouth. When Kay Starr recorded "Wabash Cannonball," a train song, the producer called him to play guitar on the session. While he was there he also did the train whistle, like an old steam locomotive. He made the sound of the cracking whip on "Tennessee" Ernie's recording of "Mule Train."

Travis was an extremely creative human being. As you know, he designed the thin, solid body guitar with all the keys on the same side. He said he got the idea from Joaquin Murphy's steel guitar, which was a board with pickups and strings. He thought, "If that works for a steel, I don't see why it wouldn't work for a guitar." It did.

He usually sat and laid the guitar on his lap to change strings. He noticed how easy it was to loosen the bass strings on the side next to him, and how difficult it was to reach to the other side. So he asked Mr. Bigsby to make his guitar with all the keys on that particular side. Of course, Travis designed the style and shape of the head. Today, most electric guitars are thin, solid bodies with all the keys on one side. Merle said he was in a music store in Oklahoma (I believe it was Tulsa), and some early teenagers were looking at guitars. He asked them if they liked the solid body. They answered, "Oh, sure." He then asked if they liked all the keys on the same side. They said, "Yes, that's great." He then told them he designed the guitar years ago. He said they gave him some quizzical looks and later when they thought he couldn't hear, one of them exclaimed, "That old guy is crazy. He thinks he designed this guitar."

When Leo Fender said in a Rolling Stone article that he got the idea for his guitar from Travis, Merle was so excited that he called Thom Bresh at three a.m. and told him to get up and go to the newsstand and get a copy and read about it.

Travis had been using a Rickenbacker vibrola which was notorious for causing the strings to go out of tune (although it was the best thing at the time). He got the idea for an attachment that would raise or lower pitch of the strings, but would allow them to return to the correct pitch. He asked Mr. Bigsby if he could build it for him. Being a confident man, Bigsby answered, "Hell yes, I can build anything." A few days later he showed up with the very first Bigsby vibrato, on which he had used a valve spring from a Harley Davidson motorcycle. Thom Bresh now has this vibrato, serial number 001, patent pending.

The Bigsby vibrato has been one of the most well known of such devices for many years.

Travis was experimenting with multiple or multi track recording, in half speed etc., during the same period of time that Les Paul's multiple recordings were released. He first recorded on a disc, then played it back and played along with it while recording both on another disc. Later he used a four track recorder. "Merle's Boogie Woogie" was a good example of this. Also, several things on "The Merle Travis Guitar" and "Strictly Guitar" albums were overdubbed and he played harmony and rhythm with himself on some things.

Merle loved to play pop standards. He would record a rhythm track, then play it back and improvise with it, just mess around with it. He recorded some wonderful music on a four track recorder while visiting his brother John in Indiana several years ago. It's interesting that he usually played the verse as well as the chorus when he did the standards.

Merle sometimes toured in the summer with Gene Autry's western show. Gene always used some musicians from Indiana, Carl Cottoner on fiddle, Bill Pierpont on accordion and, this particular year, he used Art Bishop on bass. I believe it was the first time he used electric bass. Art and I had been working together in a club in Indianapolis before he went with Autry. The western show had played New York and was working its way west, when they stopped overnight in Indy. I went to the motel to visit Merle and saw a raccoon that someone had given him. He told what had happened a day or two before. The raccoon had a collar and leash and liked to ride on the side, rear view mirror. They got in heavy traffic and Travis couldn't see in the mirror very well with the raccoon sitting on it. He tried to pull the little animal inside but it didn't want to come in. Merle gave it a yank and as it came in it bit his finger and did what raccoons normally do in the woods, right on his lap.

And there was the time Merle was alone on the stage before a large auditorium full of people. He introduced the next tune and mentioned that it was from an album that had won a grammy. He said, "I recorded this with some kid from Nashville. Now what was his name? Oh, it was Chet Atkins." Then he went on to say, "I was only kidding. I think Chet Atkins is the greatest guitar player in the world. I wonder if he is somewhere bragging on me tonight?"

When Travis was in his prime in the 1940's and 50's, he was an awesome guitarist and talent. He played with so much soul, so much authority, it was pure feeling, raw emotion. I believe that during that period the music he played, some of which was recorded, was probably the greatest music that ever came from a guitar.

I believe Travis was a genius. He was one of the most, if not the most, creative individuals I have ever known. His world view, his outlook on life was not the usual run of the mill. His viewpoints were remarkable. He always came from a different angle, a different direction. I never tired of talking with him, asking questions and getting answers that were so logical I was amazed. Others seemed to defy logic.

I have talked with many people who share this opinion. Once on tour out west with Thom Bresh and The Sons Of The Pioneers, I enjoyed listening to trail boss, Dale Warren, tell about time spent with Merle in music, the movies, fishing trips, etc. He told Thom, "You know, your dad was a genius." Then he proceeded to tell how Travis could write a song with as many verses as he wanted, on any subject. He always began at the end and went forward. He said if one knows how the story ends, it's no problem to know what happened to get to that point.

Merle loved people. One of his greatest pleasures in life was spending time, sharing thoughts, good food and drink, with good friends and those he loved.

I sometimes wonder what he could have accomplished if he had felt the burning desire, or drive to be famous or, go down in history as being famous. He really had no idea how great he was, how influential, or how much he was loved by so many people.

One thing that always bothered me about Travis was the fact that he never wanted to take credit for what he did and would put himself down. He seemed embarrassed by compliments. If someone said, "I love that song you wrote," he would say, "Oh, I can't write good songs, now Tom T. Hall is a great songwriter."

He is probably looking back and saying, "Why are they making such a big fuss about me? I can't play a guitar right. Now, Chet Atkins is a guitar player. He's the best in the world."

I remember well, "Merle Travis Day" in 1956 when a monument was erected in his honor, at his boyhood home of Ebenezer, Kentucky. Over 10,000 people stood in the oppressive heat of the summer sun to see the unveiling of the monument, to hear the telegram from President Eisenhower read on the sound system or to catch a glimpse of Travis, Chet Atkins or Gene Autry.

That evening when the festivities had ended, some of us went to Mose Rager's home where Merle, Mose and Ike Everly sat on the lawn and talked and passed a guitar around between them. Ike's sons, Don and Phil were there. They didn't yet have a recording contract.

I was there again in 1983 for Merle's memorial service. His children, brother and sister as well as Joe and Rose Maphis, Grandpa and Ramona Jones, Chet and Leona Atkins, Joe Edwards, Odell Martin, Marty Stuart and Cindy Cash and many other old and new friends were there. That is where I met Marge and Debby Rhoads and Eddie Pennington.

It was a blue day as we stood under the grey October sky, surrounded by the red and gold oak and gum trees. Thom Bresh picked up the old Travis Martin with the Bigsby neck and said, "This is for you Merle," and then played "I'll See You In My Dreams." No one was embarrassed by the tears that flowed.

I was once again in Ebenezer for the dedication of the Merle Travis Highway. The state highway begins at Ebenezer near the monument, and runs through the old town of Beech Creek, where Merle's father had worked in number nine mine (my father also worked there in number eleven mine), and connects with Highway 431 in Beechmont.

Before the ribbon cutting ceremony, there were speeches and tributes by various officials, Travis' children and siblings, friends and second cousin Claude Travis, who was instrumental in bringing about the naming and dedication of the highway. It was an honor and I felt much gratitude for being on the stage with Merle's children Thom Bresh, Pat Travis-Eatherly, Merlene Travis-Maggini, and Cindy Travis-Tolk as well as his brother John and sister Vada Adler.

After the speeches, there was some fine music by guitarists such as Don Dean, Dave Stewart, the great James "Spider" Rich and many others. I played a beautiful Travis song, "Dance of the Goldenrod."

Although it was a happy event, it was also a very sad occasion. Just before Lane Brody went on to sing "Amazing Grace," which she had also sang at the memorial service, she was notified by a state trooper of her father's death. I don't know how she did it, but she managed to get through almost the entire song before here voice broke with grief. Bresh closed with "Sixteen Tons," which was written about these same hills and hollers and the people who worked under and around them.

Today I am pleased and honored that Thom Bresh is a very close friend, one of my two best friends. We have traveled many miles together, enjoyed many great conversations, made observations, gained insights, shared some great jokes and much, much laughter. Thom is a fine legacy, left in this world to carry on his father's talent.

Merlene, Merle and Cindy

AFTERWORD

The preceding chapter was simply a collection of random thoughts that came to mind when I began revising and updating the Merle Travis guitar style.

I have saved newspaper and magazine articles, photographs, periodicals and various items about Travis, as well as articles and stories written by him since the very early 1950's. Because of my interest in Travis and his music, my memories of time spent with him, as well as his mentor, Mose Rager, who narrated in detail to me much of Merle's early life in Kentucky, I have a sizeable amount of information about him.

A few years ago, Mr. John Rumble, who is oral historian for the Country Music Foundation, which operates the Country Music Hall of Fame and Museum, Library and Media Center, conducted interviews with me about Travis, Rager, my early life in Muhlenberg County and my career.

I was also happy to loan my collection of Travis material to the Foundation for over a year, for archival duplication. In fact, it was a great help to me because they organized the material, separating it from material on Mose, Chet Atkins, Ike Everly and other jazz, country and classical guitarists, putting each in its own place.

The interviews and all materials are on tape, microfiche, microfilm, etc. in the library and media center. A more in-depth historical reference may be obtained from the Country Music Foundation, Nashville, Tennessee.

Thanks to Margie Joines-Rhoads for the time spent and energy exerted in her meticulous proofreading and editing of this material.

Tommy Flint

Merle Travis, Tommy Flint and Mose Rager

NOTES OF INTEREST

I learned "Amos Johnson Rag" from Mose Rager before Merle recorded it under a different title. Travis lived in California, but was visiting friends back in Kentucky. He and Mose, and some other guys were sitting on the floor in a circle, passing around a guitar and taking turns playing. When it was Mose's turn, he played a tune he had learned from Amos Johnson, a black guitarist who lived in Drakesboro. Merle liked it so well he began laughing, slapped his leg and rolled back flat on the floor. Mose called it "Amos Johnson Rag."

Rager said it wasn't long until he heard it on the radio. Merle had changed it, written a new bridge, put his own interpretation on it, and had written words which were about Mose. He called it "Guitar Rag." Mose told me that Travis sent him the royalties from the tune.

Mose played a bridge for the tune which has never been recorded. I will do that one day soon.

Travis said he got the idea for "Walking the Strings" from a tune that Mose played called "Kansas City Rag." The first part of the solo where Travis slides up to high F chord in the tenth position and plays the roll, F, B♭, etc. is the only part that is like the "Kansas City Rag." Also, the rag contained only a few bars of "walking" on the bass strings, which is the main theme of "Walking the Strings."

In the 1930's and 40's and even the 50's, which I can remember, when the musicians of Muhlenberg County would get together to play, others would come to listen, talk, and some to dance. There were some very good dancers in the area. Houston Dickerson was a great tap dancer and buck dancer. Sometimes, when we played pop standards and waltzes, he and his lovely wife whom he called "Miss Lindy" were an impressive sight to behold.

Mose played a tune called "Merle's Buck Dance." He said that he and Travis used to play it for dancers before my time. They would sometimes do a chorus in stop time, i.e., play a staccato chord on the first beat of each measure or, every other measure. The sound of the dancer's shoes would fill in the empty spaces much like a drummer would do.

This was one of the first tunes I learned from Mose, before I heard Travis do it. But it wasn't long until I heard Merle play it leading into a station break on the Supper Time Frolic on WJJD Chicago. Then I believe it was called the "Saturday Night Shuffle."

Later, I heard Merle tell the story of why he changed the title. When he recorded it with Hank Penny's band it was titled "Merle's Buck Dance" on the record label, Penny told him, "That's a terrible name for a tune, you need to find a better title for it. So he changed it to "Saturday Night Shuffle."

For the version with Penny's band, Merle used an electric guitar, I believe it was the L-10 with a DeArmond pickup. He used a capo on the fifth fret which put it in the key of F.

He used the Martin D-28 for the transcription version and played it in the key of C.

In the mid 1950's, when the Merle Travis Guitar album was released, he had recorded it using the Gibson Super 400 Special. This time he had changed the arrangement again. He used a capo on the second fret and played it in the key of D. He modulated down a half step to D♭ before modulating back to D to end the solo.

HOW TO TUNE THE GUITAR

If you are a beginner, I would advise using an electronic tuner for now, while your ears are developing. The tuner will allow you to tune visually, while your tuning skills (pitch recognition) are being honed. A tuner can be purchased at most music stores.

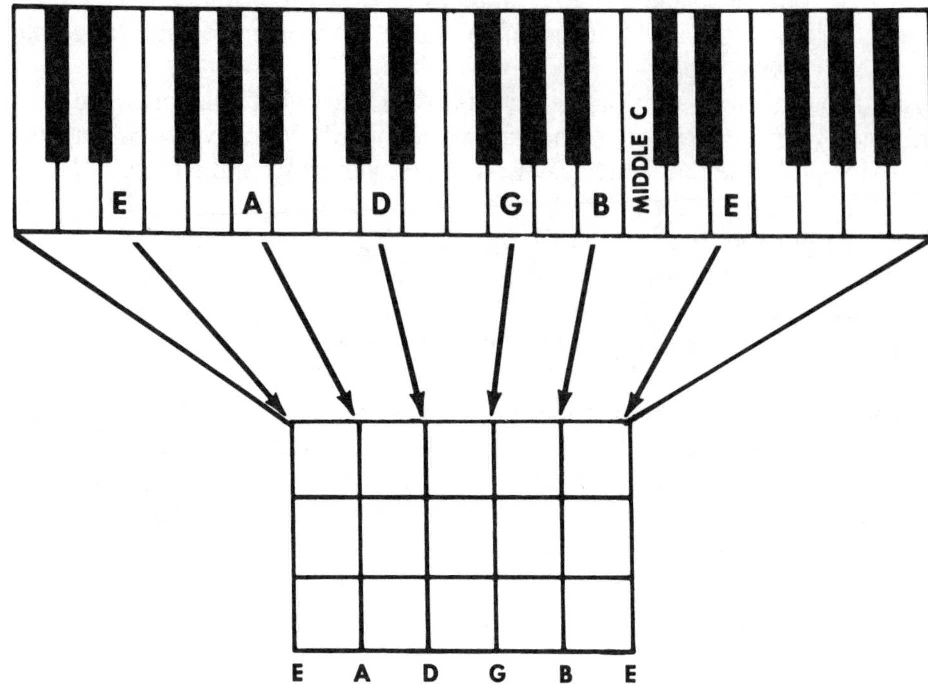

The six open strings of the guitar are the same pitch as the six notes shown on the piano keyboard. The first ① string is E above Middle C. The other five strings are below Middle C on the piano keyboard.

THE PITCH PIPE

Each pipe has the correct pitch of the individual string.

IF BOTH THE PITCH PIPE AND PIANO ARE UNAVAILABLE:

1. Tighten the ⑥th string until you get a good clear tone.
2. Place the finger on the ⑥ string behind the 5th fret. This will give you the pitch of the open ⑤ string.
3. Tighten or loosen the ⑤ string until it sounds the same.
4. Place finger on the ⑤ string behind the 5th fret to get the pitch of the open ④ string.
5. Place finger on the ④ string, 5th fret to get pitch for open ③ string.
6. Place the finger on the ③ string, 4th fret to get the pitch for the open ② string.
7. Place the finger on the ② string, 5th fret to get the pitch for the open ① string.

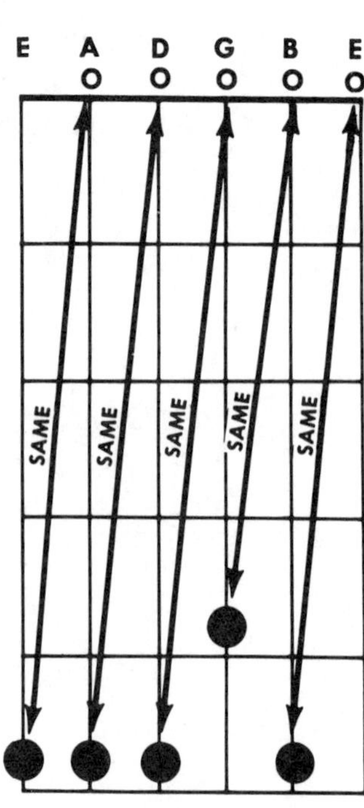

HOW TO READ TABLATURE

Using tablature is a fast and easy way to learn the exact location of the notes and chords on the fingerboard. It is easy to read, understand and transfer from the page to the strings and frets of the guitar. It is as easy to read in the high positions as the first fret.

Tablature is nothing more than a diagram of the strings and frets. There are three things you need to remember:

- The lines represent the strings.
- Numbers indicate the frets.
- 0 means open string.

The top line is the ①st or, small E string. The bottom line is the ⑥th or large E bass string. When a number is on the top line it is on the ①st string. If a number is on third line down it is on the ③rd string.

The tab is divided into measures by bar lines. There are usually four beats or counts per measure. Sometimes, there are only three counts per measure. The counts are spaced evenly.

In the following example, the first 0 in the first measure is on the fourth line from the top so you play the ④th string open. The next 0 is on the third line so, play the ③rd string open. The next 0 is the second string open. The three is on the first line so place your finger on the ①st string, third fret. Notice the four numbers are spaced evenly. Using only the right thumb, pluck the strings shown while counting slowly and evenly, 1 2 3 4.

In the second measure, the same four numbers are in a vertical column. That tells you all four strings are plucked, or strummed together as a chord on the first beat. There is nothing written on the second beat. Move your finger to the seventh fret and play the strings together on the third beat. There is nothing on the fourth beat.

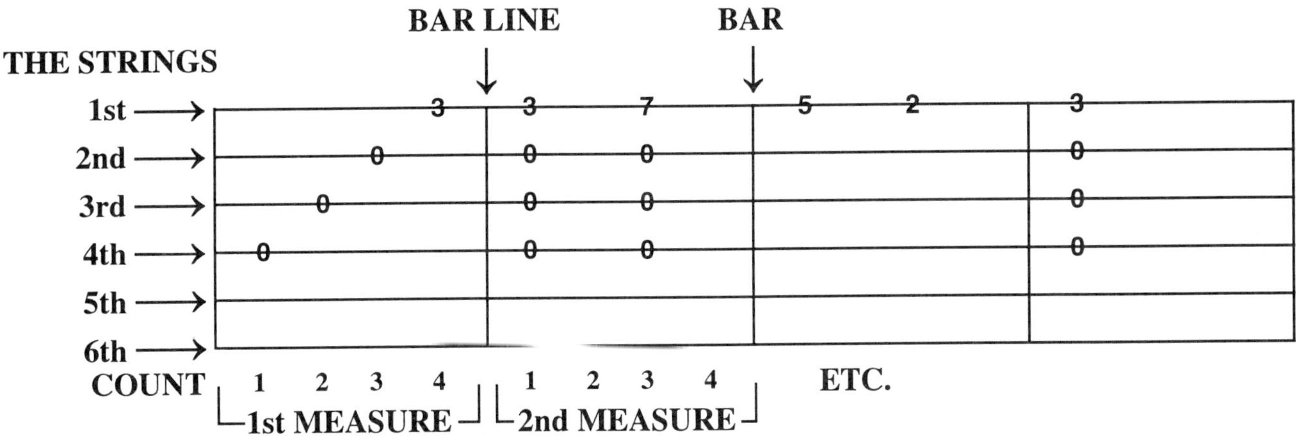

Sometimes there are notes on the beats and between the beats. These are called eighth notes. In the following example, play the notes indicated slowly and evenly, while counting 1 & 2 & 3 & 4 &. Sometimes eighth notes are indicated by a heavy horizontal line with short stems pointing downward toward the numbers. In any case, the tab numbers are written directly below the corresponding notes of standard music notation.

EIGHTH NOTES

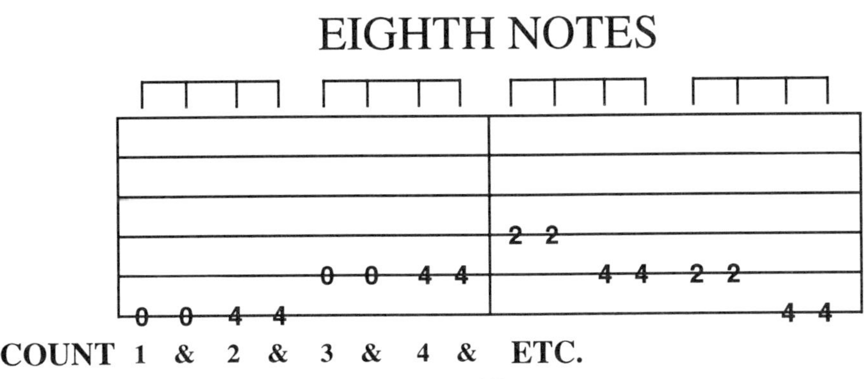

THE CHORDS USED IN THIS SECTION

Major Chords

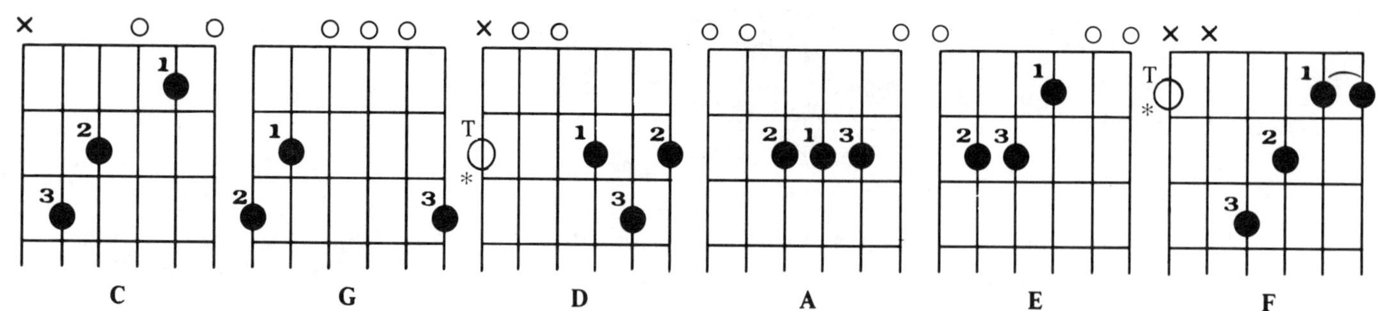

7th Chords

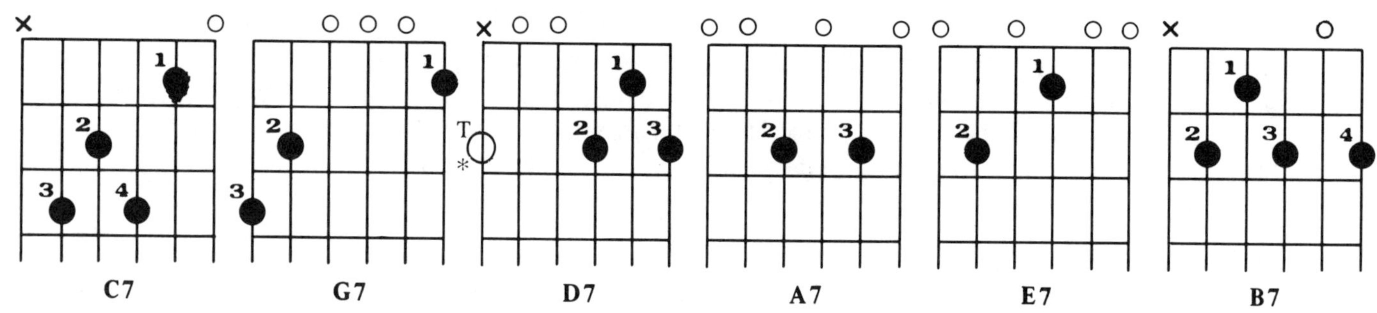

Minor Chords

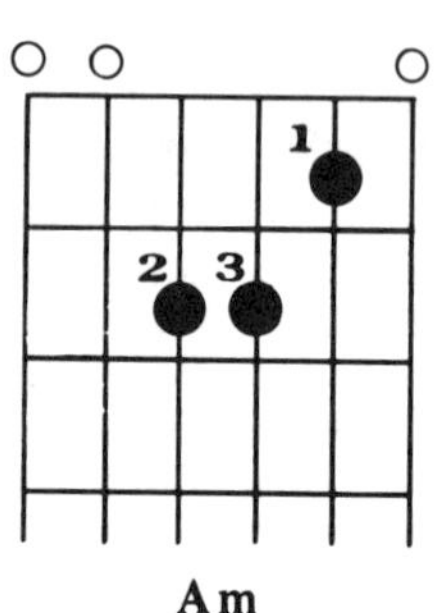

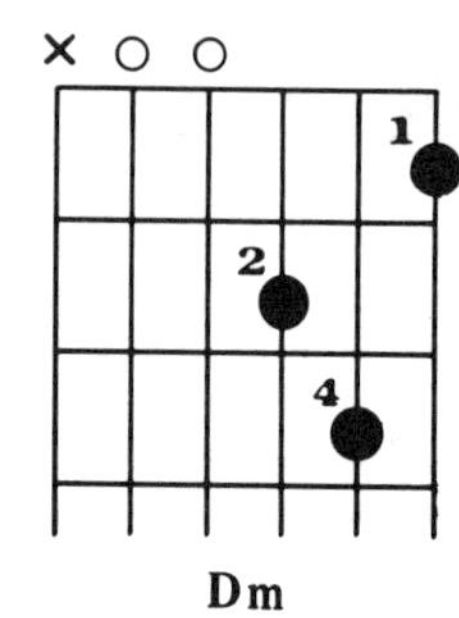

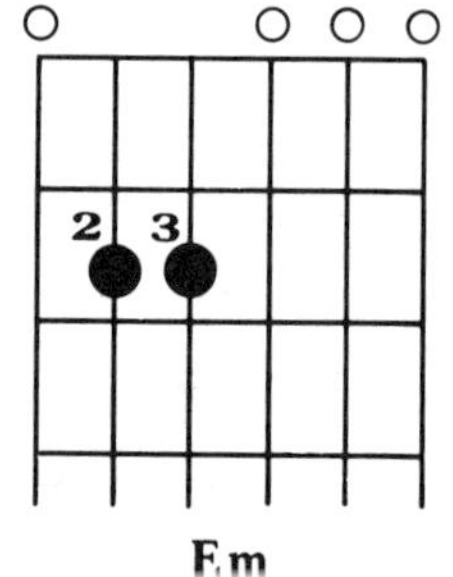

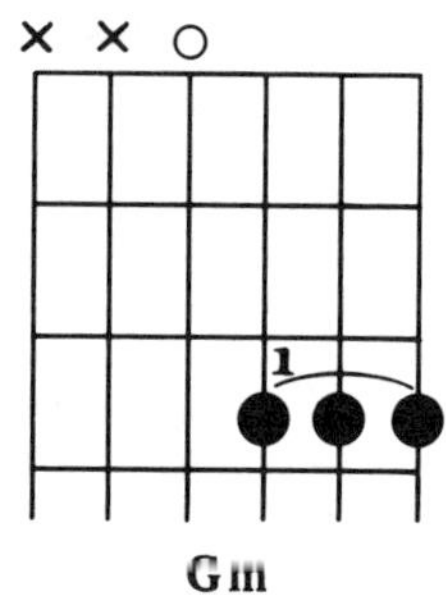

I would suggest that you practice playing the three principal chords in the basic "Open String" keys. The principal chords are simply the three most commonly used chords in a given key. They just seem to fit together and sound very pleasant to the ear. Knowing how the chords fit together is an invaluable asset when playing by ear. It eliminates much of the guesswork and saves a great deal of time.

The three principal chords are called:

the TONIC	SUBDOMINANT	and	DOMINANT 7th	
or the 1	4	and	5	Chords

It is very easy to find the three principal chords on the chord circle on the following page.

*Thumb may be used on ⑥th string.

THE THREE PRINCIPAL CHORDS

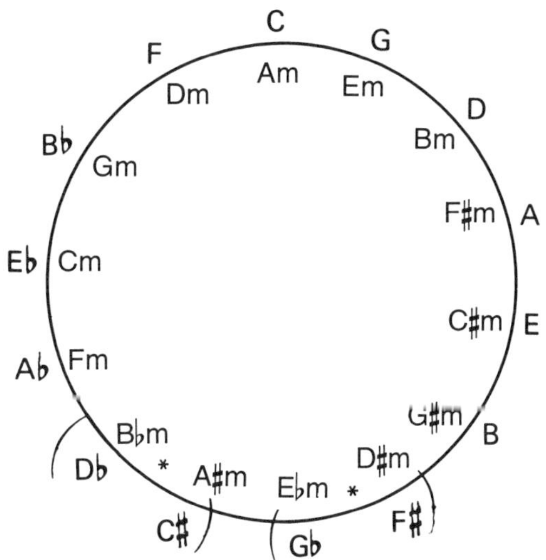

HOW TO FIND THE CHORDS

The three principal chords are called:

	TONIC	SUBDOMINANT	and	DOMINANT 7th
or	1	4	and	5

Pick out any chord on the circle. This is the tonic chord. Now move counterclockwise to the next chord.
This is the subdominant chord.
The first chord clockwise to the tonic is the dominant 7th chord.
The dominant 7th naturally is a seventh chord.
As an example, the chords in the key of C are: C, F and G7.
In the key of G: G, C and D7 or the key of E: E, A and B7.
You now know enough chords to play in the keys of C, G, D, A and E.
The small letters inside the circle are the minor keys relative to the adjacent major keys outside the circle.

HOW TO PRACTICE

Play the tonic, subdominant, dominant 7th and tonic. Use the thumb and strum each chord four beats spacing the counts as evenly as a clock.

EXAMPLE

Each diagonal line represents a strum with the thumb.

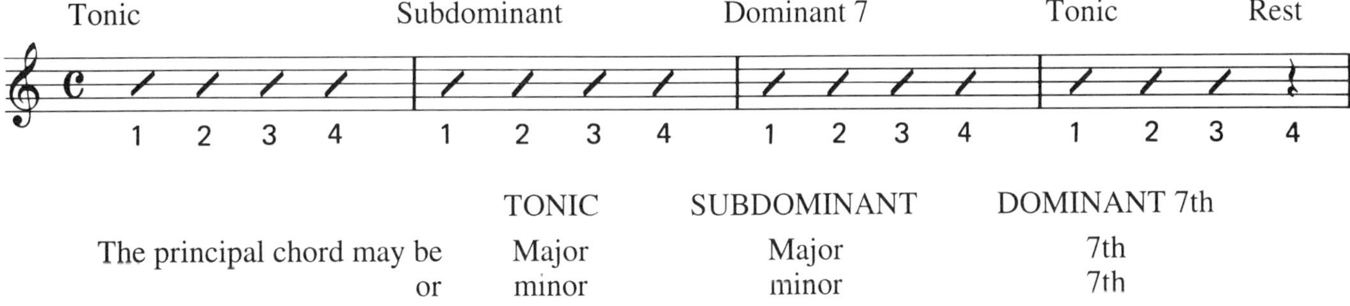

	TONIC	SUBDOMINANT	DOMINANT 7th
The principal chord may be	Major	Major	7th
or	minor	minor	7th

*The fingering for D♭ and C♯ is identical. Also G♭ and F♯ are identical.

THE TRAVIS RHYTHM IN TABLATURE

Be sure to read the chord symbols above each measure!

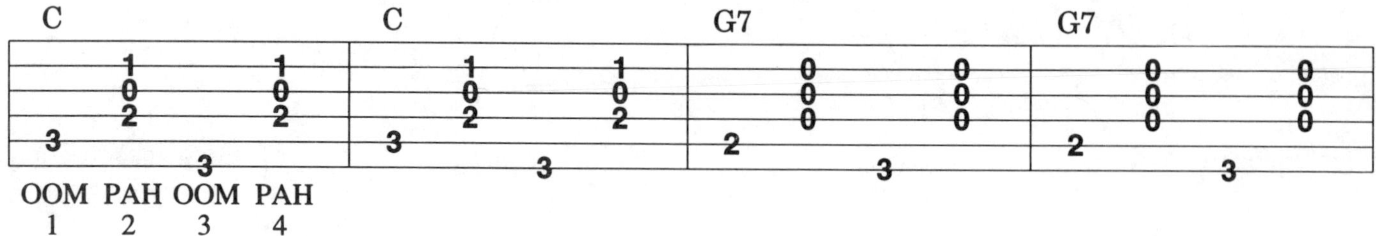

In order to facilitate reading and avoid cluttering of the tablature it will be written as follows.
The thumb will still play the ④③ and ② strings on the PAHS, or the counts of 2 and 4.

WRITTEN

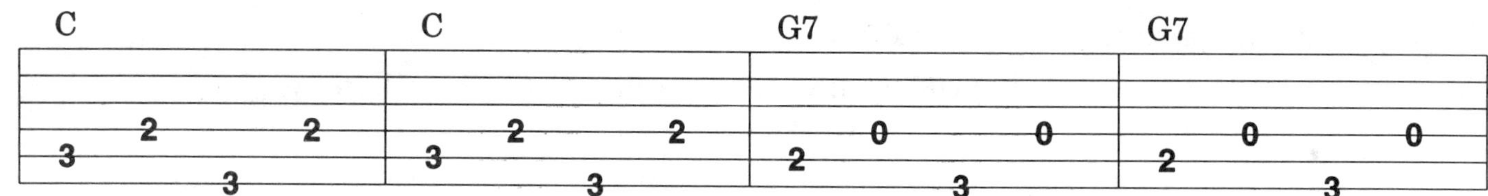

WRITTEN

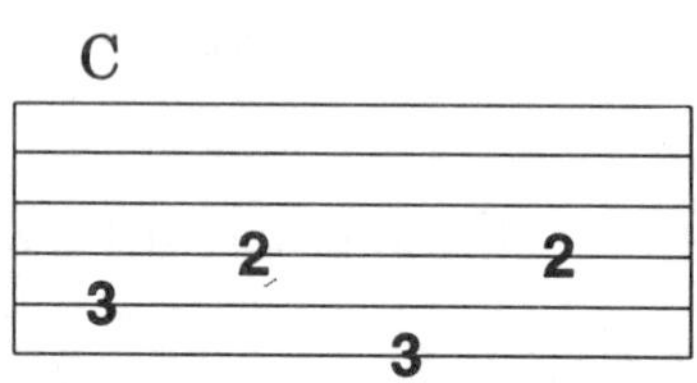

PLAYED

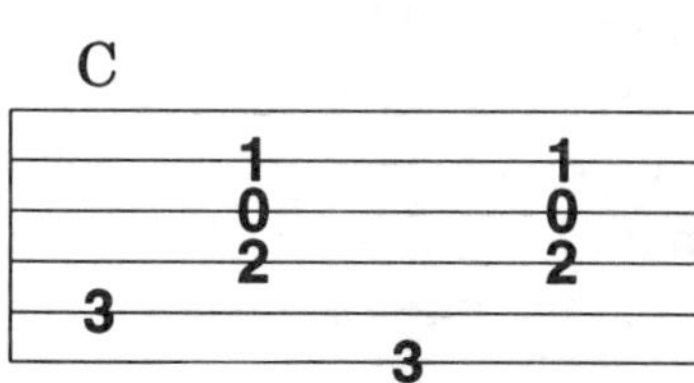

A PROGRESSION

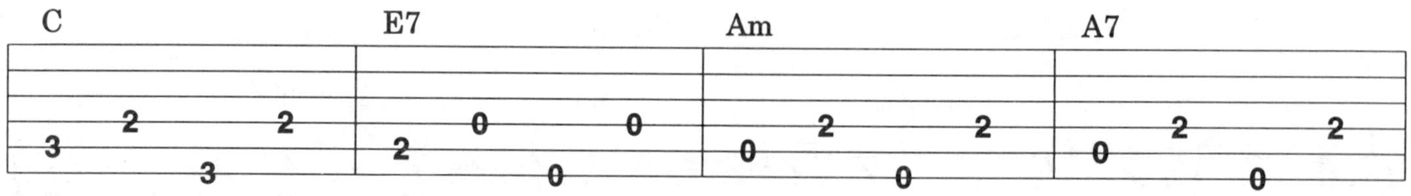

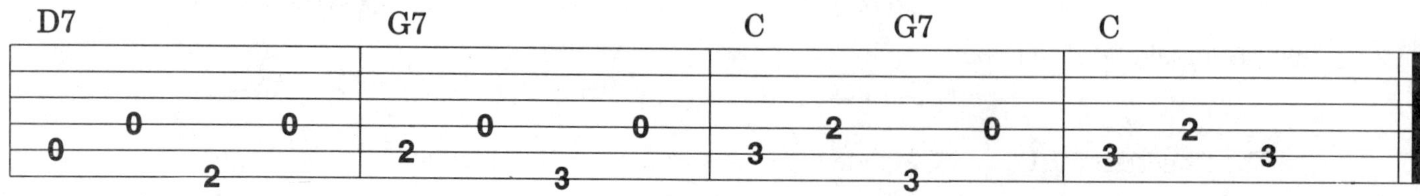

USING THE THUMB AND FINGER TOGETHER

The Merle Travis Style is actually two or more parts played simultaneously on one instrument. The thumb keeps a steady rhythm on the bass strings and chord while the fingers pick out the melody on the treble strings. This style is very effective in solo playing. The bass notes on the ooms or the first and third beats take the place of the electric or acoustic bass. The rhythm strokes on the pahs or the second and fourth beats take the place of the snare drum or rhythm guitar.
It is very important that you play the rhythm stroke on the pahs or 2 and 4. Start at the ④ string and let the thumb glide over two or three strings. In the following exercise the finger plays on the count of 1 or the first oom in each measure. Use index finger only.
p=thumb i=index

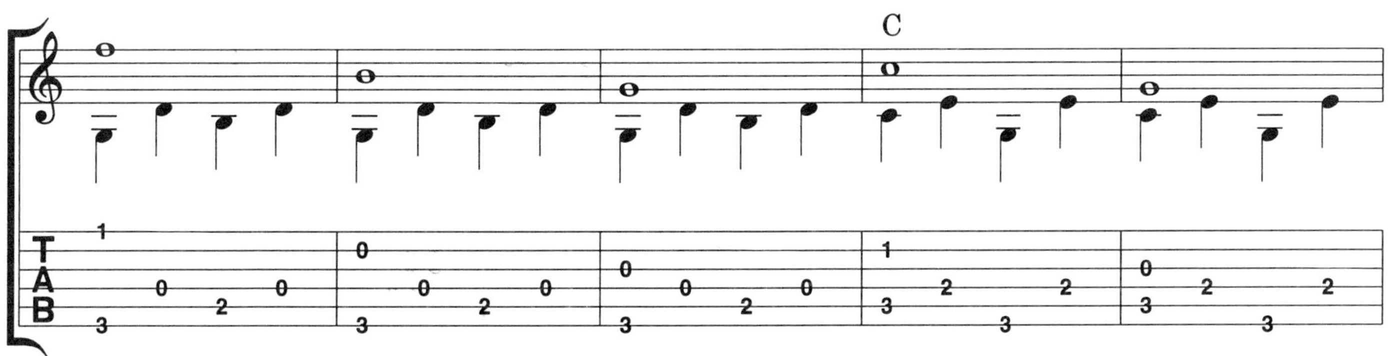

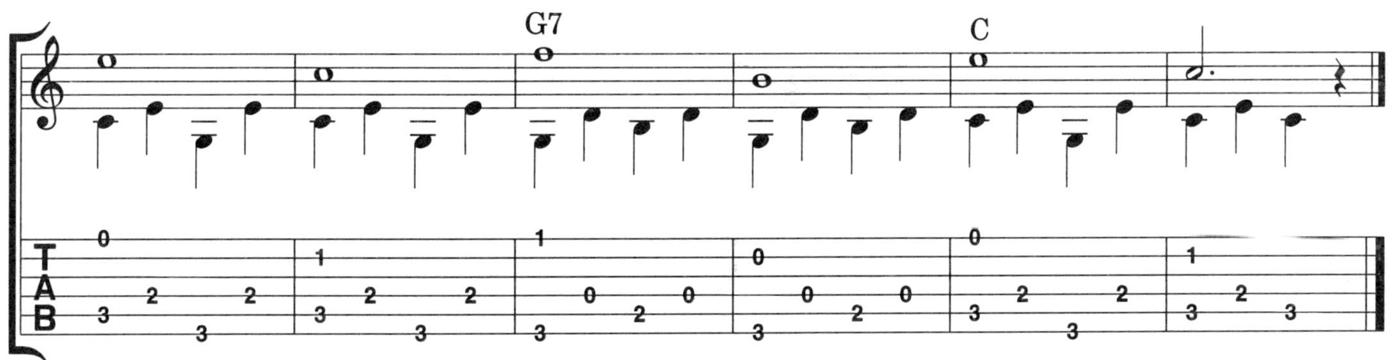

SOME PRELIMINARY STUDIES

In the following exercise the index finger plays on the first beat, (the first oom) in each measure. The thumb will keep a steady oom pah rhythm while the finger is playing the melody.

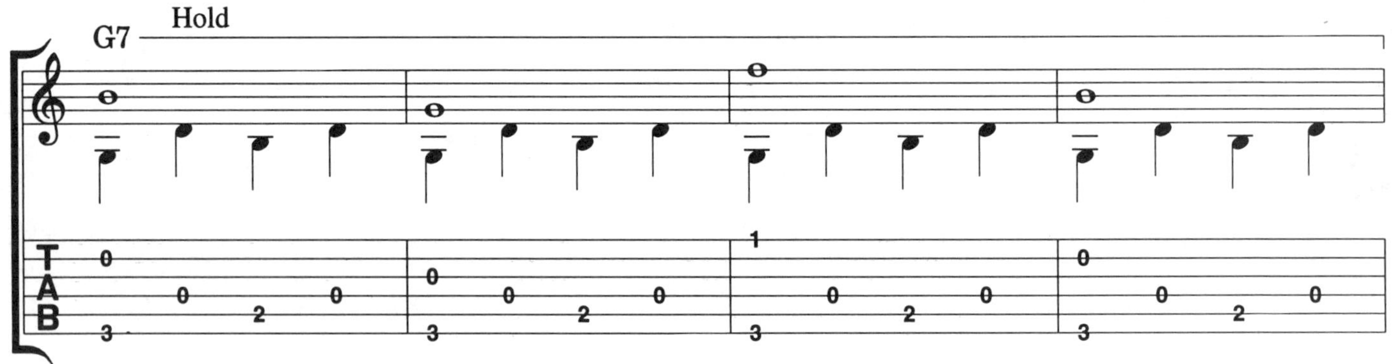

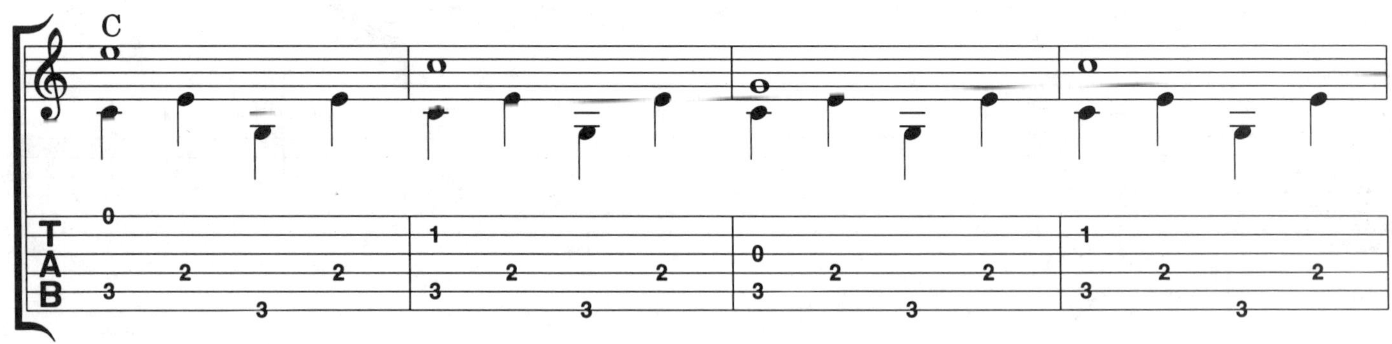

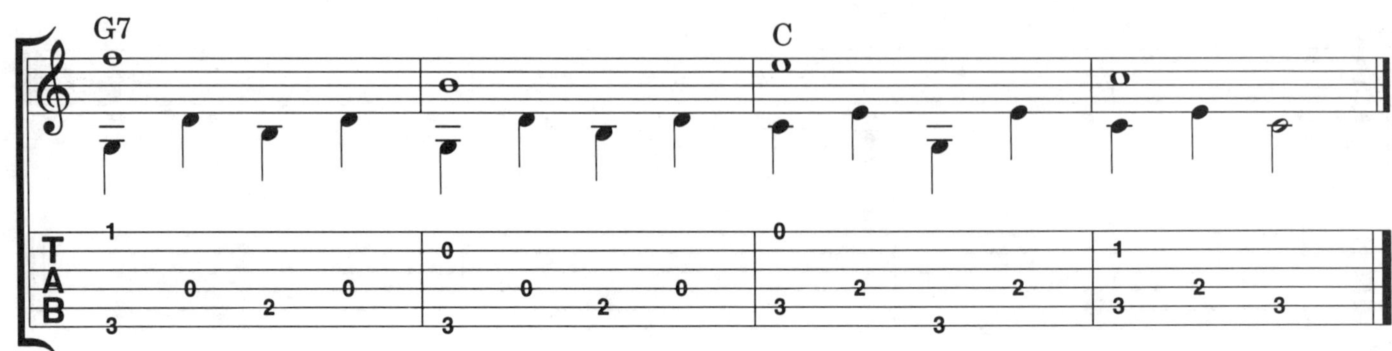

A CHORD PROGRESSION

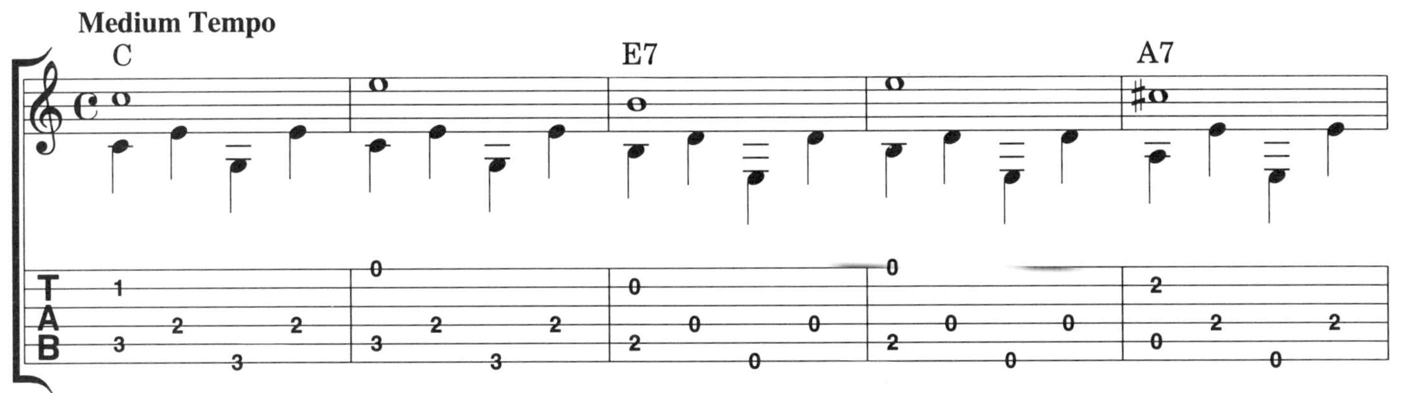

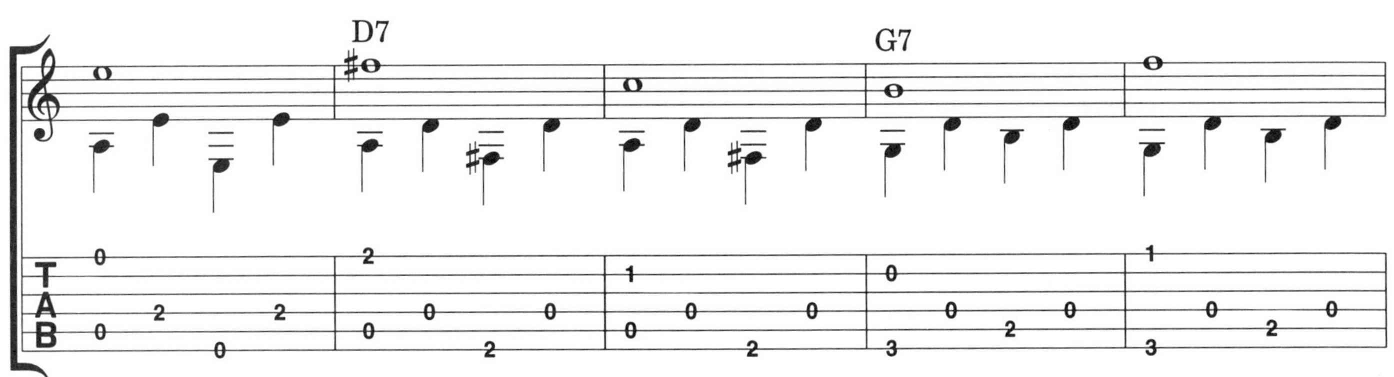

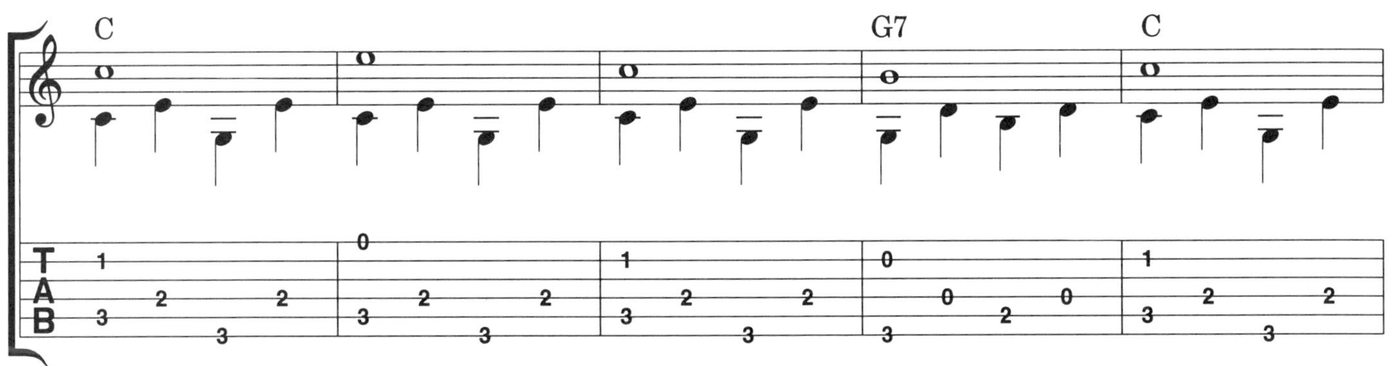

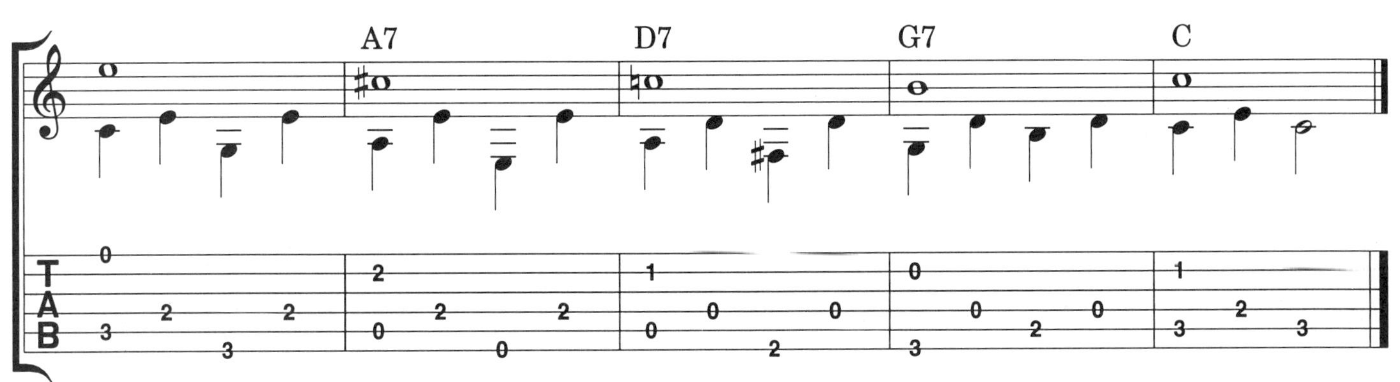

The finger will play the melody on the first, third and fourth beats, or oom, oom pah. When the melody note is on the ③ string on the second or fourth beats or the pahs, the thumb will strike the ④ string only on the rhythm stroke.

TAKE IT AWAY

MIXED RHYTHM EXERCISES

Tempos - most songs played in the Merle Travis Style have a loose, easy swing feeling to them. The tempos are brighter than average but should never feel stiff, rigid or rushed. Strive to maintain an easy swing to the exercises and solos presented.

GOT IT

Tommy Flint

ADDING NOTES TO THE CHORD

It is possible to play additional notes with the fourth finger while holding the basic chord. The third fret on the ① and ② strings can be used with G7 chord. The open ① string may also be used.

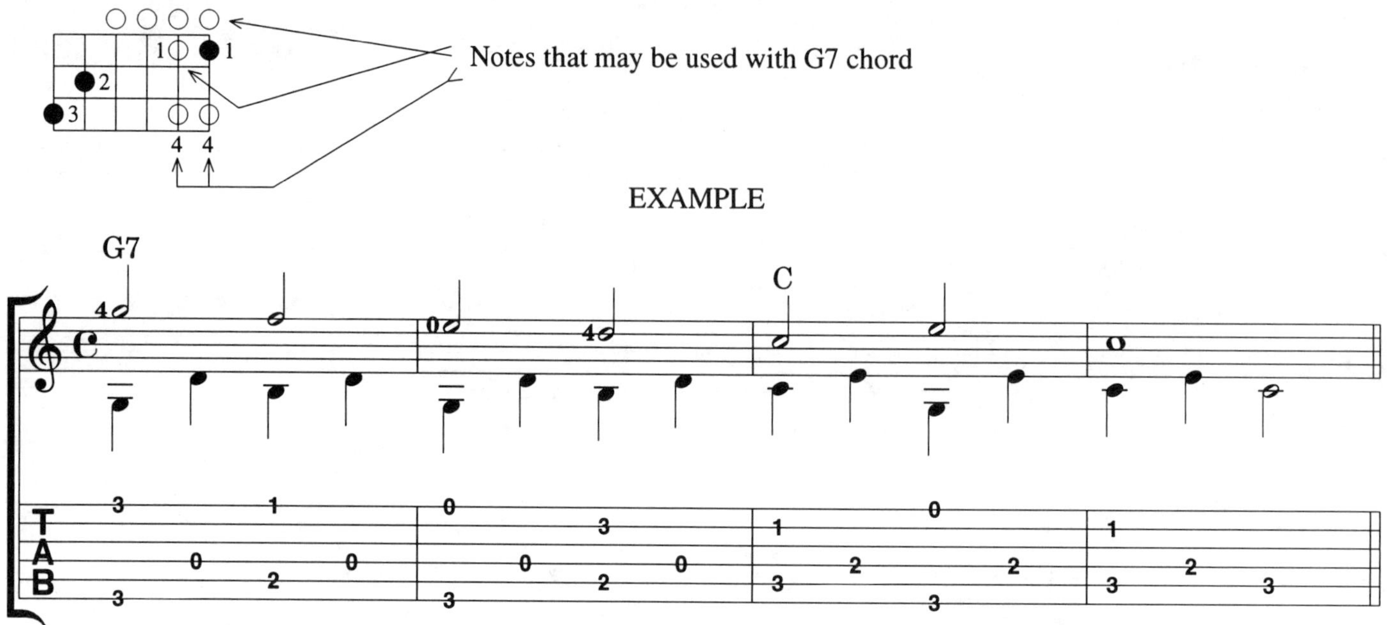

Use fourth finger on ② string in the fourth measure.

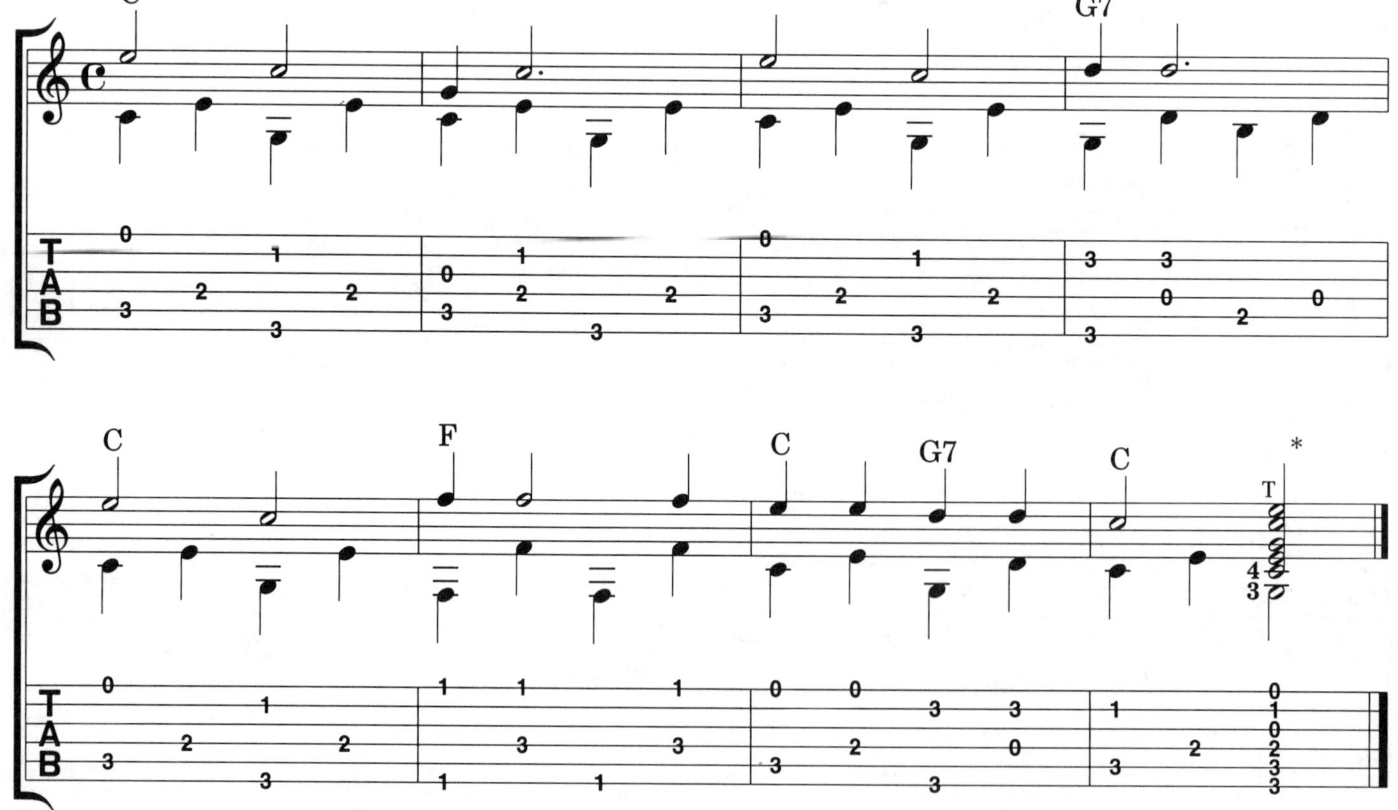

* Strike all six strings with thumb pick.

The third fret on the ① and ② strings may also be used with the C chord. In order to keep the fourth finger free to play the additional melody notes, it will now become necessary to make C chord with three fingers. If you find it too difficult at this time to hold both the ⑤ and ⑥ strings with the third finger as shown in the diagram, then hold the ⑤ string only. It is possible to play alternate basses by bouncing the third finger back and fourth from the ⑤ to the ⑥ string. ⑤ on the first oom or the count of one. ⑥ on the second oom or the count of three.

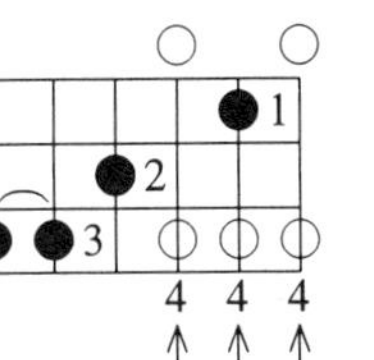

Can be used.

GO TELL AUNT RHODY

Easy Tempo

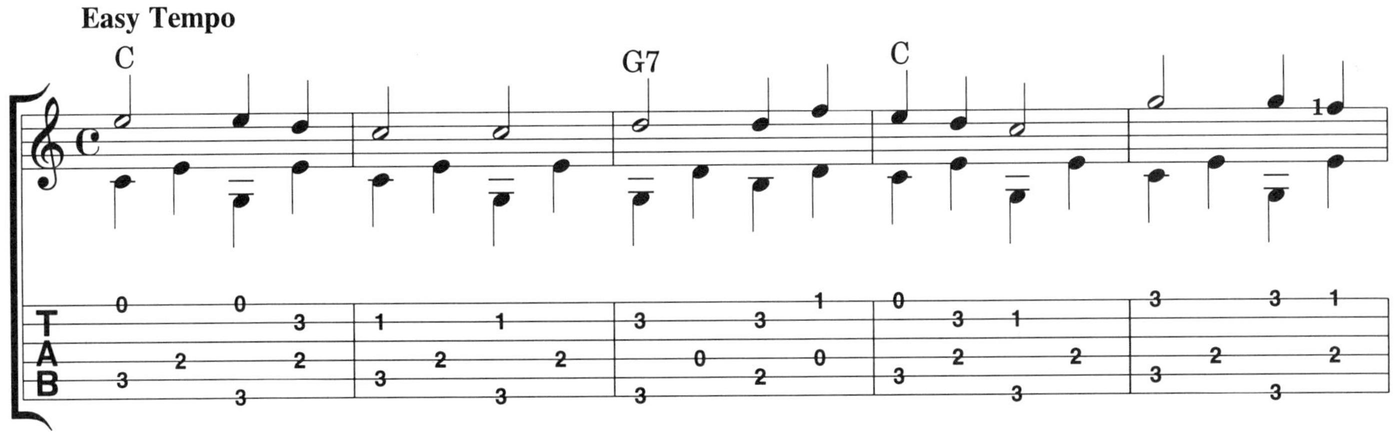

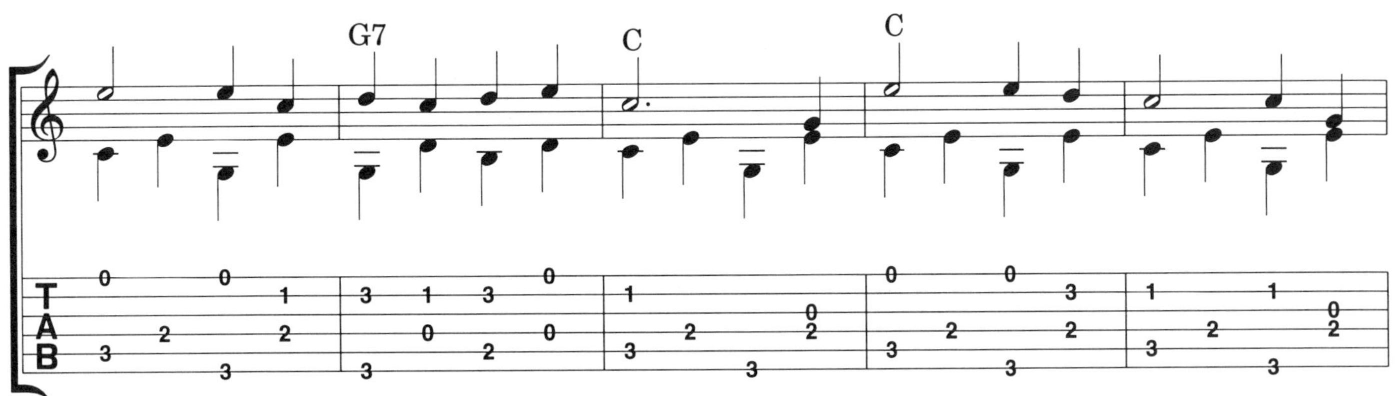

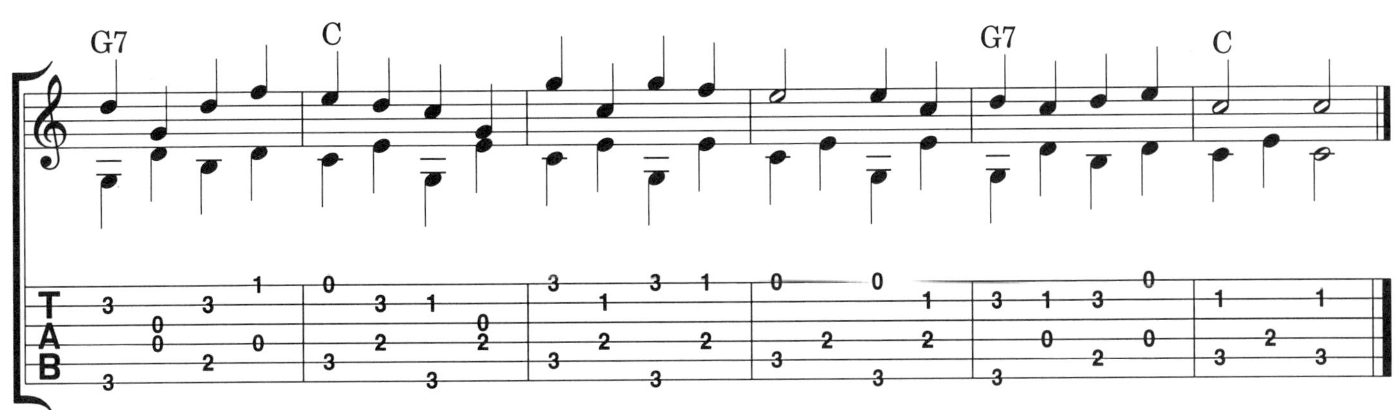

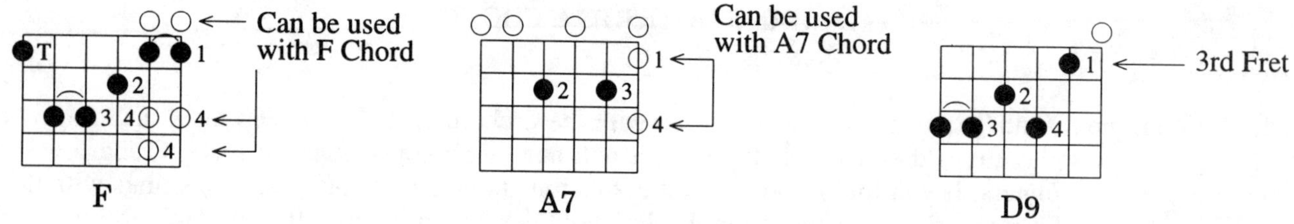

The ⑤ string may be omitted from F and D9 chords if it is too difficult to hold two strings with the third finger.

NASHVILLE EXPRESS

Tommy Flint

Fairly Bright Tempo

F C A7 D9

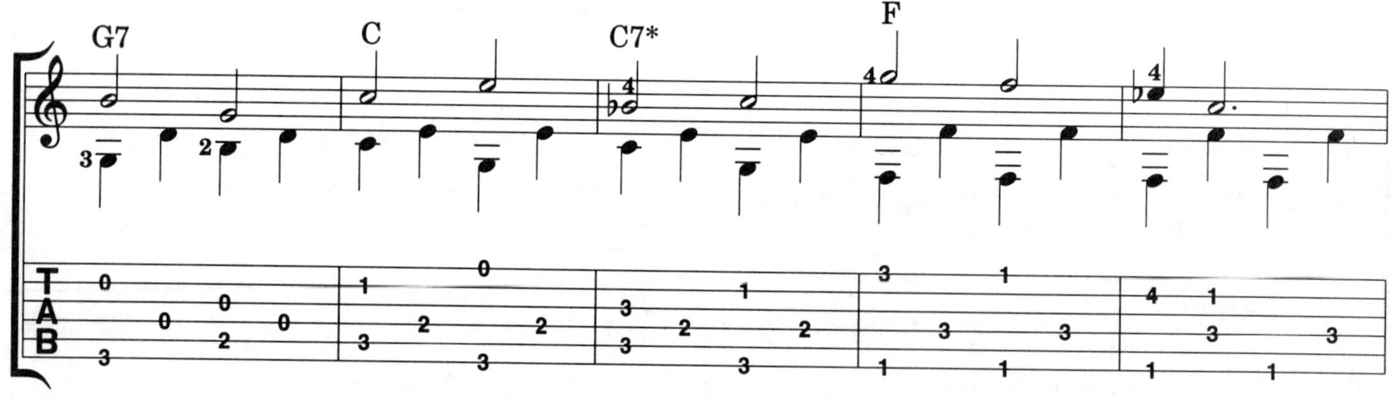

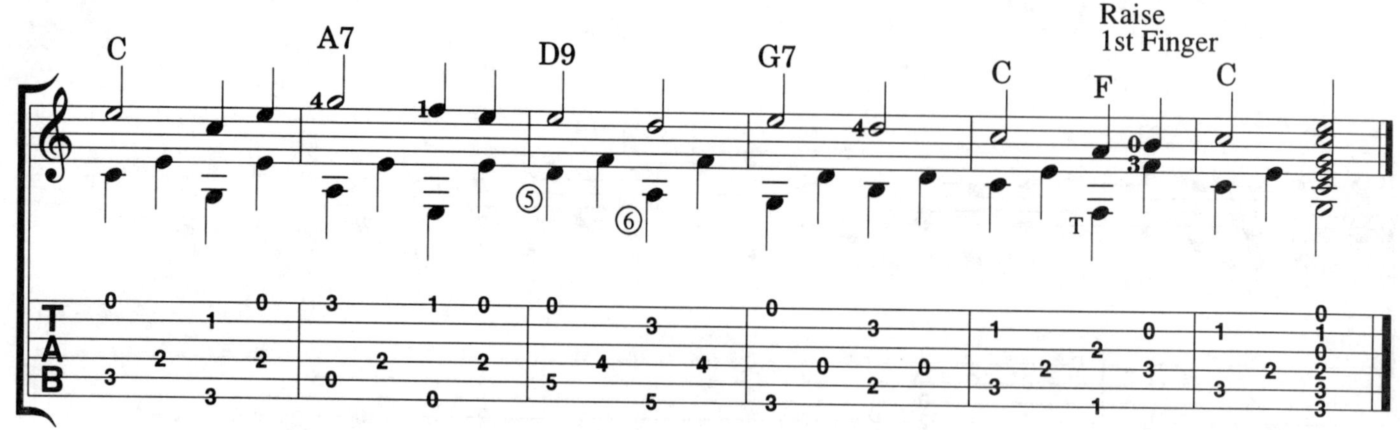

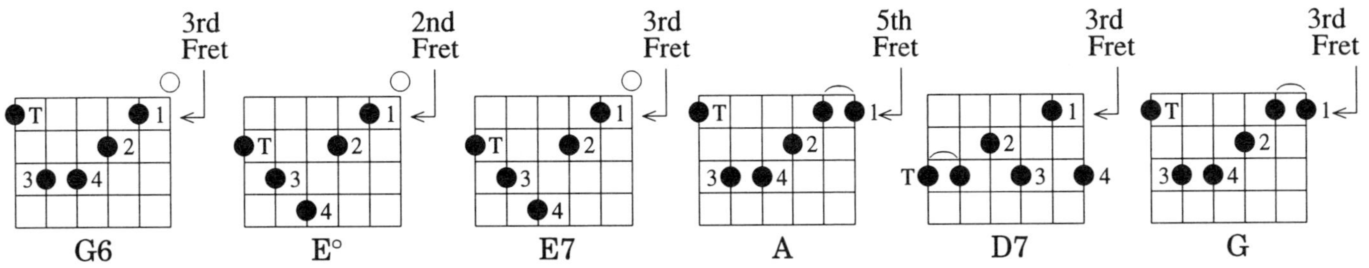

COUNTRY SHUFFLE

TOMMY FLINT

Easy Swing Tempo

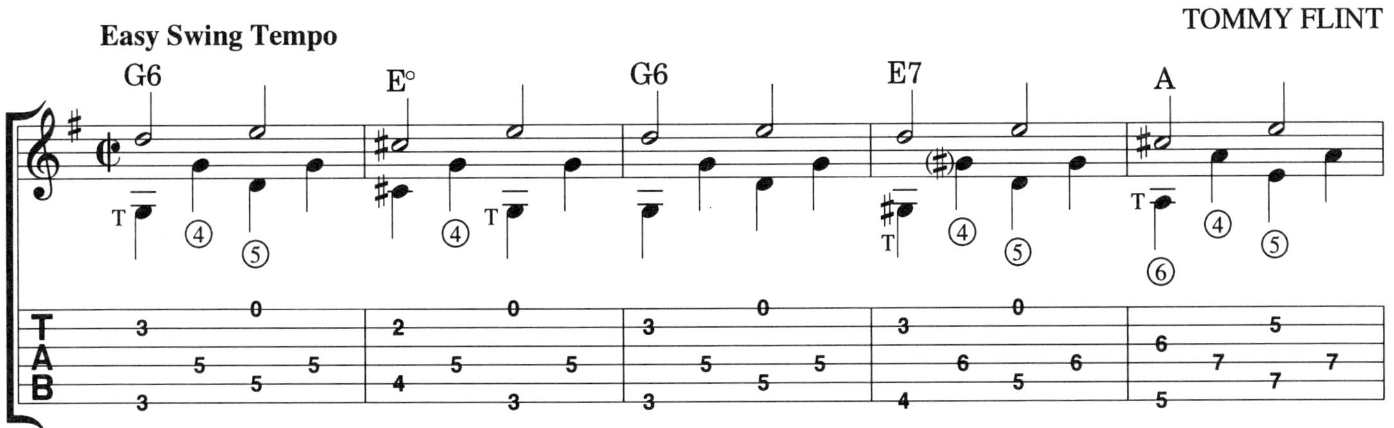

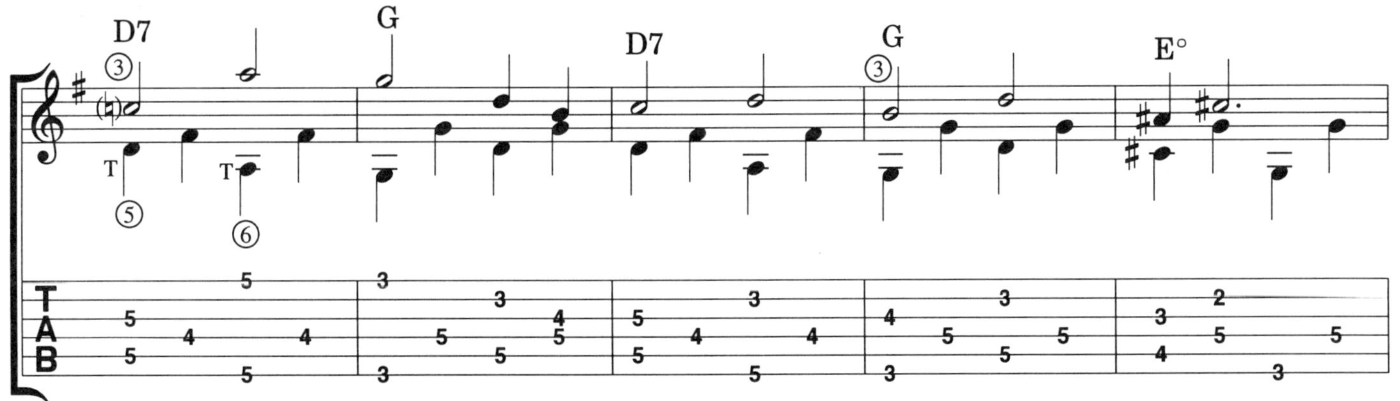

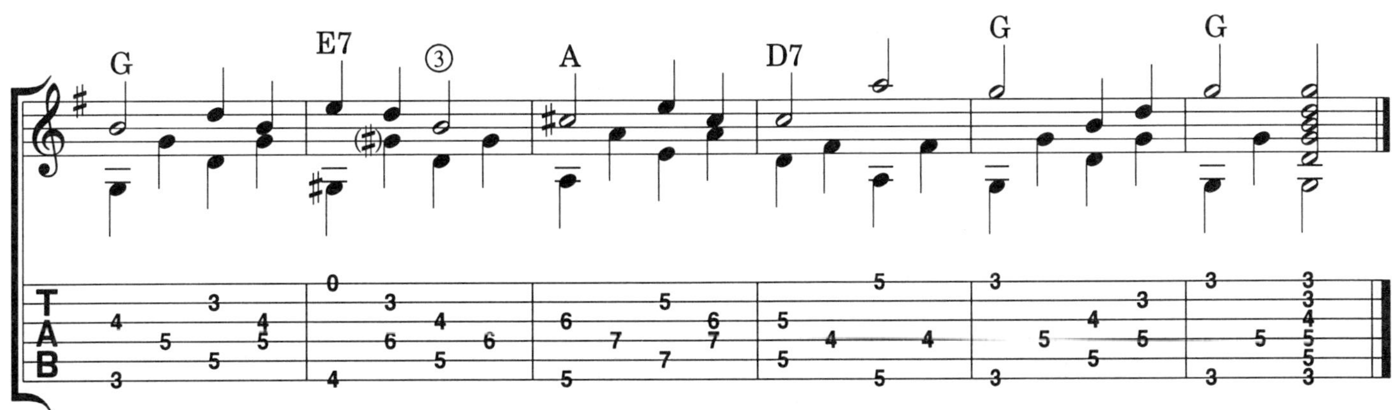

THE CHORDS USED ON THIS PAGE

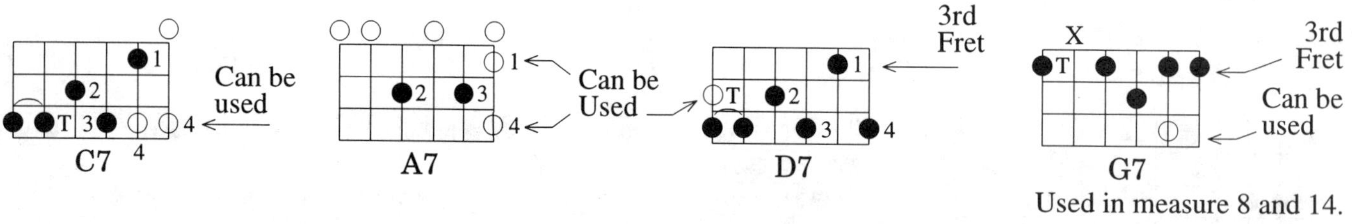

Used in measure 8 and 14.

C, F, E7 and G7 in the thirteenth measure are the open string chords at the first fret.

RED RIVER VALLEY

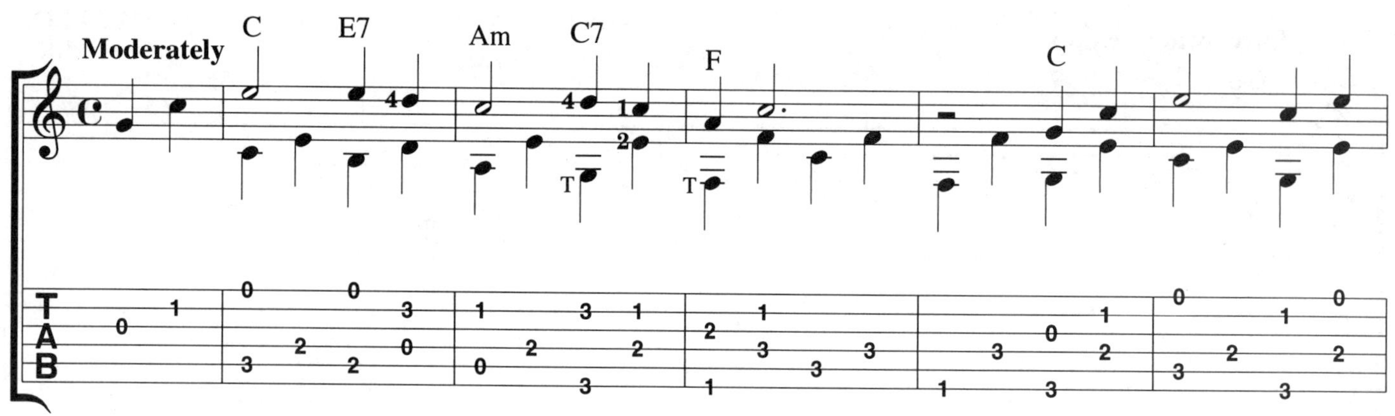

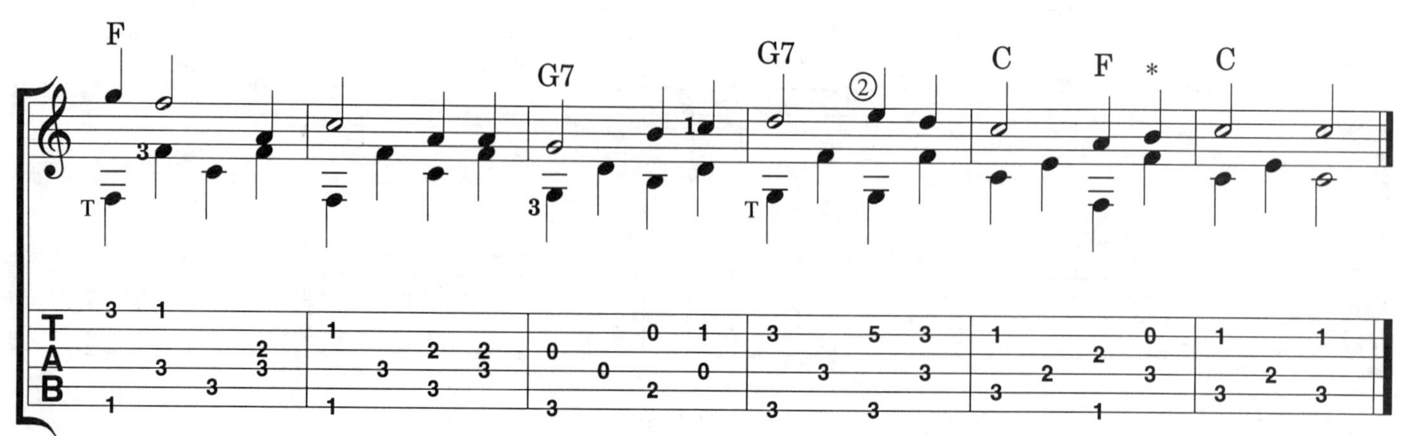

SYNCOPATION

One important and colorful ingredient of the Travis style is the flowing, spontaneous feel of the melody above the hard driving oom pah rhythm. This is achieved by syncopation or playing between the beats. Syncopation means irregularity of rhythm. In this book, syncopation means that the melody notes played with the finger fall between the rhythm beats played with the thumb.

The following patterns should be memorized and practiced until a steady even rhythm has been obtained. The syncopated notes are between oom and pah.

In the 1st measure, play after the first Pah and second Oom. In the 2nd measure play after the first Oom and first Pah.

SOME TRAVIS LICKS

No. 1

No. 2

No. 3

The finger plays after every thumb stroke or oom pah. The chords change on the "And" after the counts of 2 and 4 or the first Pah and second Oom in every measure.

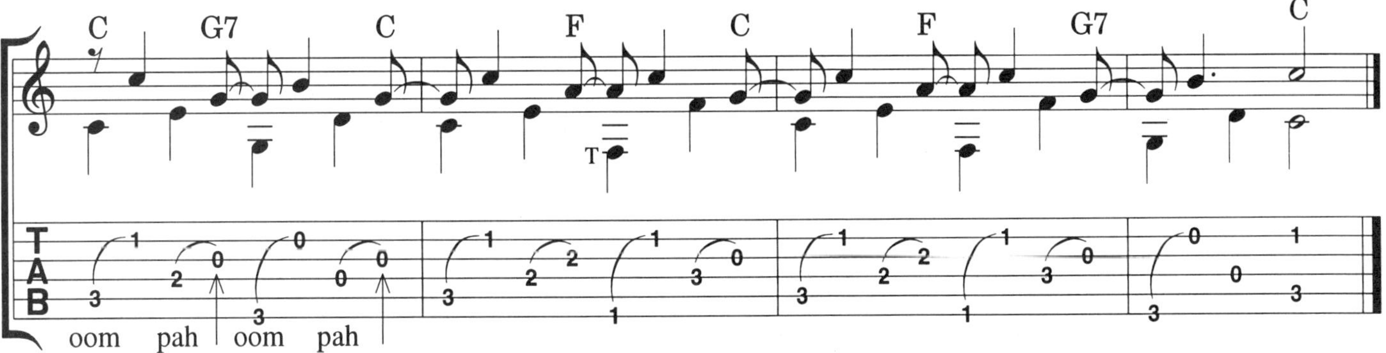

THE CHORDS USED IN THE FOLLOWING SOLO

C, E7, Am and F are the common forms at the first fret.

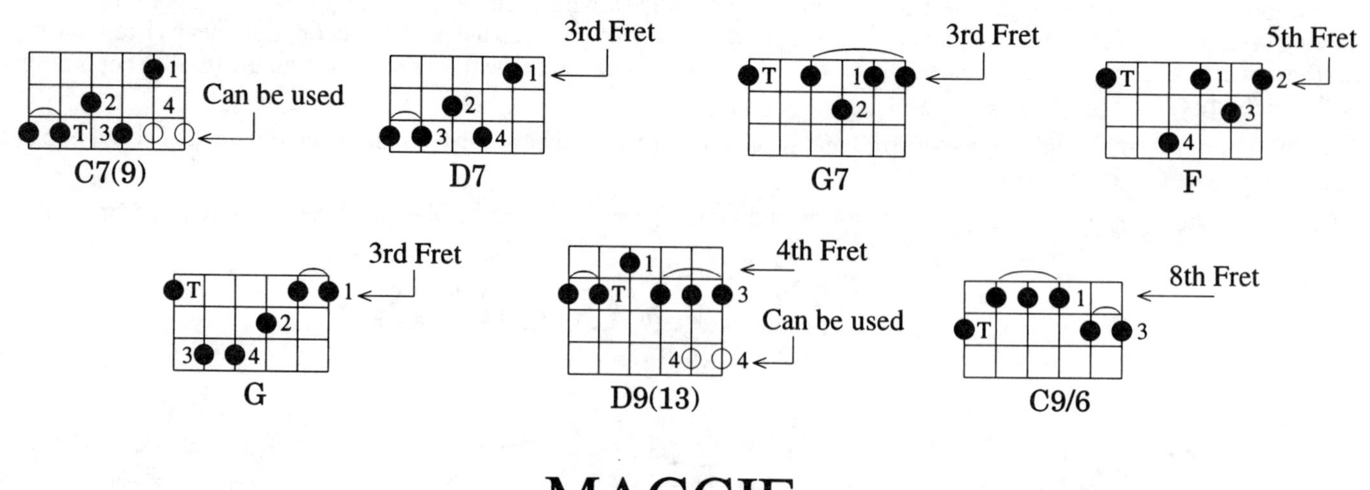

MAGGIE

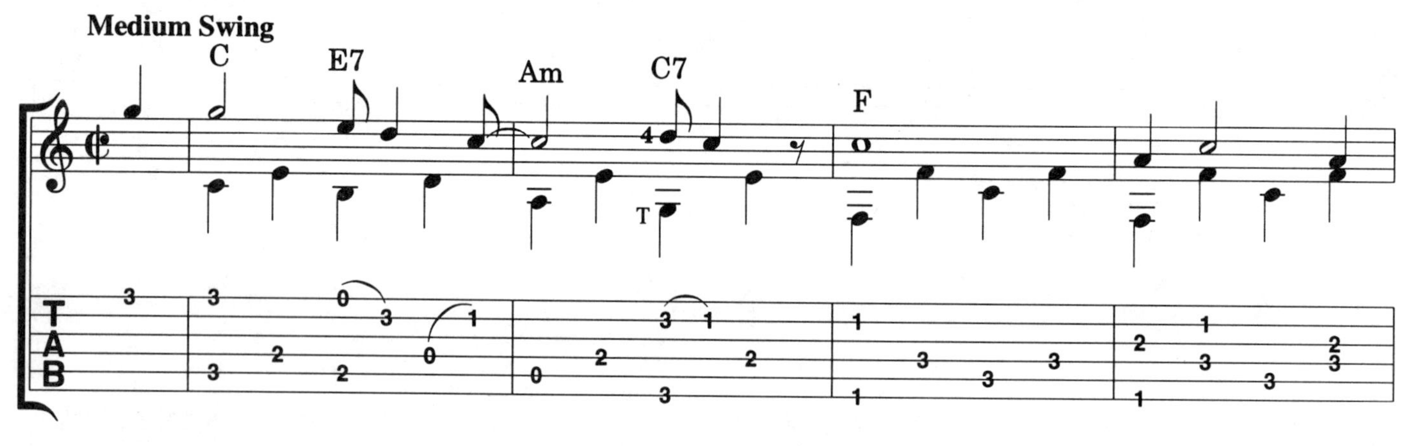

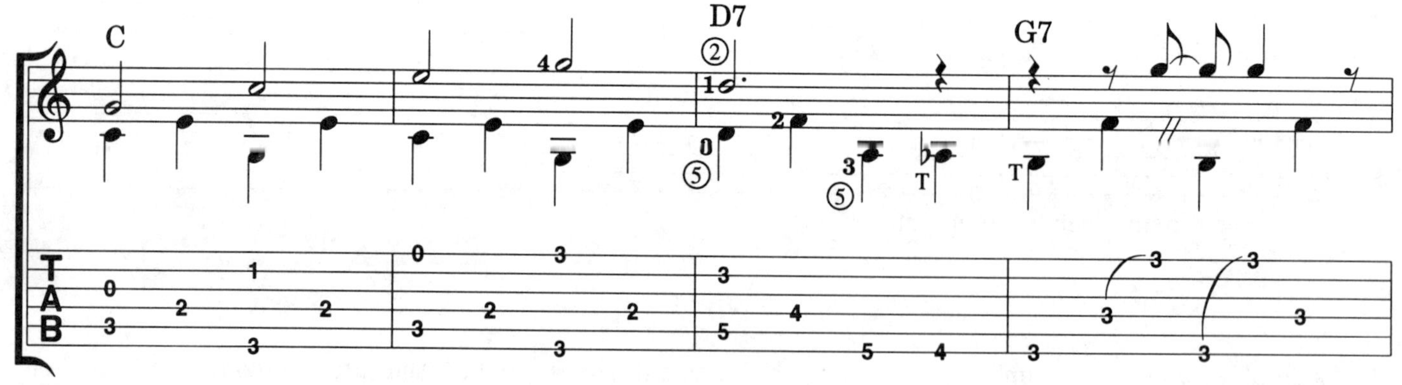

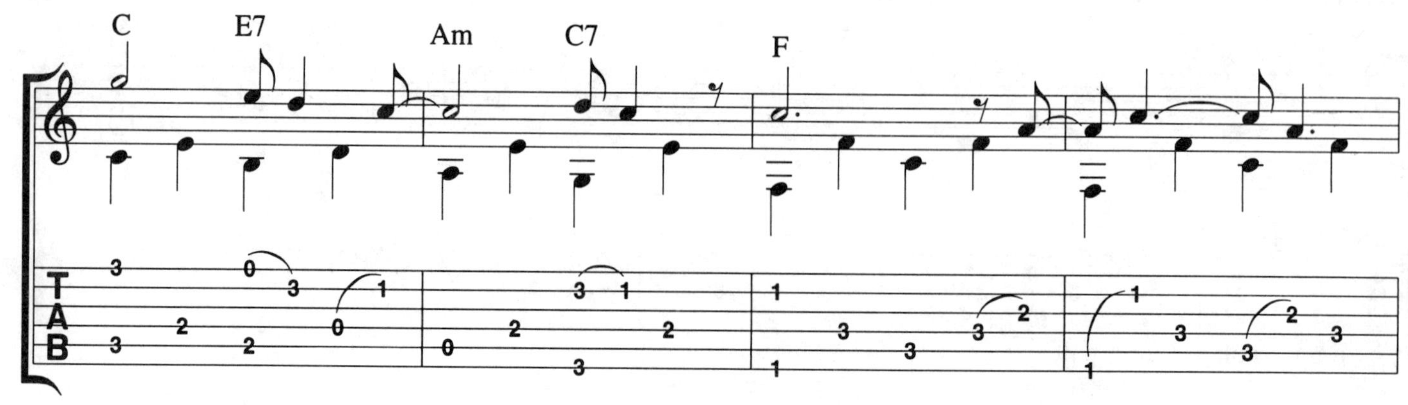

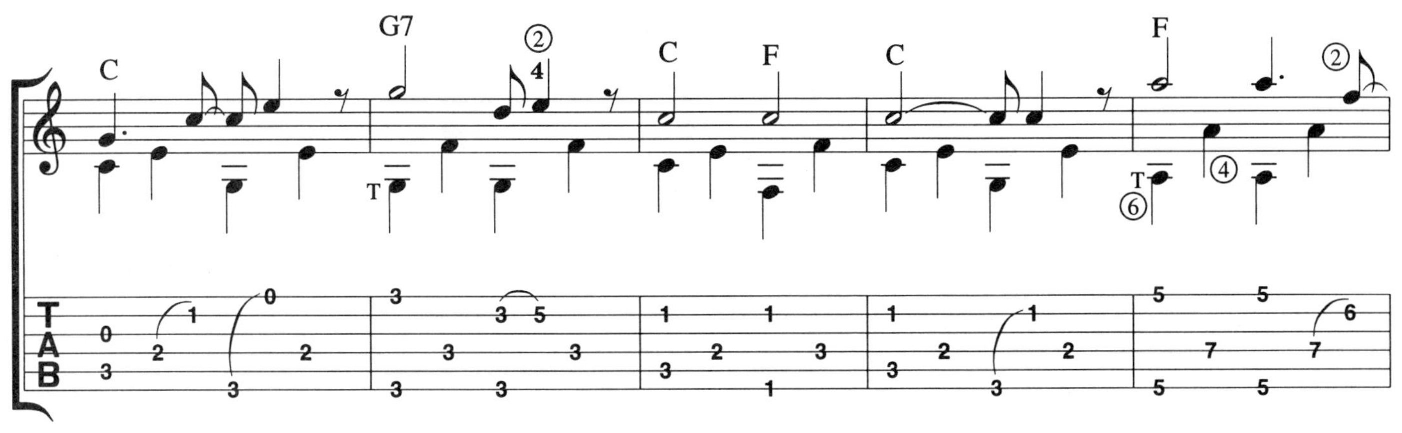
C
G7
C
F
C
F

C
G
D9

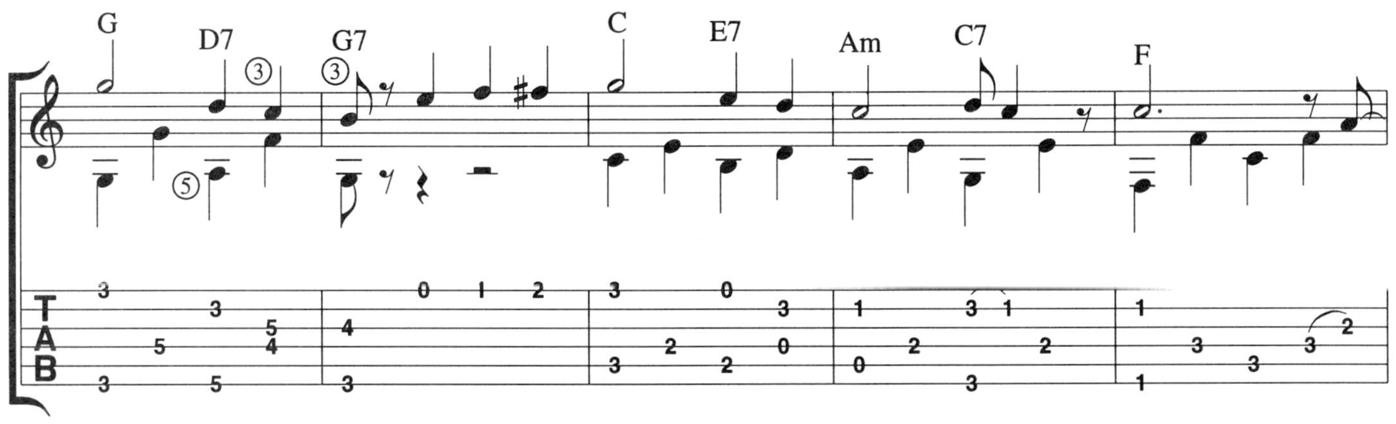
G
D7
G7
C
E7
Am
C7
F

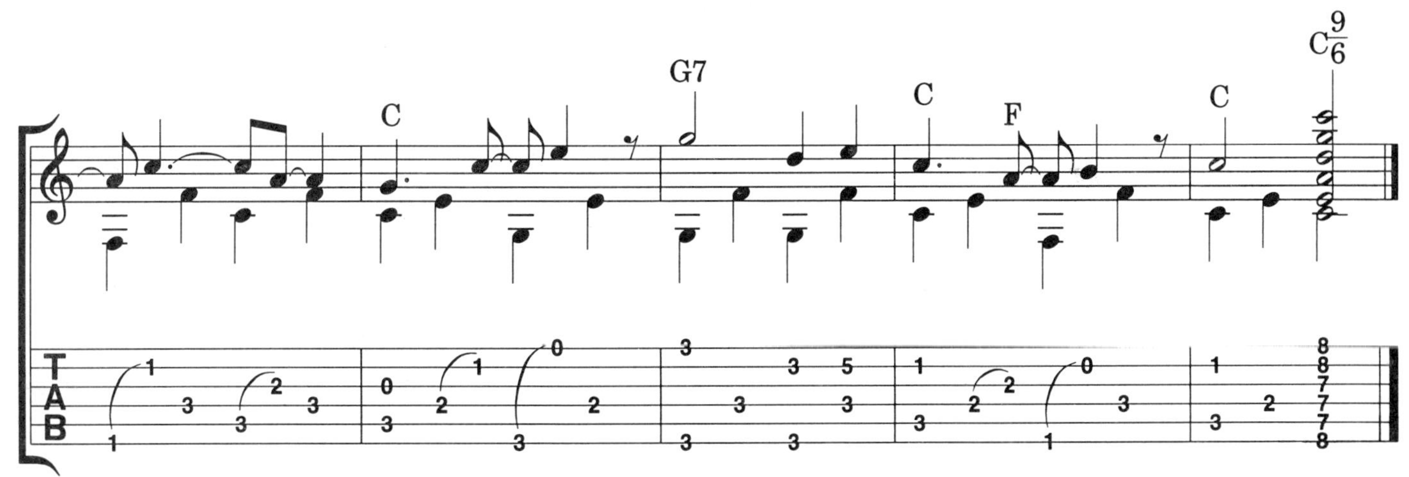
C
G7
C
F
C
C 9/6

THE CHORDS USED ON THIS PAGE

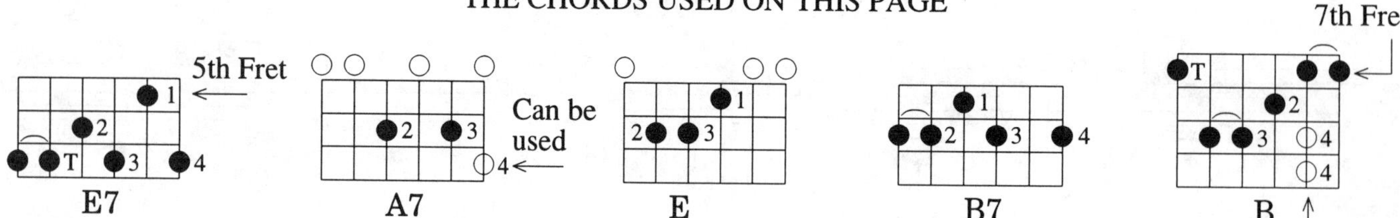

GOING DOWN THE ROAD FEELING BAD

Medium Fast

E7 Bend Bend

A7 Bend slide Bend E B7 E slide

A Bend slide Bend E B7 E slide slide

B slide E C7 * B7 E

*One fret higher than B7. Same fingering.

THE GUITAR BLUES

Tommy Flint

THE THREE FINGER ROLL

Beginning with the thumb, pluck the bass string. Then roll over the chord striking the ③ ② and ① string consecutively. Use i finger on ③ string, m finger on the ② string and a finger on the ① string.

SOME TRAVIS ENDINGS

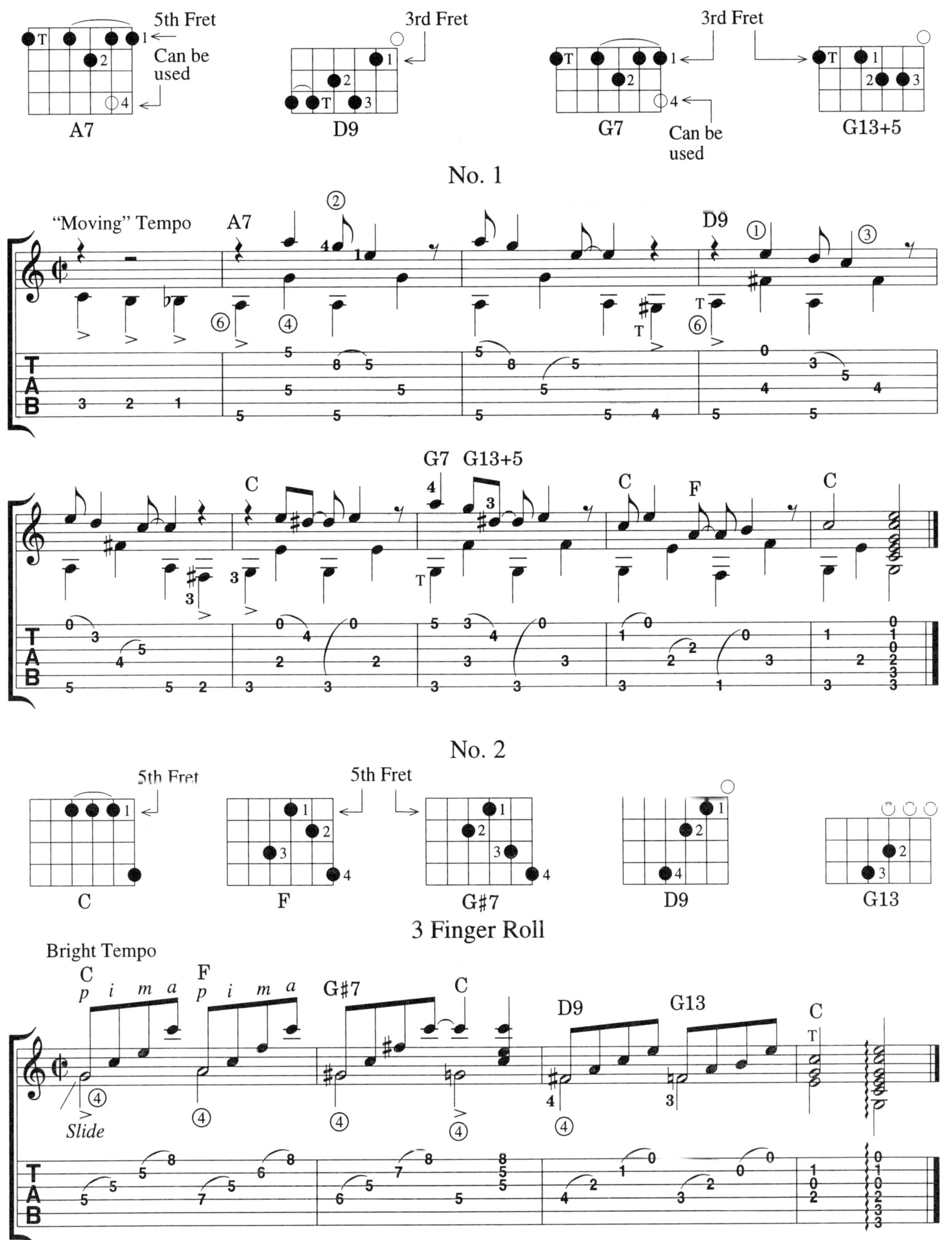

THE TRAVIS STYLE

As the Travis style is primarily a chord style, it would be wise at this point to learn some chords the way Merle makes them, using the thumb. The inversions may seem difficult at first, but with perseverance you can master them. Most of the chords shown here are unique and original.

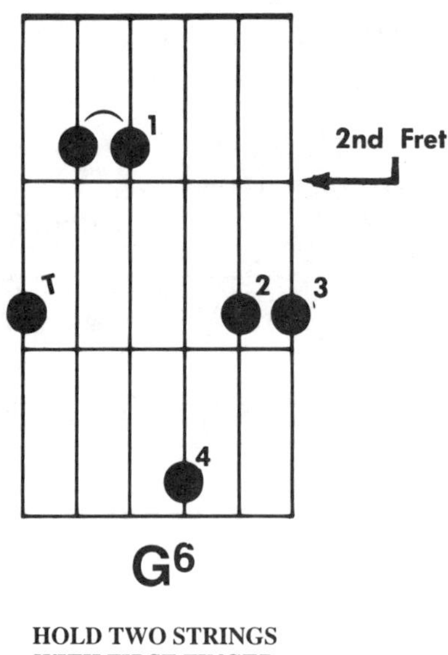

G^6

HOLD TWO STRINGS
WITH FIRST FINGER

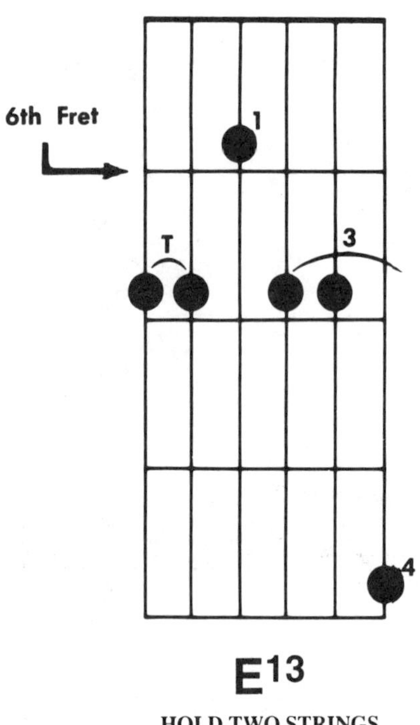

E^{13}

HOLD TWO STRINGS
WITH THE THUMB

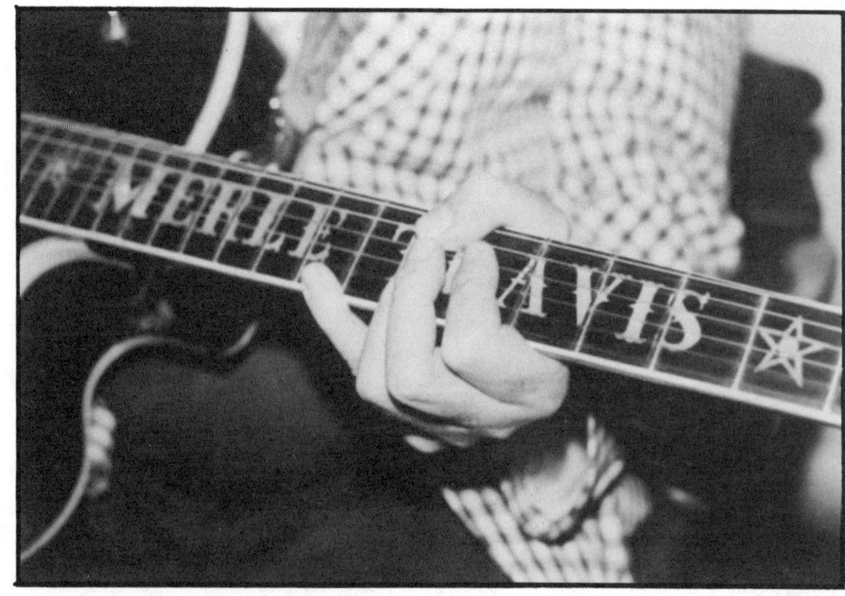

Remove the fourth finger from the ① string and bar the ③, ② & ① strings with the third finger. The chord becomes E9.

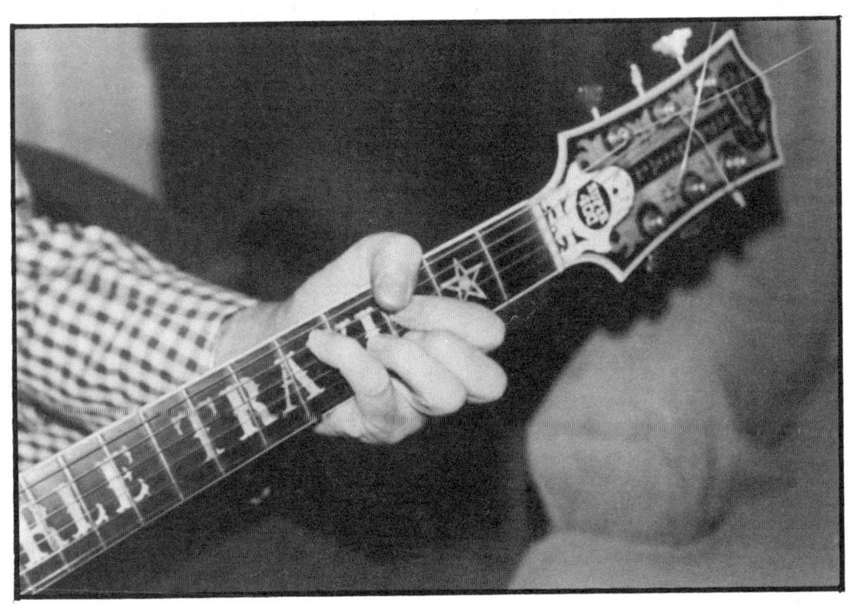

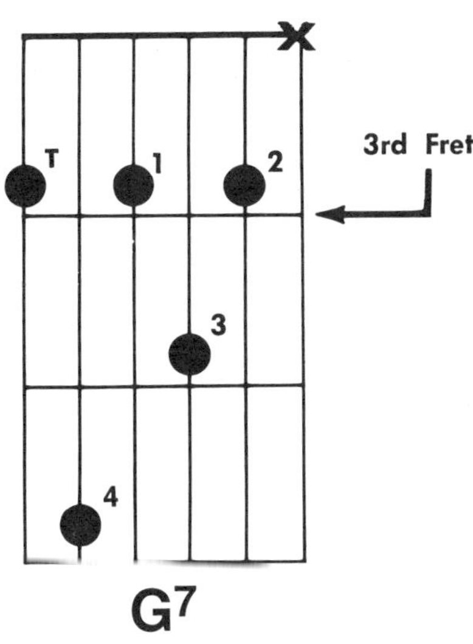

G7

WHEN THE OPEN ① STRING IS ADDED
TO THE CHORD IT BECOMES G13.

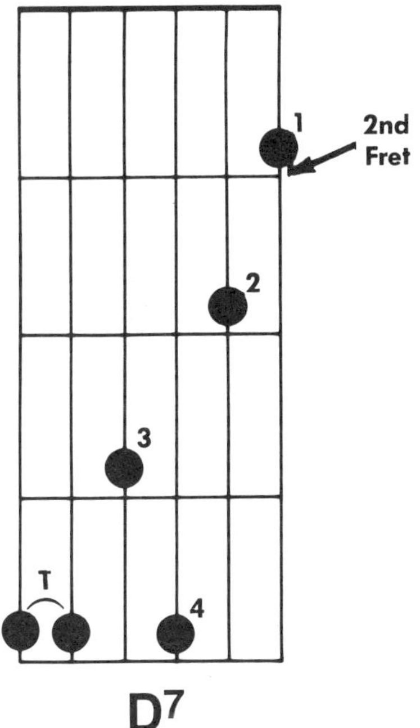

D7

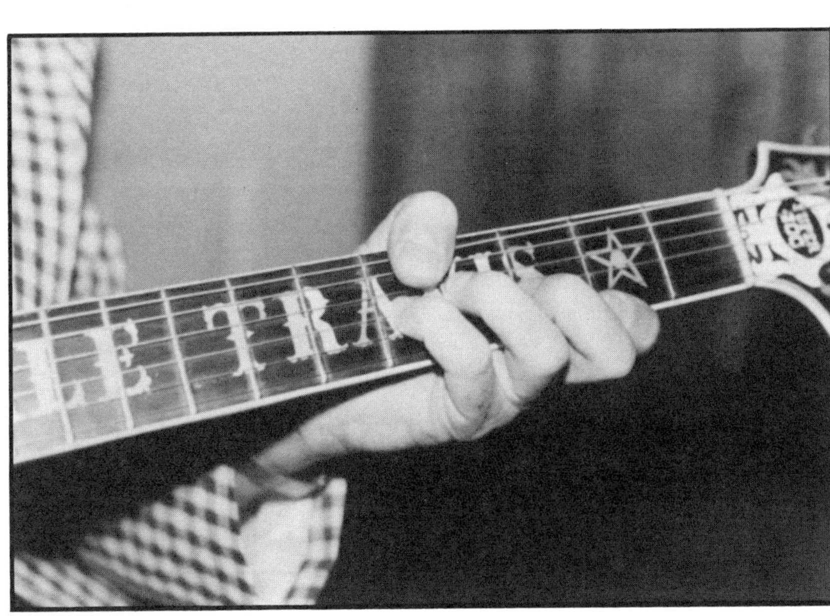

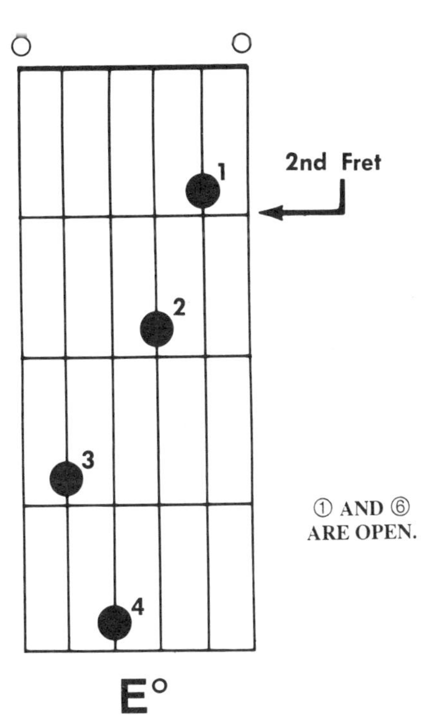

① AND ⑥
ARE OPEN.

E°

SIX STRING DIMINISHED

SOME TRAVIS CHORDS USING OPEN STRINGS

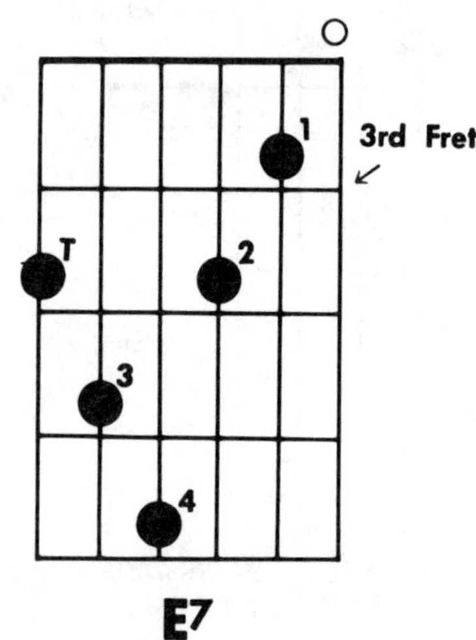

E7

⑥ STRING MAY
BE PLAYED OPEN.

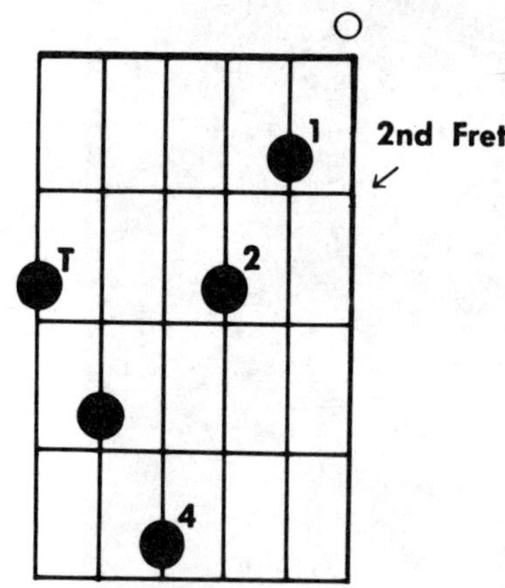

SIX STRING DIMINISHED

⑥ STRING MAY
BE PLAYED OPEN.

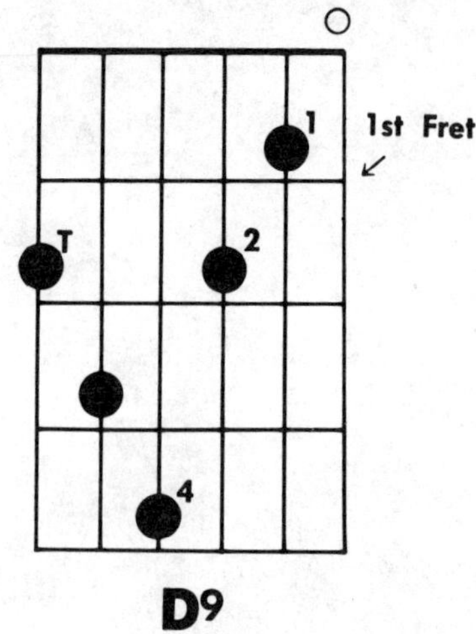

D9

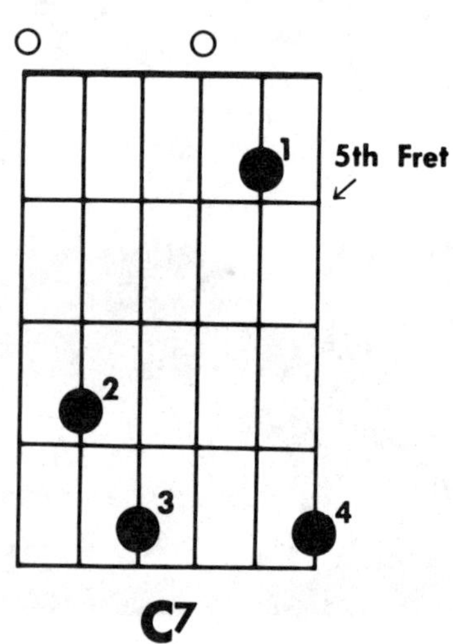

C7

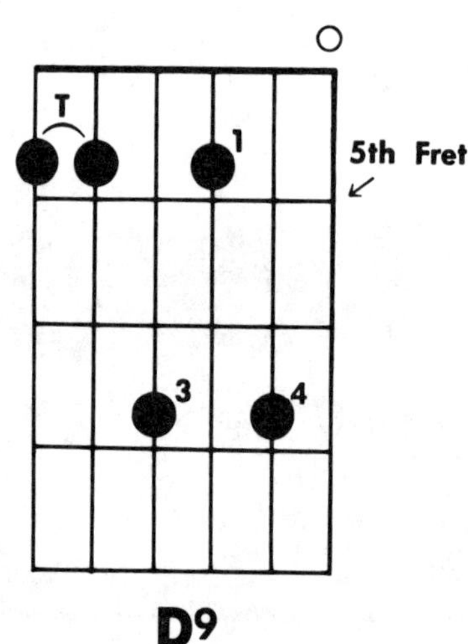

D9

HOLD DOWN TWO
STRINGS WITH THUMB.

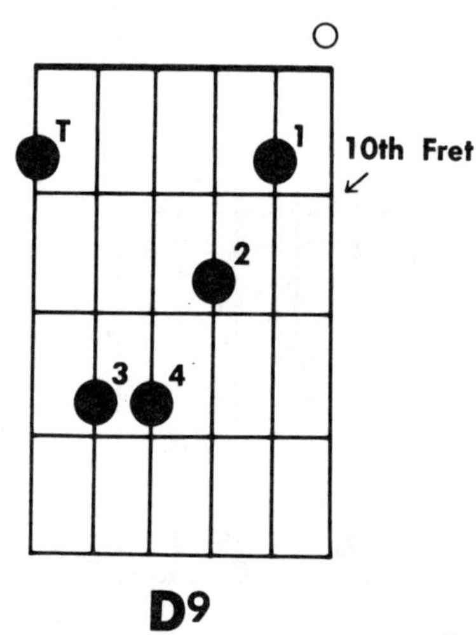

D9

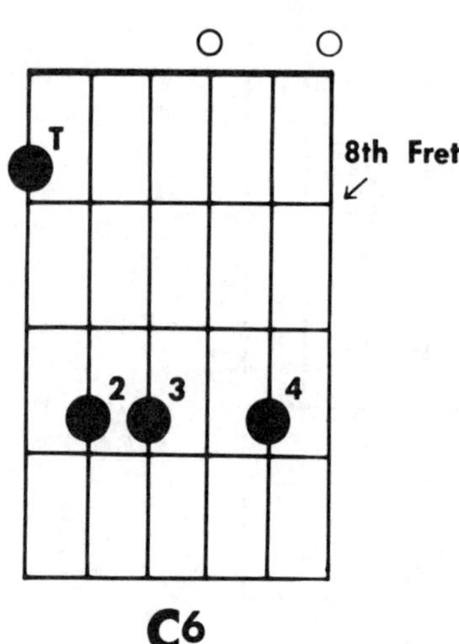

C6

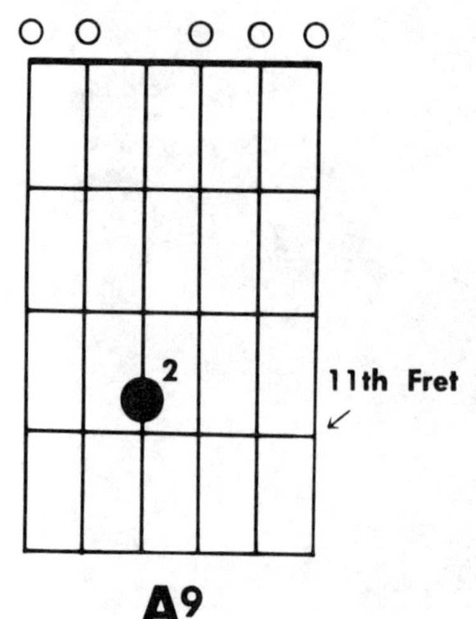

A9

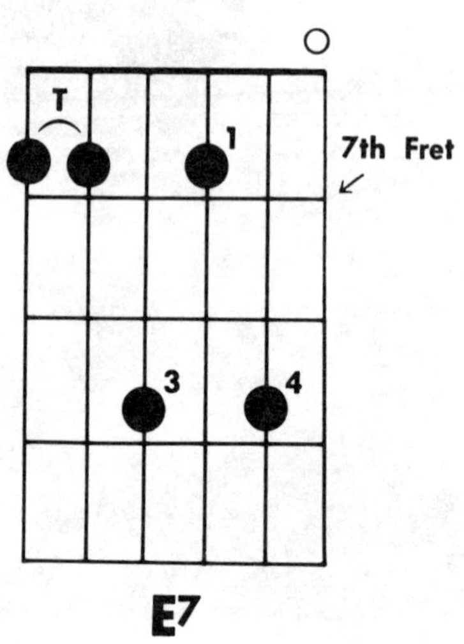

E7

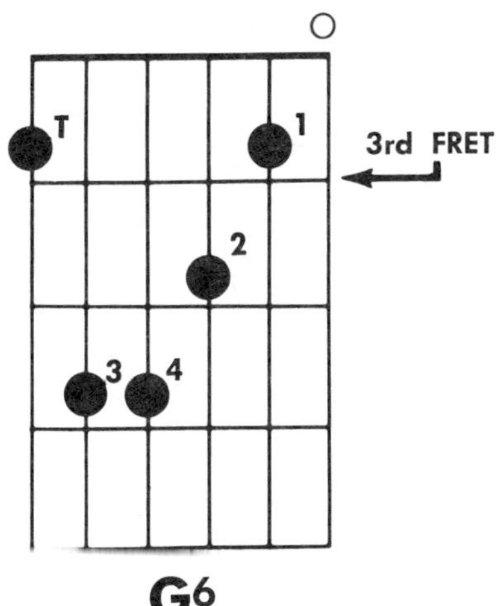

G6

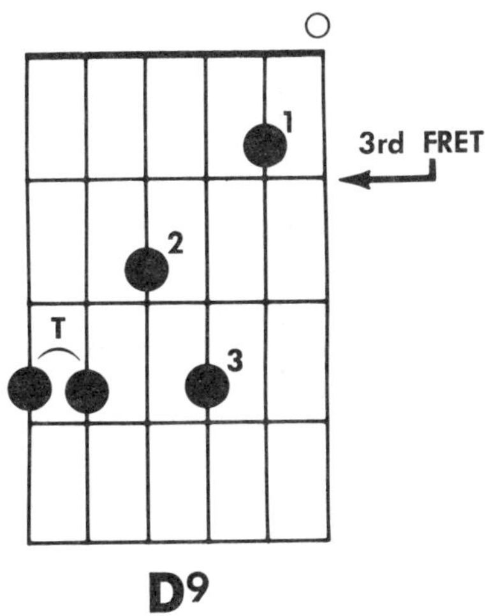

D9

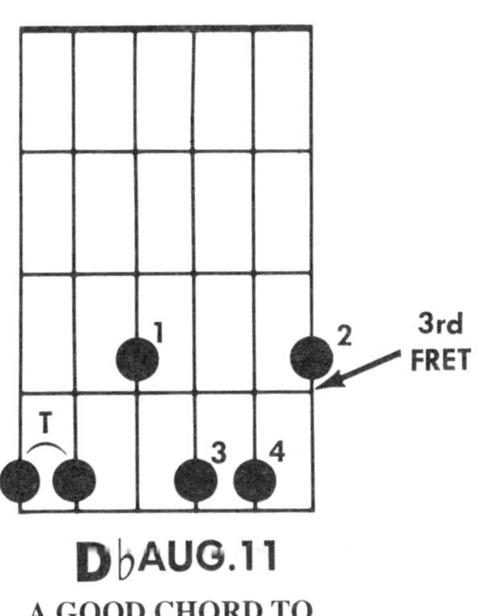

D♭AUG.11

A GOOD CHORD TO USE JUST BEFORE ENDING IN C.

The following chords are moveable and may be played in any position. (Any fret).

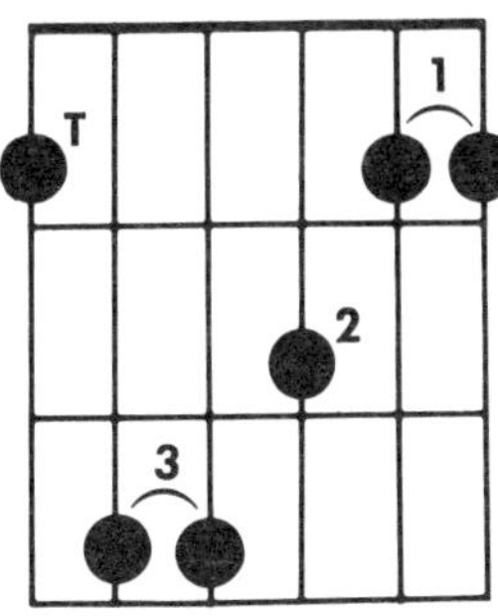

BOTH STRINGS WITH THIRD FINGER.

1st FRET .... F
2nd FRET .. F♯ or G♭
3rd FRET .... G
4th FRET .... A♭
5th FRET .... A
6th FRET .... B♭
7th FRET .... B
8th FRET C

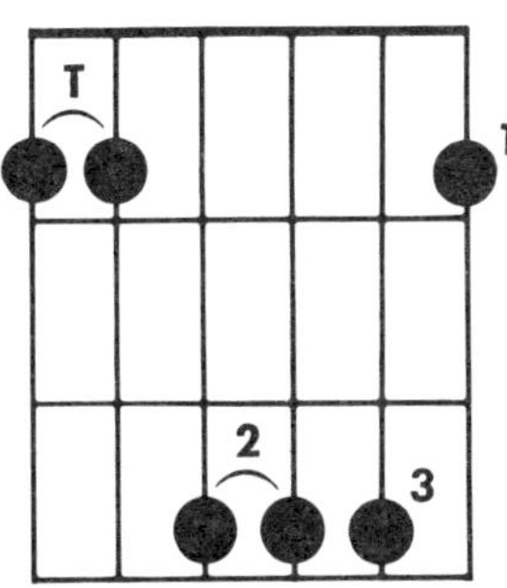

BOTH STRINGS WITH SECOND FINGER.

1st FRET .... B♭
2nd FRET .... B
3rd FRET C
4th FRET .. C♯ or D♭
5th FRET .... D
6th FRET .... E♭
7th FRET .... E
8th FRET .... F

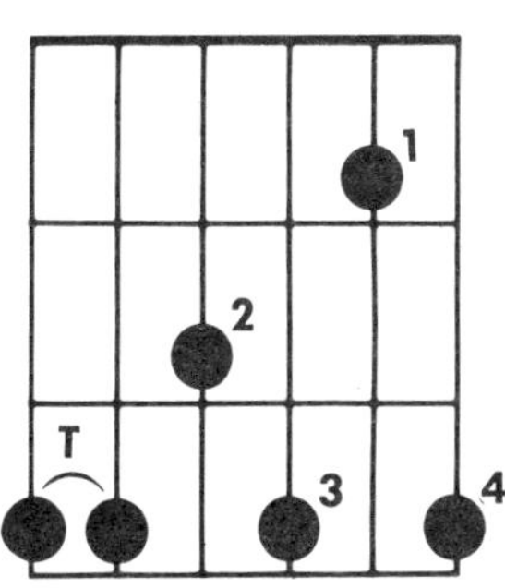

1st FRET C7
2nd FRET C♯7 or D♭7
3rd FRET D7
4th FRET .... E♭7
5th FRET E7
6th FRET F7
7th FRET F♯7 or G♭7
8th FRET G7

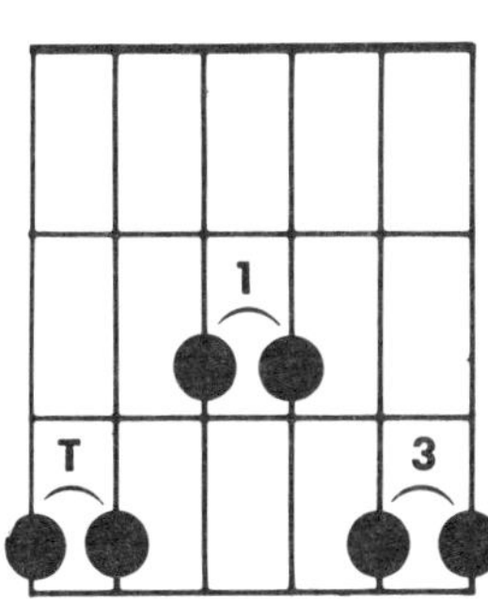

A GOOD CLOSING CHORD

1st FRET B9/6
2nd FRET C9/6
3rd FRET C♯ or D♭9/6
4th FRET D9/6
5th FRET .... E♭9/6
6th FRET E9/6
7th FRET F9/6

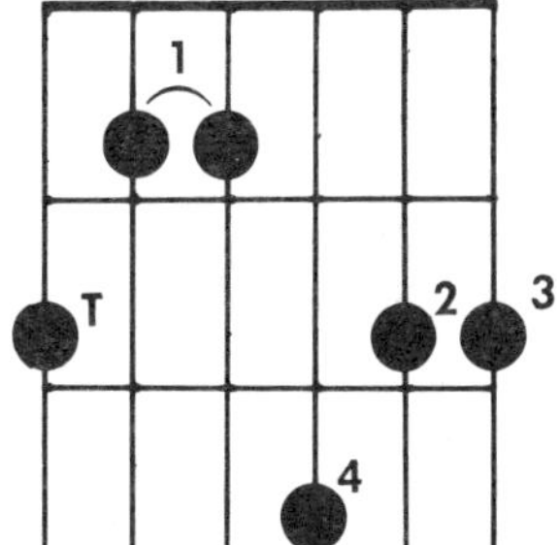

1st FRET F♯6 or G♭6
2nd FRET G6
3rd FRET .... A♭6
4th FRET A6
5th FRET .... B♭6
6th FRET B6
7th FRET C6

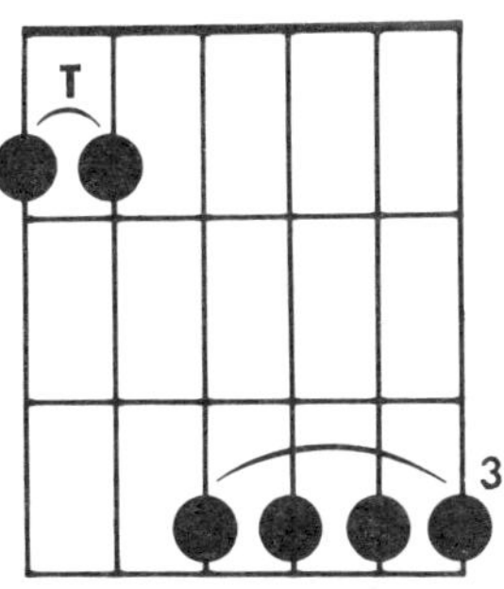

1st FRET .... B♭6
2nd FRET B6
3rd FRET C6
4th FRET C♯6 or D♭6
5th FRET D6
6th FRET .... E♭6
7th FRET E6

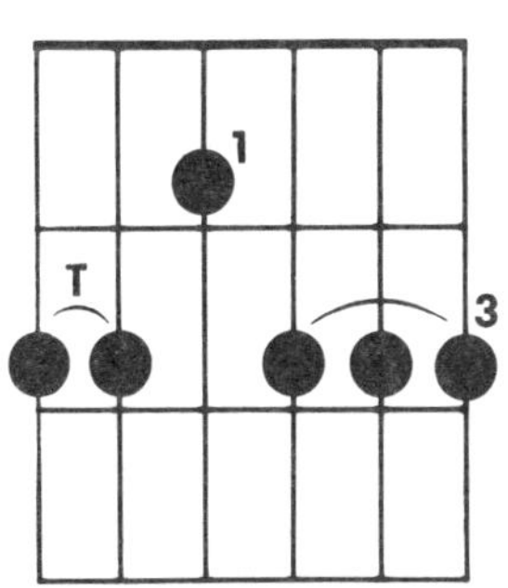

1st FRET B9
2nd FRET C9
3rd FRET C♯9 or D♭9
4th FRET D9
5th FRET .... E♭9
6th FRET E9
7th FRET F9

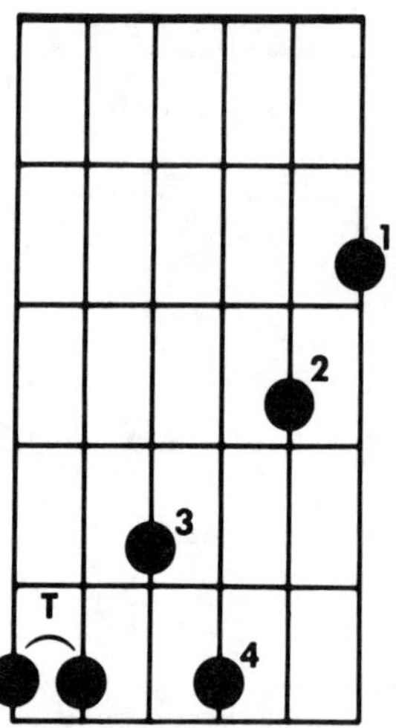

1st FRET C♯7 or D♭7
2nd FRET D7
3rd FRET .... E♭7
4th FRET E7
5th FRET F7
6th FRET F♯7 or G♭7
7th FRET G7

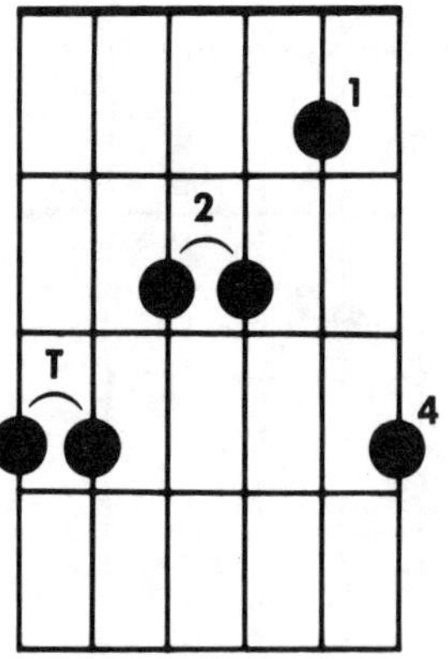

1st FRET C6
2nd FRET C♯6 or D♭6
3rd FRET D6
4th FRET .... E♭6
5th FRET E6
6th FRET F6
7th FRET F♯6 or G♭6
8th FRET G6

THE ABOVE CHORD MAY BE USED AS A MINOR 7th. 1st FRET WOULD BE Am7 ETC.

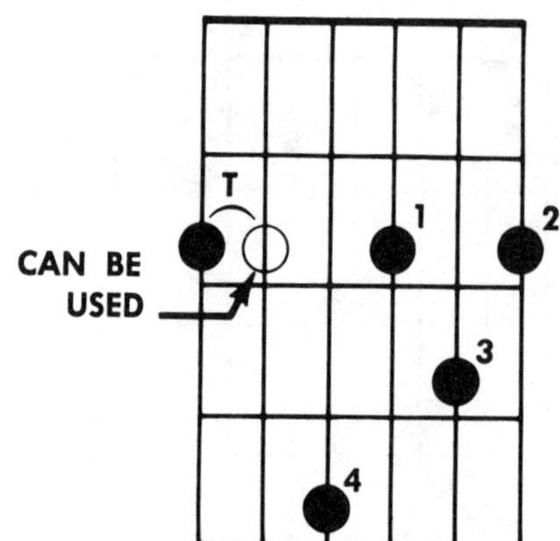

1st FRET .. C♯ or D♭
2nd FRET .... D
3rd FRET .... E♭
4th FRET .... E
5th FRET .... F
6th FRET .. F♯ or G♭
7th FRET .... G

WHEN THE THUMB HOLDS DOWN BOTH THE ⑥ AND ⑤ STRINGS. THE ABOVE CHORD BECOMES A SIXTH OR MINOR 7th CHORD. 2nd FRET D6 or Bm7.

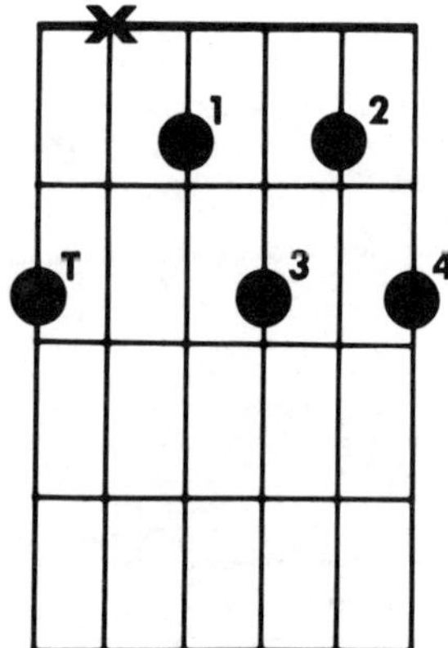

1st FRET E♭°, A°, C°, F♯°
2nd FRET E°, B♭°, C♯°, G°
3rd FRET .. F°, B°, D°, A♭°

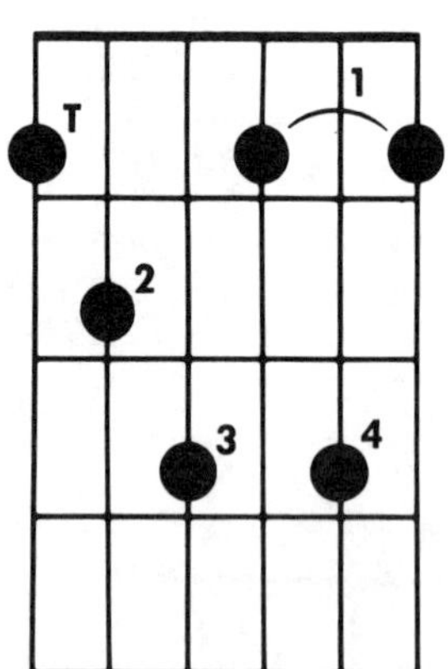

1st FRET .. B°, F°, A♭°, D°
2nd FRET C°, F♯°, A°, E♭°
3rd FRET C♯°, G°, B♭°, E°

THE DIMINISHED SEVENTH (°) CHORD HAS FOUR NAMES. THE 0 CHORD REPEATS ITSELF EVERY FOUR FRETS (MINOR THIRD) UP THE FINGERBOARD. THE ABOVE CHORDS HAVE THE SAME NAME IN THE FIRST AND FOURTH POSITIONS. (FIRST AND FOURTH FRETS.)

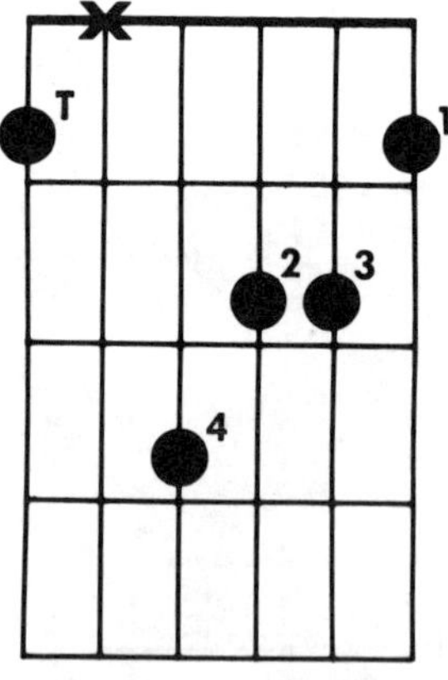

1st FRET A+, C♯+, F+
2nd FRET B♭+, D+, F♯+
3rd FRET B+, E♭+, G+
4th FRET C+, E+, A♭+

THE AUGMENTED FIFTH CHORD HAS THREE NAMES. IT REPEATS ITSELF EVERY FIFTH FRET (MAJOR THIRD). IT HAS THE SAME NAME AT THE FIRST AND FIFTH FRET.

MY OLD KENTUCKY HOME

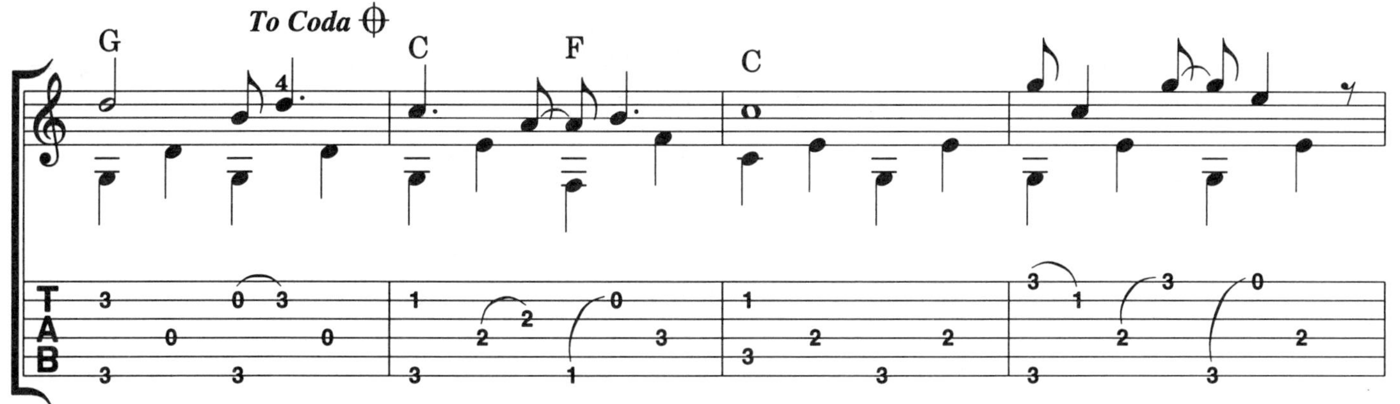
G
To Coda
C
F
C

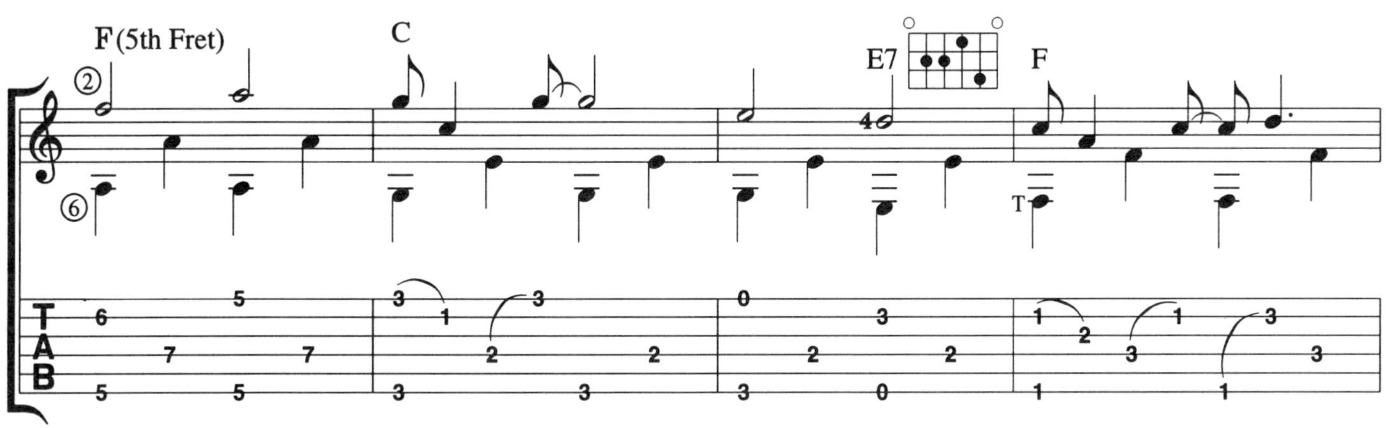
F (5th Fret)
C
E7
F

C
C
E7

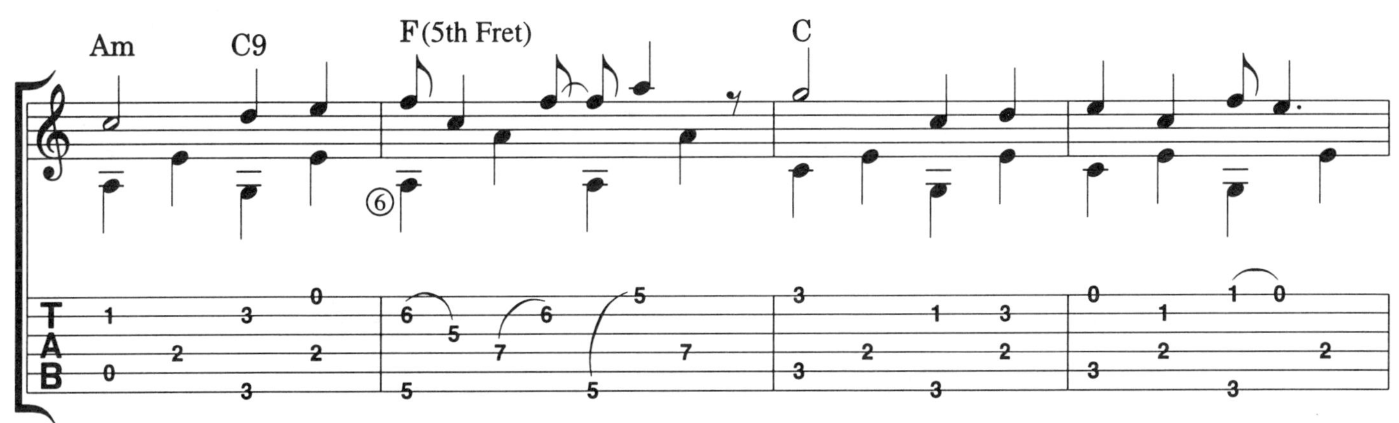
Am
C9
F (5th Fret)
C

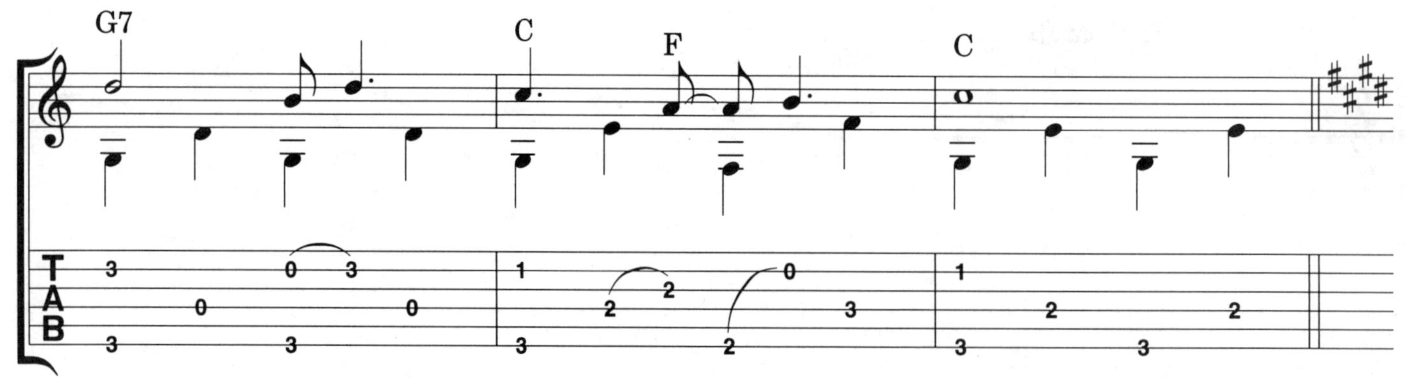
G7
C
F
C
TAB

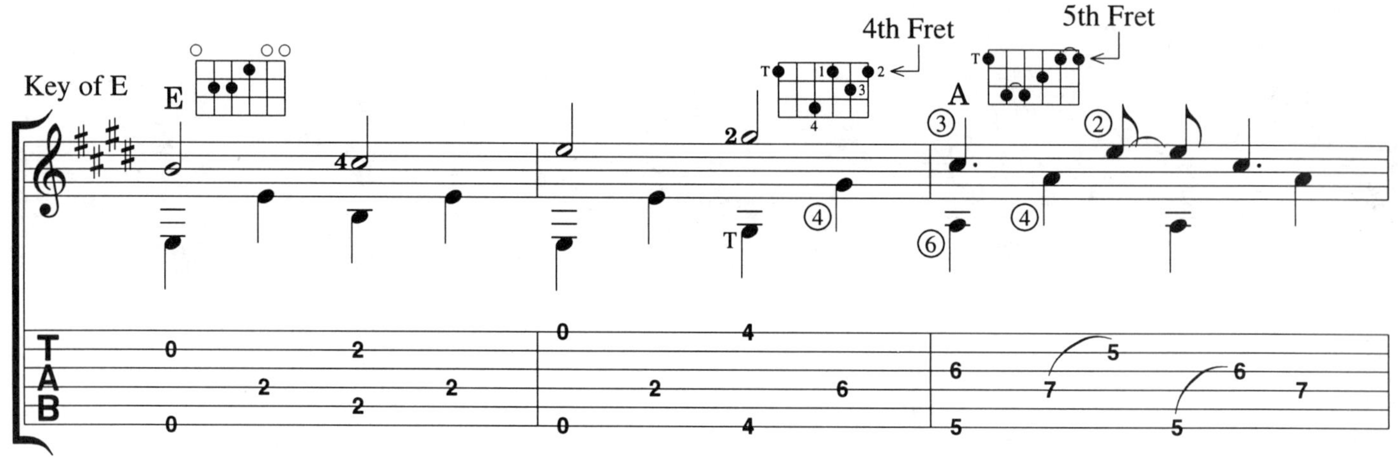
Key of E
E
4th Fret
5th Fret
A
TAB

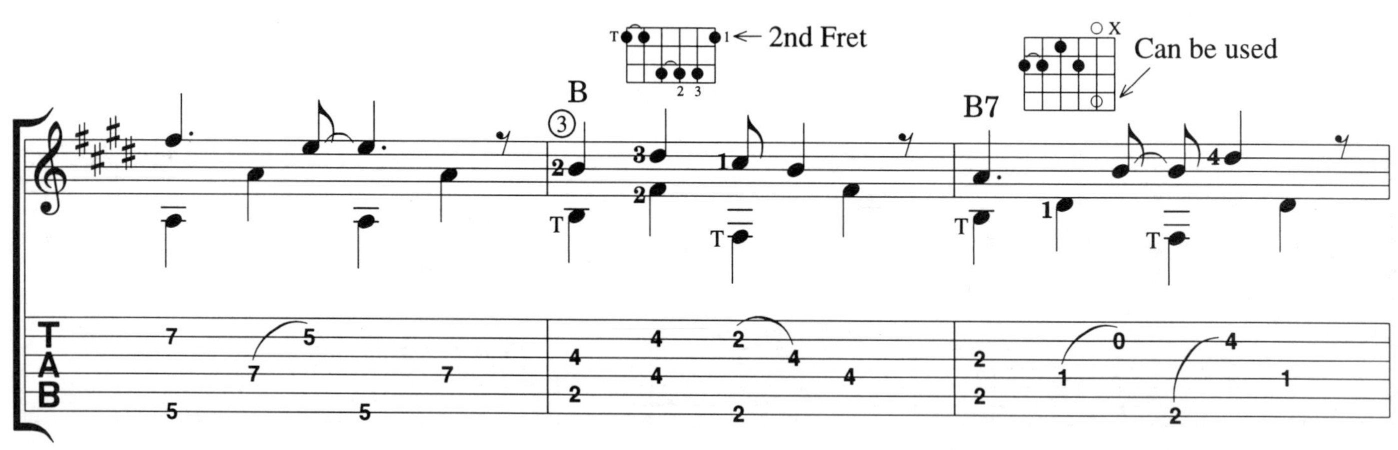
2nd Fret
B
Can be used
B7
TAB

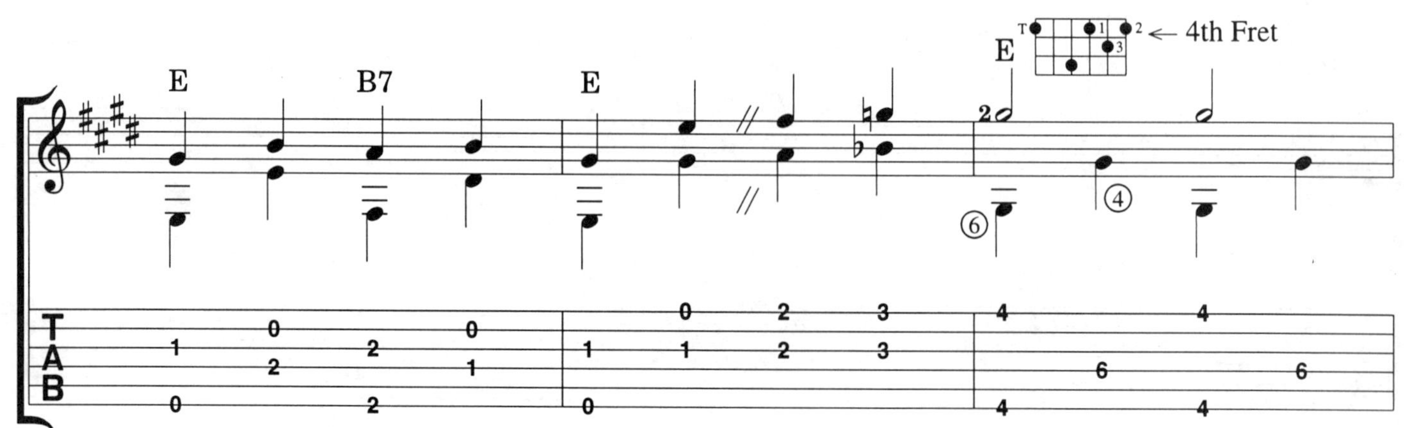
E
B7
E
E
4th Fret
TAB

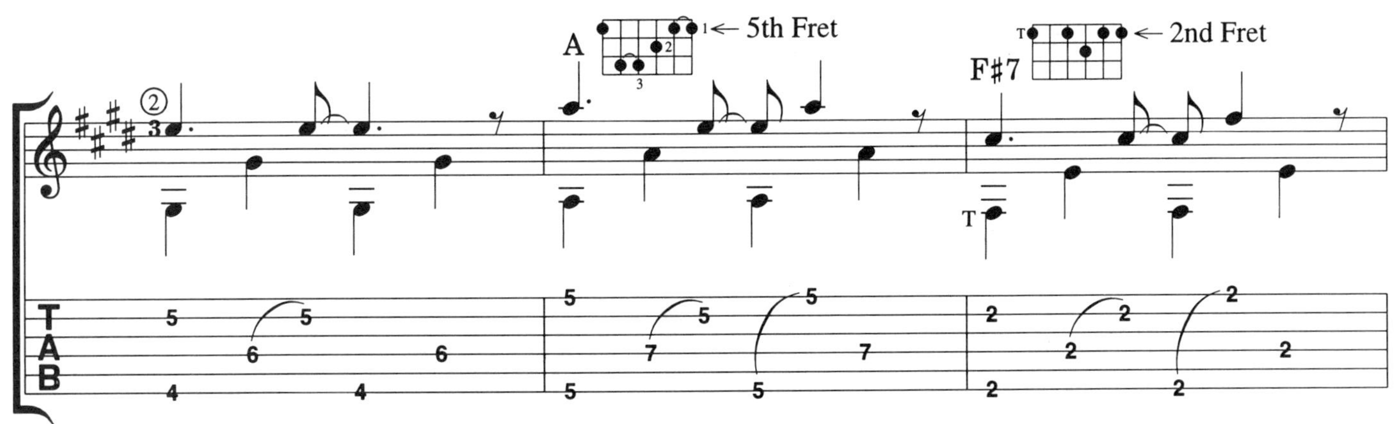

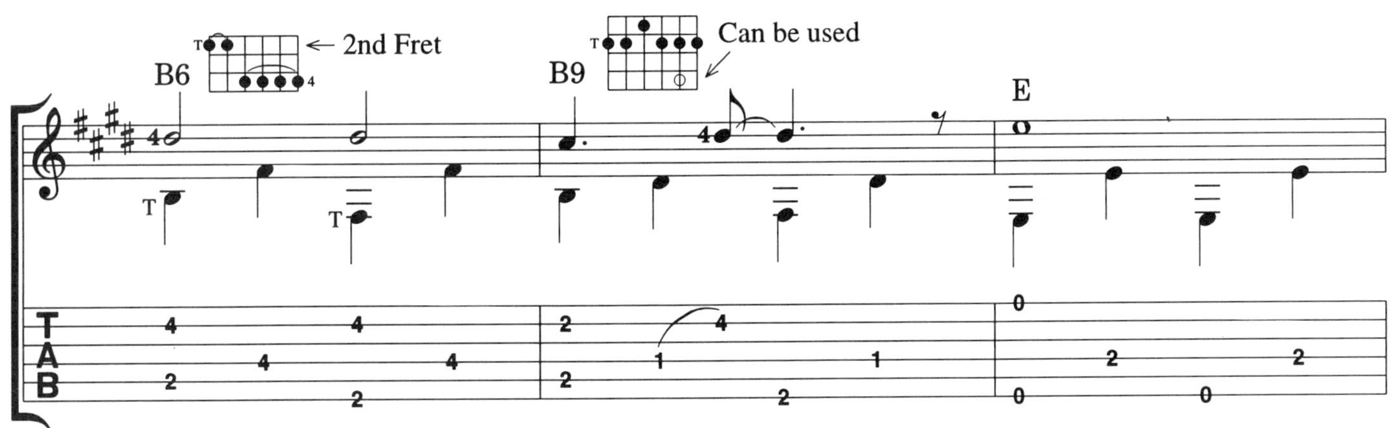

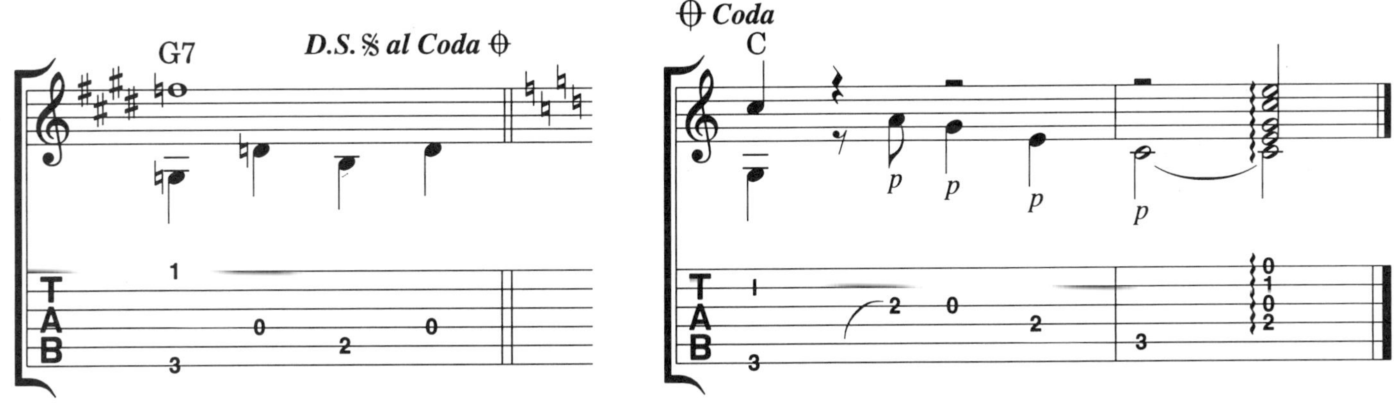

A BLUES INTRO

BICYCLE BUILT FOR TWO

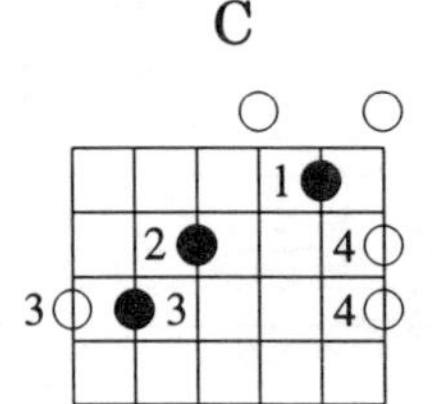

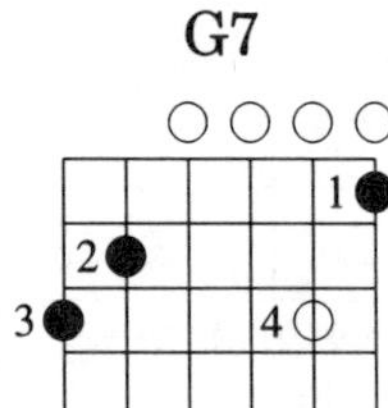

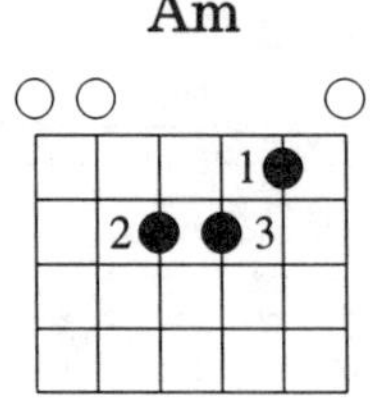

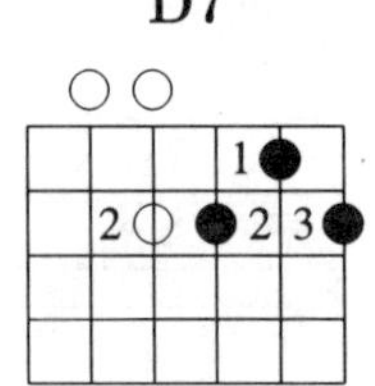

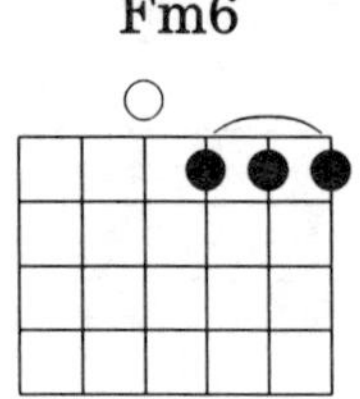

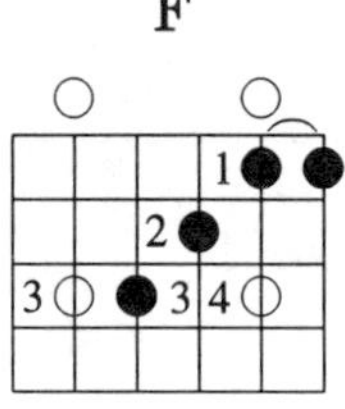

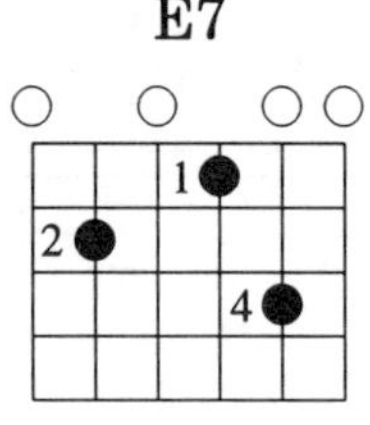

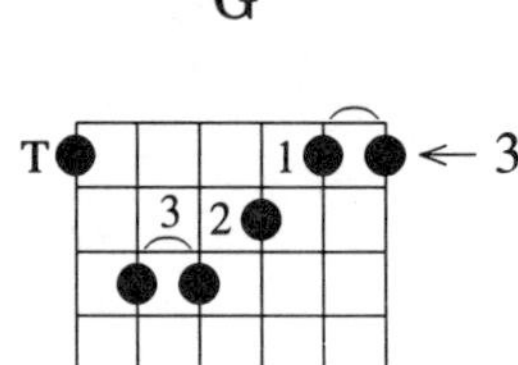

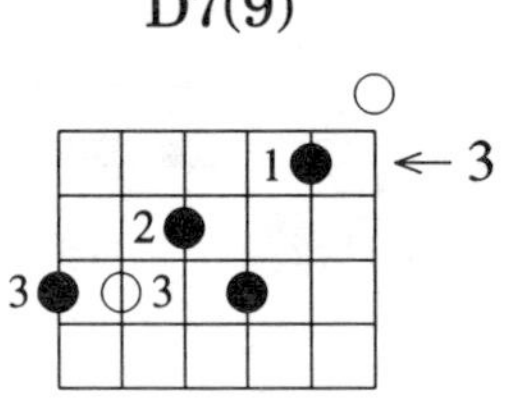

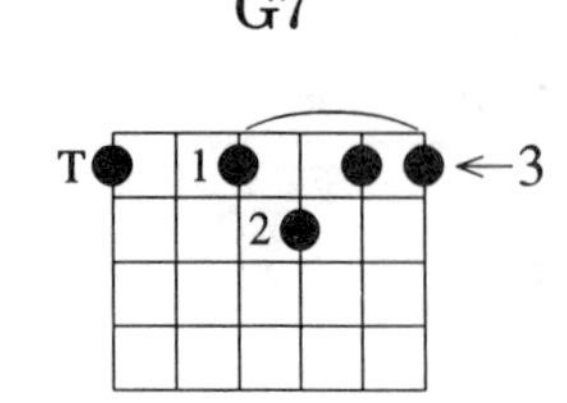

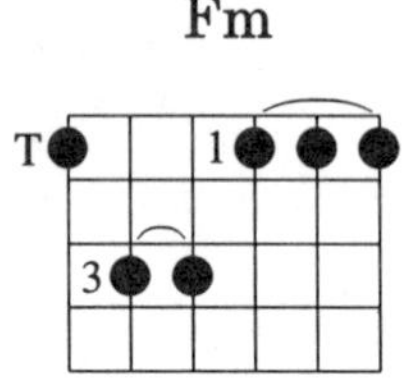

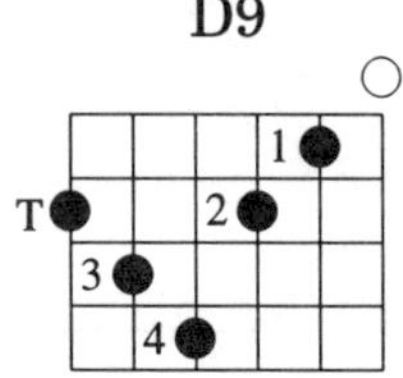

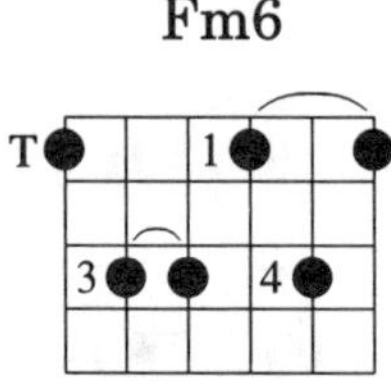

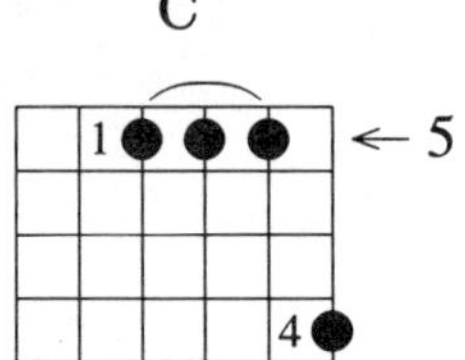

BICYCLE BUILT FOR TWO

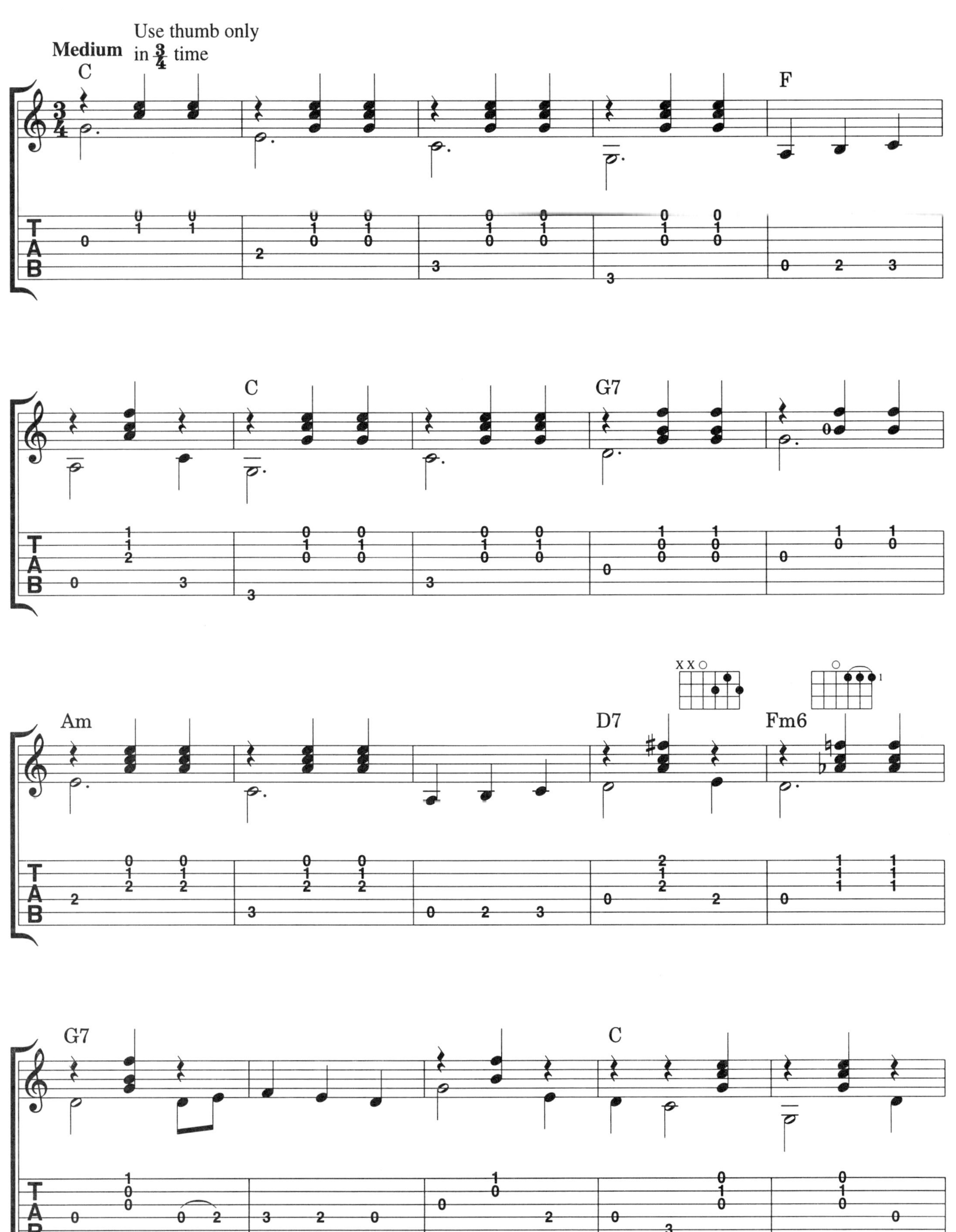

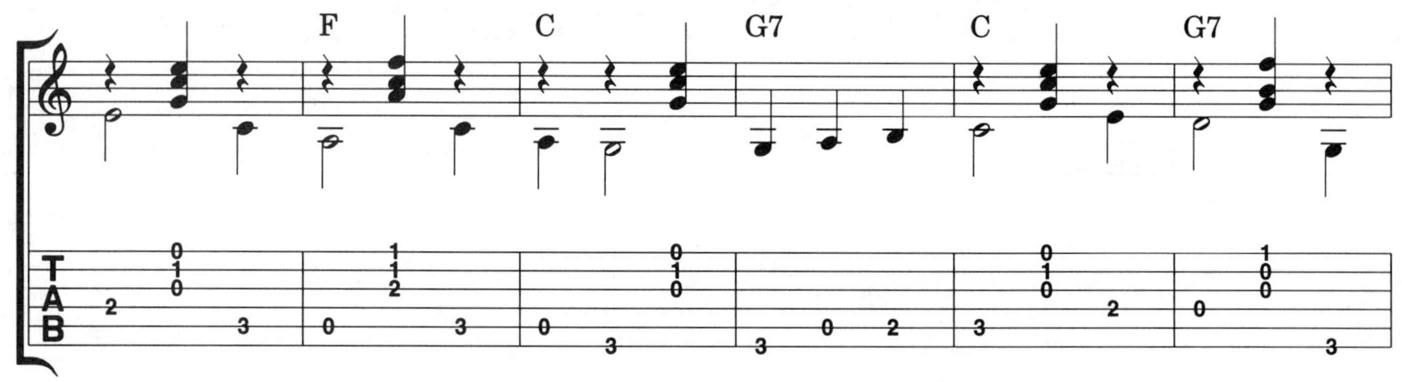

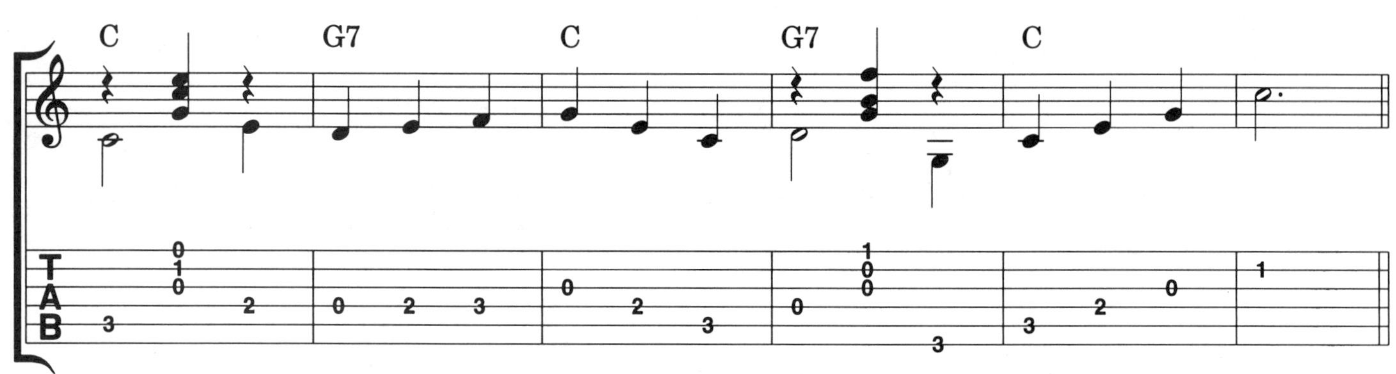

Verse
Bright

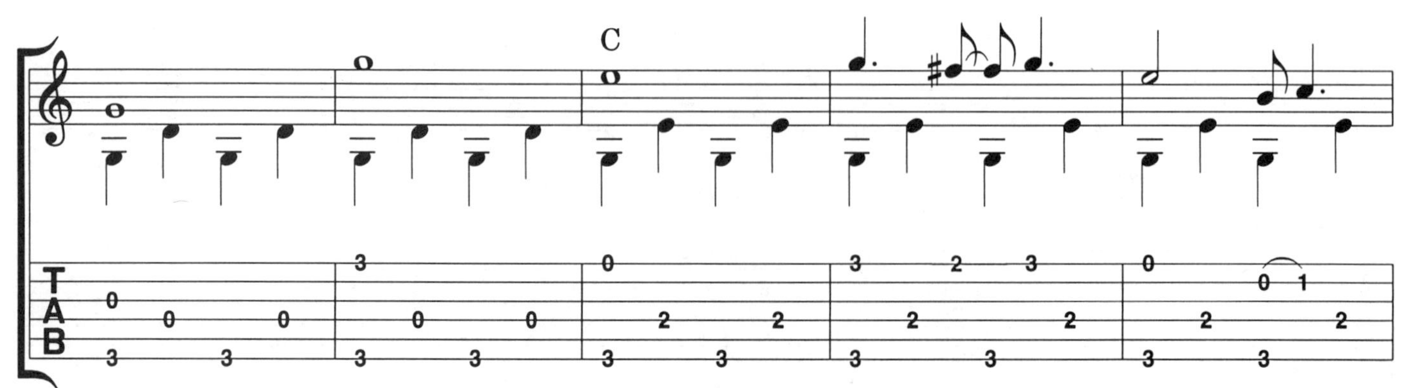

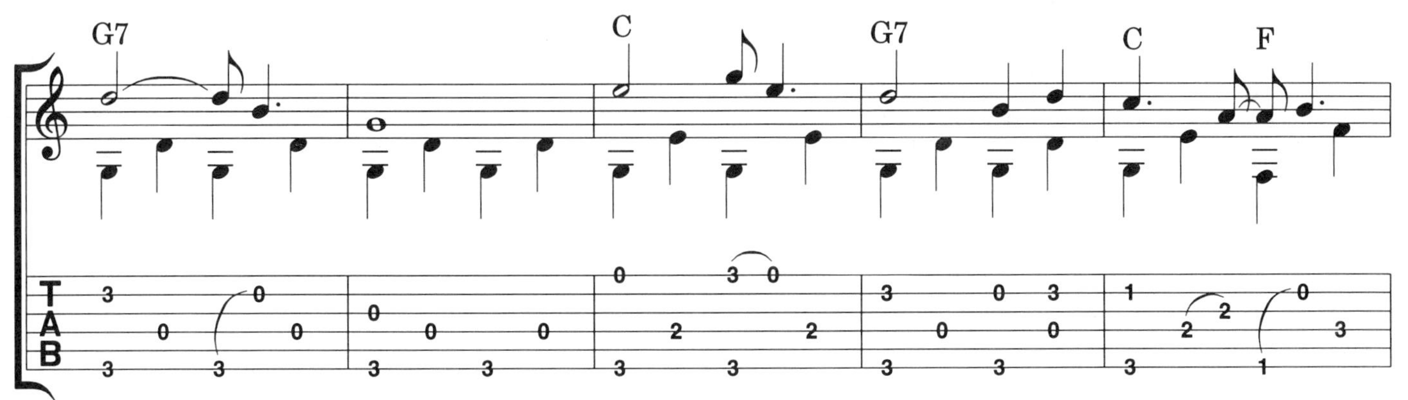
G7
C
G7
C
F
TAB

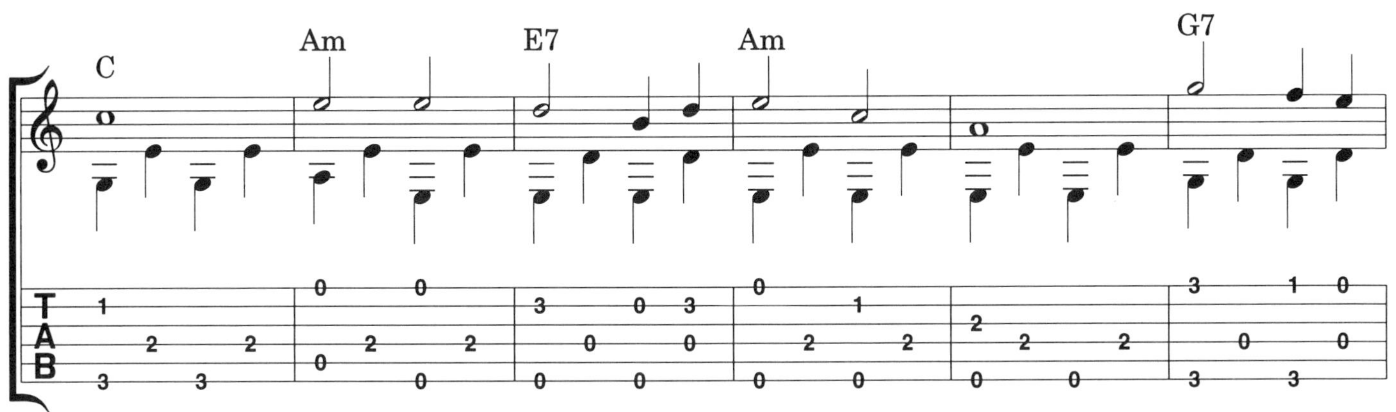
C
Am
E7
Am
G7
TAB

C
Am
E7
Am
TAB

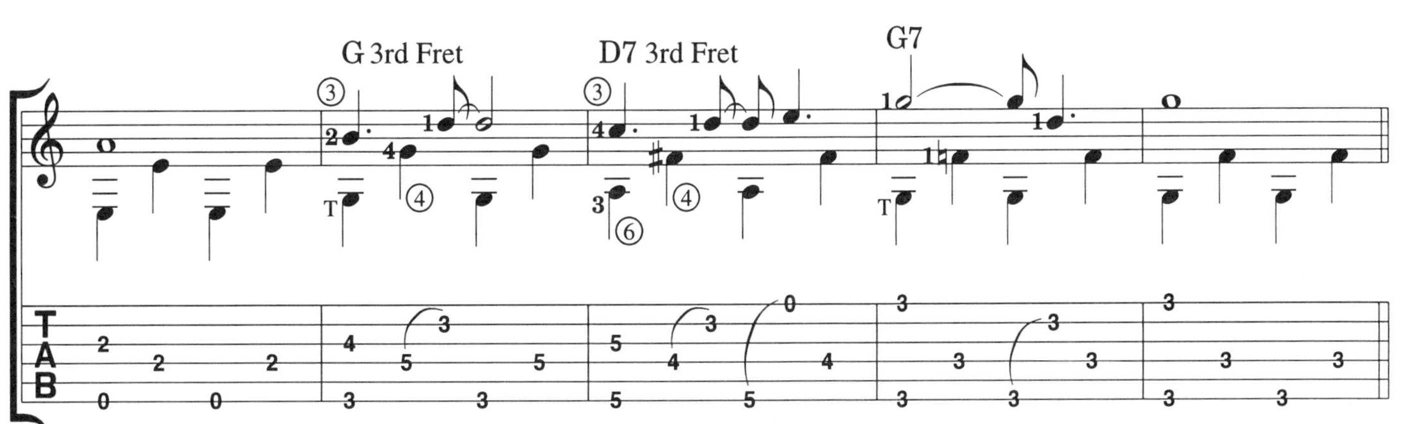
G 3rd Fret
D7 3rd Fret
G7
TAB

Chorus

C
C7
TAB

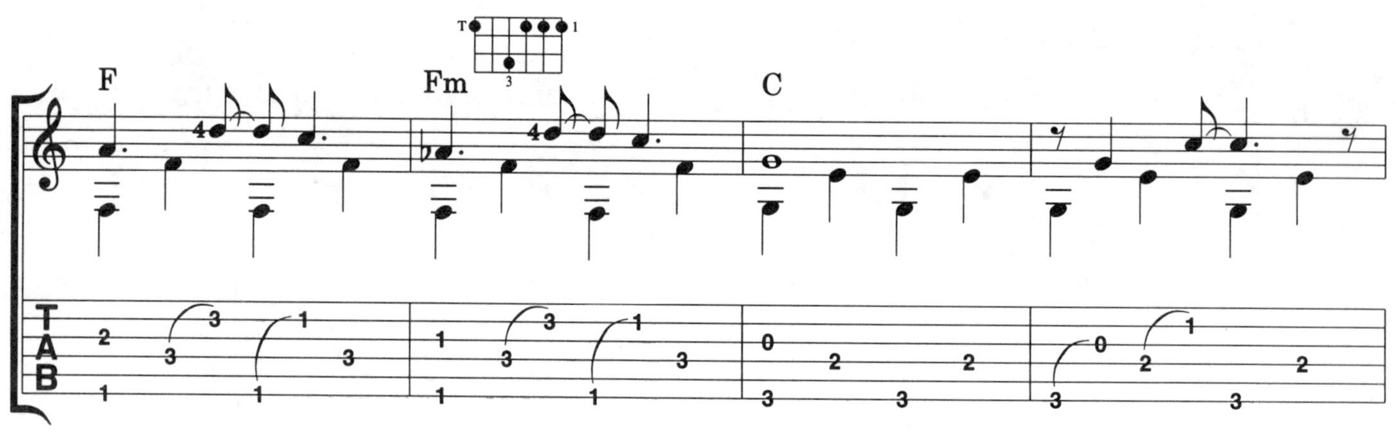
F
Fm
C
TAB

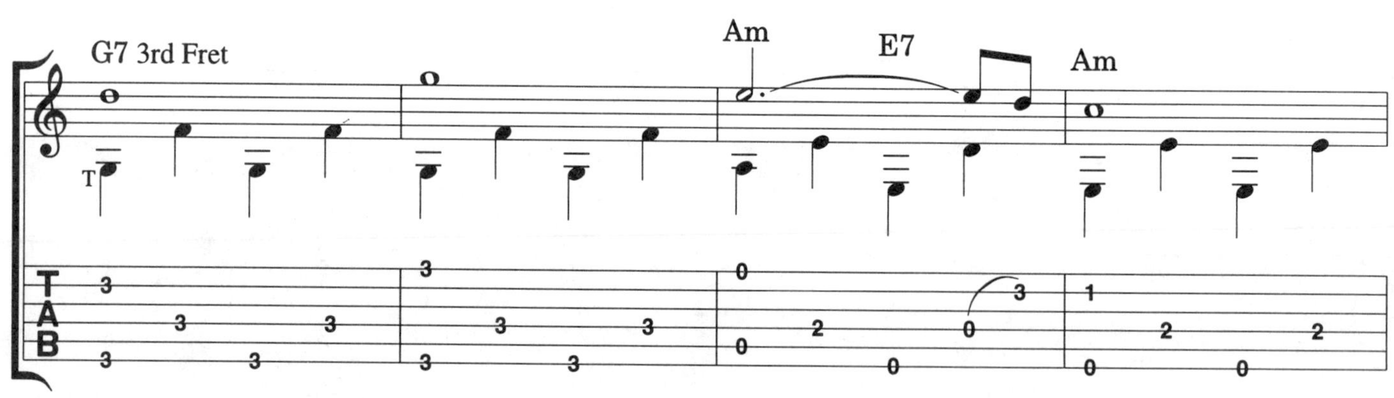
G7 3rd Fret
Am
E7
Am
TAB

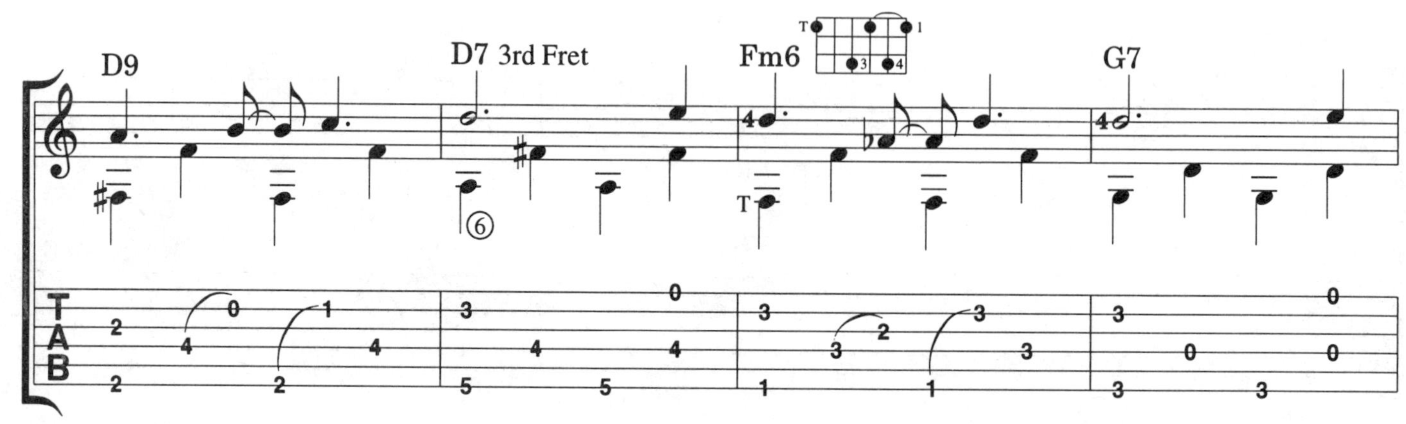
D9
D7 3rd Fret
Fm6
G7
TAB

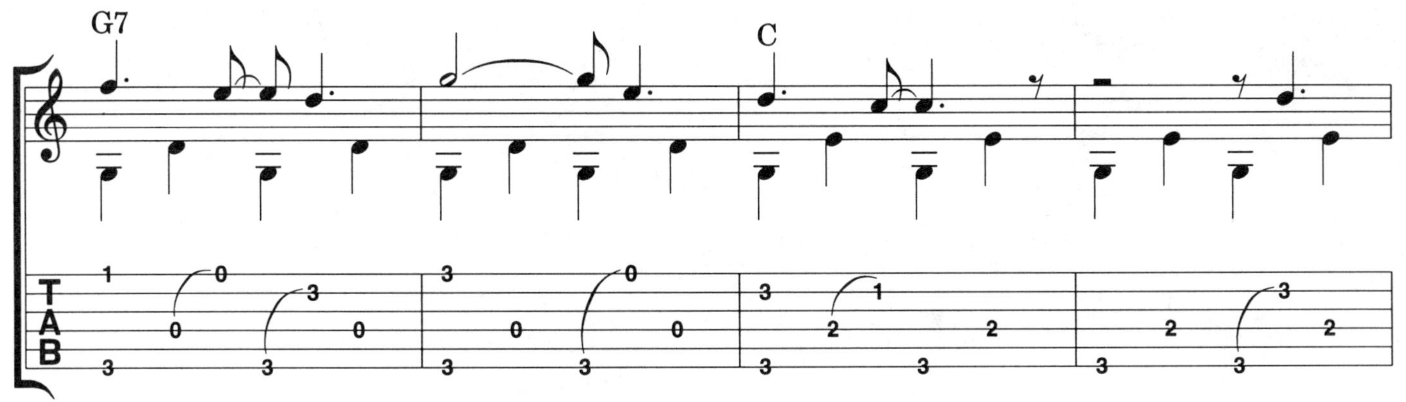

G7
C

F
Fm
G7

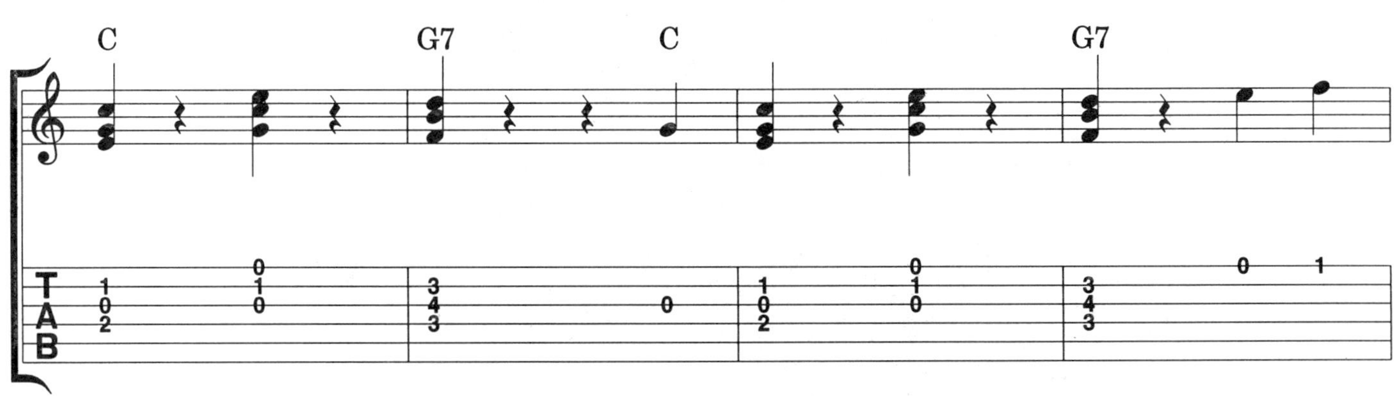

C
G7
C
G7

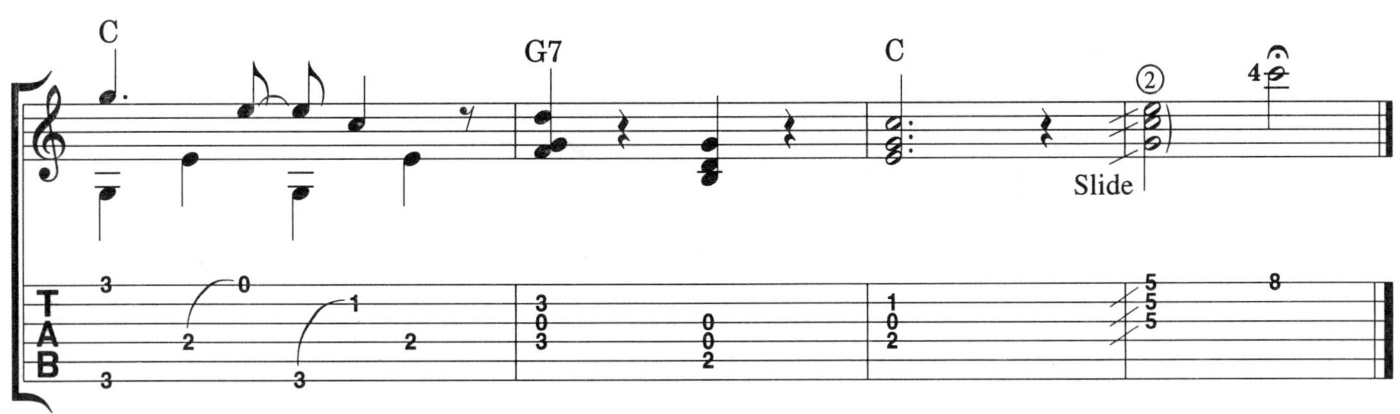

C
G7
C
Slide

Ike Everly, Merle Travis and Mose Rager

SATURDAY'S SONG

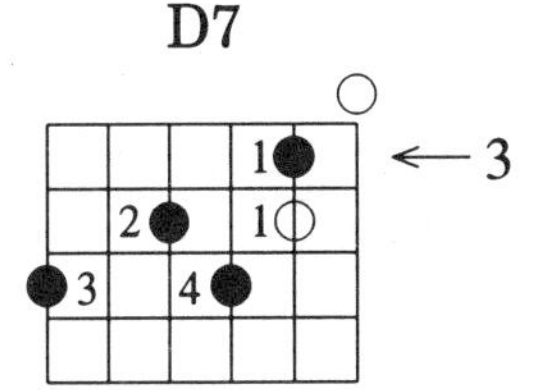

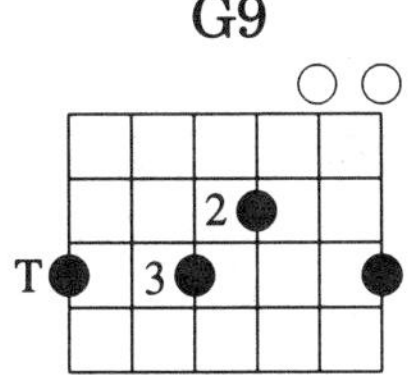

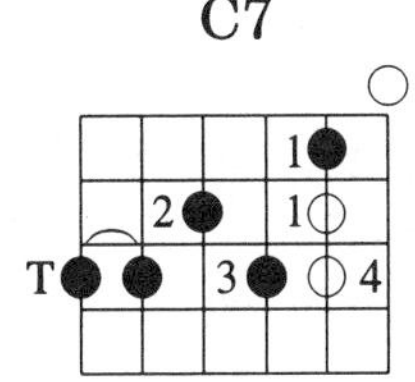

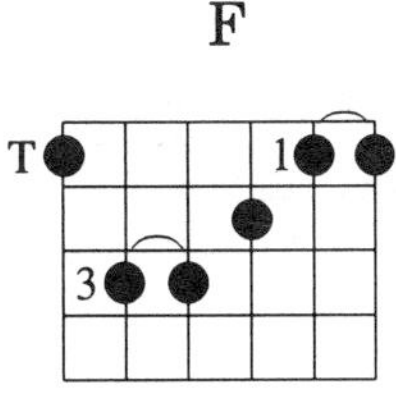

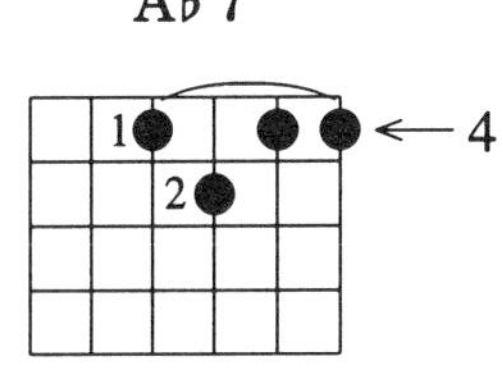

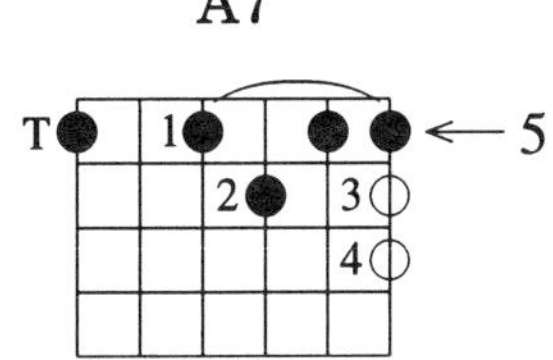

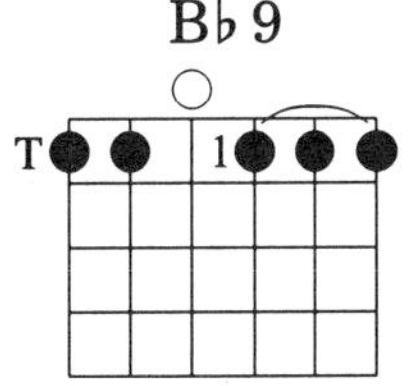

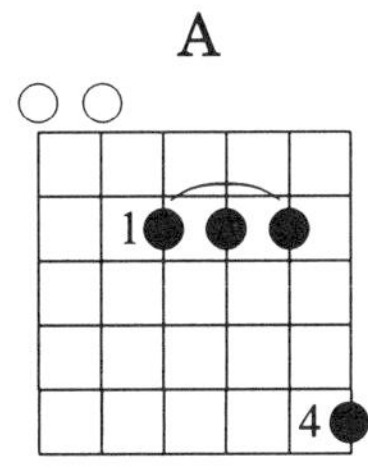

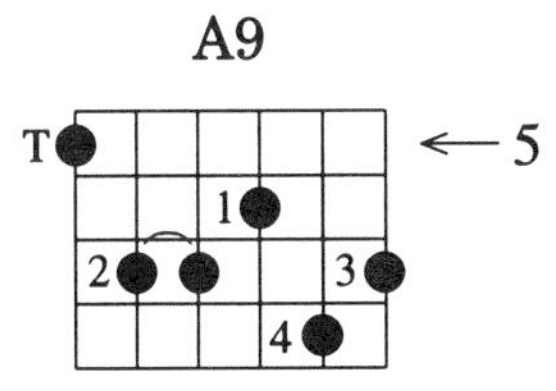

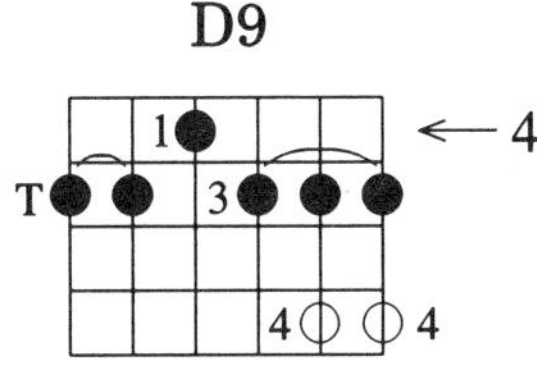

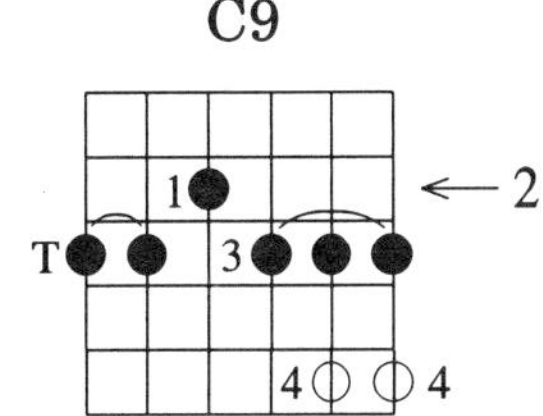

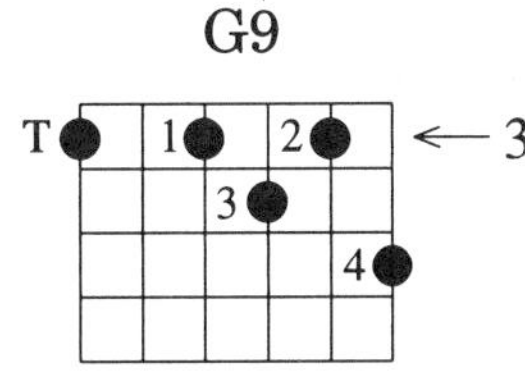

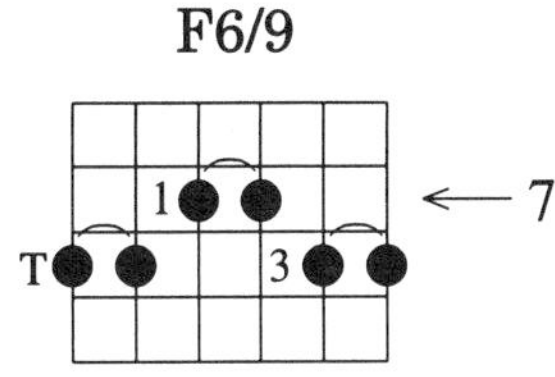

SATURDAY'S SONG

Tommy Flint

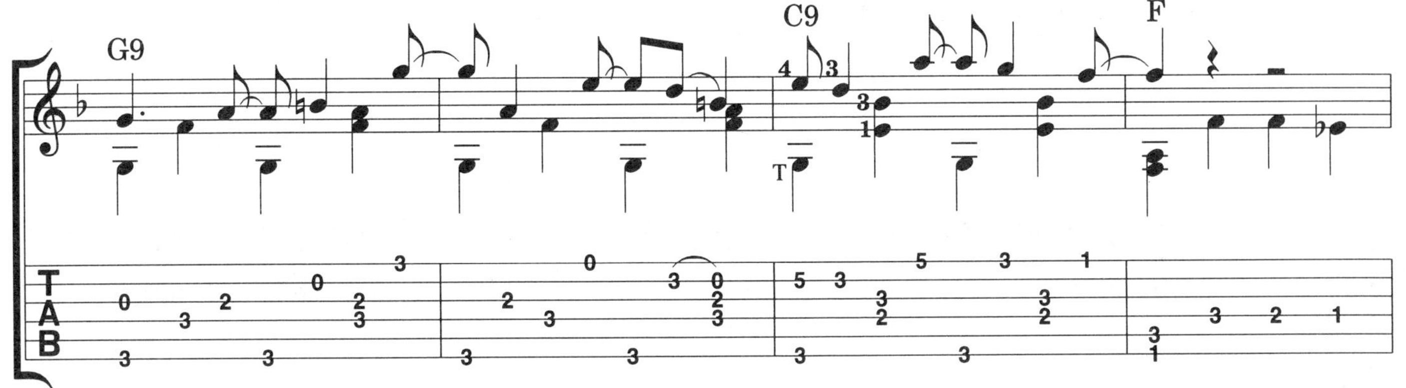
G9
C9
F
TAB

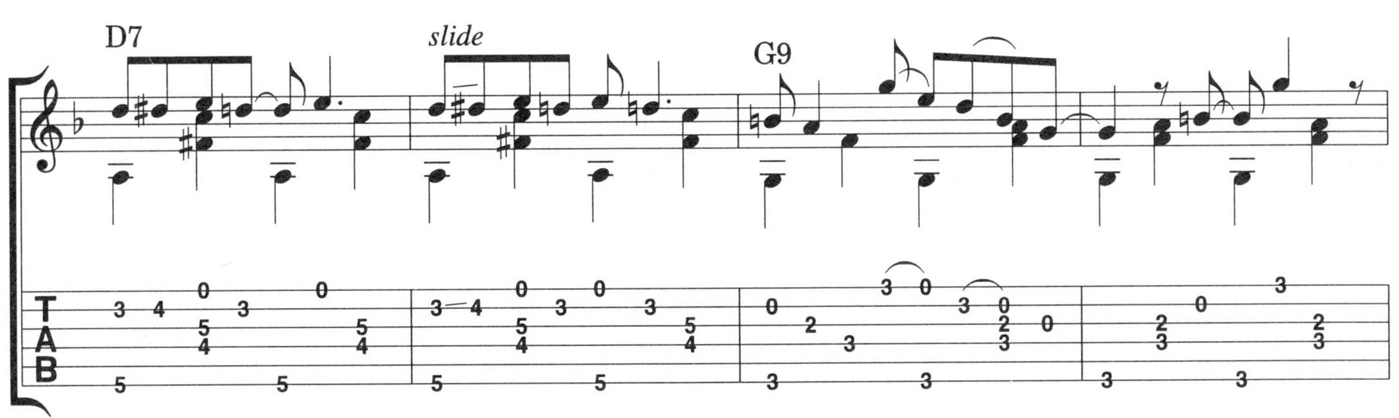
D7
slide
G9
TAB

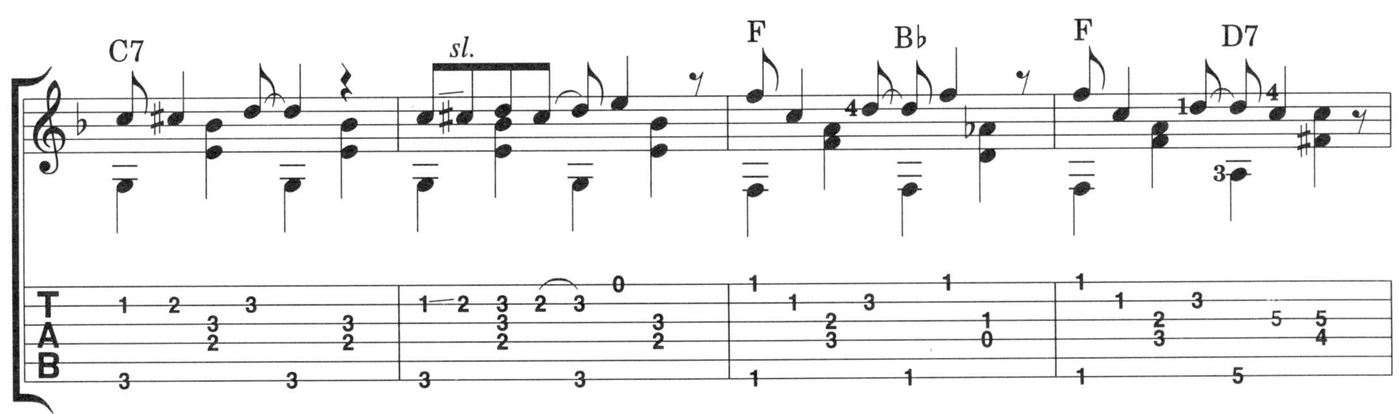
C7
sl.
F
B♭
F
D7
TAB

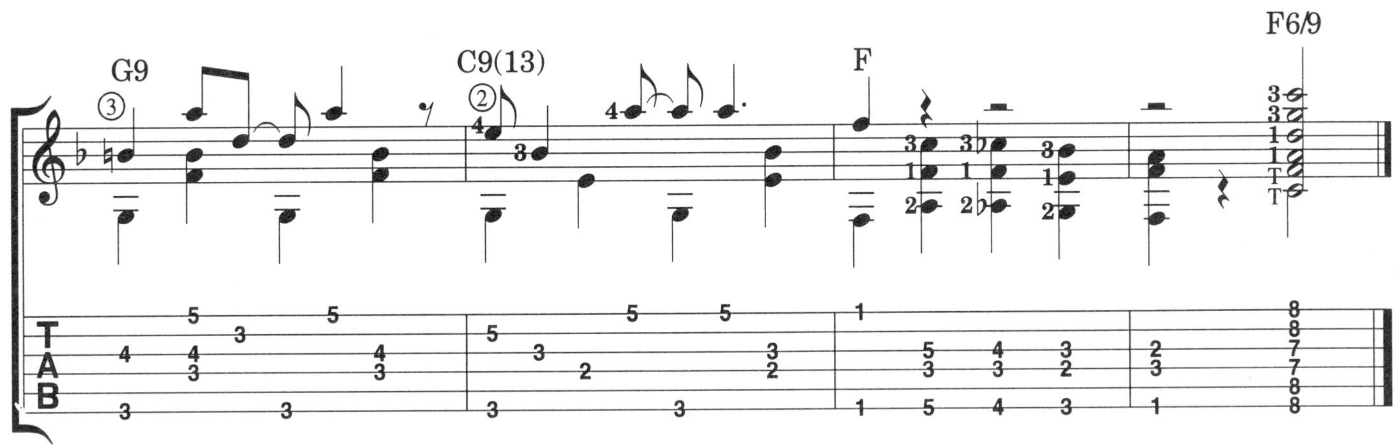
G9
C9(13)
F
F6/9
TAB

KELLY'S BLUES

Tommy Flint

KELLY'S BLUES

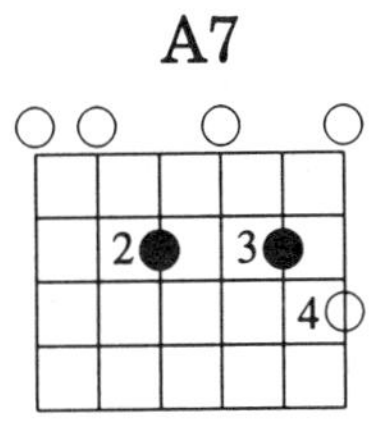

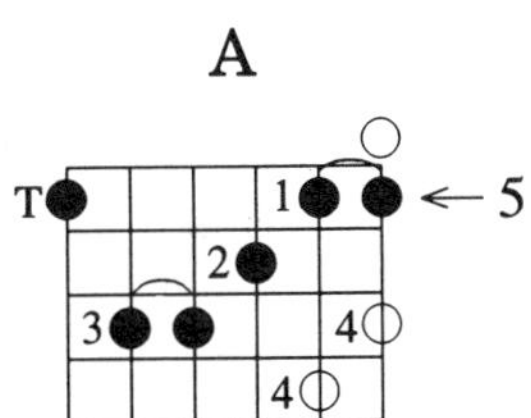

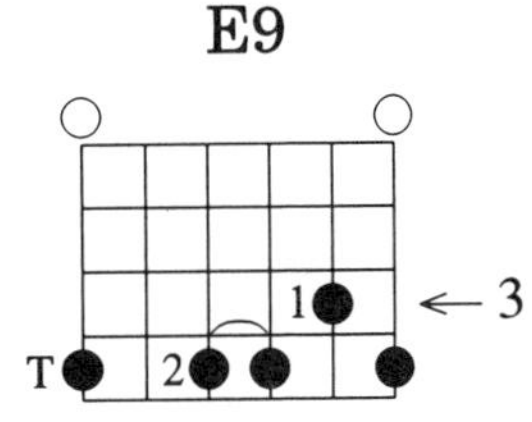

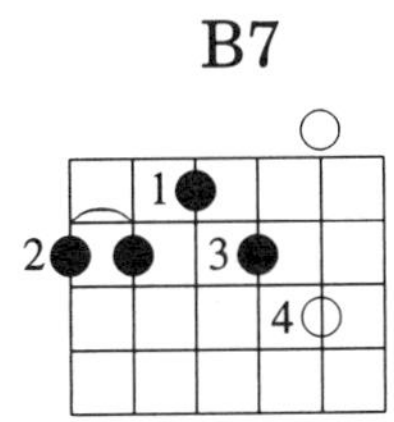

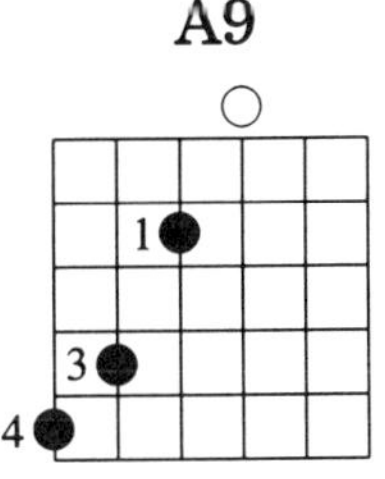

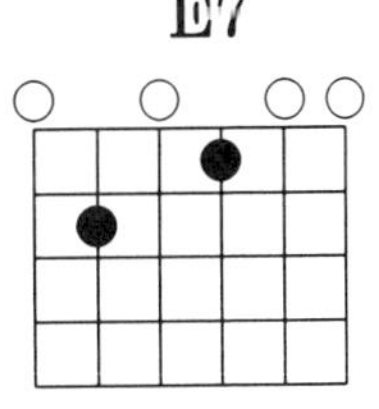

DRAKESBORO COAL DRAG

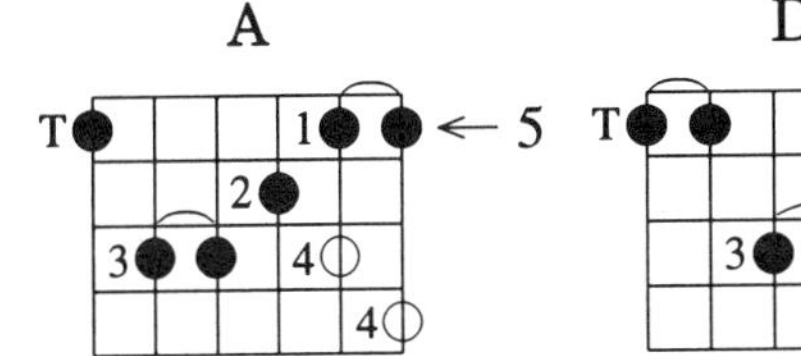

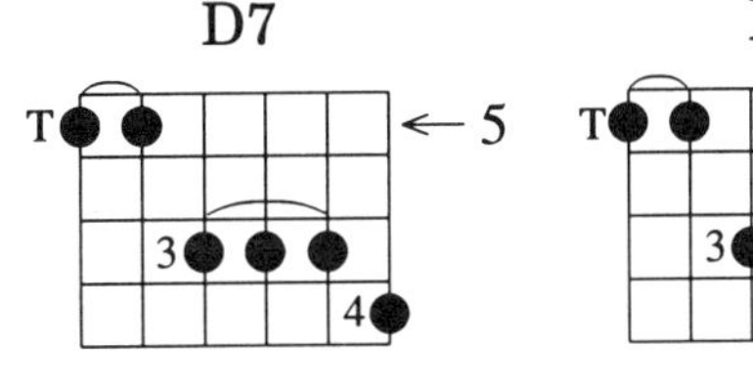

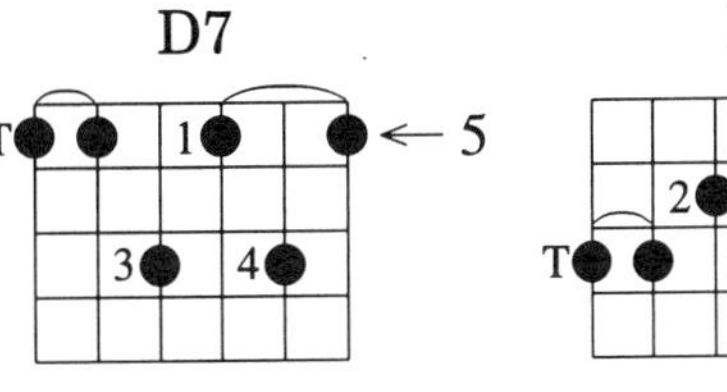

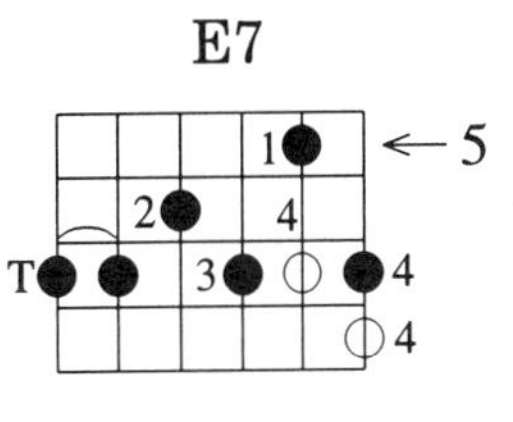

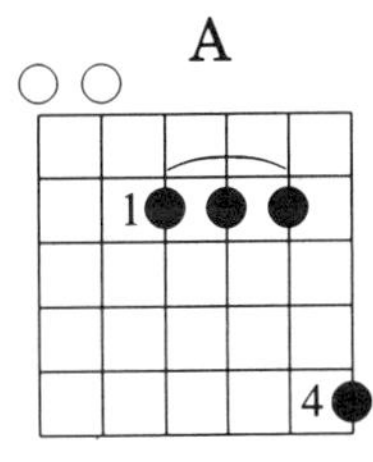

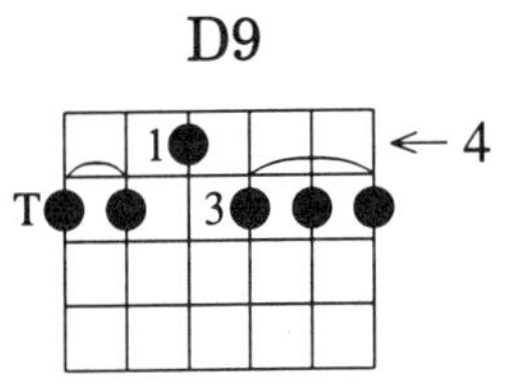

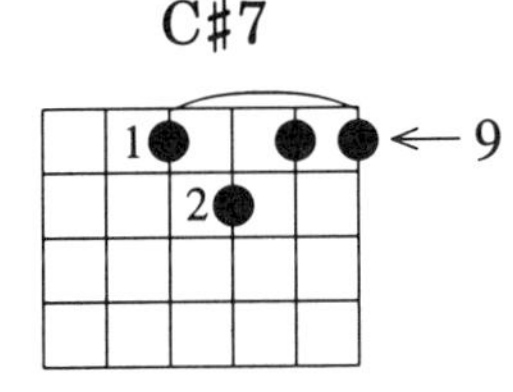

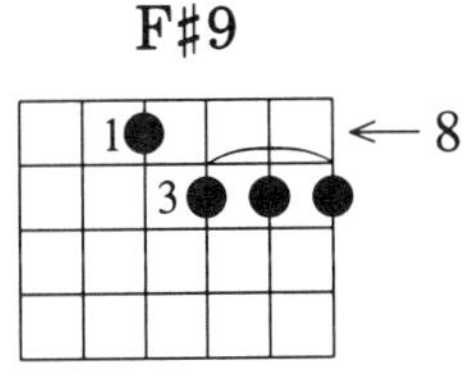

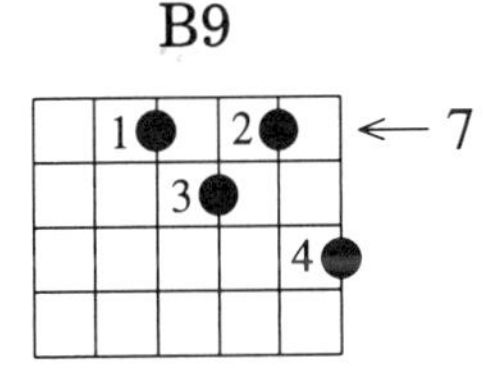

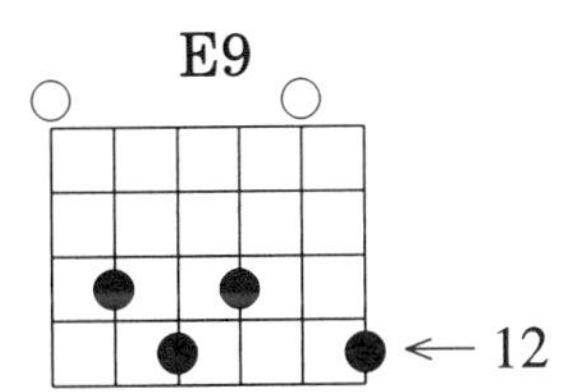

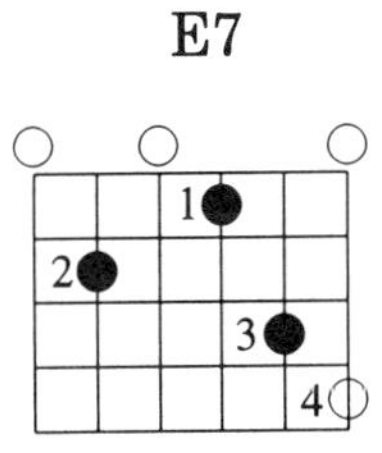

DRAKESBORO COAL DRAG

Tommy Flint

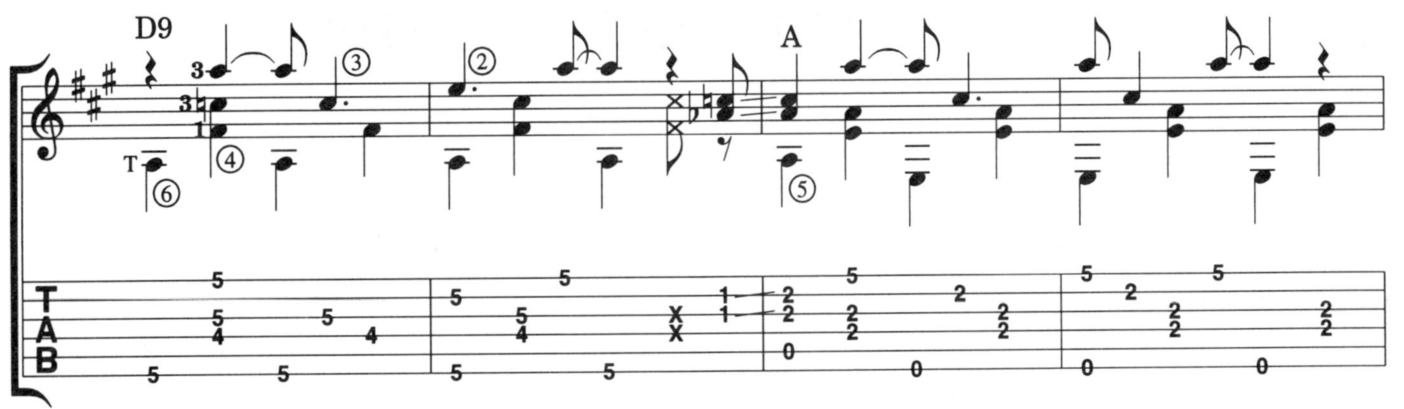
D9
A
TAB

E7
A
TAB

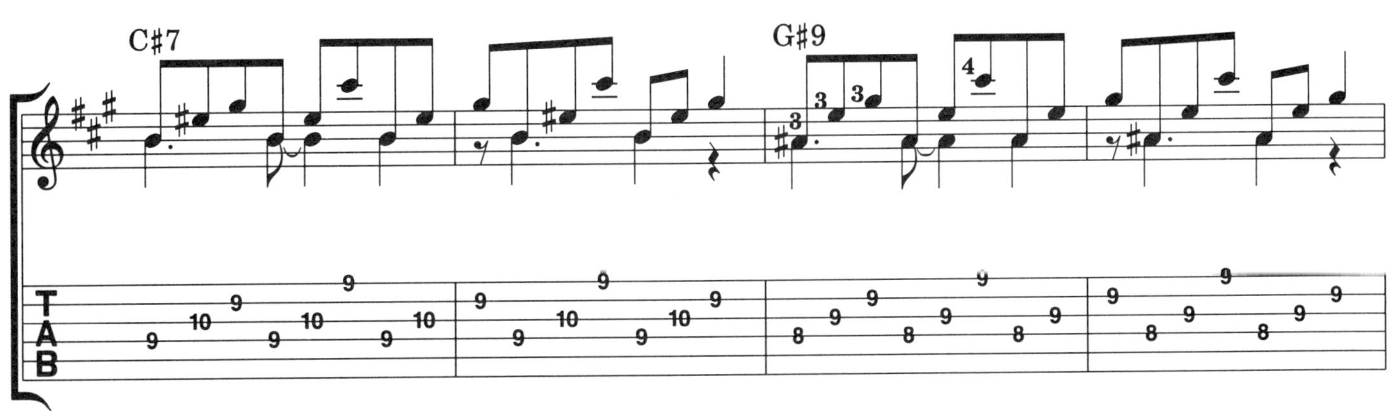
C#7
G#9
TAB

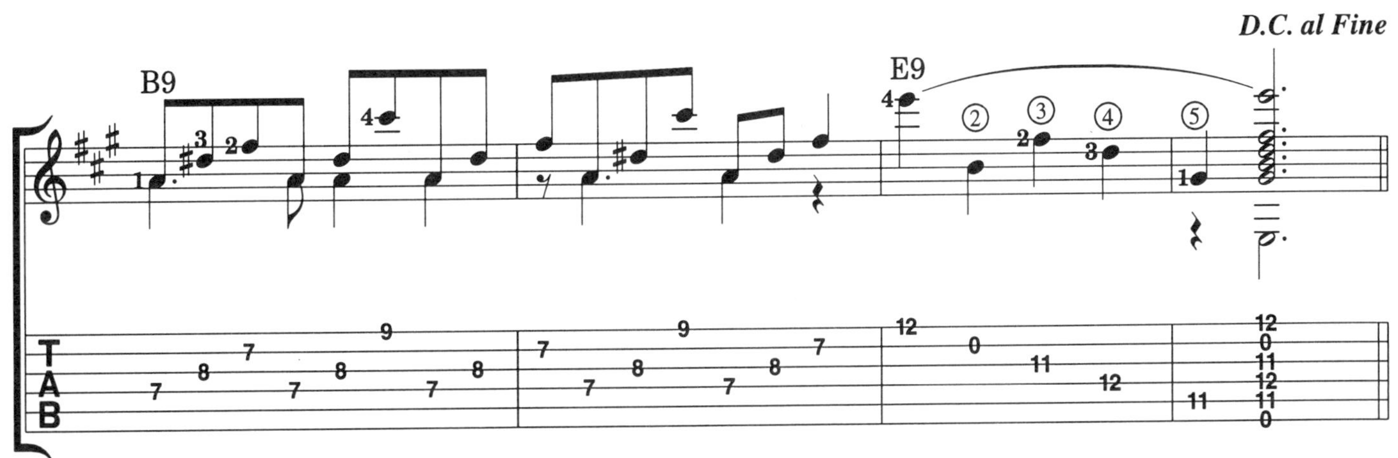
D.C. al Fine
B9
E9
TAB

HONEYSUCKLE SWEET

Tommy Flint

D9
A

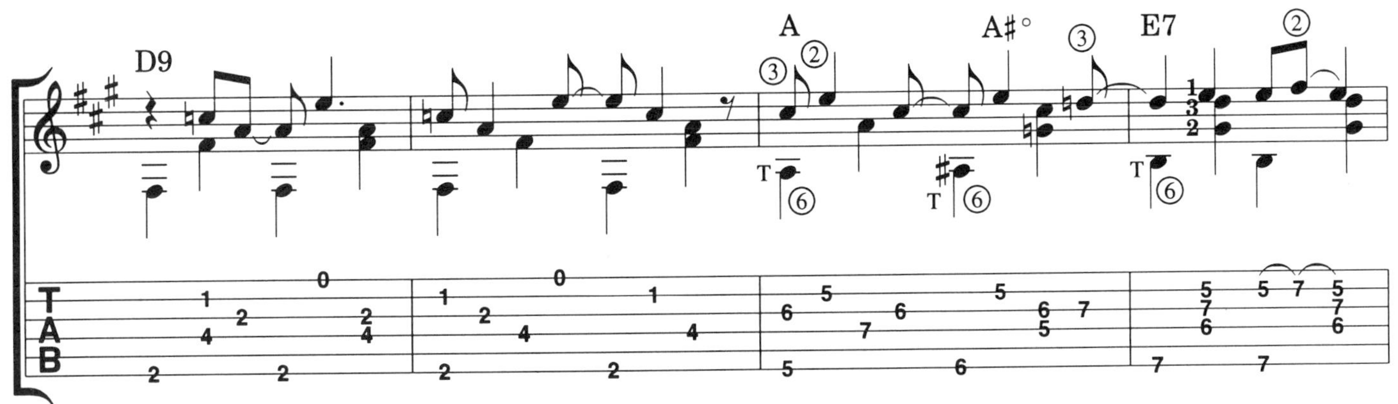
D9
A
A♯°
E7

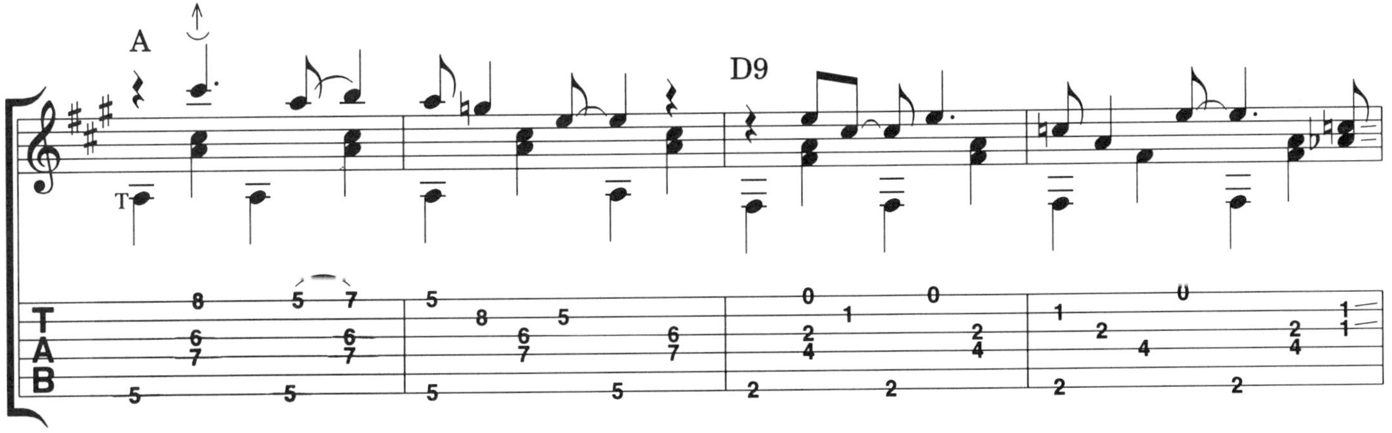
A
D9

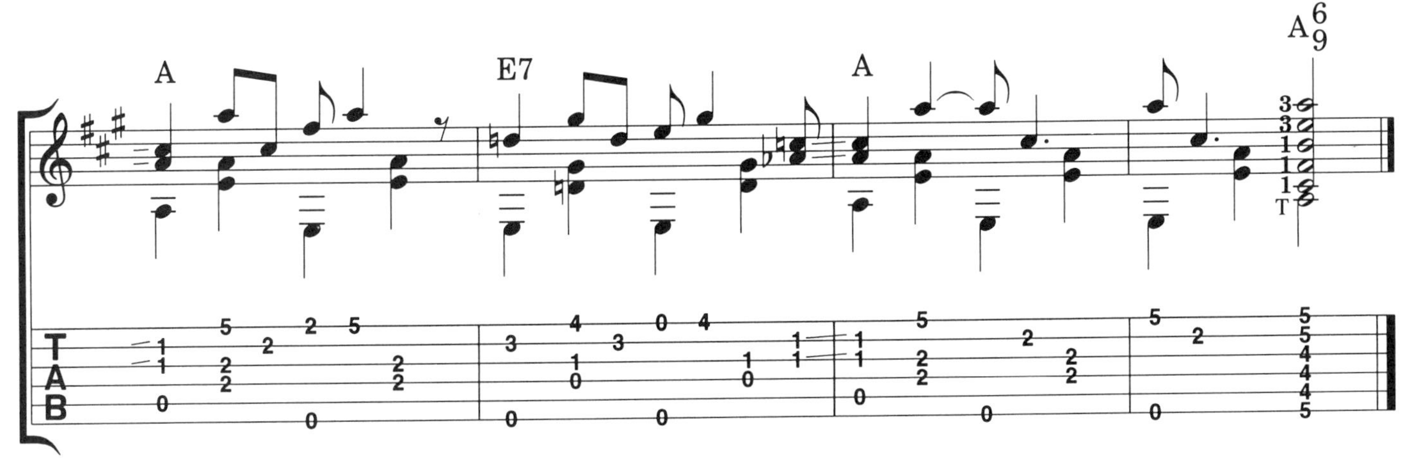
A
E7
A
A 6/9

TO
MY COUSIN
TOMMY
KEEP UP THE GOOD
PICKIN'
GUILD

The next eight solos are examples of how standard Travis licks can be used to create new melodies.

HONEYSUCKLE SWEET

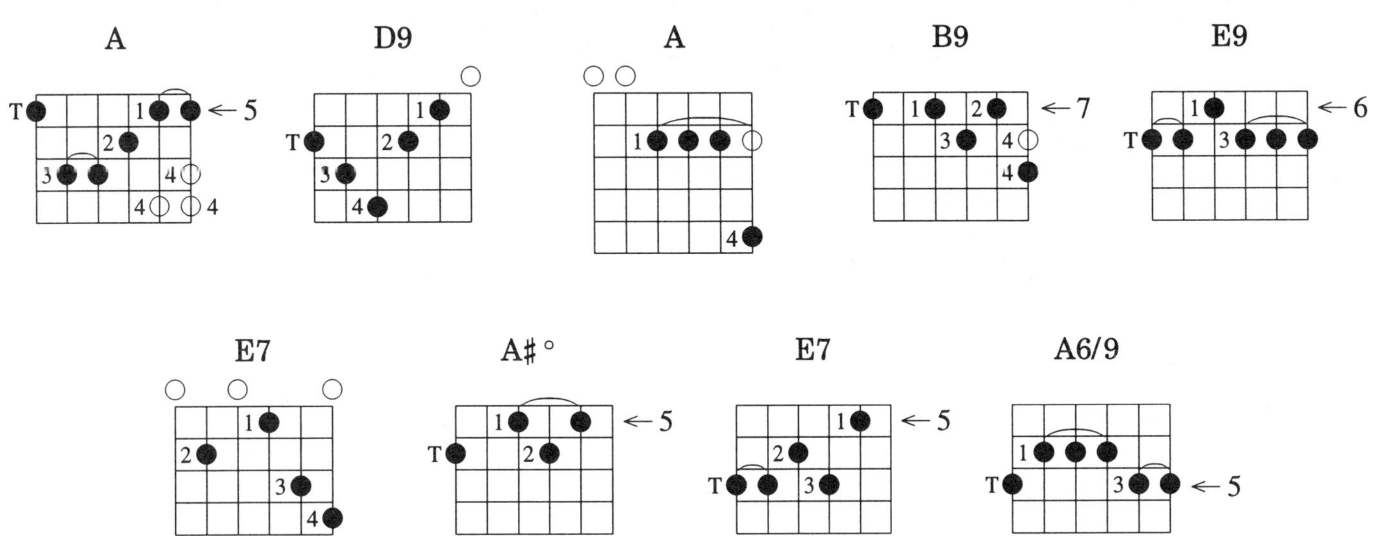

GREEN RIVER BLUES

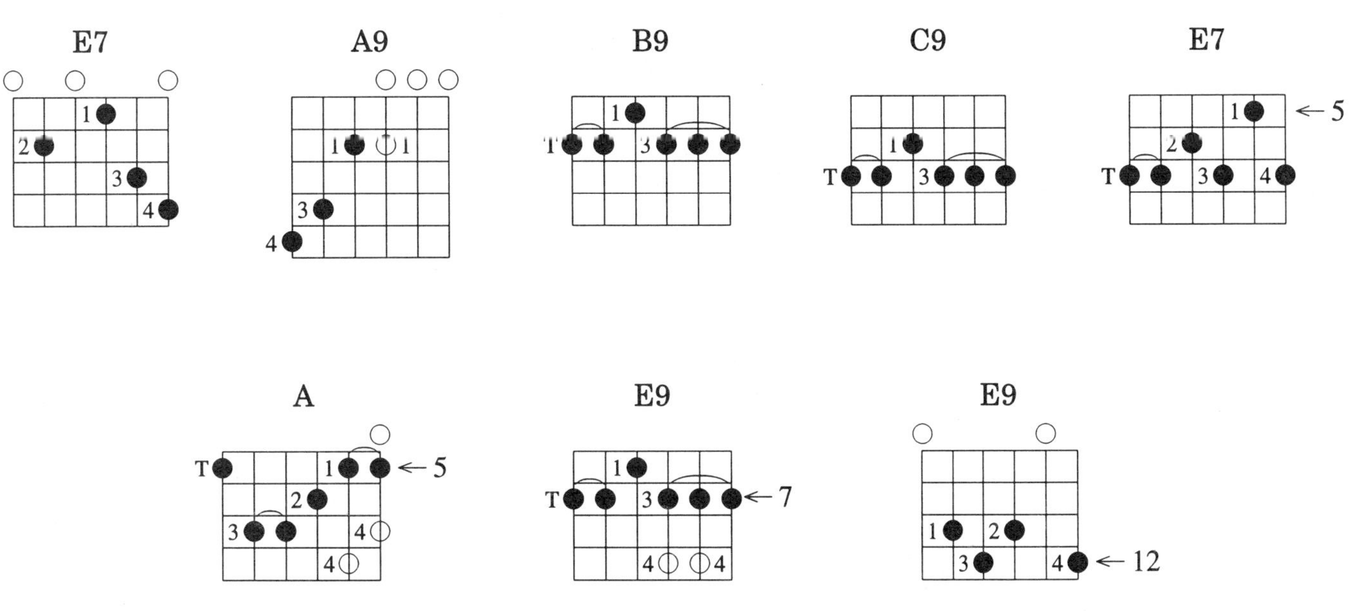

GREEN RIVER BLUES

Tommy Flint

* Slap deadened strings.

E7
A
E7
E9
A
E7
C9
B9
A9
E7
E9
TAB

This page has been left blank to avoid awkward page turns

MY MEMORY OF MERLE

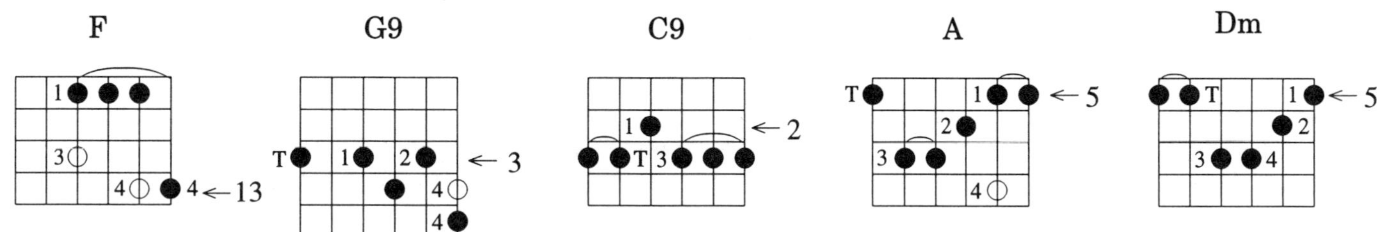

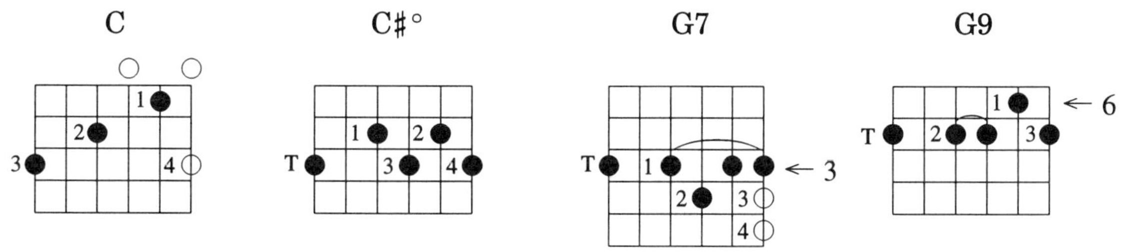

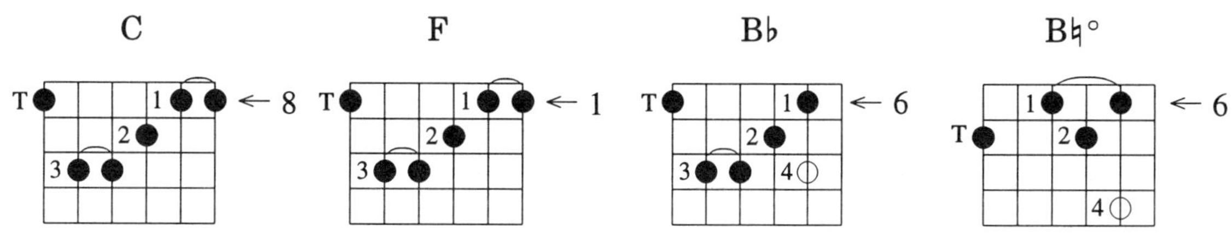

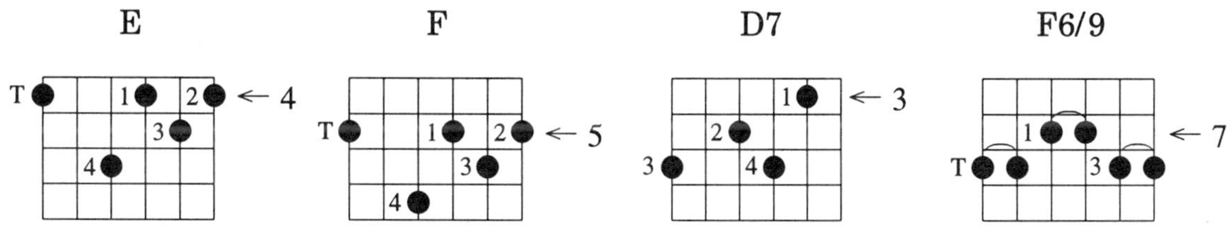

MY MEMORY OF MERLE

Tommy Flint

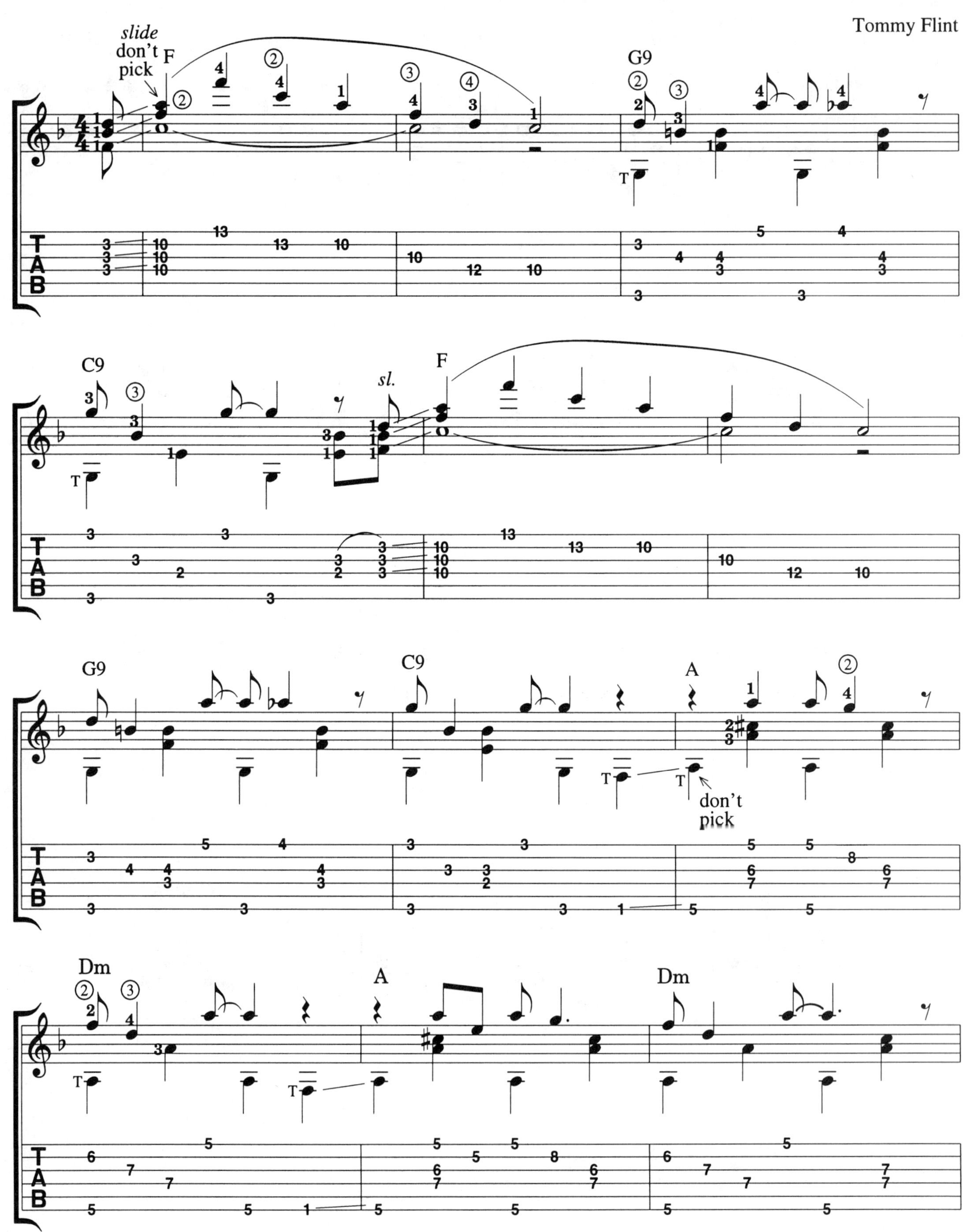

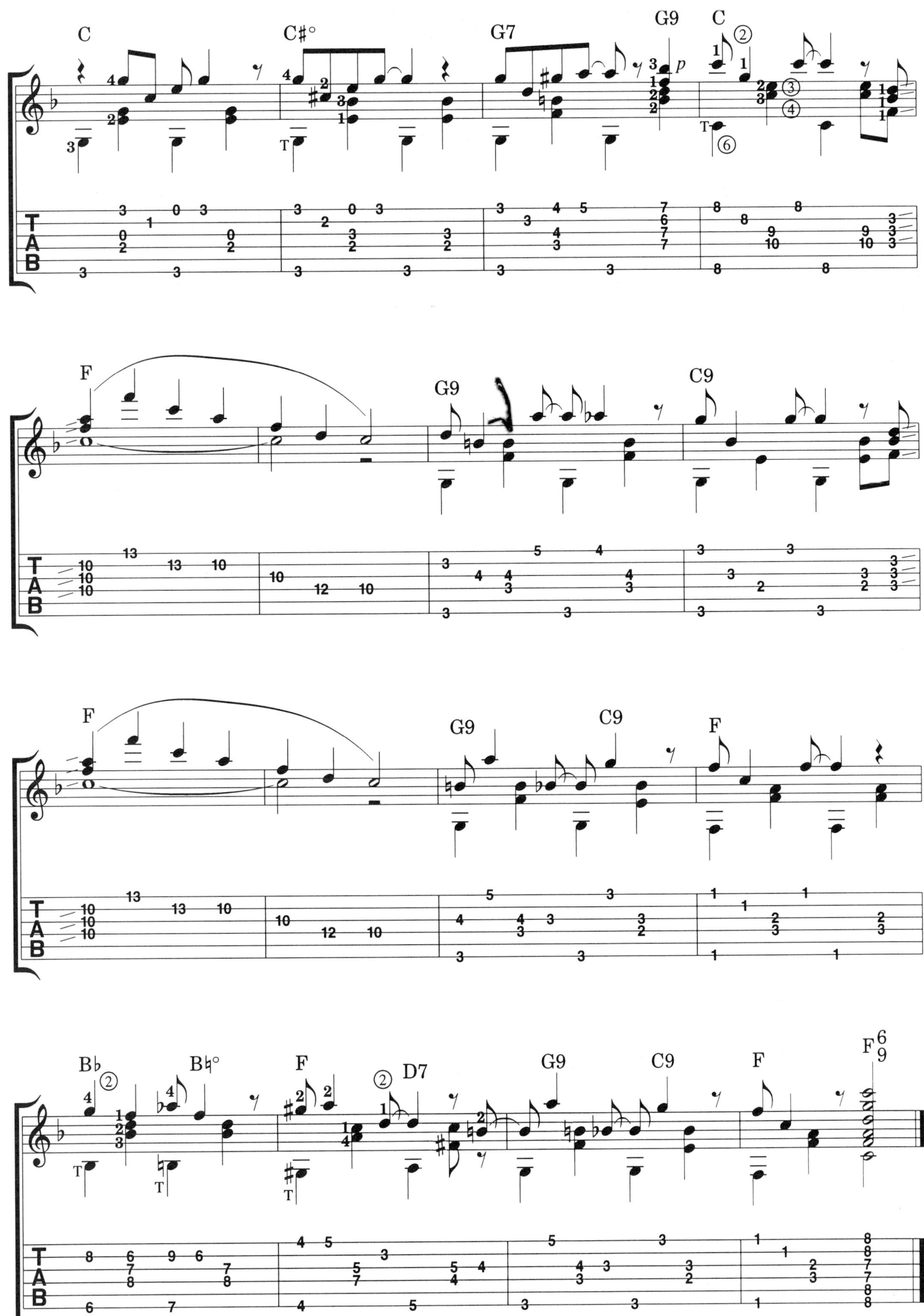
C C♯° G7 G9 C
F G9 C9
F G9 C9 F
B♭ B♮° F D7 G9 C9 F F6/9
TAB

WALKIN' IN BEECH CREEK

Tommy Flint

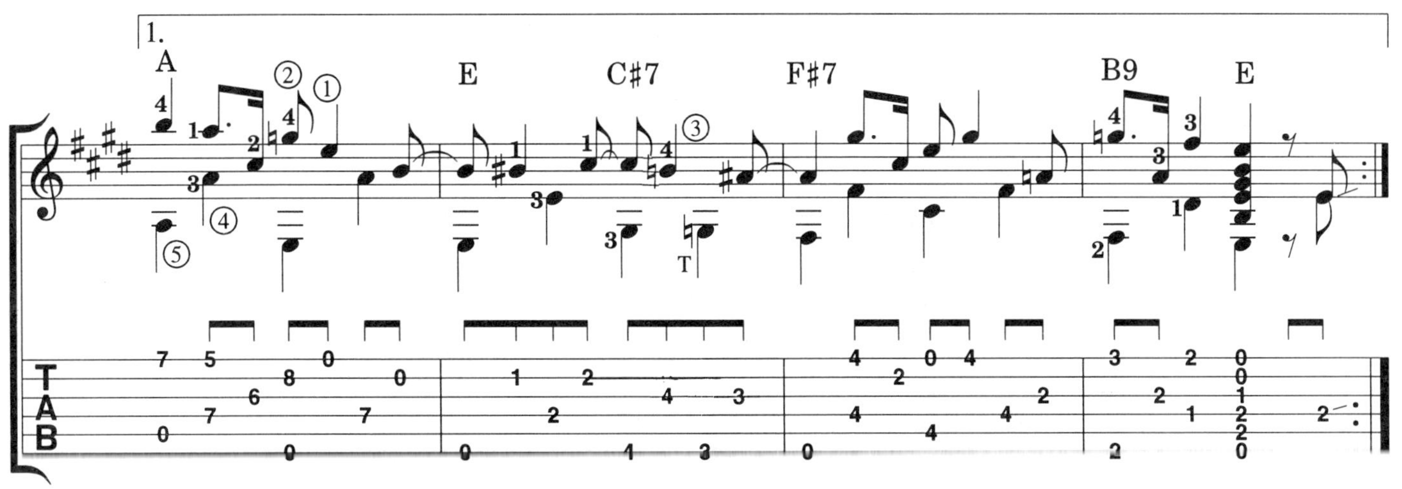
1.
A
E
C#7
F#7
B9
E
T
TAB

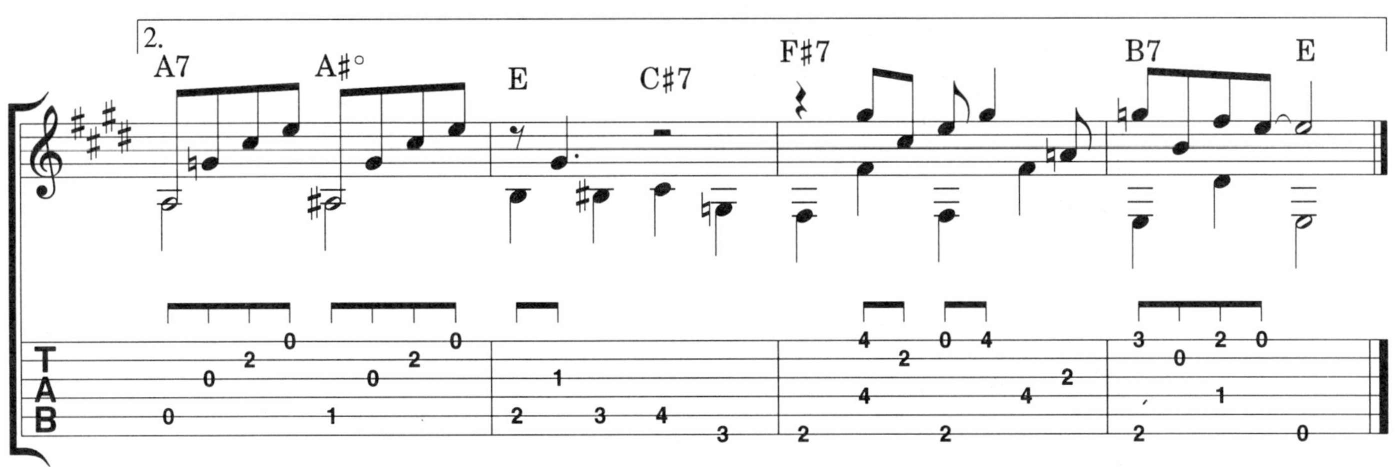
2.
A7
A#°
E
C#7
F#7
B7
E
TAB

WALKIN' IN BEECH CREEK

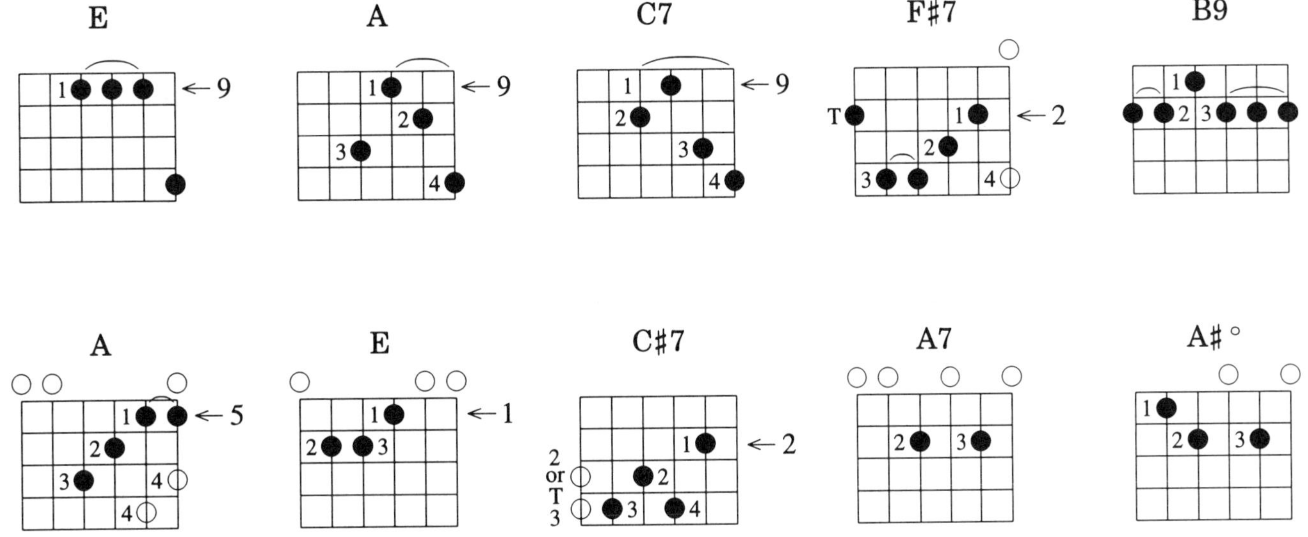

PICKIN' LIKE AMOS

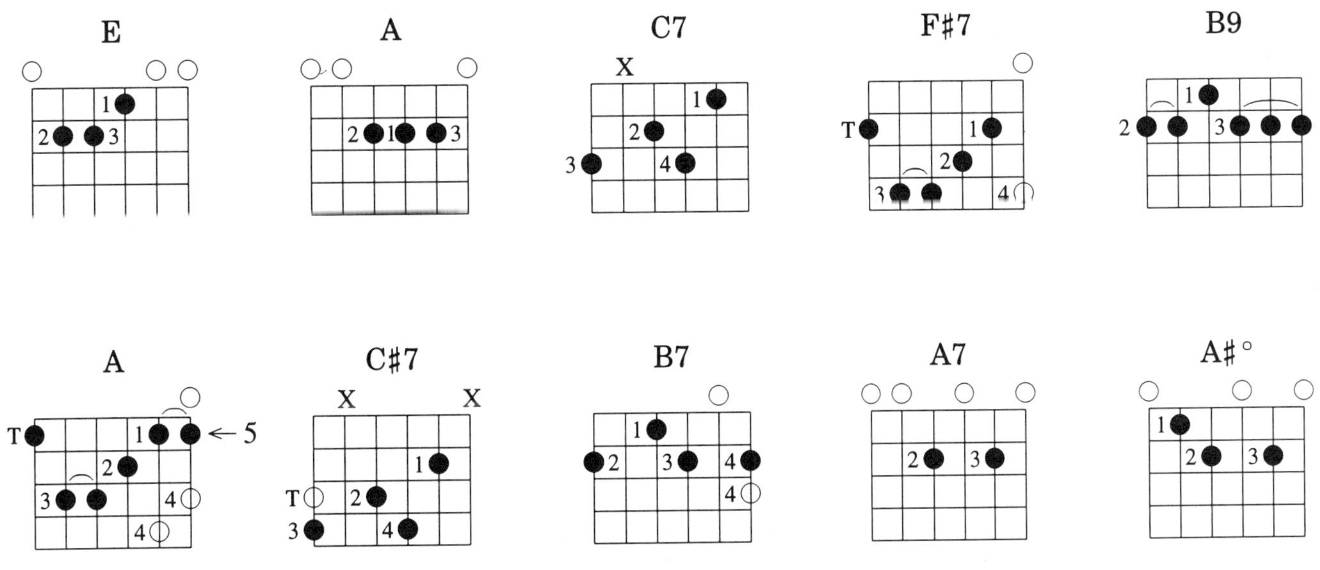

PICKIN' LIKE AMOS

Tommy Flint

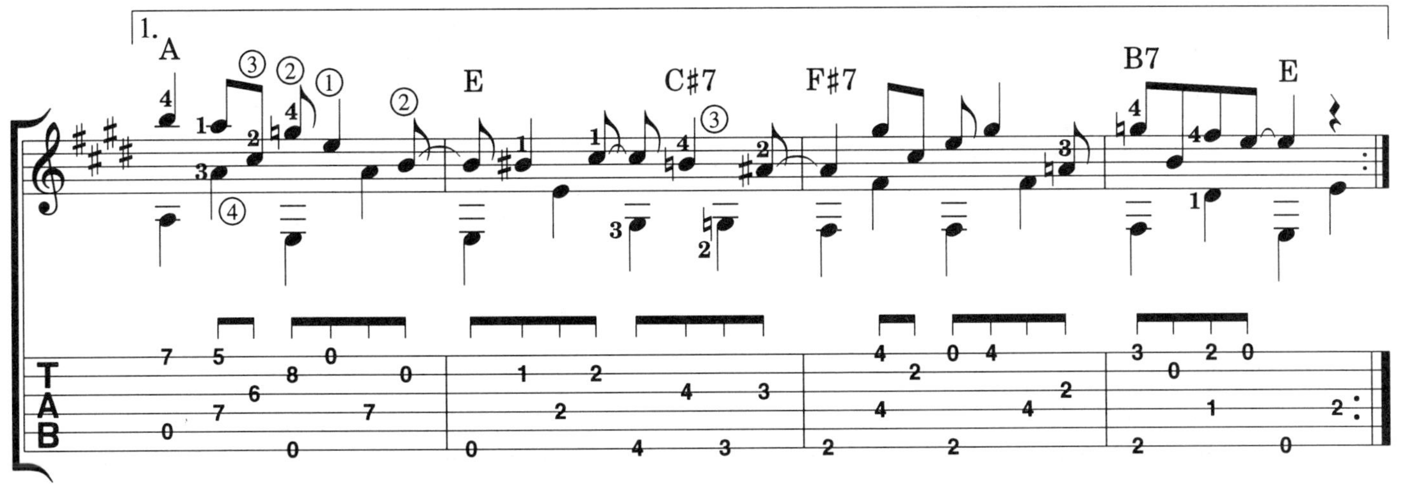
1.
A
E
C#7
F#7
B7
E
TAB

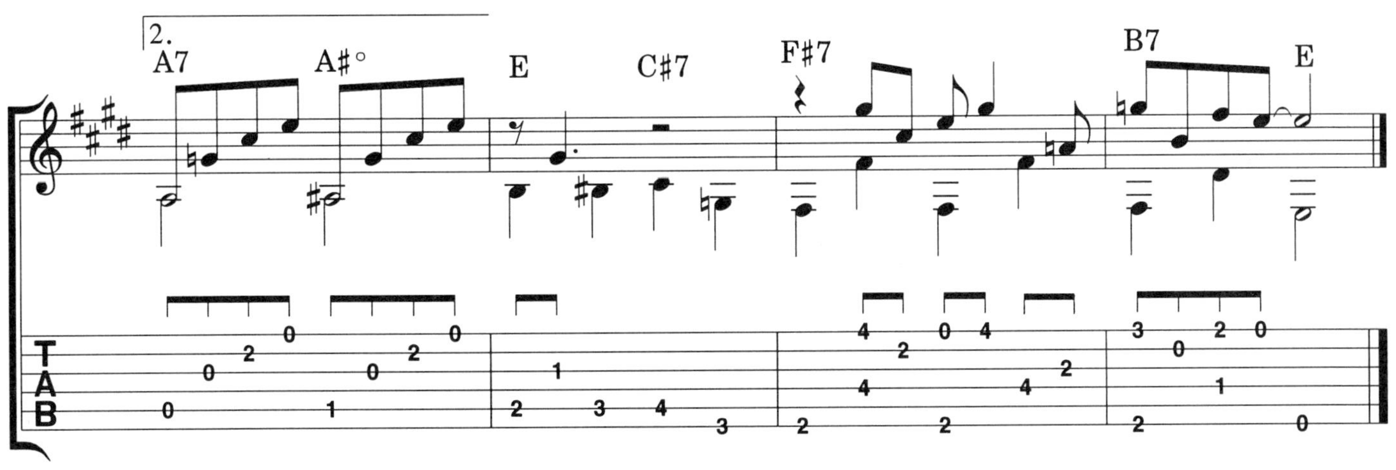
2.
A7
A#°
E
C#7
F#7
B7
E
TAB

GOODBYE MY BLUEBELL

I first heard "Goodbye My Bluebell" on the Supper Time Frolic from WJJD, Chicago, when it was used for the station break. Travis said he learned it from a harmonica player whose name I can't remember. He also said it is from the Civil War era. That's all I know about the song, other than I know it sounded great when Merle played it.

The first version in this book is the original version on which he used the Martin D28. He played it more lively, slightly faster, and used more syncopation. It has an improvised feeling about it. He played it in the key of C, without a capo.

The second version is from "The Merle Travis Guitar" album which was released a few years later. On this he used the Super 400 electric. He played it more relaxed and laid back, with less syncopation. He also used a capo on the second fret, so consequently it was in the key of D.

By comparing these two versions of Bluebell, it is easy to see how over a period of time his feelings, or thoughts, as to how the tune should be played had changed.

Joe Maphis, Chet Atkins, Merle Travis and Mose Rager

GOODBYE MY BLUEBELL

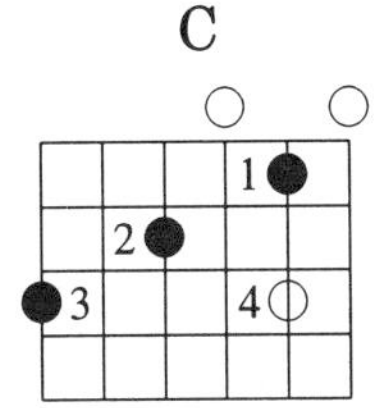

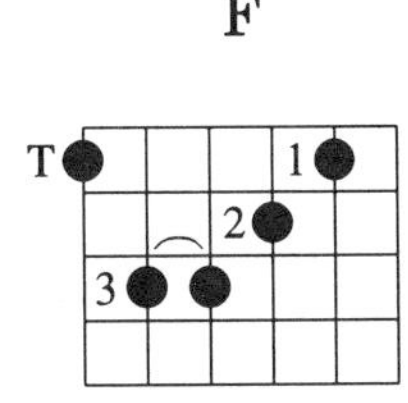

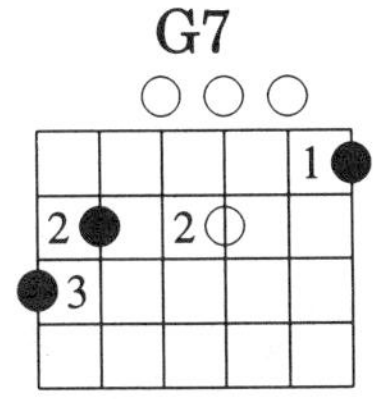

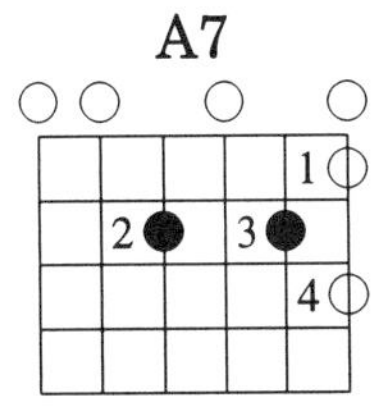

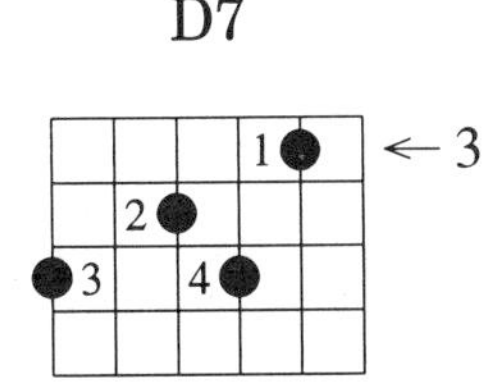

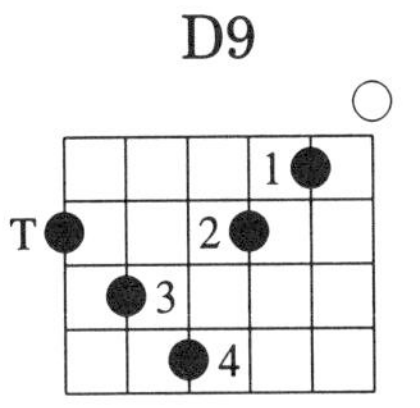

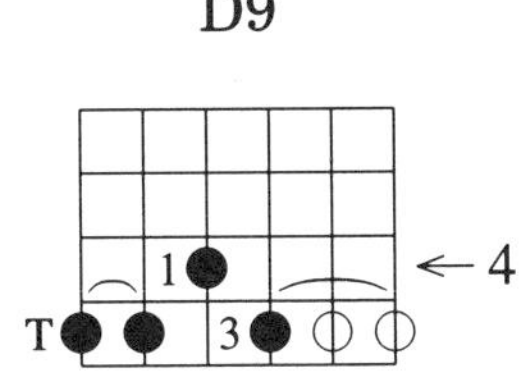

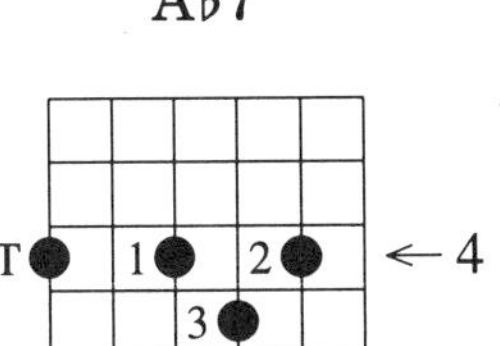

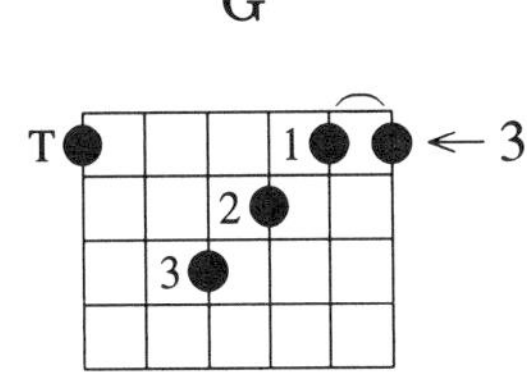

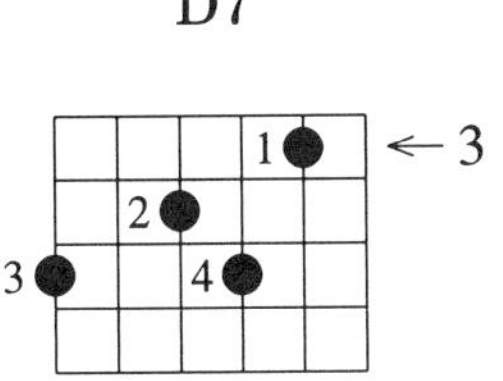

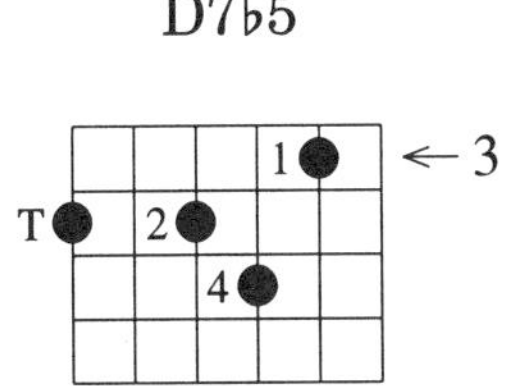

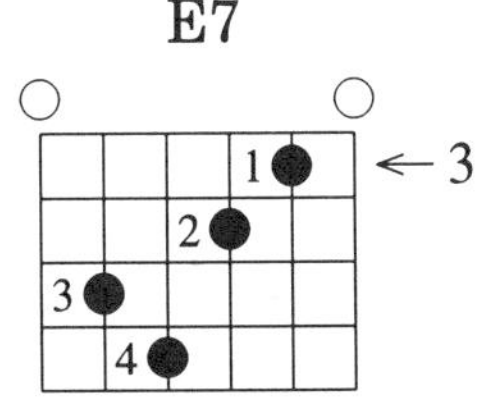

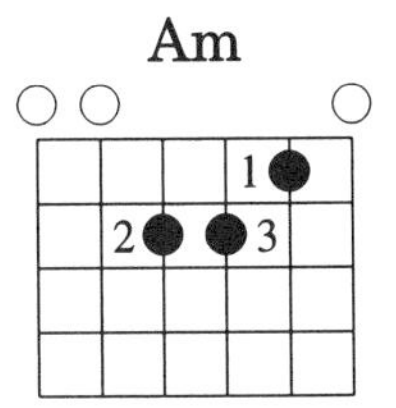

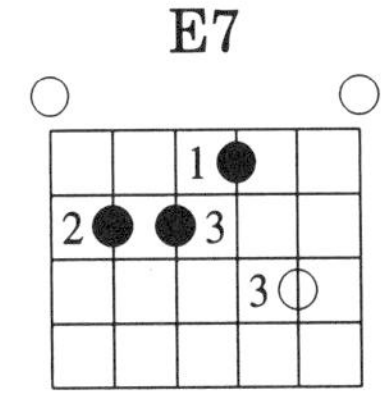

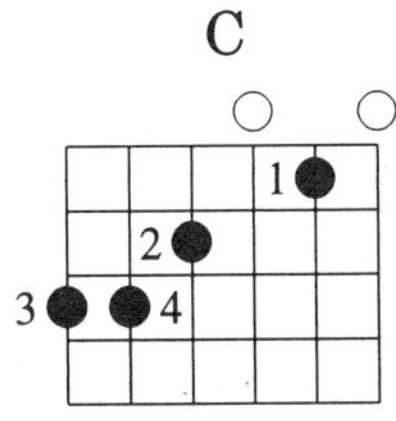

2ND VERSION

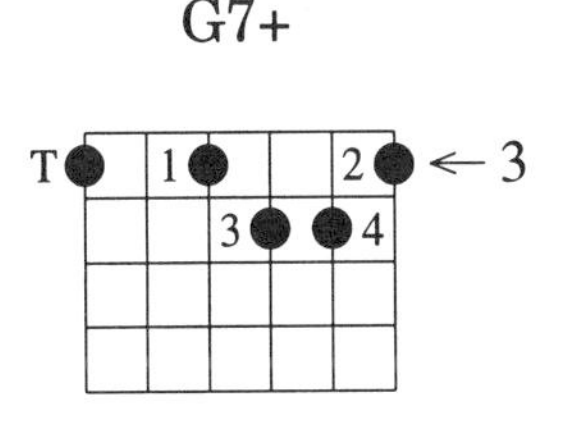

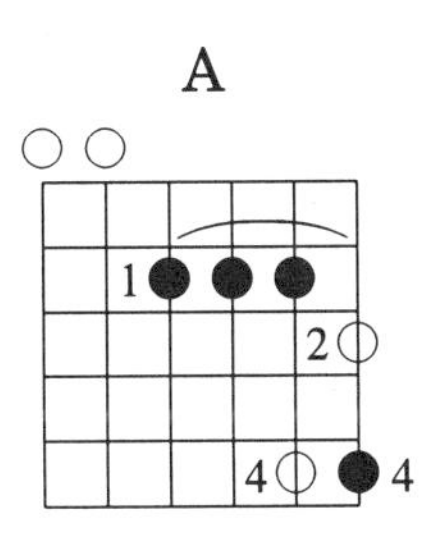

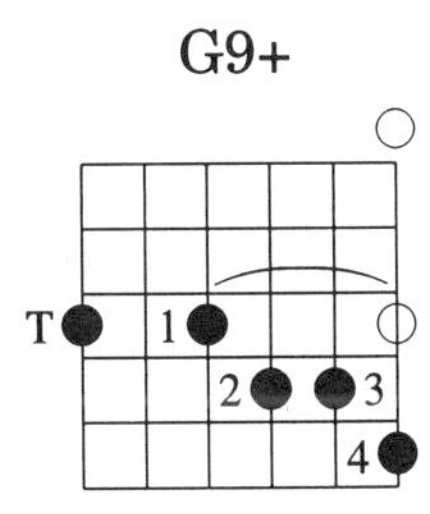

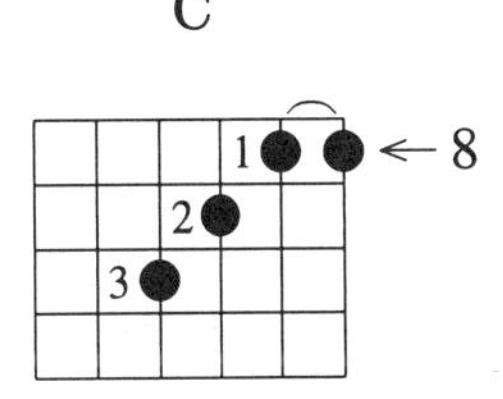

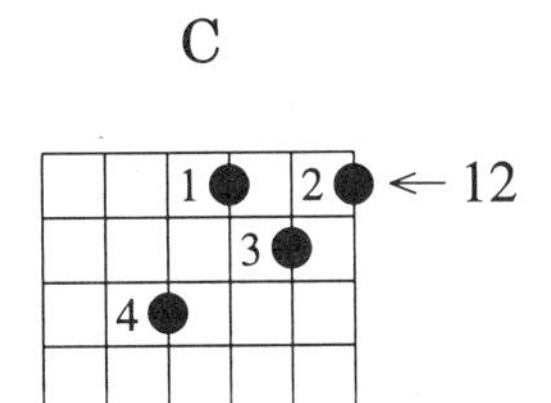

GOODBYE MY BLUEBELL

Early Version
From 1940's
on MARTIN D28

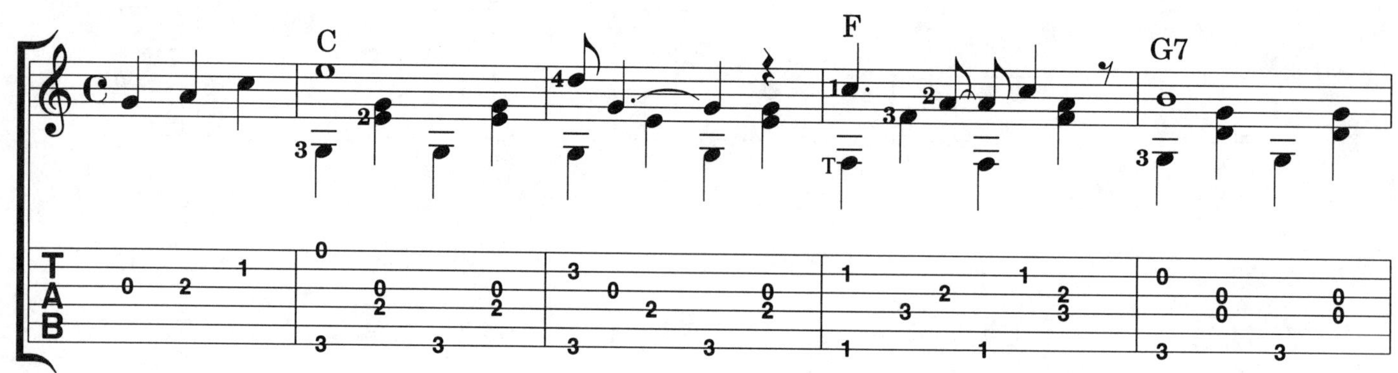

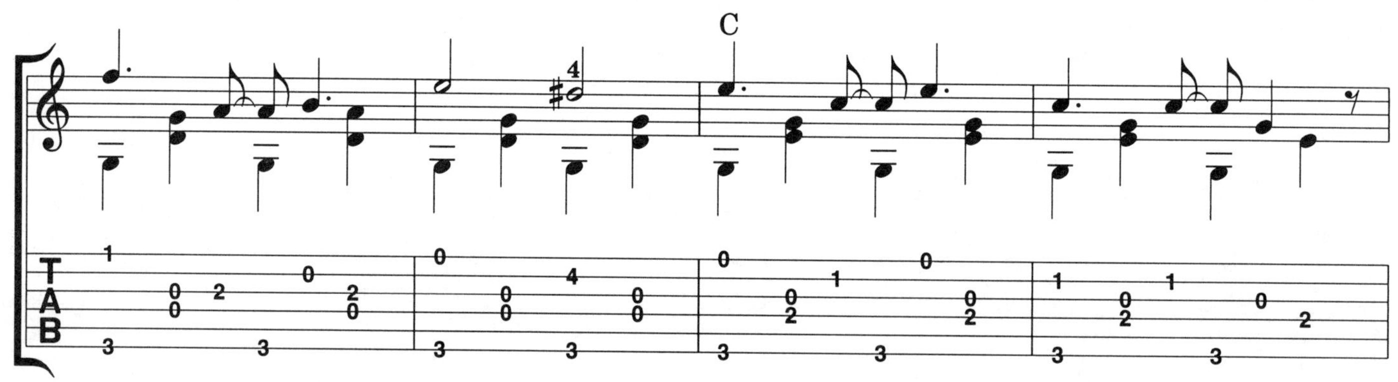

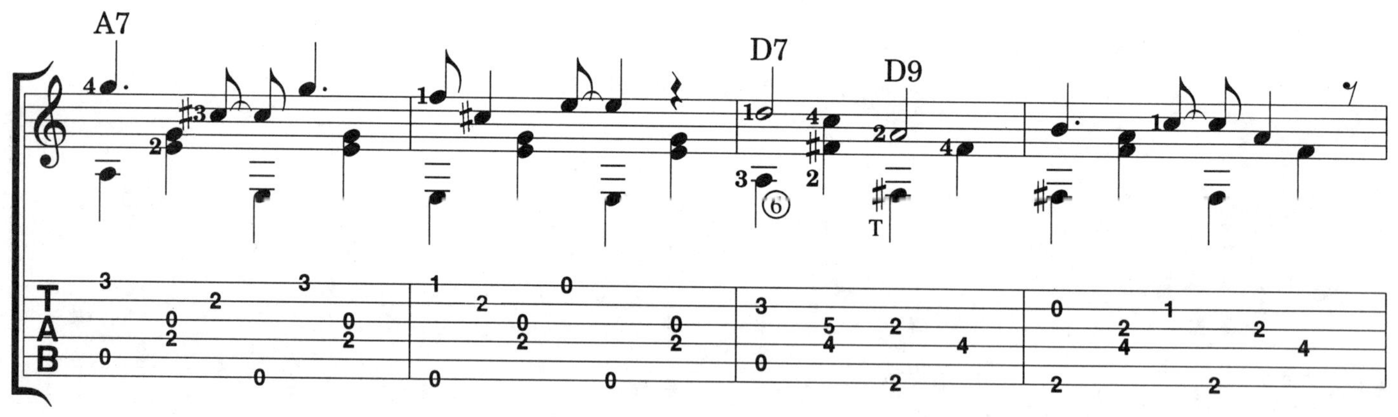

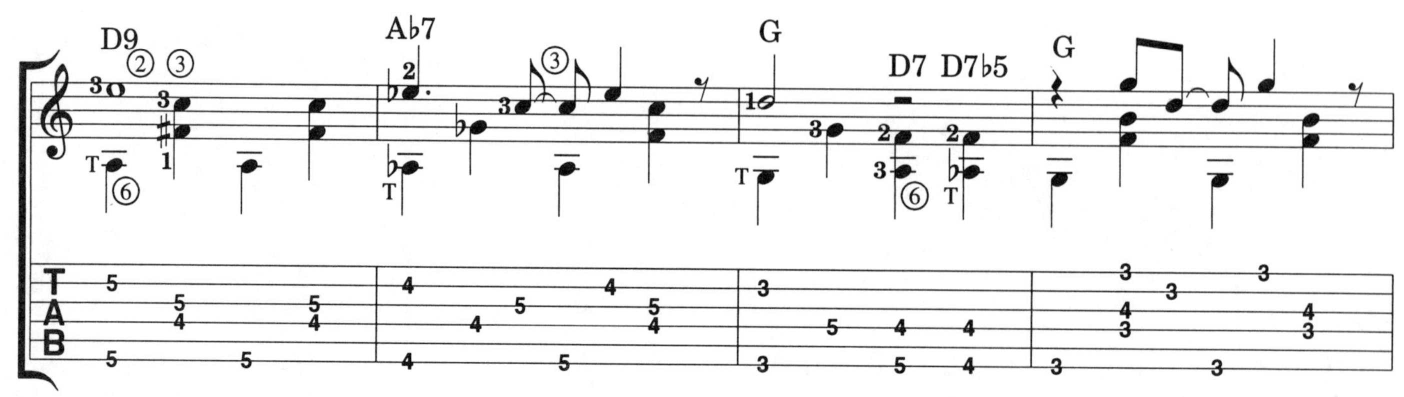

C
F
G7
TAB

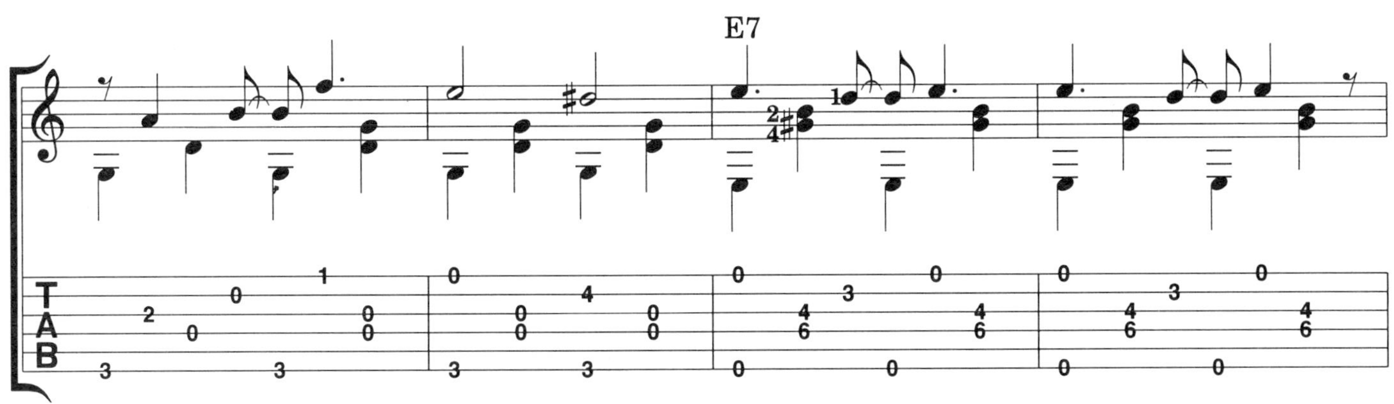
E7
TAB

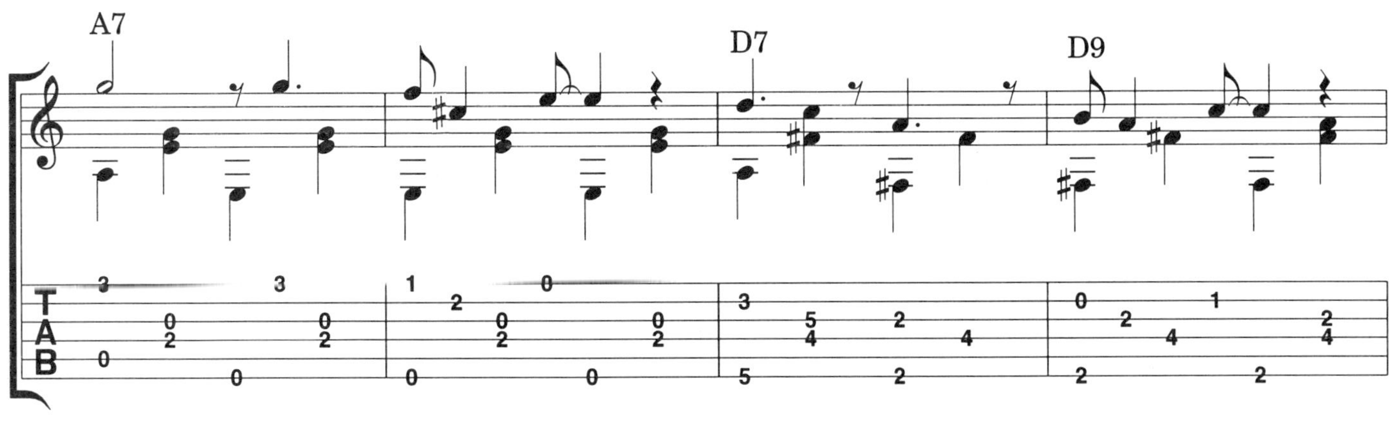
A7
D7
D9
TAB

C
G7
C
F
C
TAB

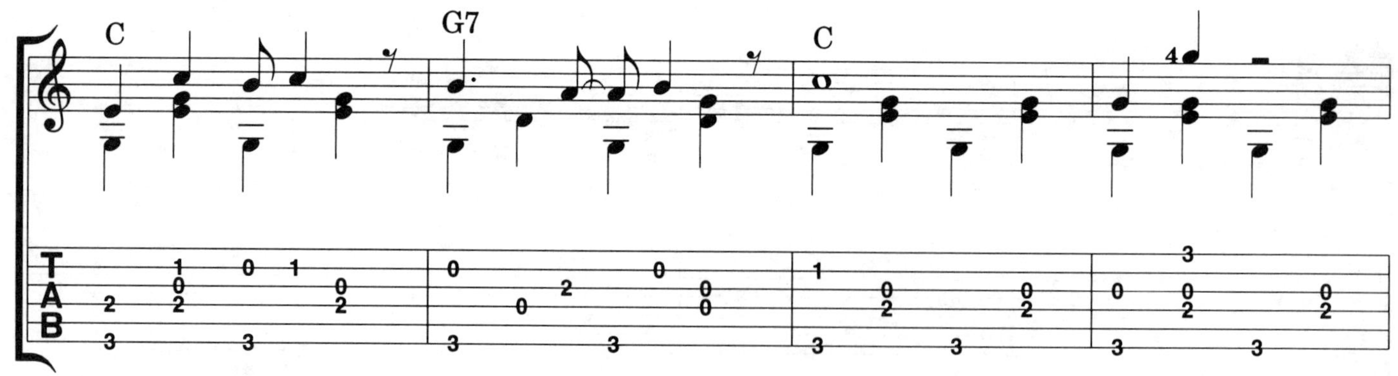
C
G7
C

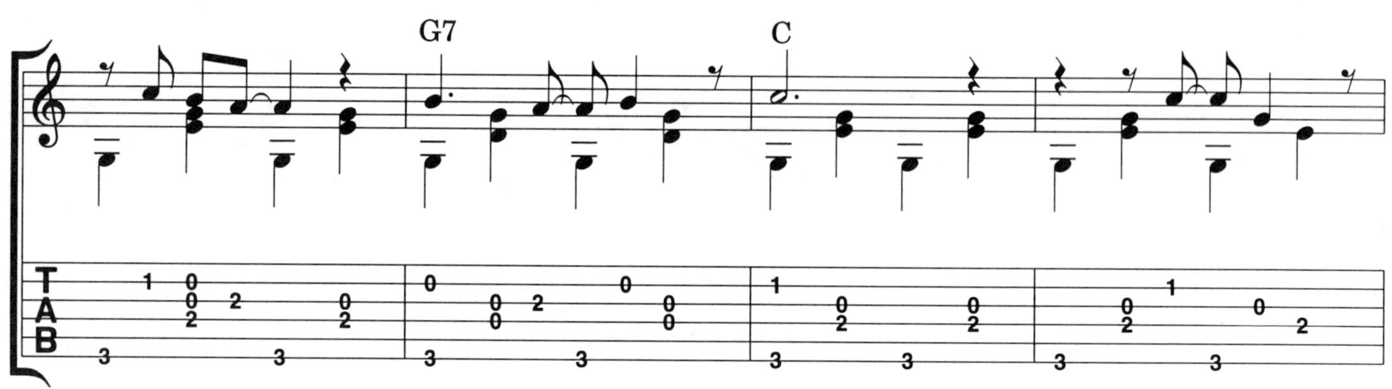
G7
C

Am
E7
Am

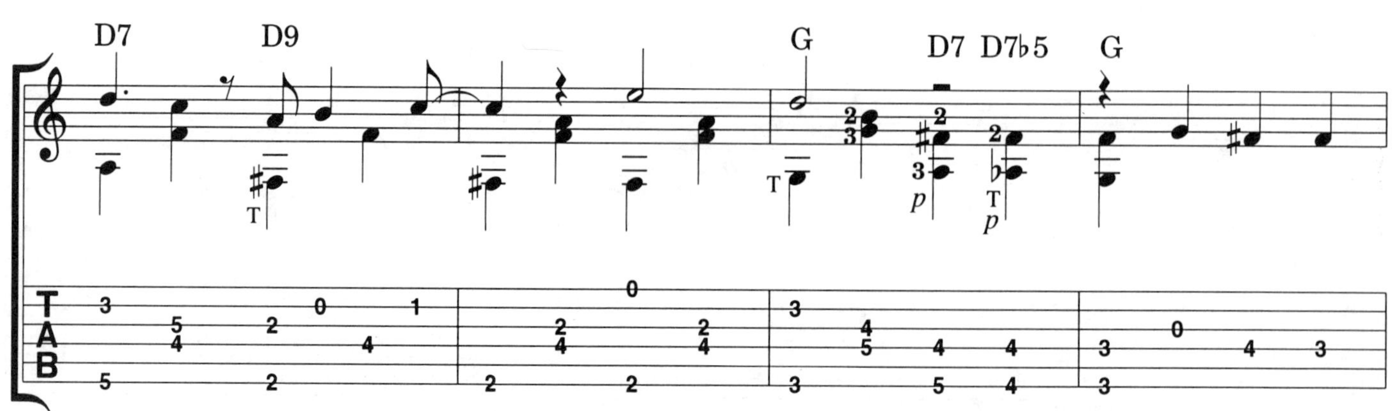
D7
D9
G
D7
D7♭5
G

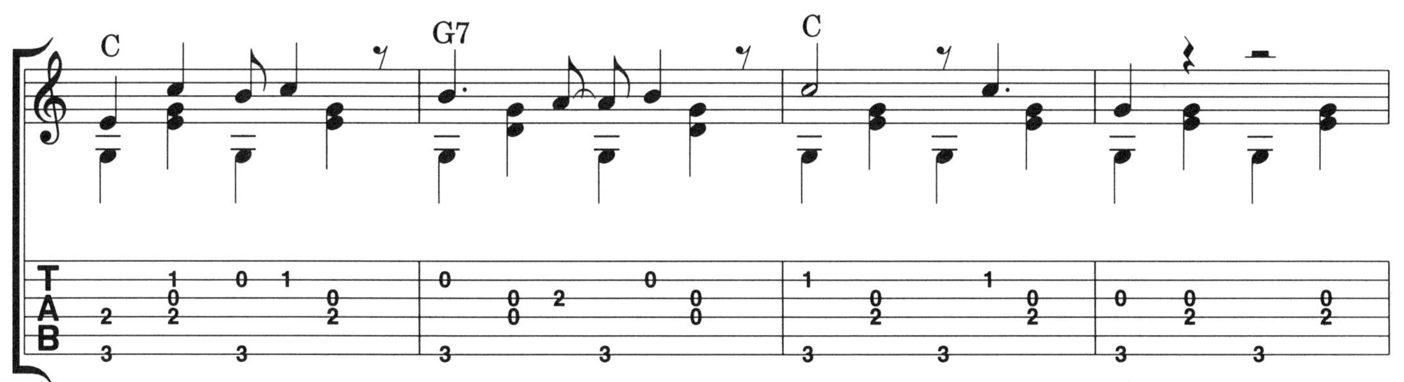
C
G7
C
TAB

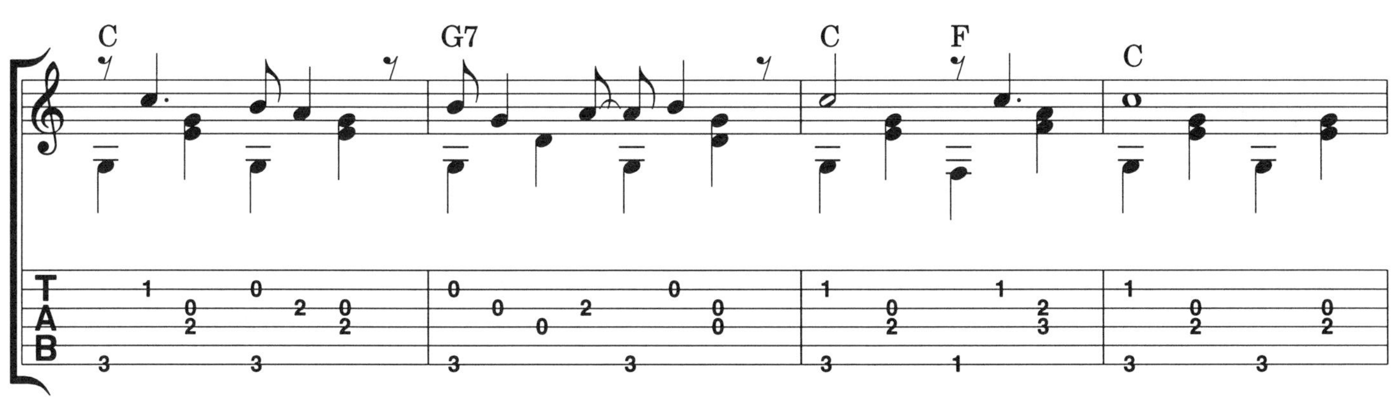
C
G7
C
F
C
TAB

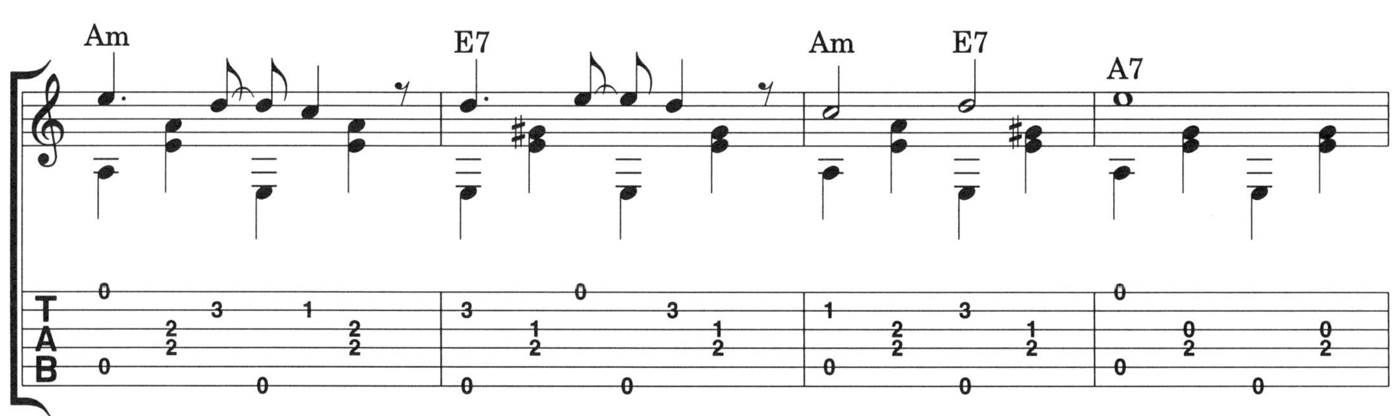
Am
E7
Am
E7
A7
TAB

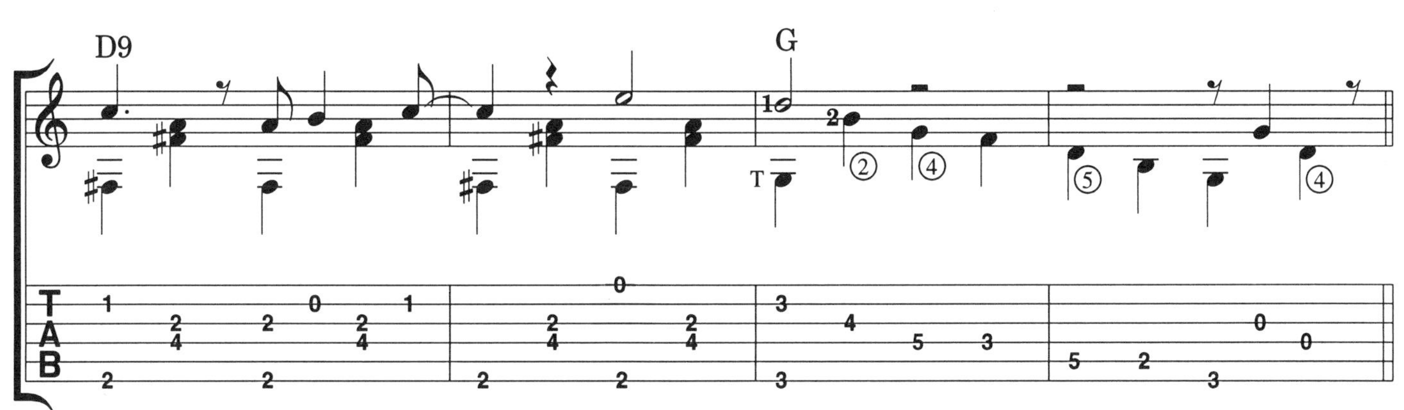
D9
G
T
TAB

C
F
G7
T
A
B

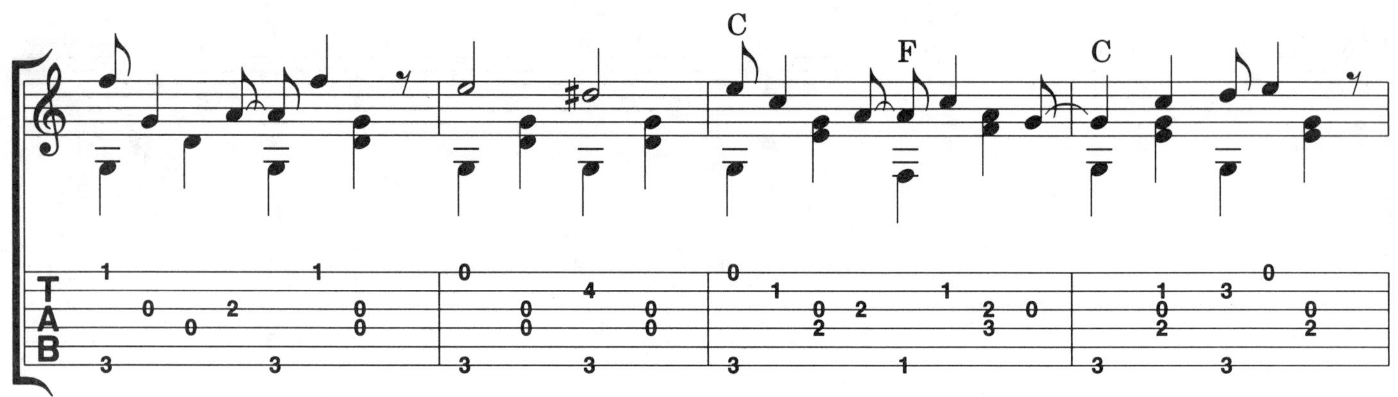
C
F
C
T
A
B

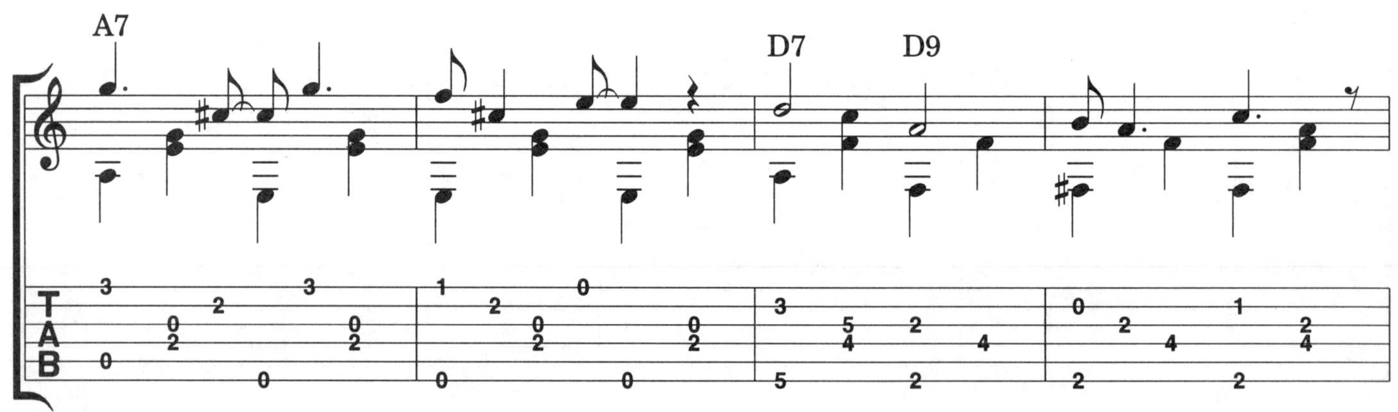
A7
D7
D9
T
A
B

D9
A♭7
G
(D7 D7♭5)
G
T
A
B

C
F
G
TAB

G(9)
G
E7
TAB

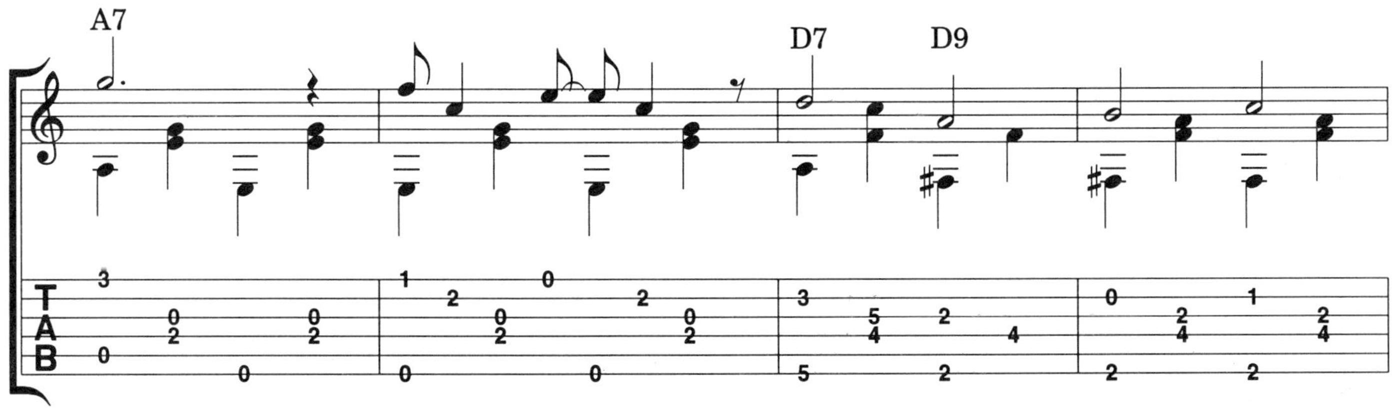
A7
D7
D9
TAB

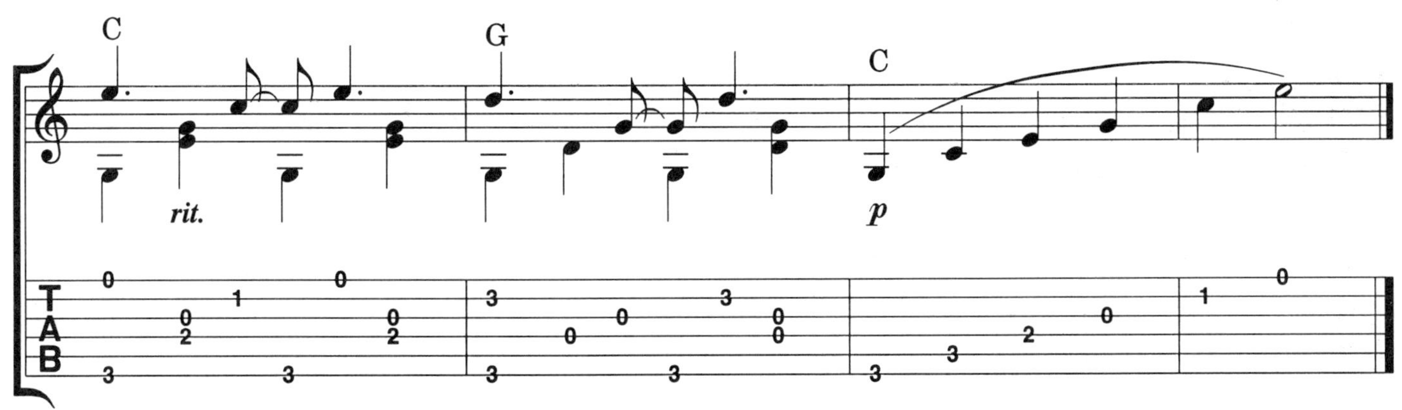
C
G
C
rit.
p
TAB

(FAREWELL MY) BLUE BELL

From Mid 1950's on Super 400
Civil War Song

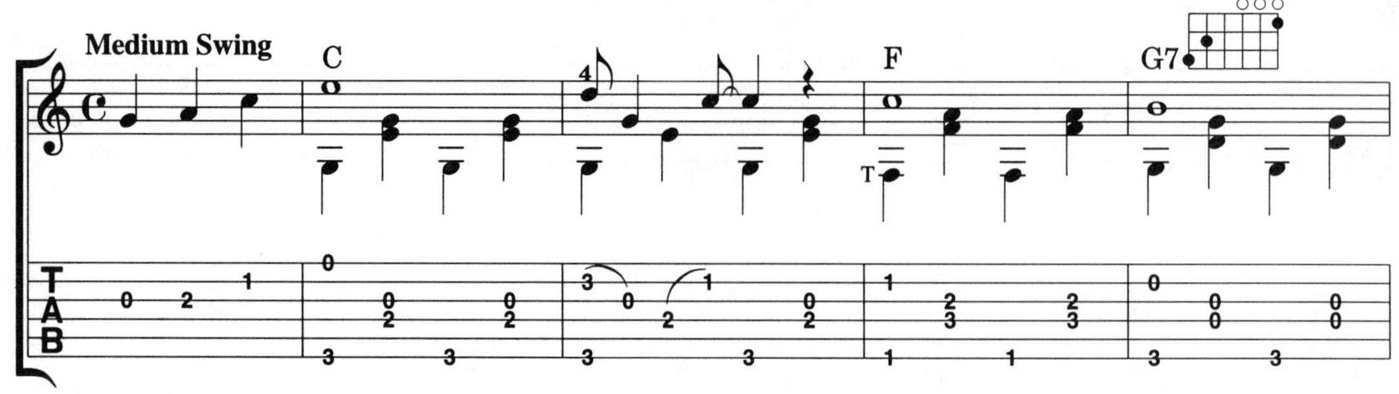

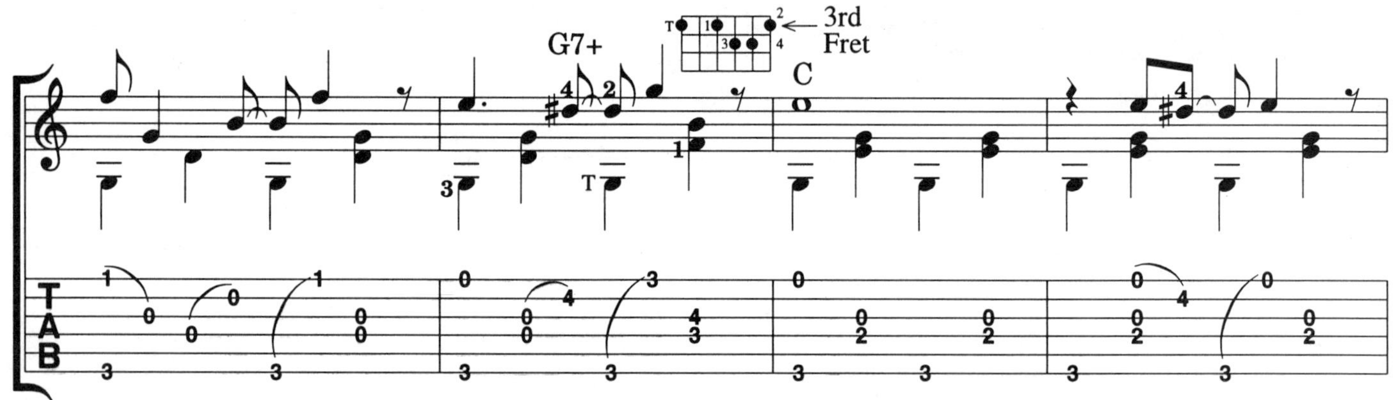

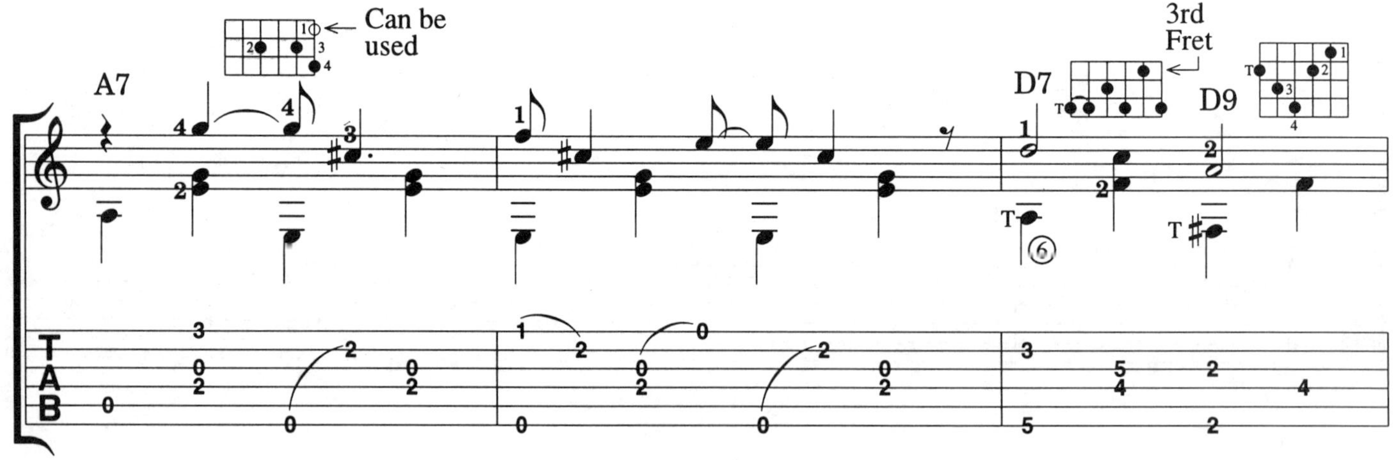

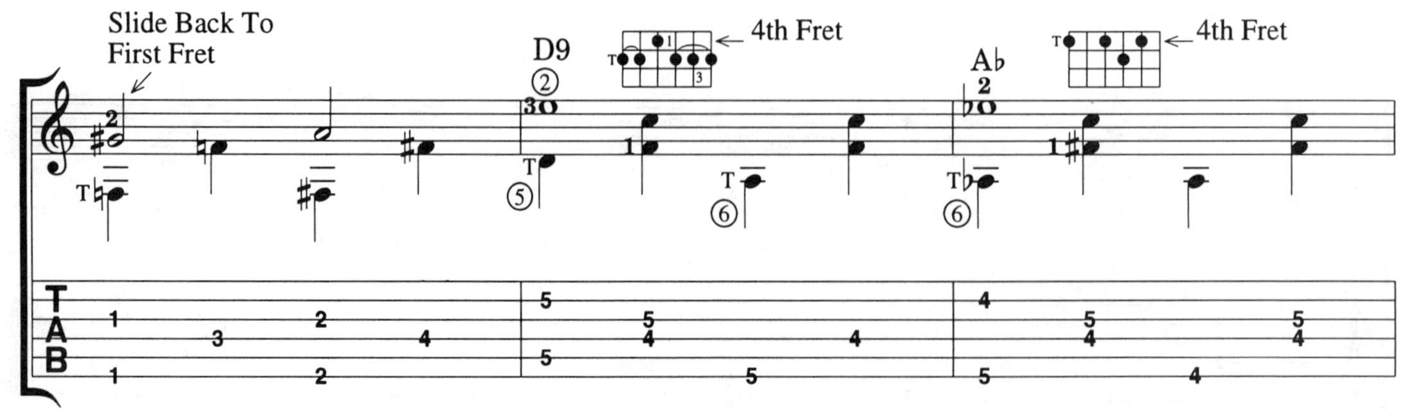

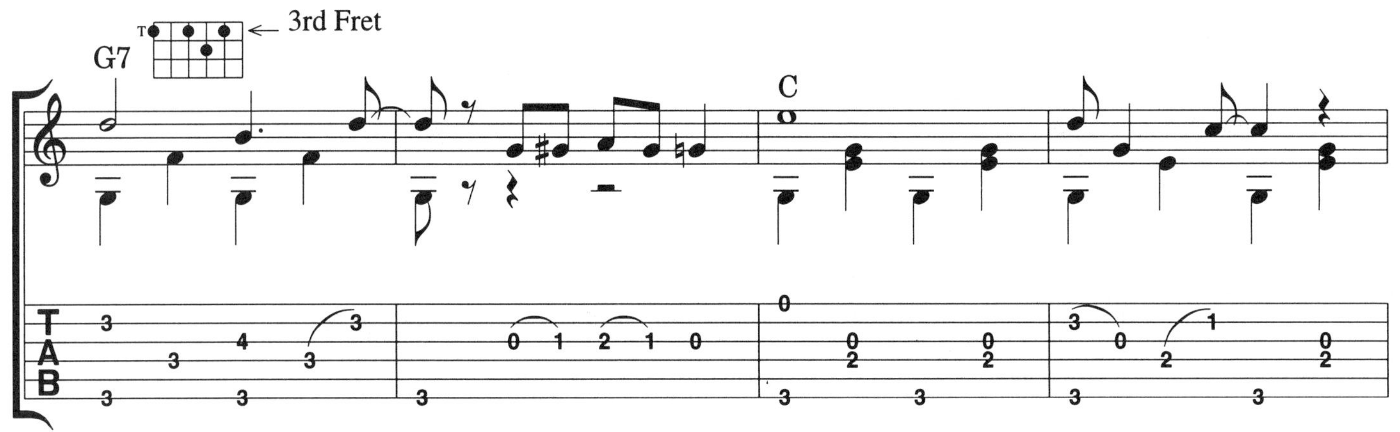
3rd Fret
G7
C
T
A
B

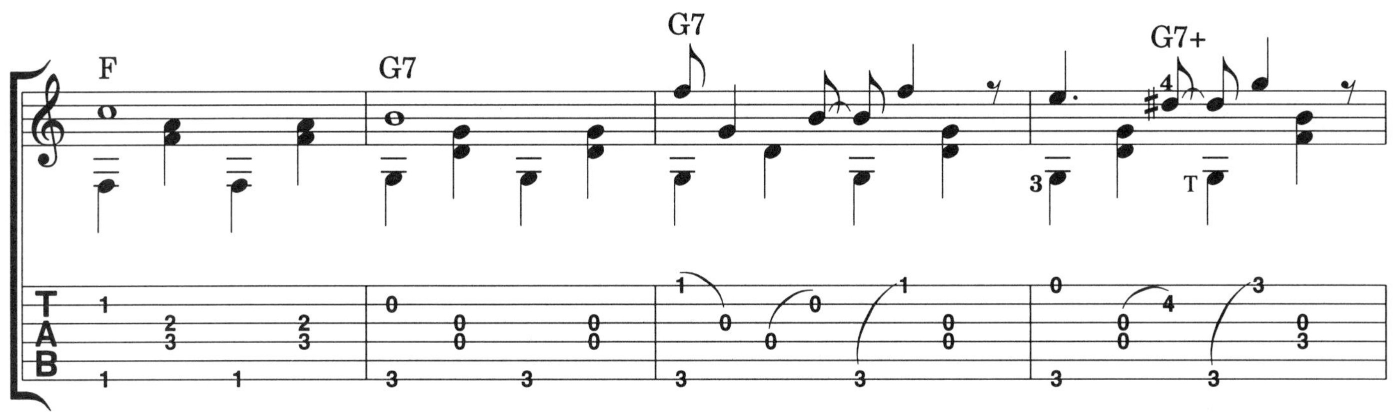
F
G7
G7
G7+
T
A
B

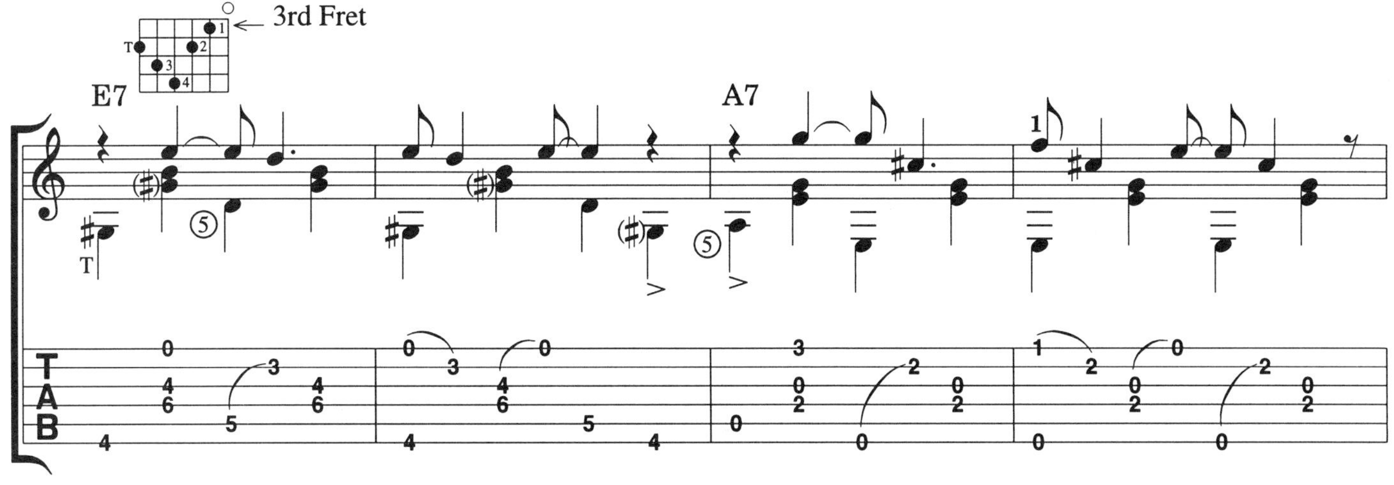
3rd Fret
E7
A7
T
A
B

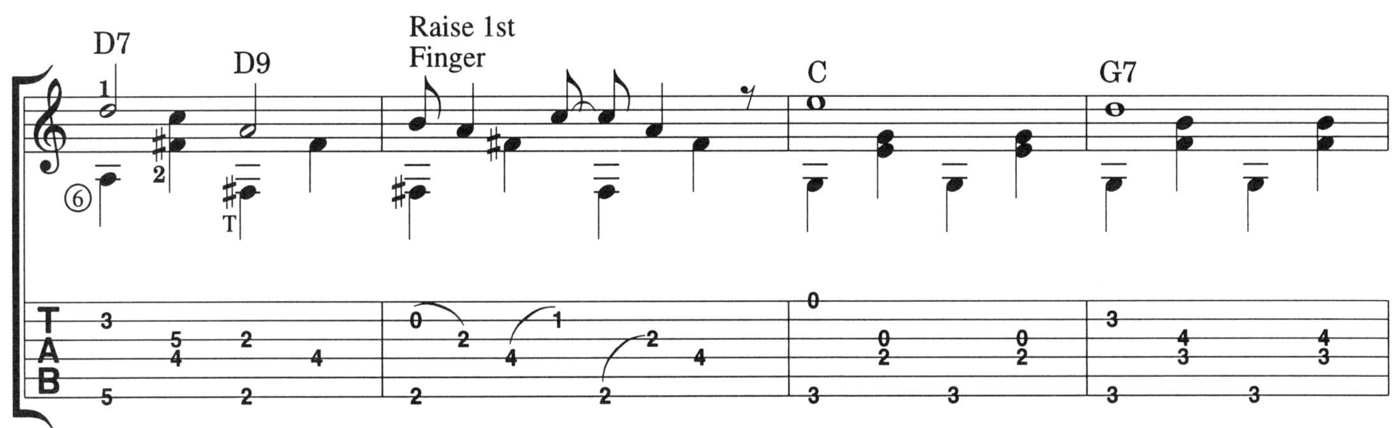
D7
D9
Raise 1st
Finger
C
G7
T
A
B

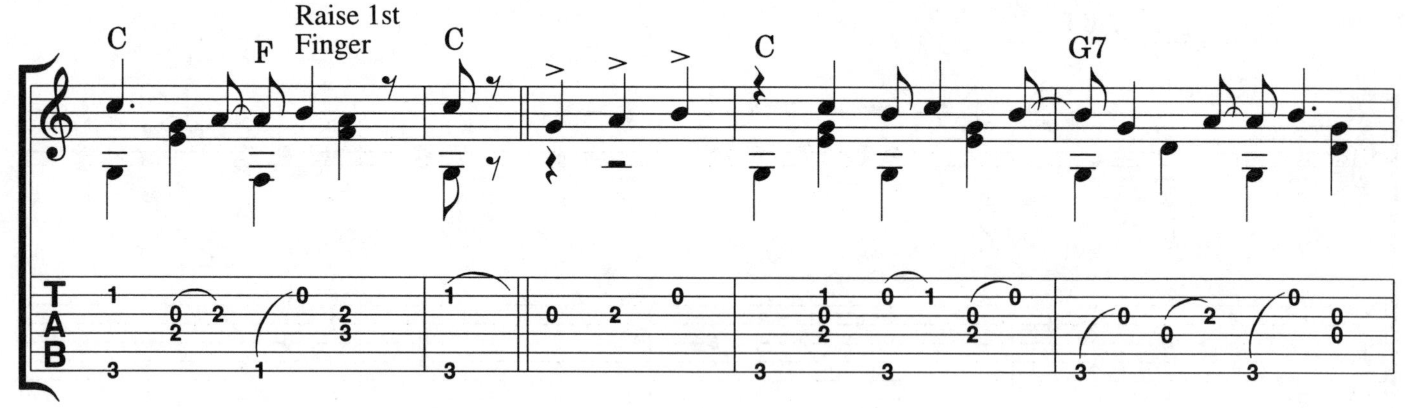
C
F
Raise 1st Finger
C
C
G7

C
G7

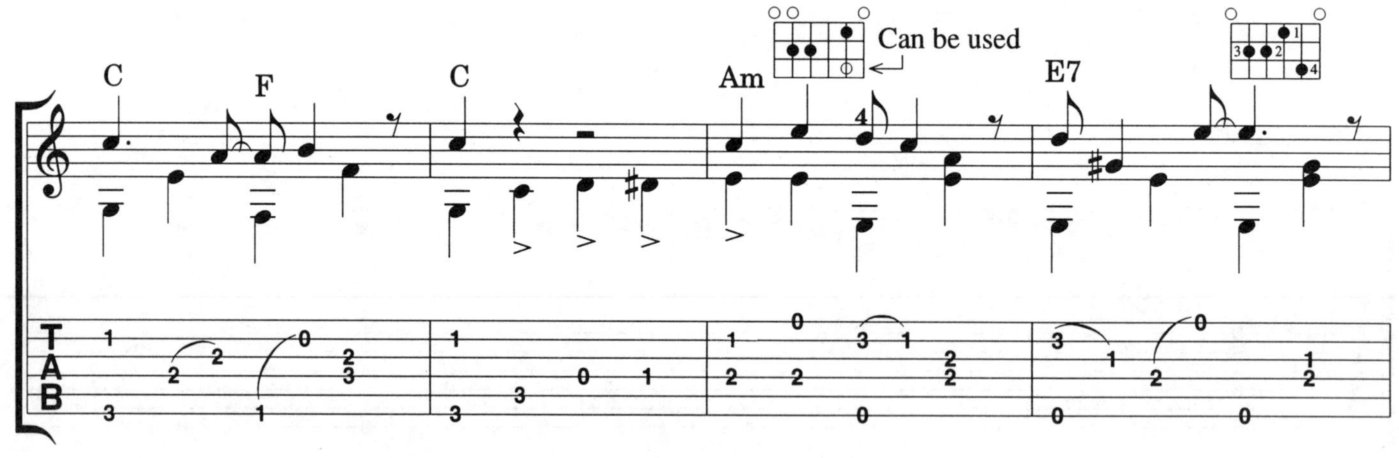
C
F
C
Am
Can be used
E7

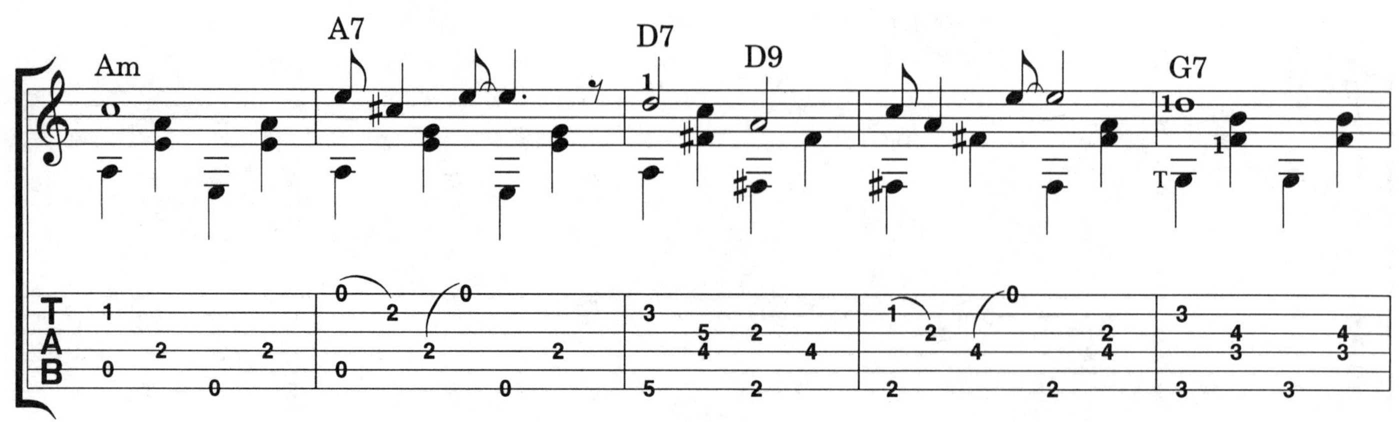
Am
A7
D7
D9
G7

C
G7
C
F
TAB

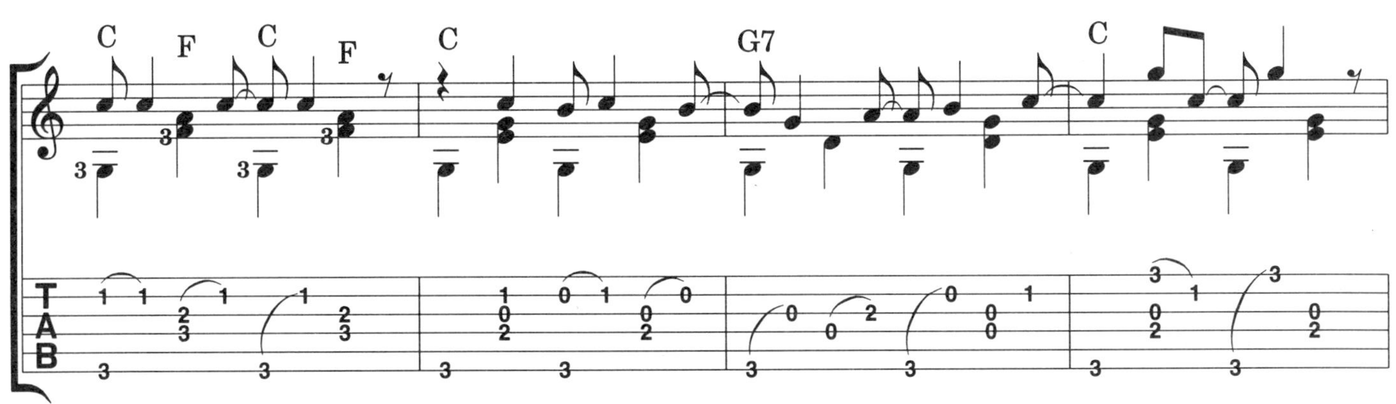
C
F
C
F
C
G7
C
TAB

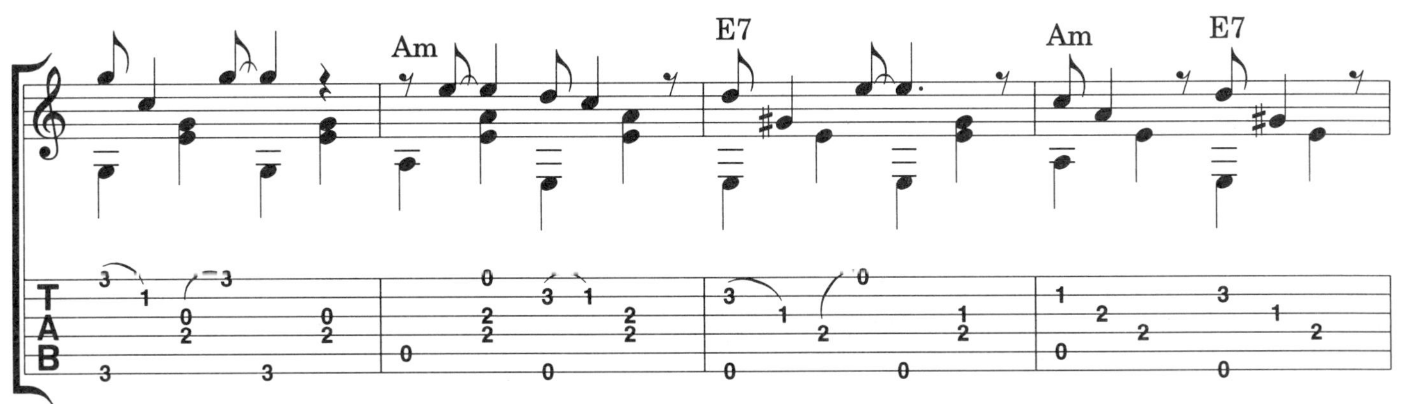
Am
E7
Am
E7
TAB

A7
D7
D9
3rd Fret
G7
TAB

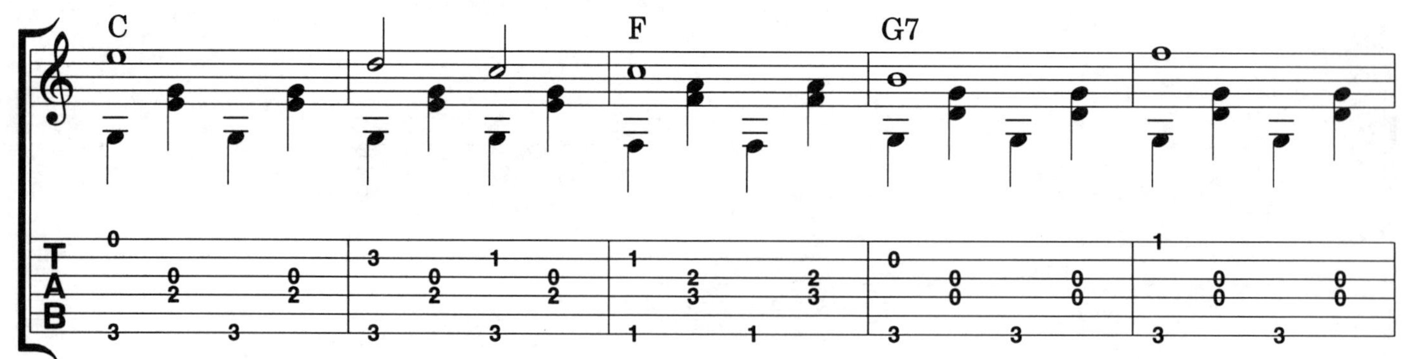
C
F
G7

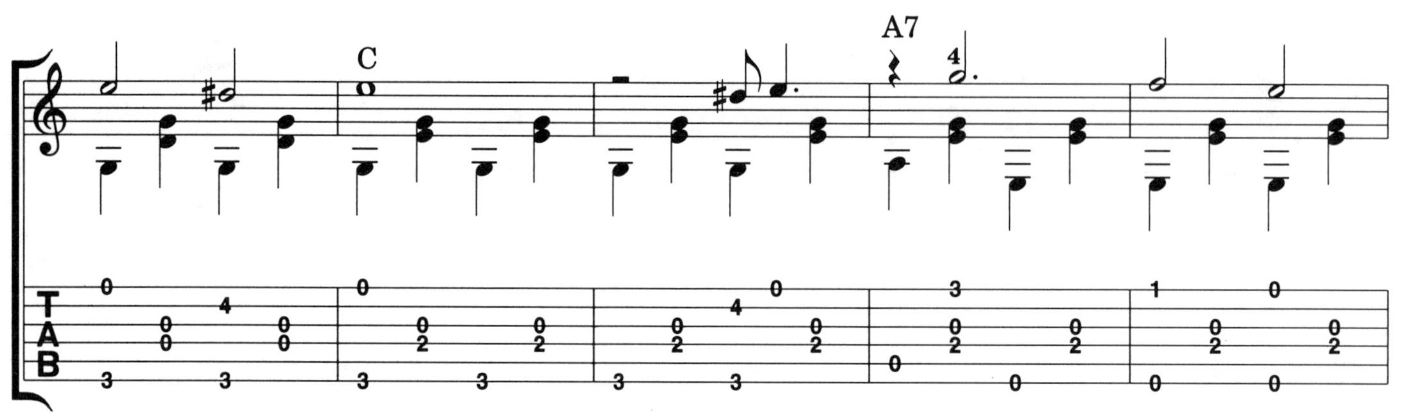
C
A7

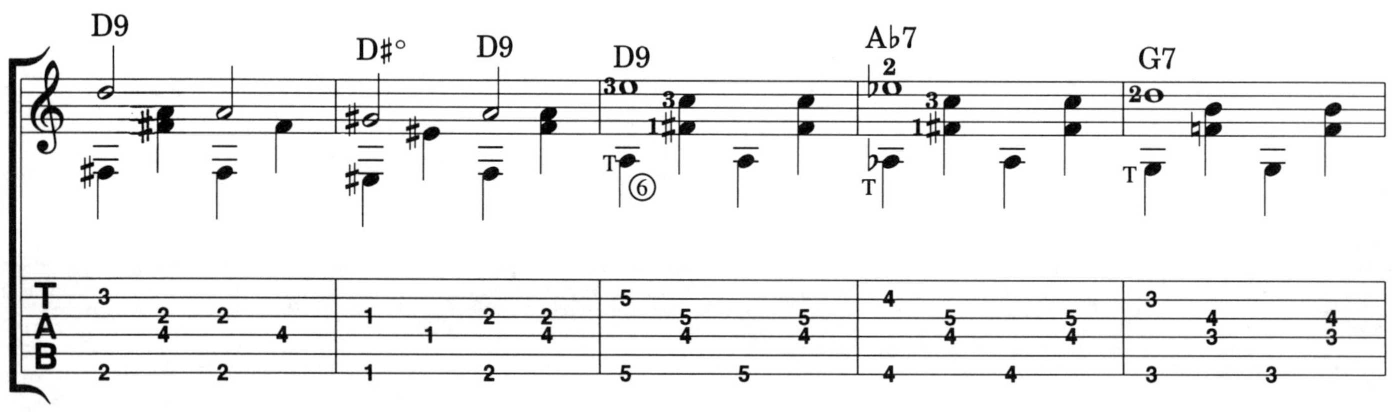
D9
D♯°
D9
D9
A♭7
G7

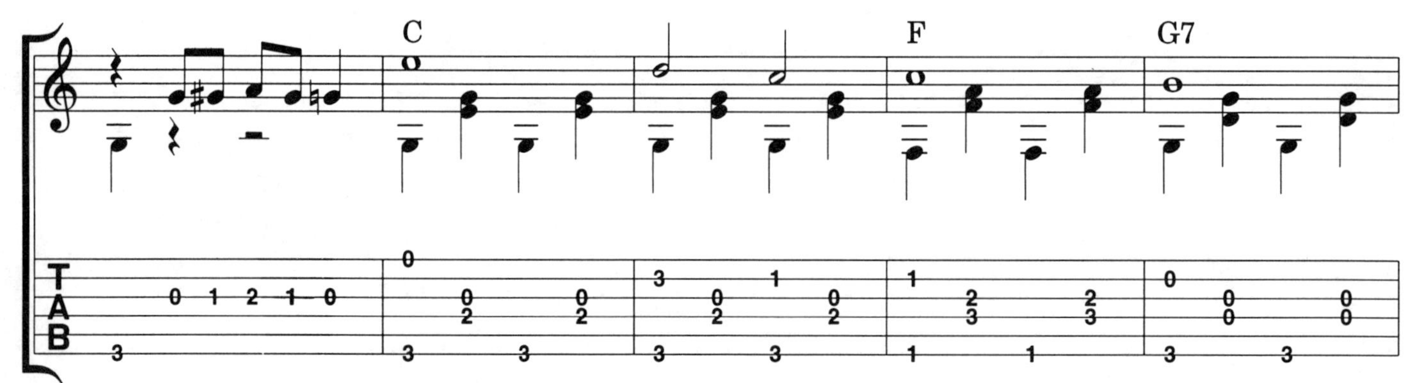
C
F
G7

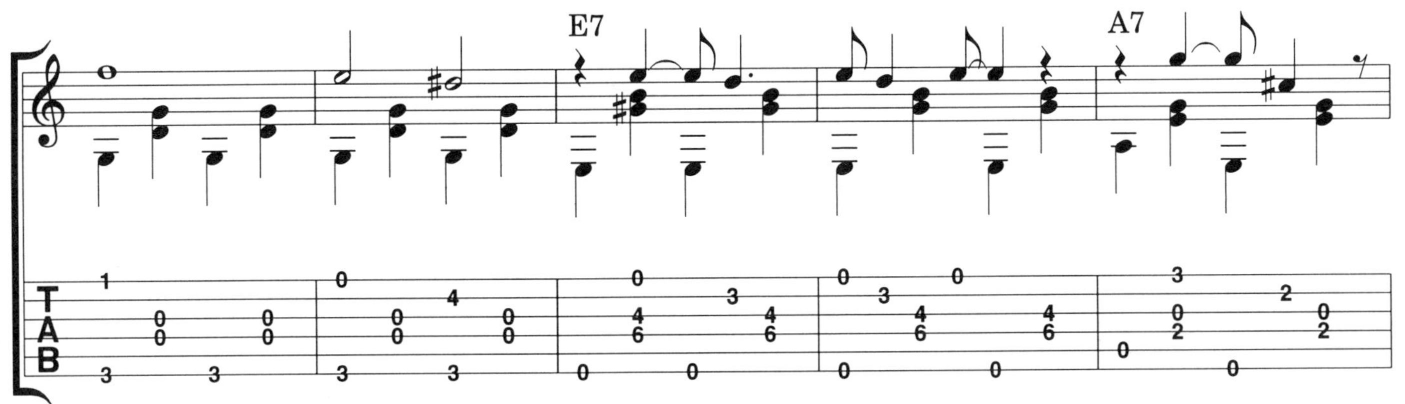
E7
A7
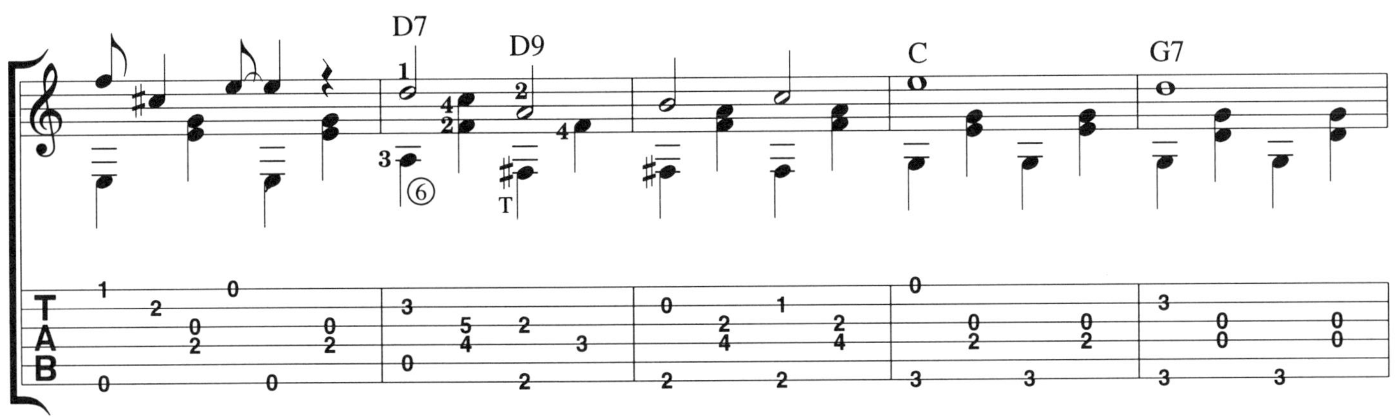
D7
D9
C
G7
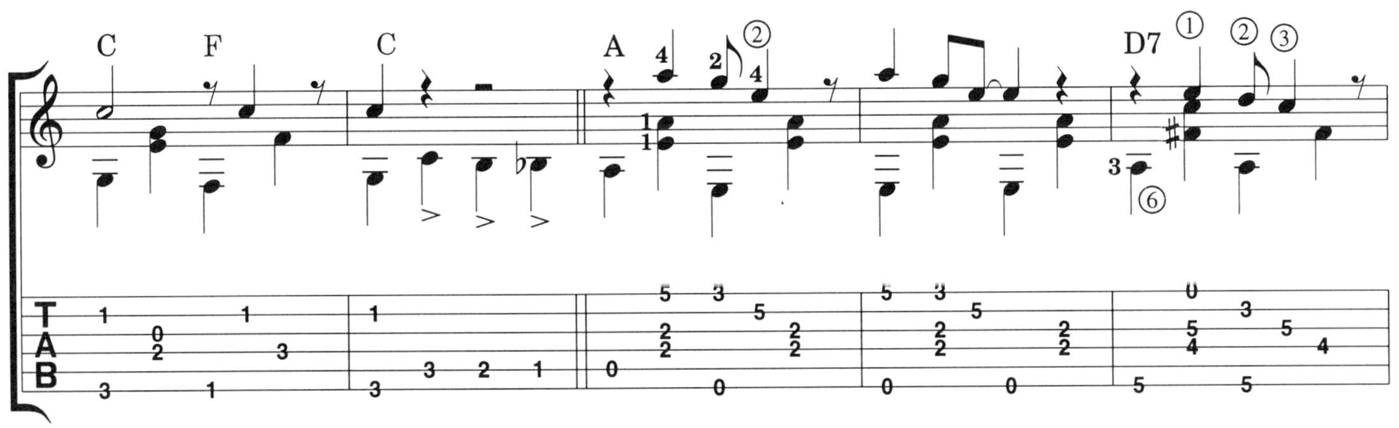
C
F
C
A
D7
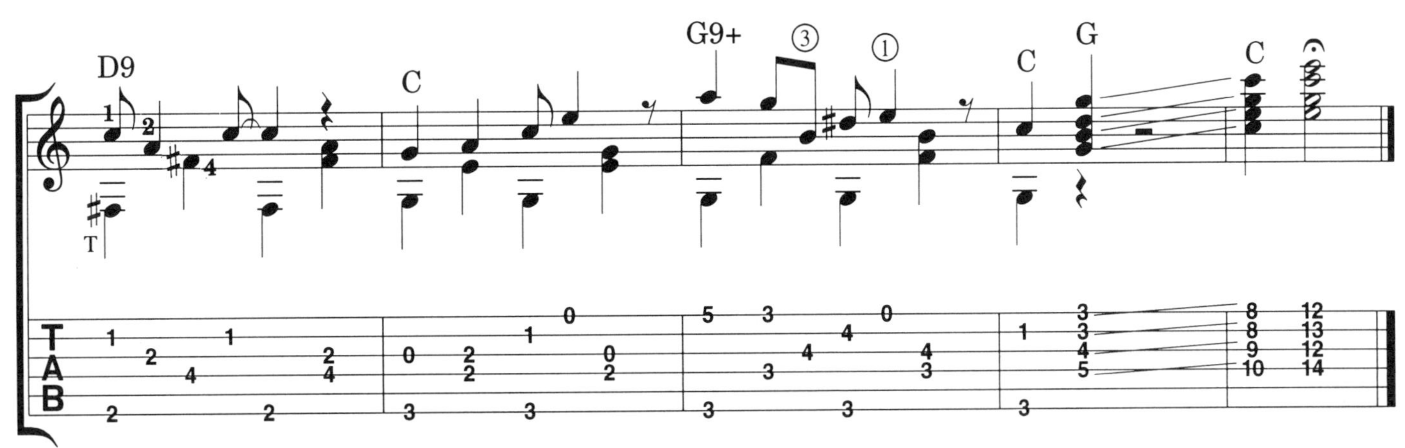
D9
C
G9+
C
G
C

BLUEBELL

Harmony line to be played with last chorus

2nd Guitar

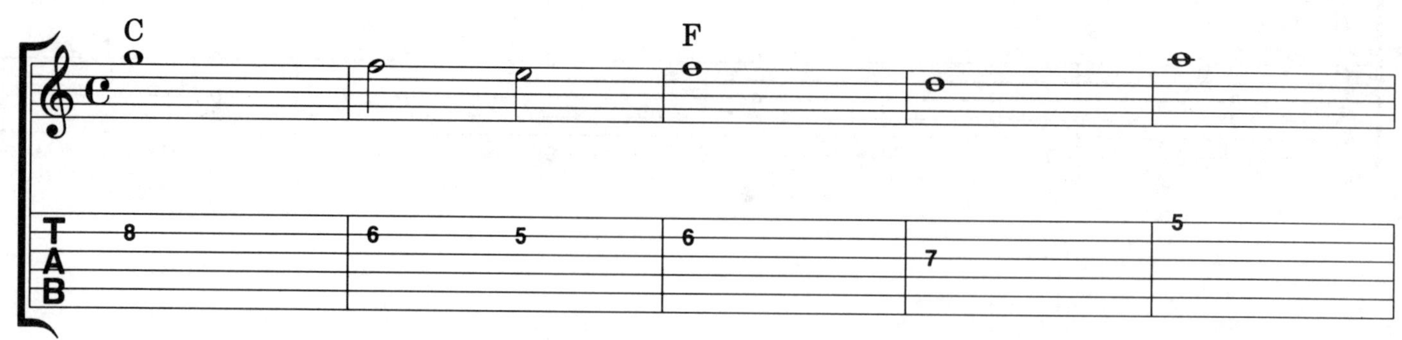

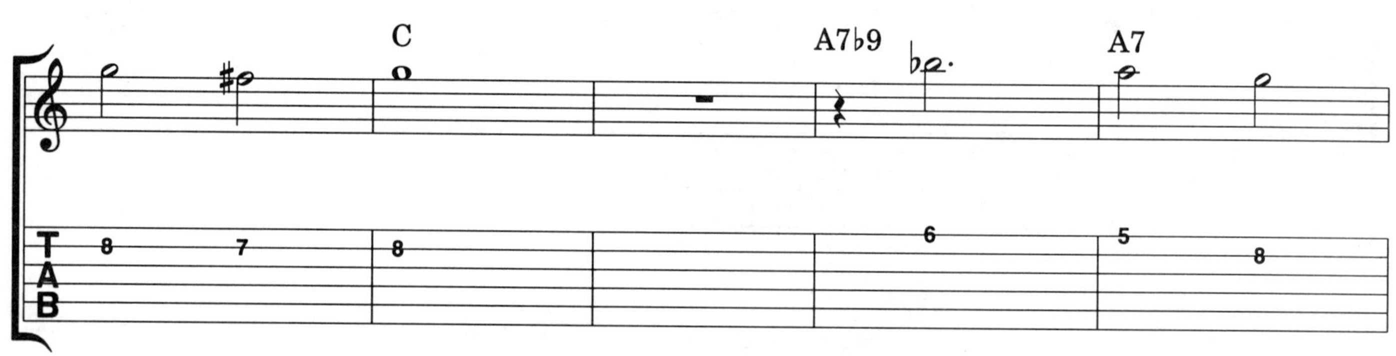

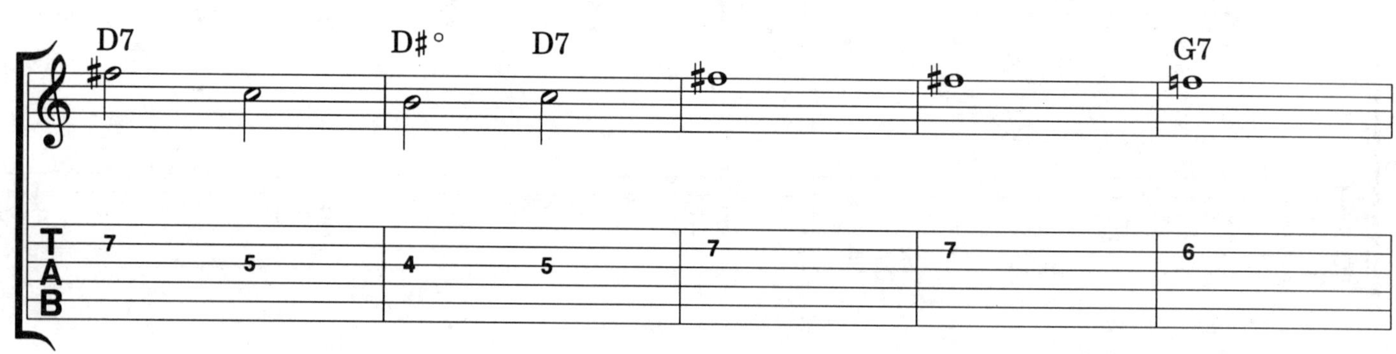

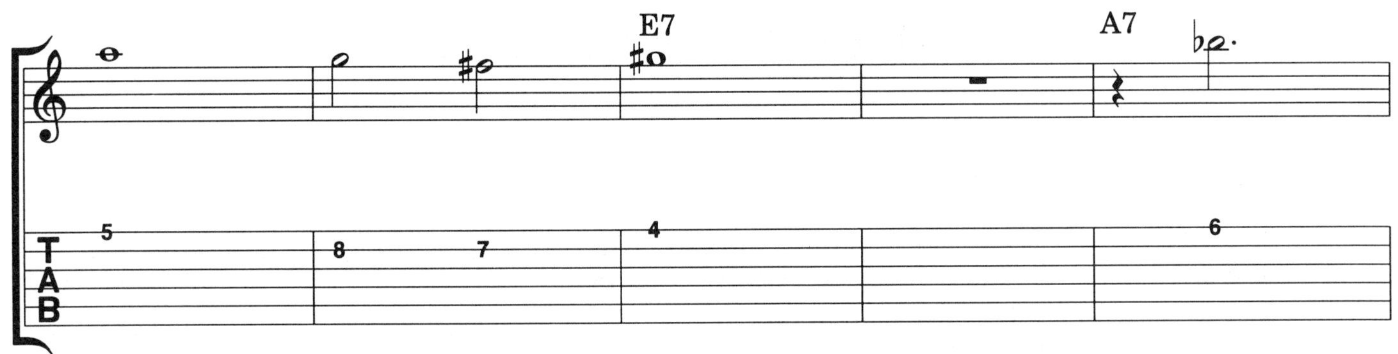
E7
A7
5
8 7
4
6

D
C
G7
5 8
7 5
4 6 7
3
1

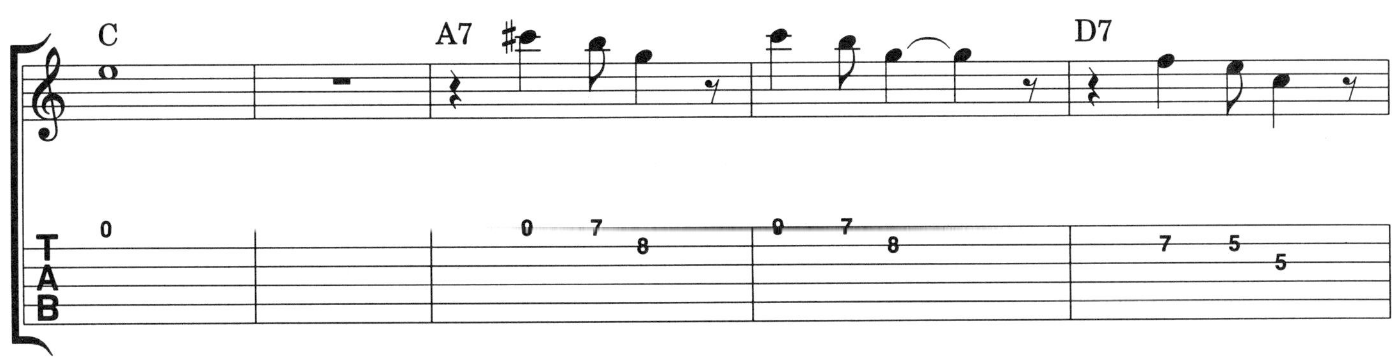
C
A7
D7
0
0 7 8
0 7 8
7 5 5

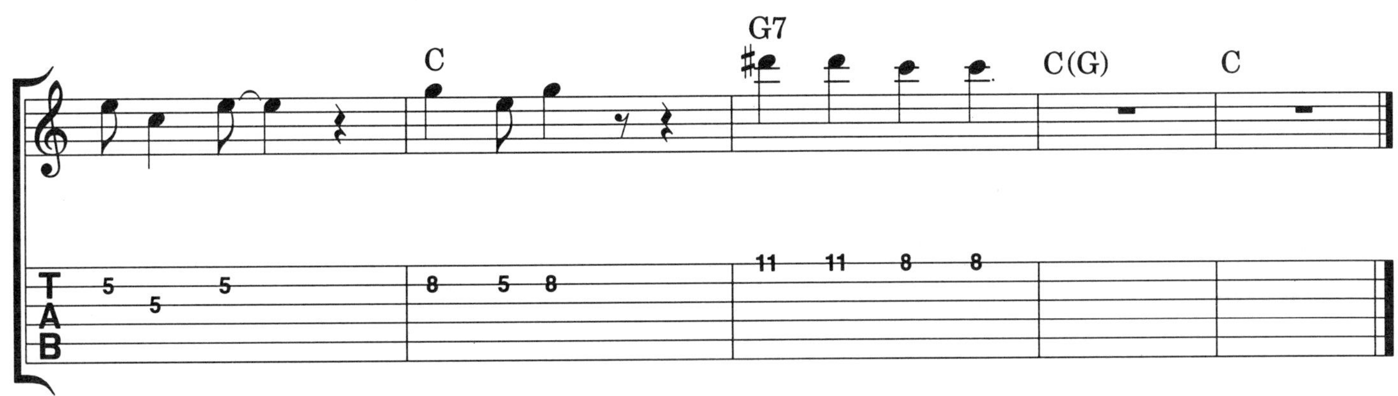
C
G7
C(G)
C
5 5 5
8 5 8
11 11 8 8

BUGLE CALL RAG

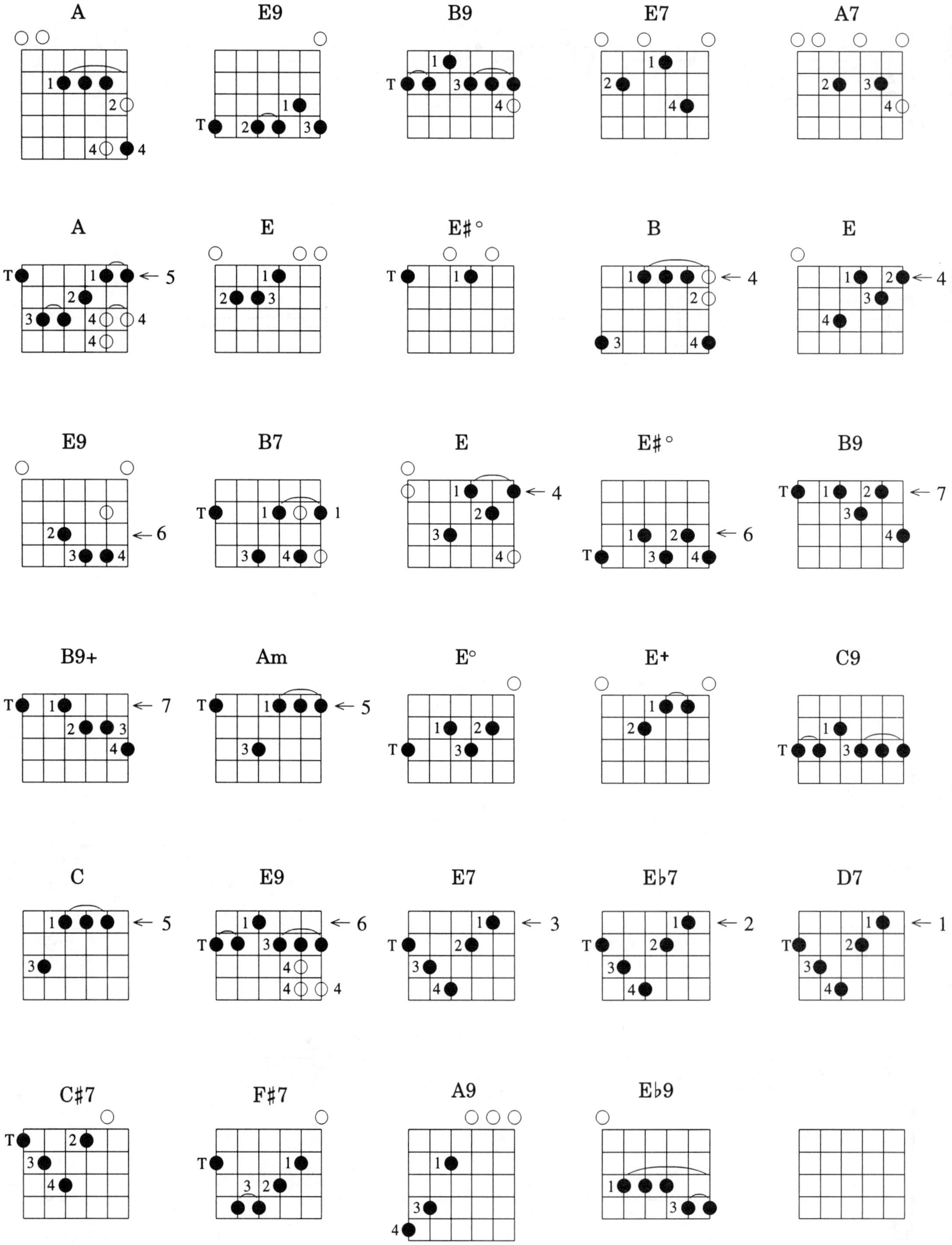

A | E9 | B9 | E7 | A7

A | E | E♯° | B | E

E9 | B7 | E | E♯° | B9

B9+ | Am | E° | E+ | C9

C | E9 | E7 | E♭7 | D7

C♯7

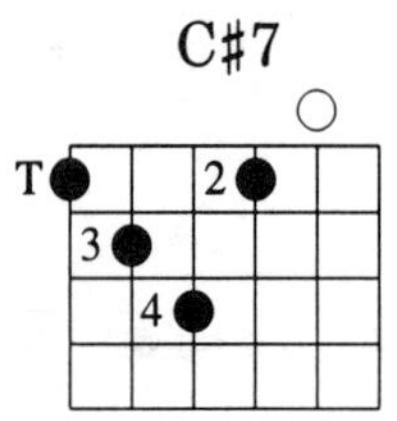

F♯7

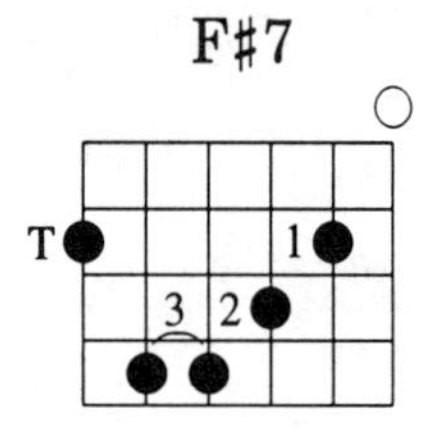

A9

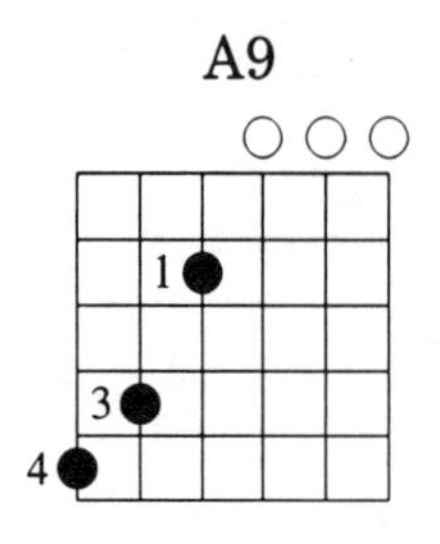

E♭9

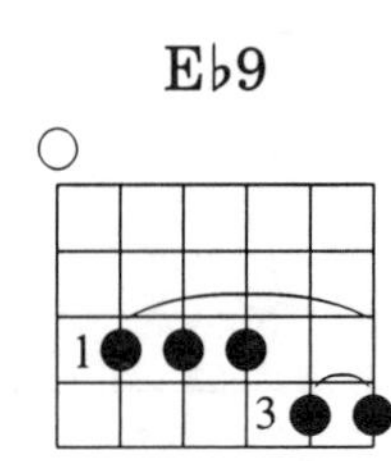

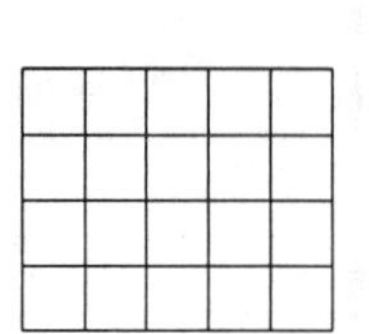

BUGLE CALL RAG

Capo on 4 to be with recording

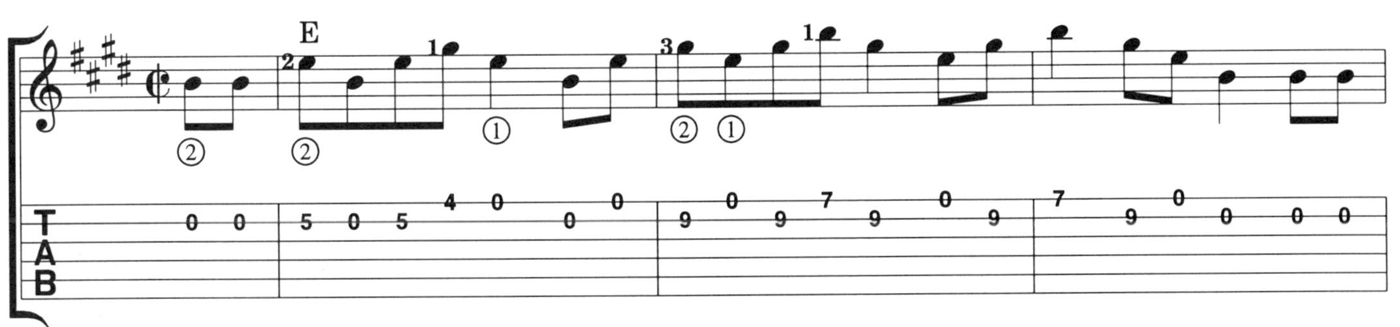

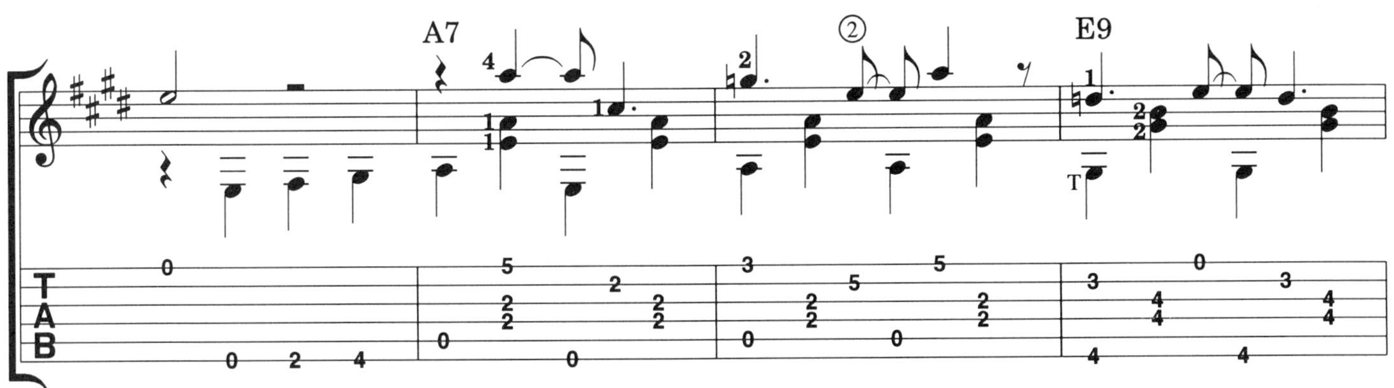

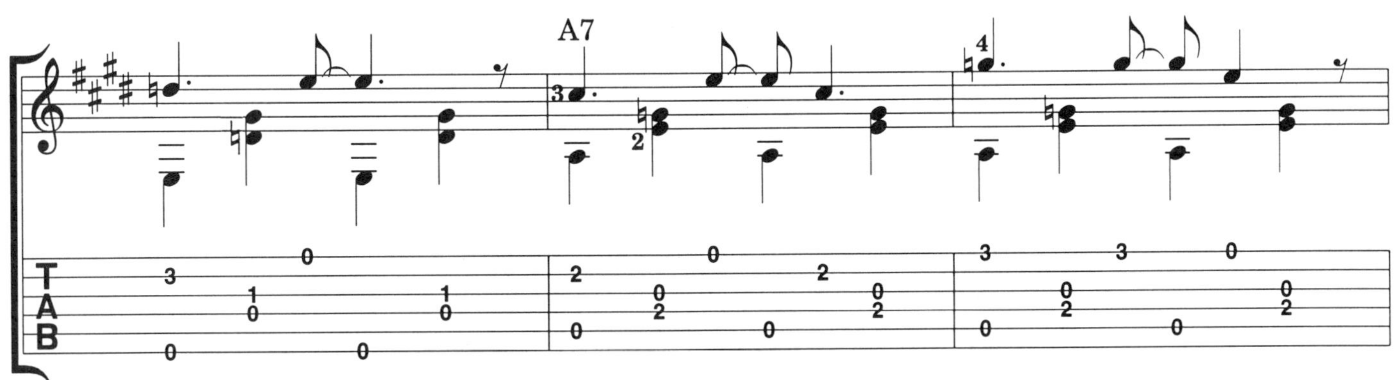

E9
B9

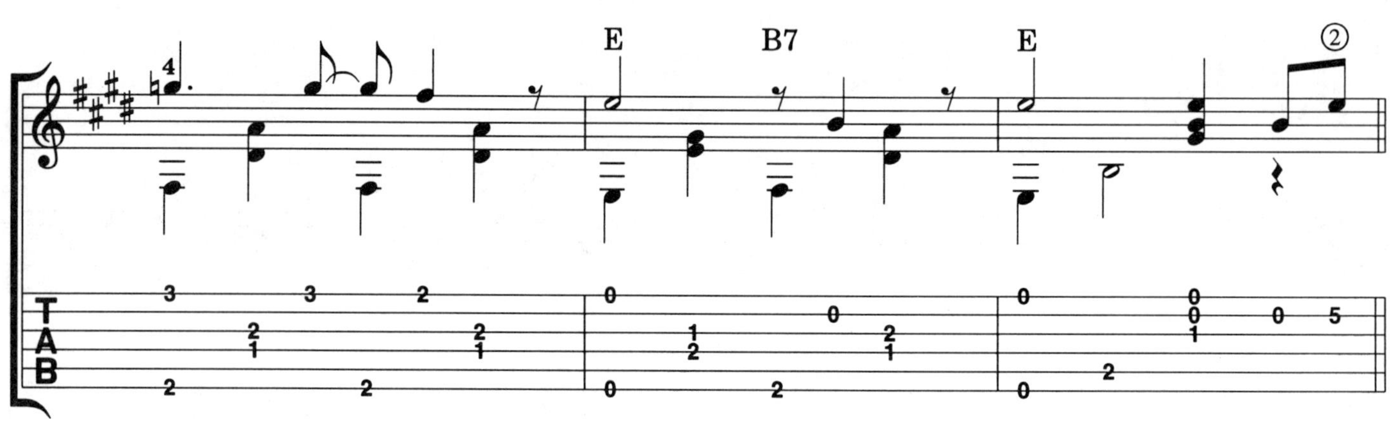
E
B7
E

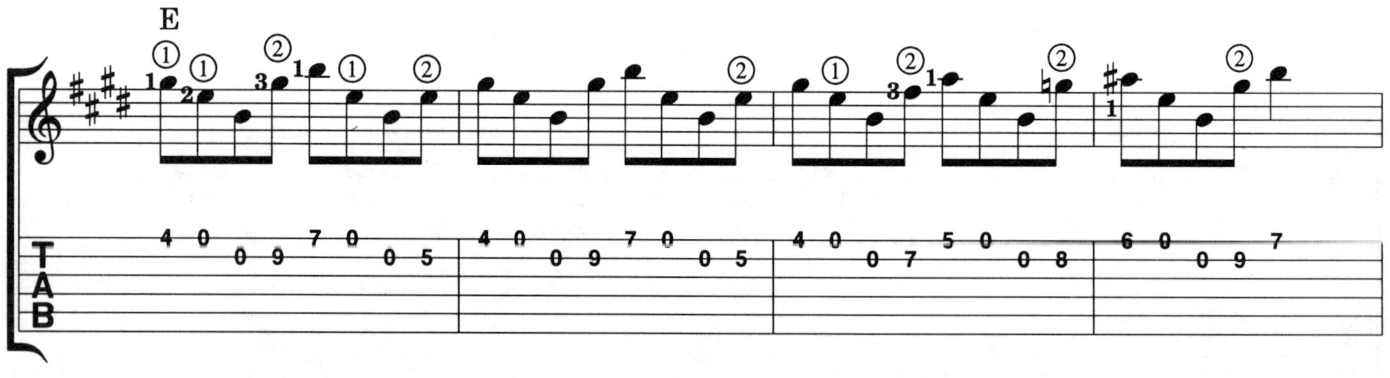
E

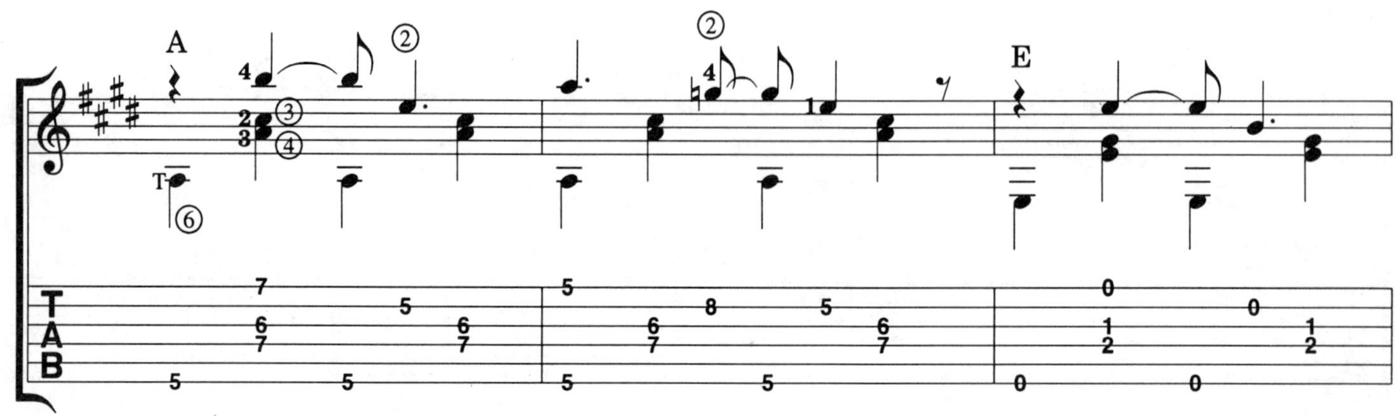
A
E

B9

E7
A

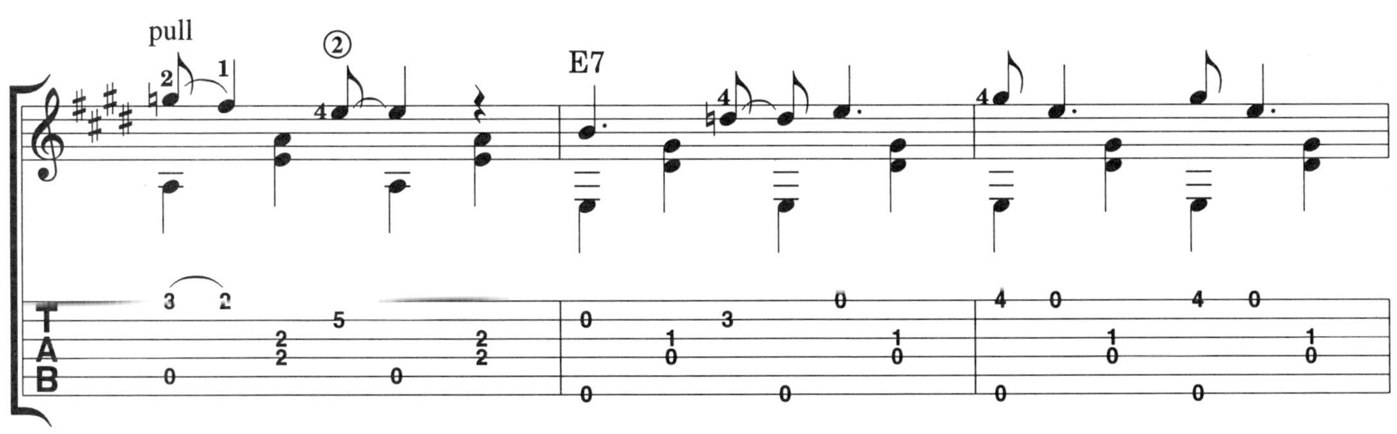
pull
E7

B9
E
B7
E

5
5
3
3
⑤
④
③
T
A
B

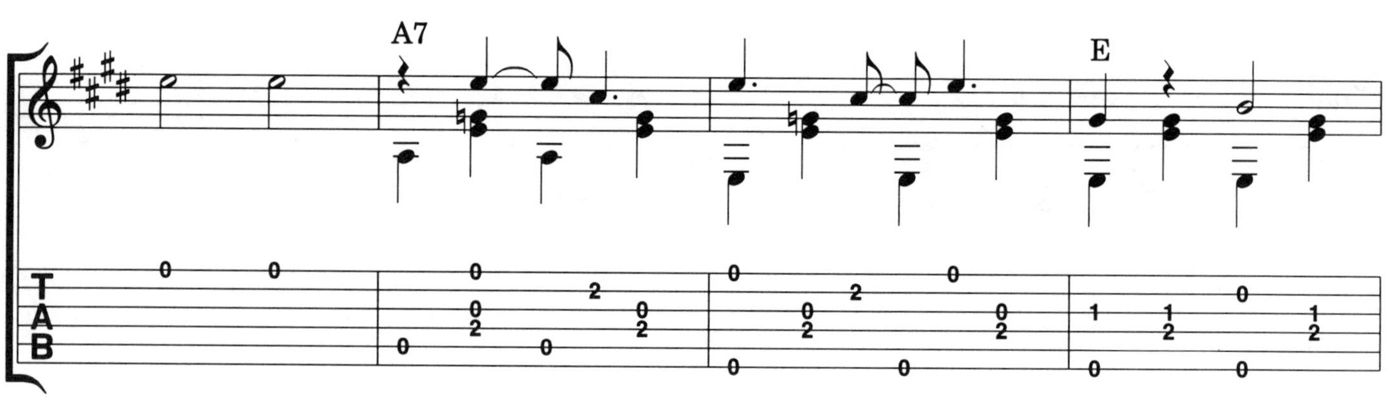

A7
E
T
A
B

B9
E
T
A
B

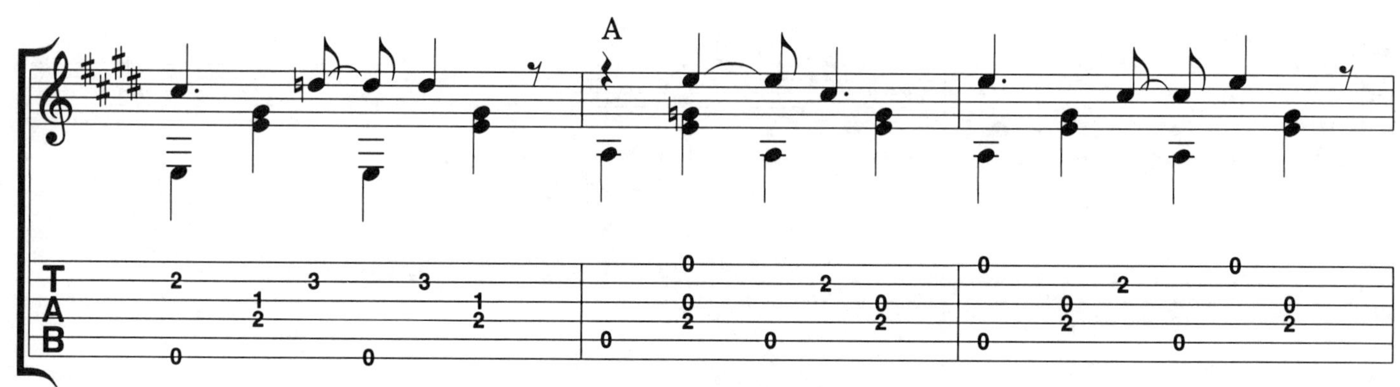

A
T
A
B

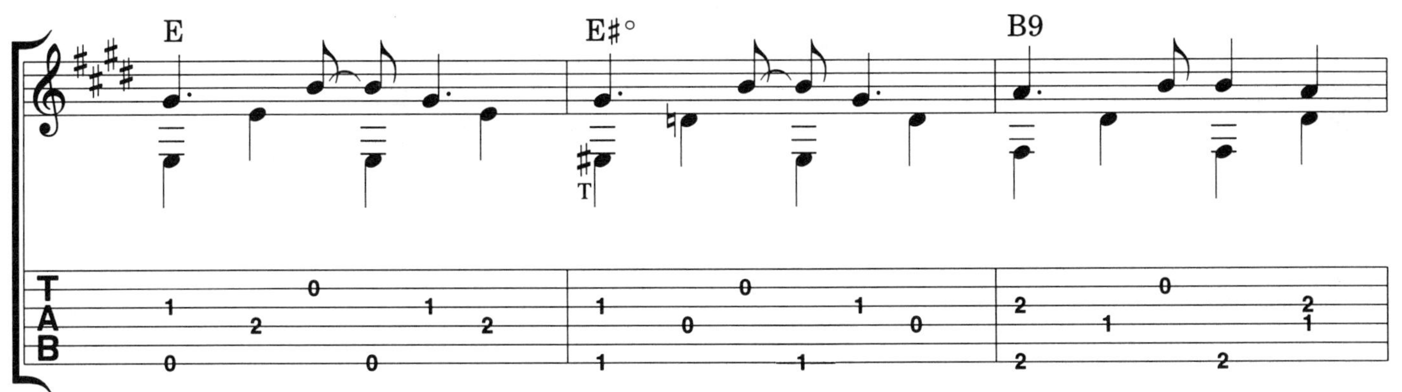
E
E#°
B9
T
T
A
B

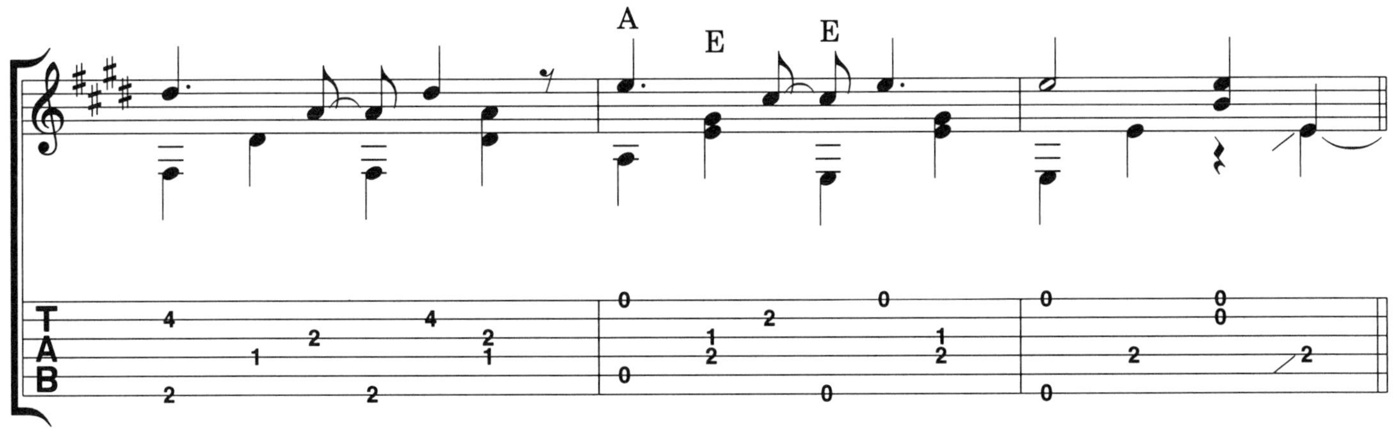
A
E
E
T
A
B

T
A
B

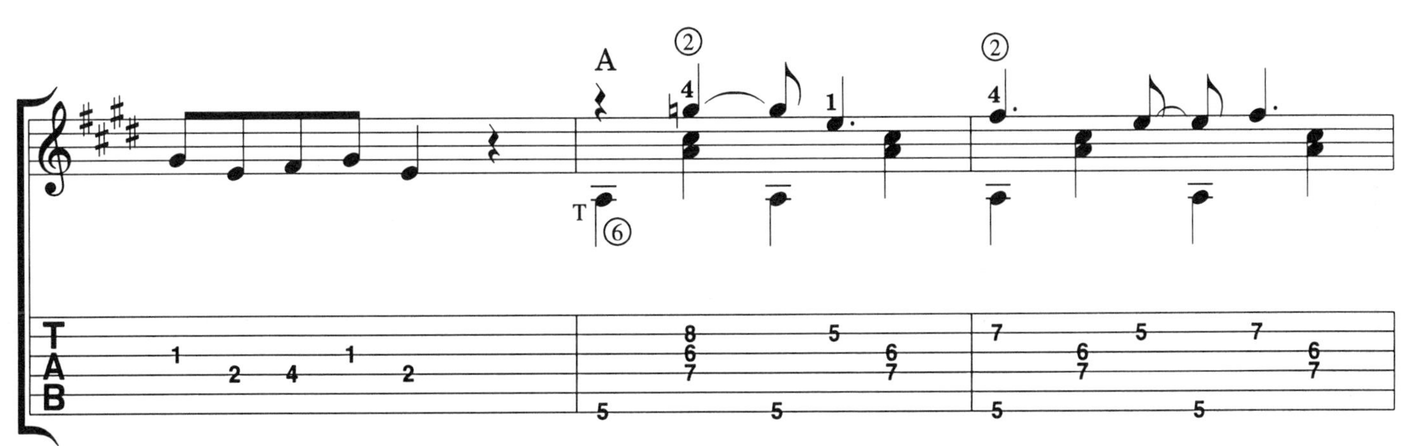
A
T
T
A
B

E
B
T
A
B

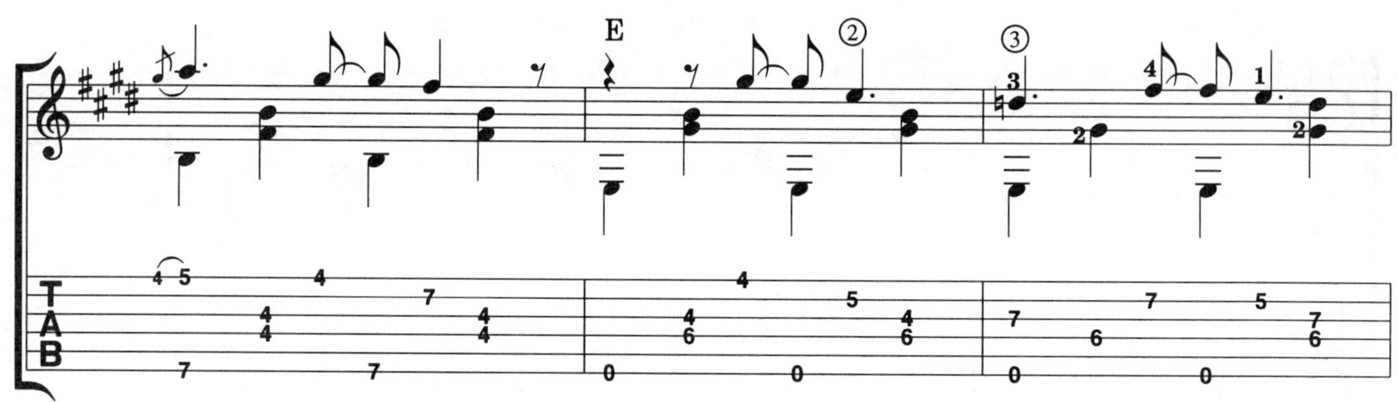
E
T
A
B

A
E
T
A
B

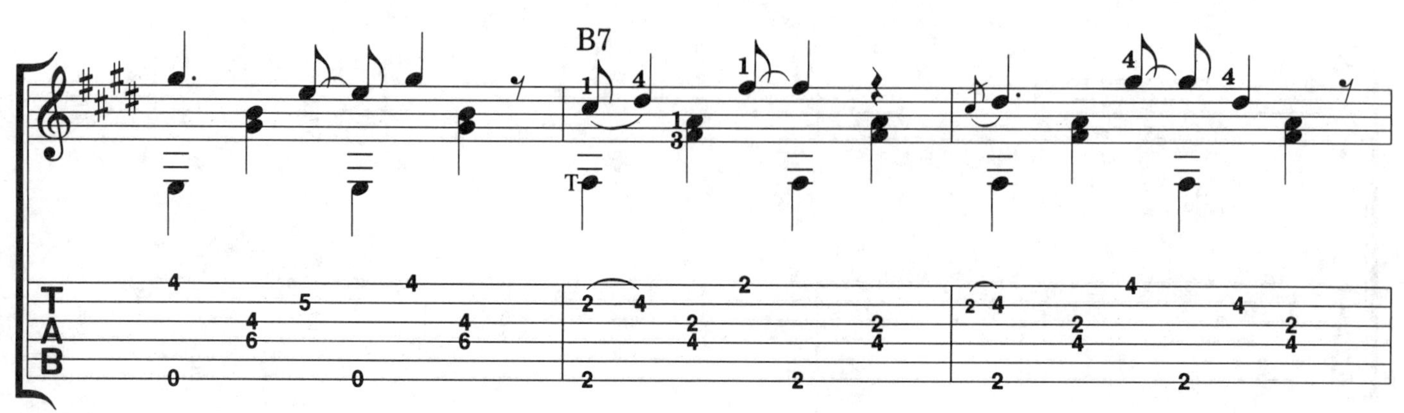
B7
T
A
B

E
E

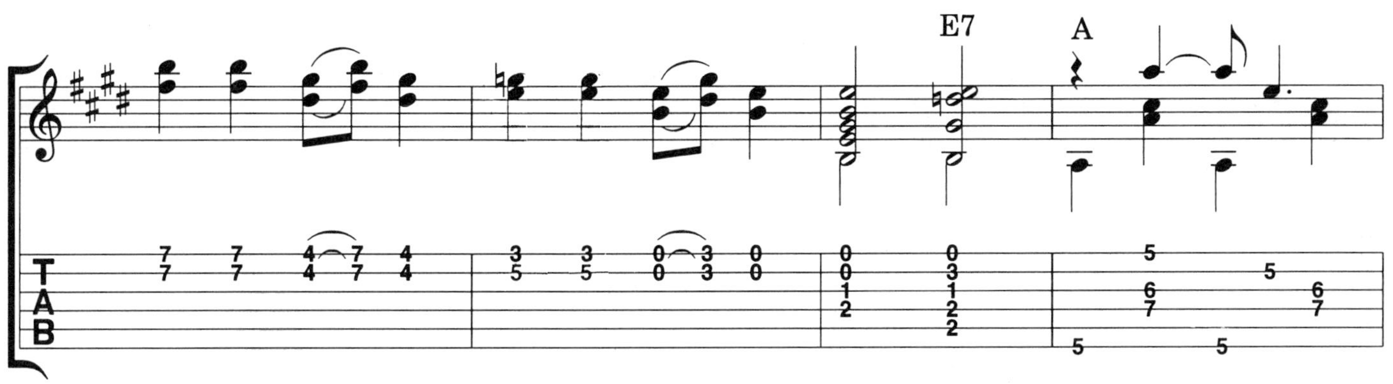
E7
A

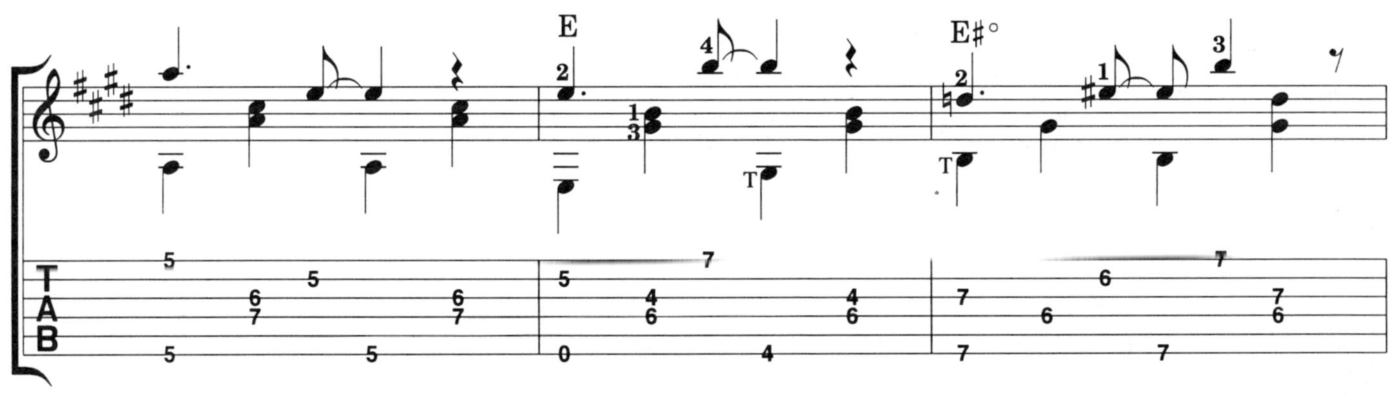
E
E#°

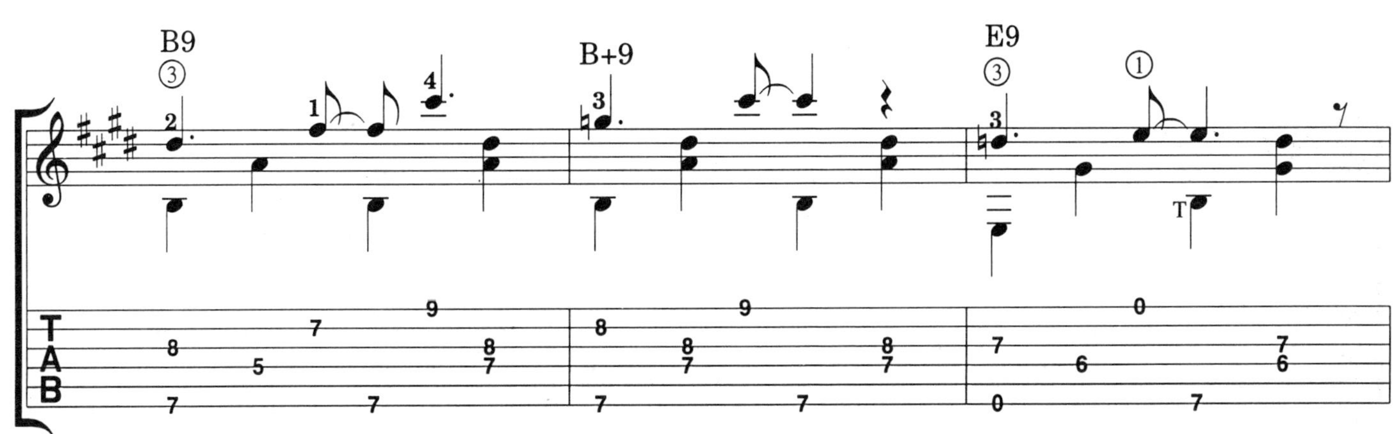
B9
B+9
E9

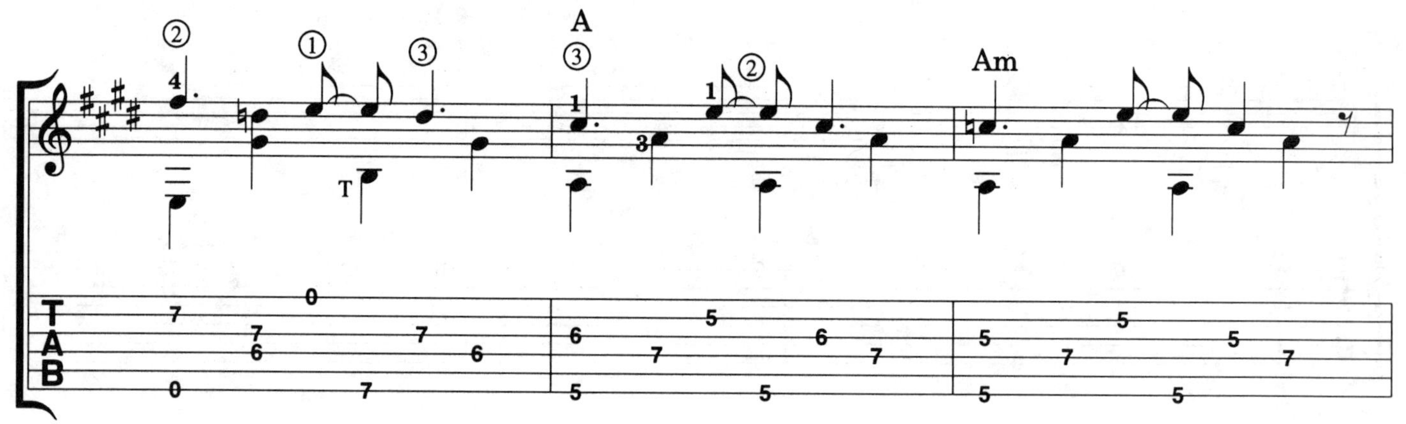
A
Am
T
A
B

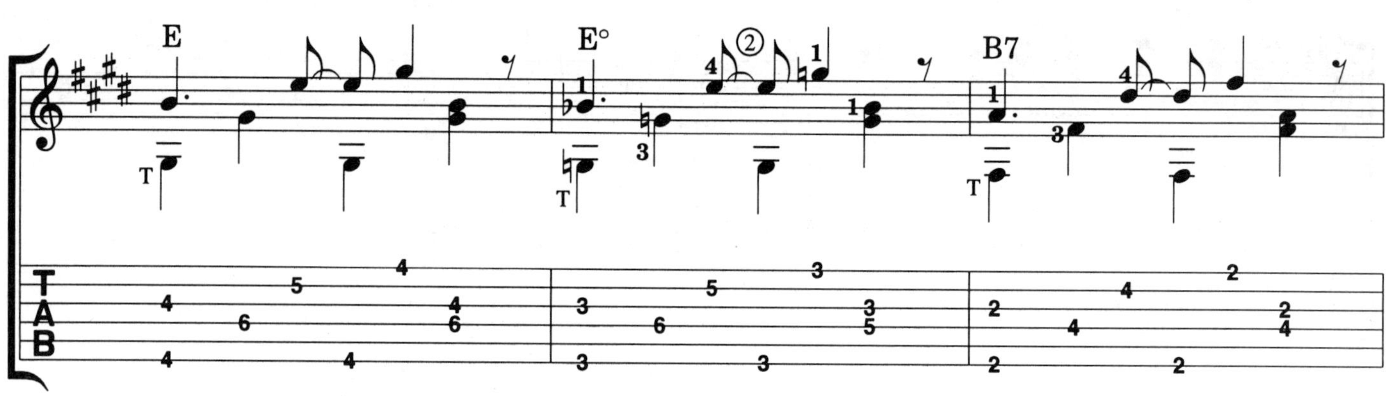
E
E°
B7
T
A
B

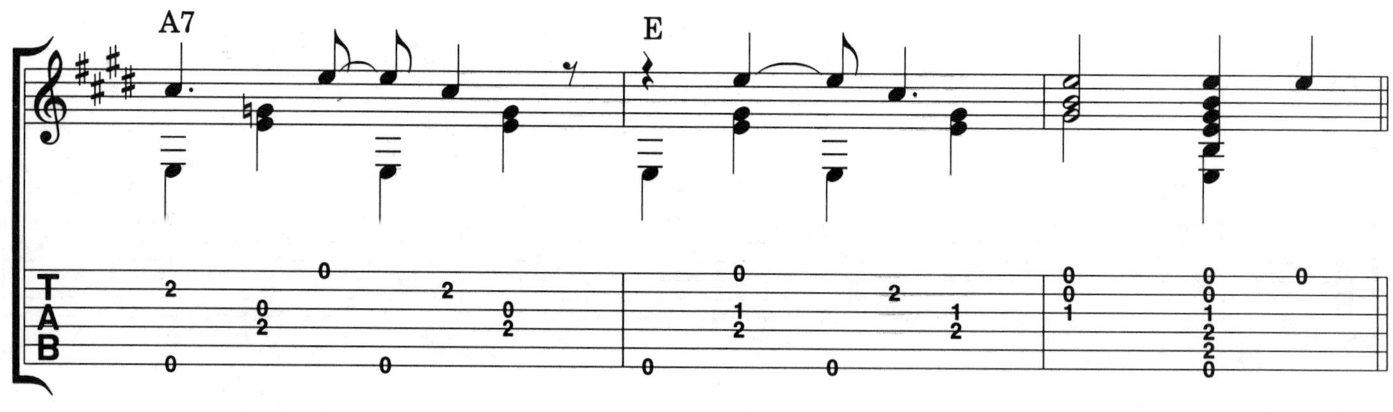
A7
E
T
A
B

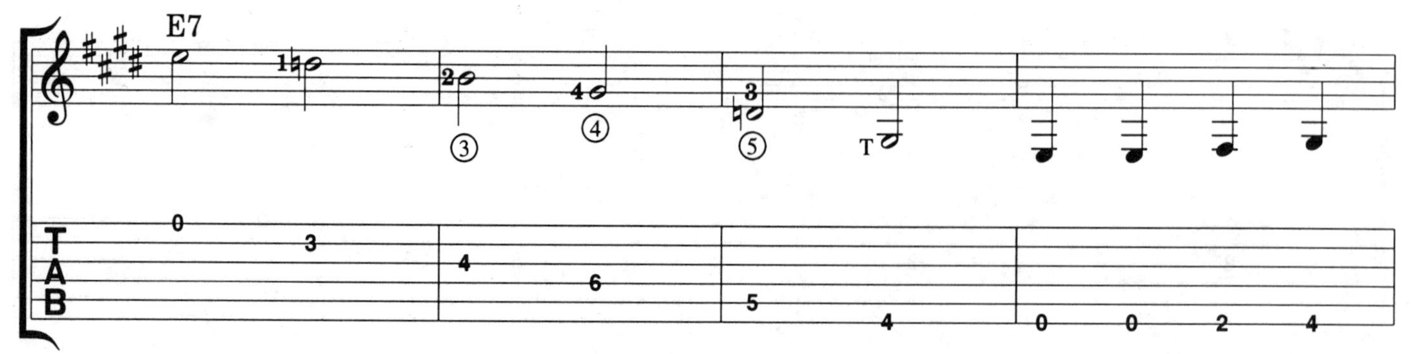
E7
T
A
B

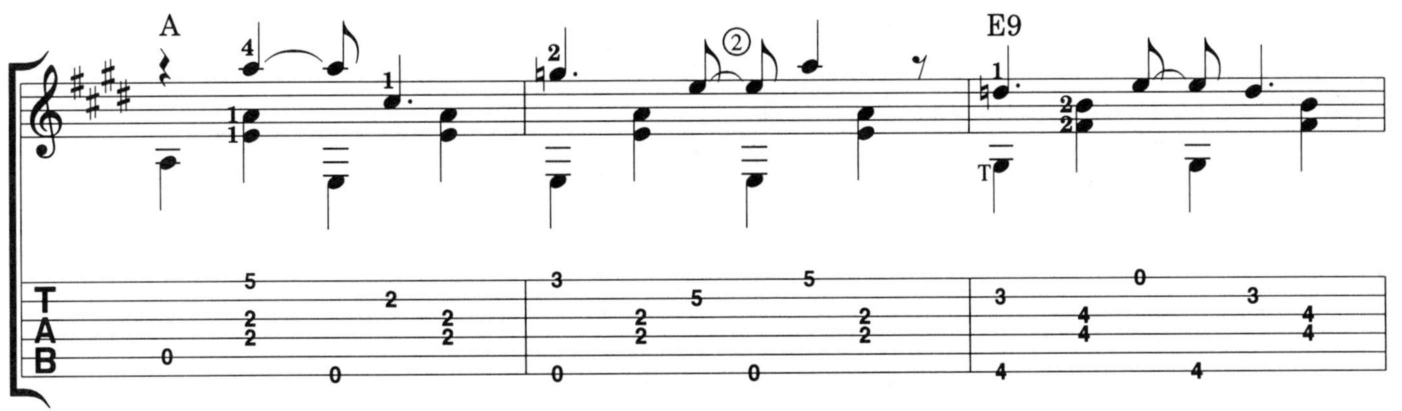
A
E9
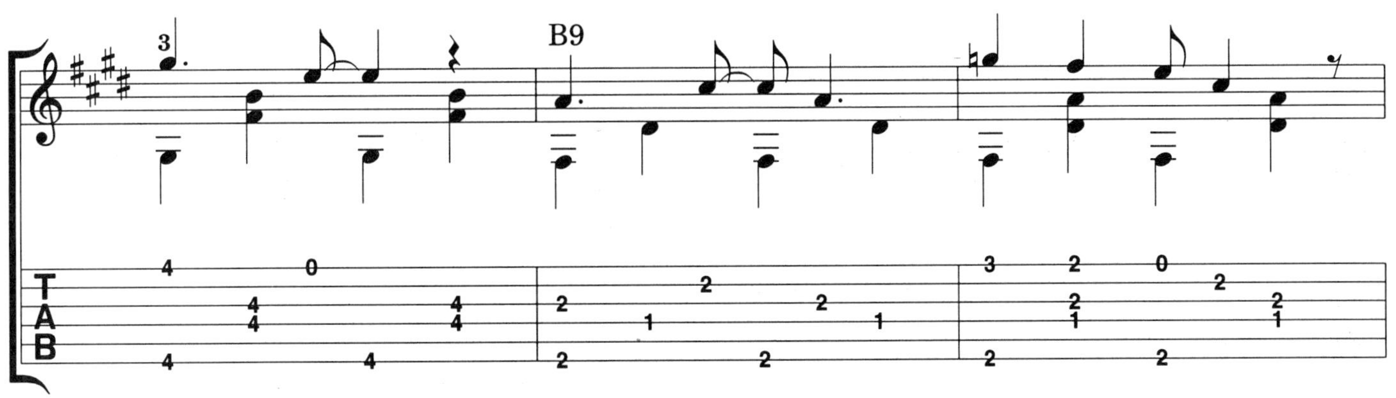
B9
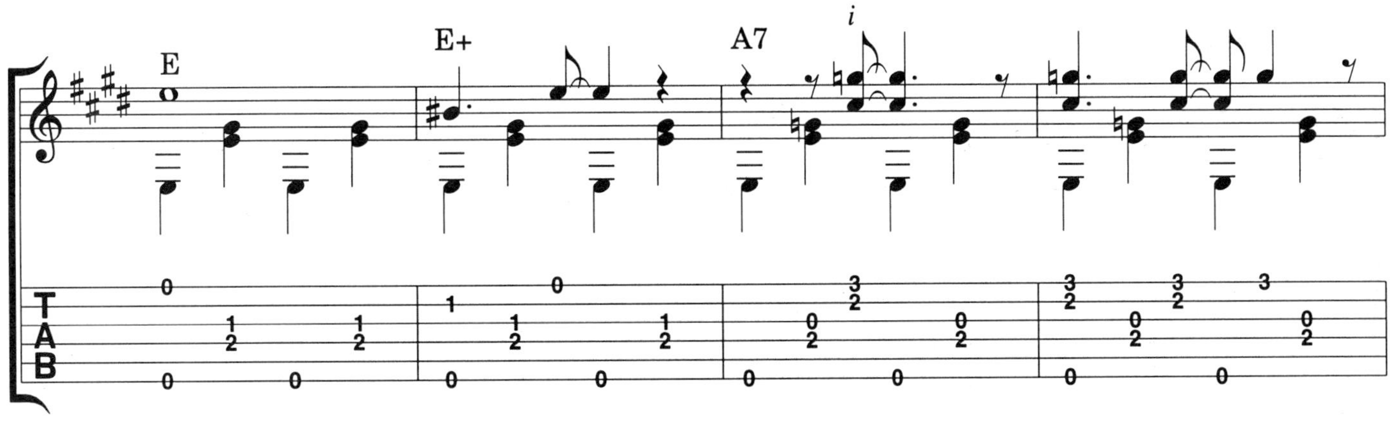
E
E+
A7

E9
B9

E
B7
E
E
TAB
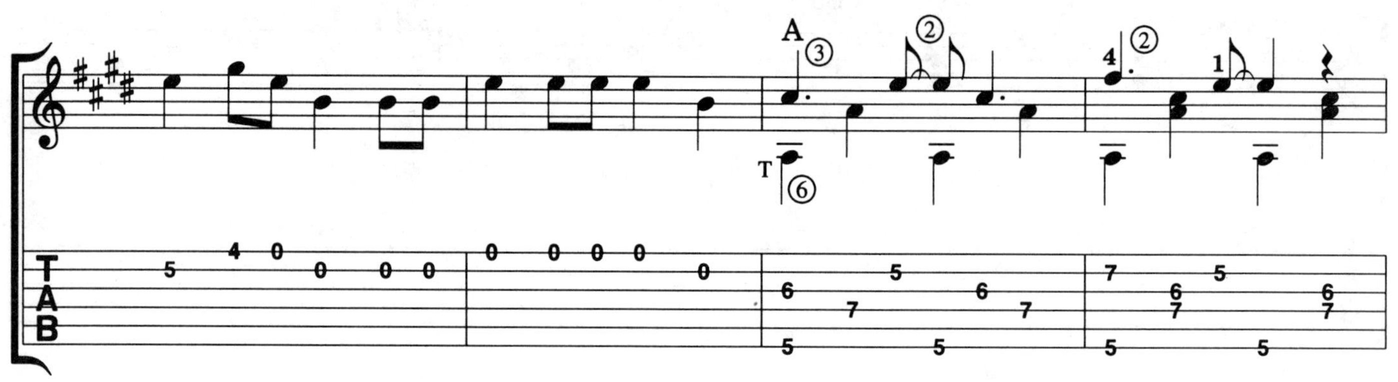
A
TAB
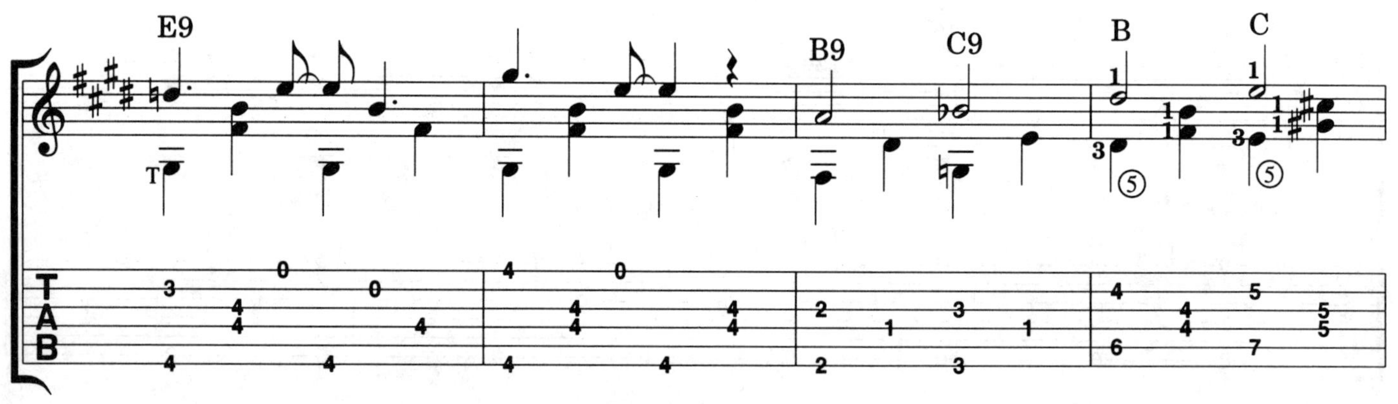
E9
B9
C9
B
C
TAB
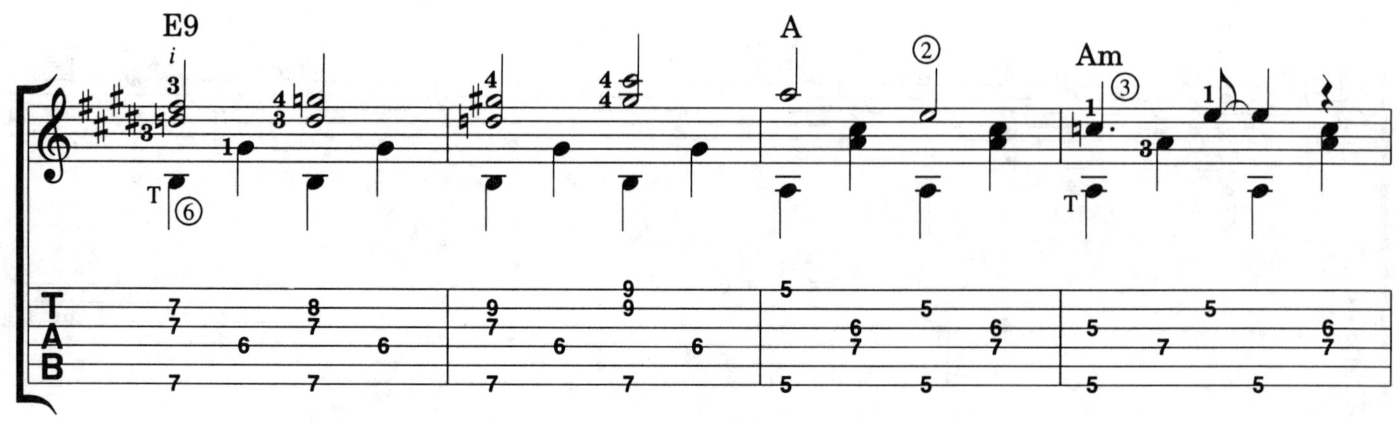
E9
A
Am
TAB

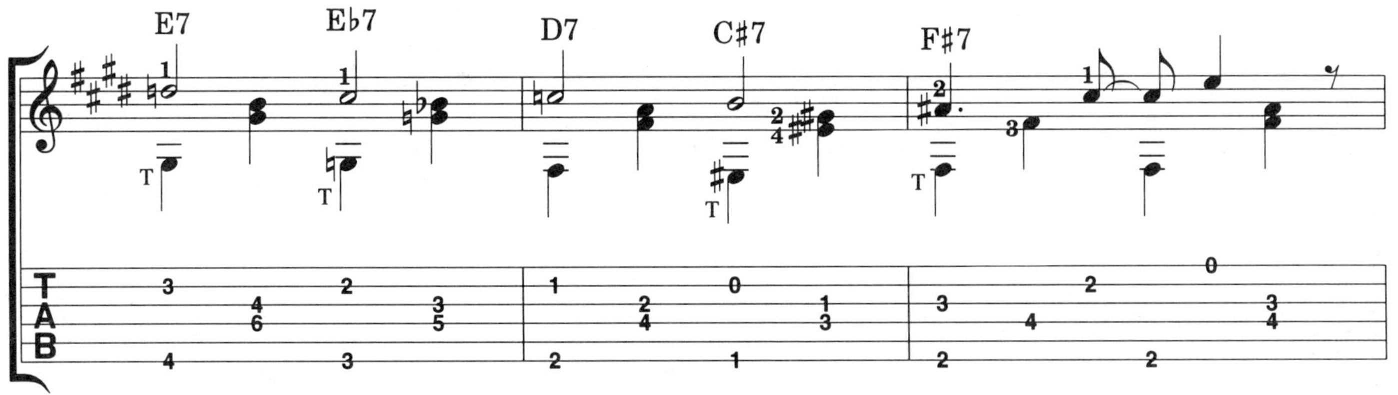
E7
E♭7
D7
C♯7
F♯7

B9
E
B7
E

E

A
E

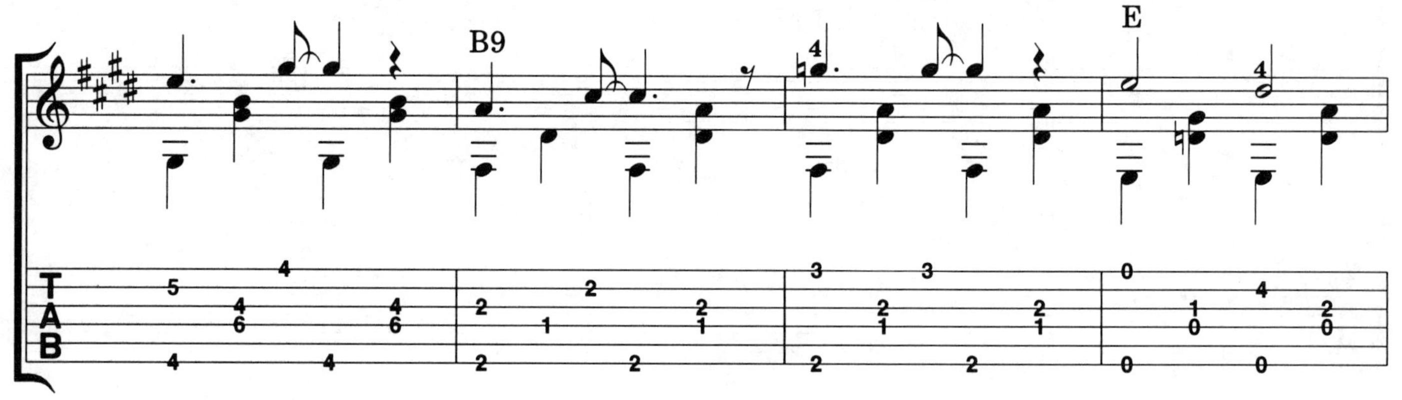
B9
E
TAB

A9
E
TAB

B9
E
B7
TAB

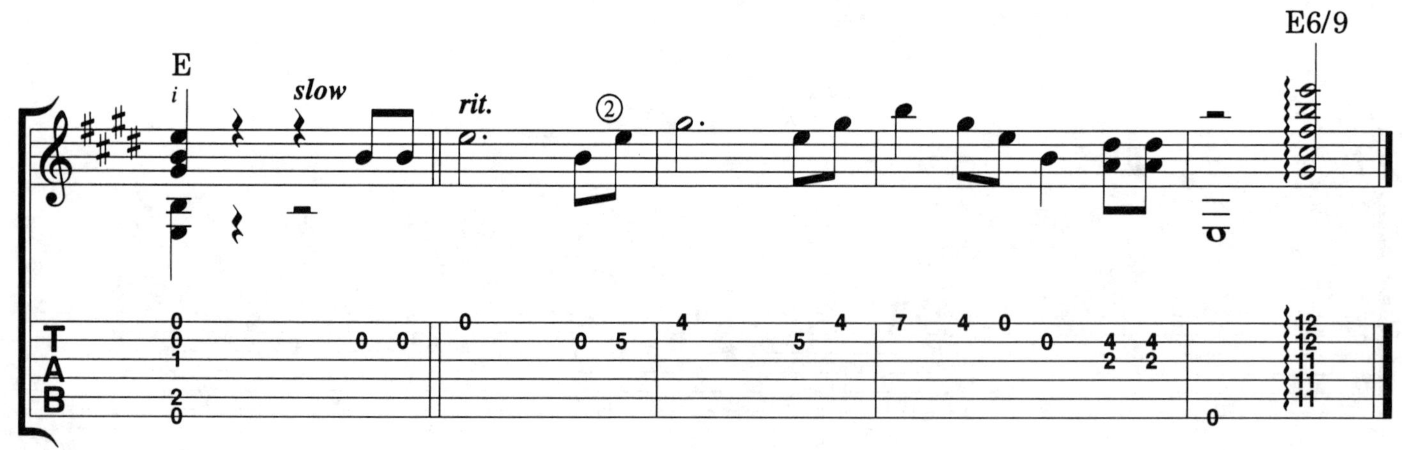
E
i
slow
rit.
E6/9
TAB

CUDDLE UP A LITTLE CLOSER

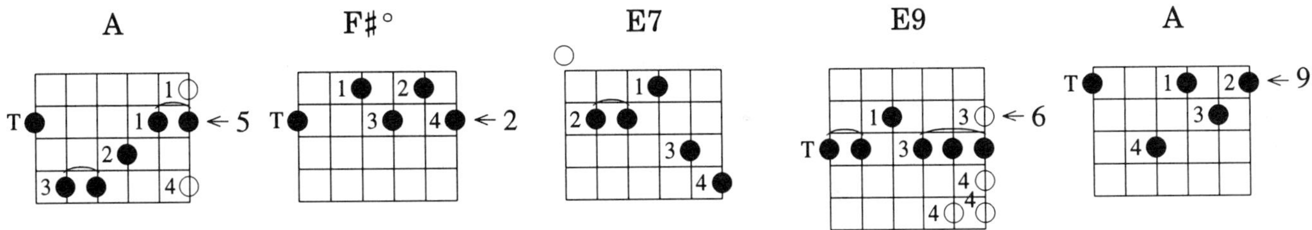

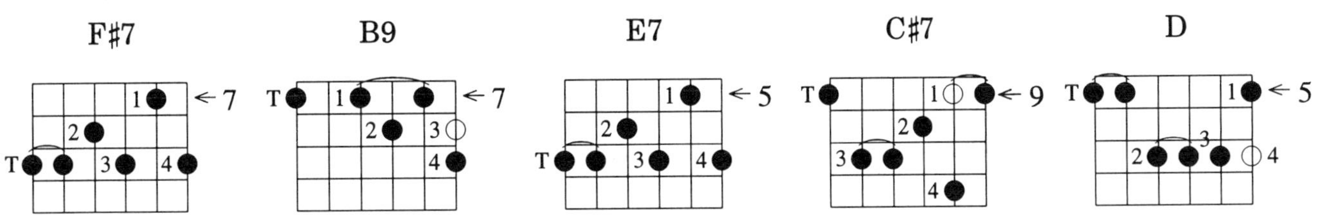

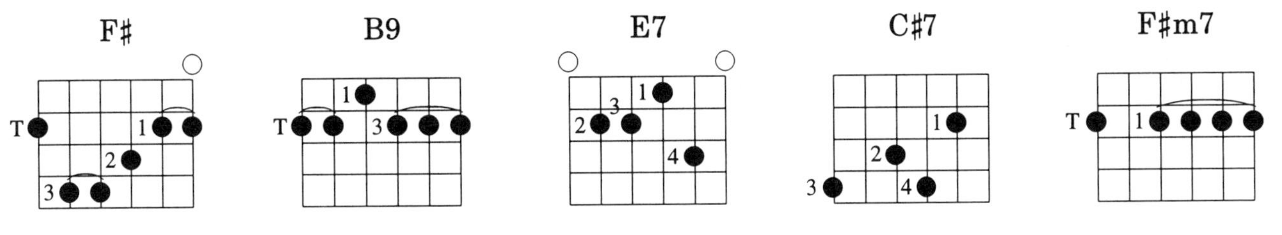

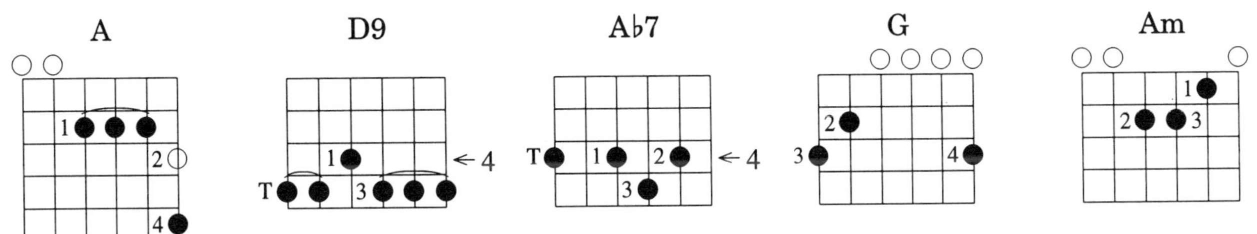

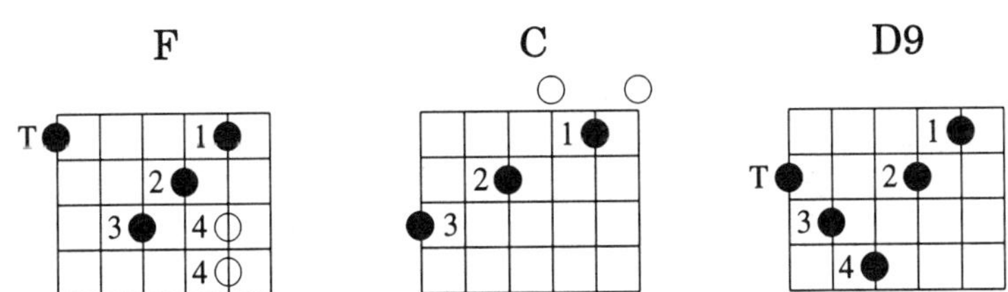

CUDDLE UP A LITTLE CLOSER

Lovey Mine

A
F♯7
TAB

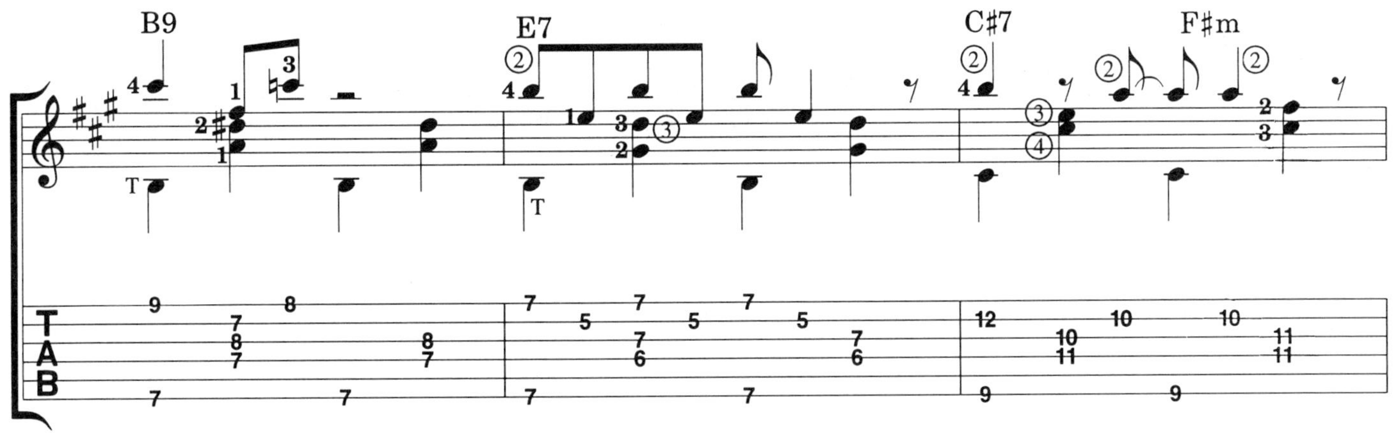
B9
E7
C♯7
F♯m
TAB

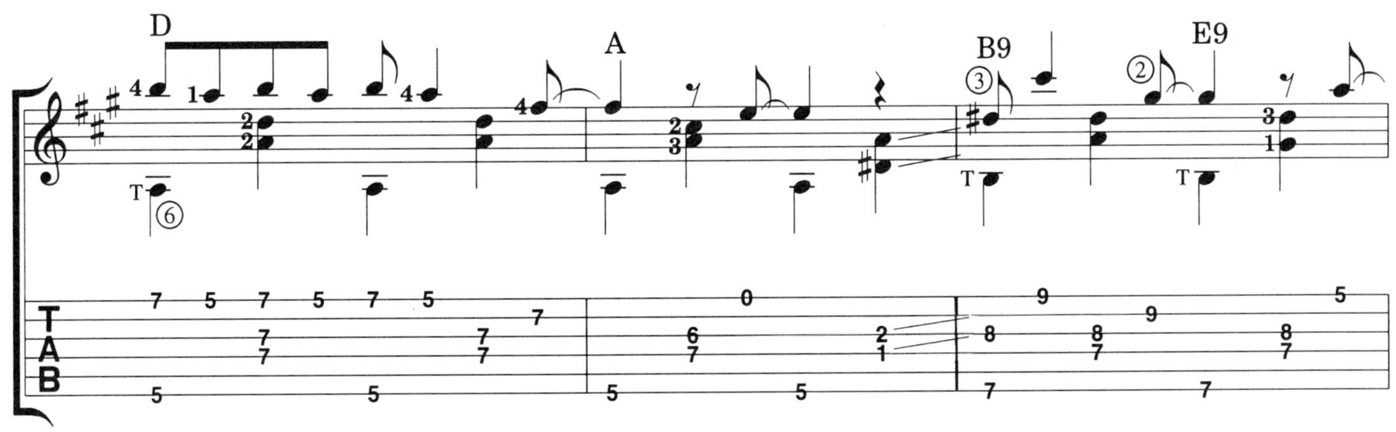
D
A
B9
E9
TAB

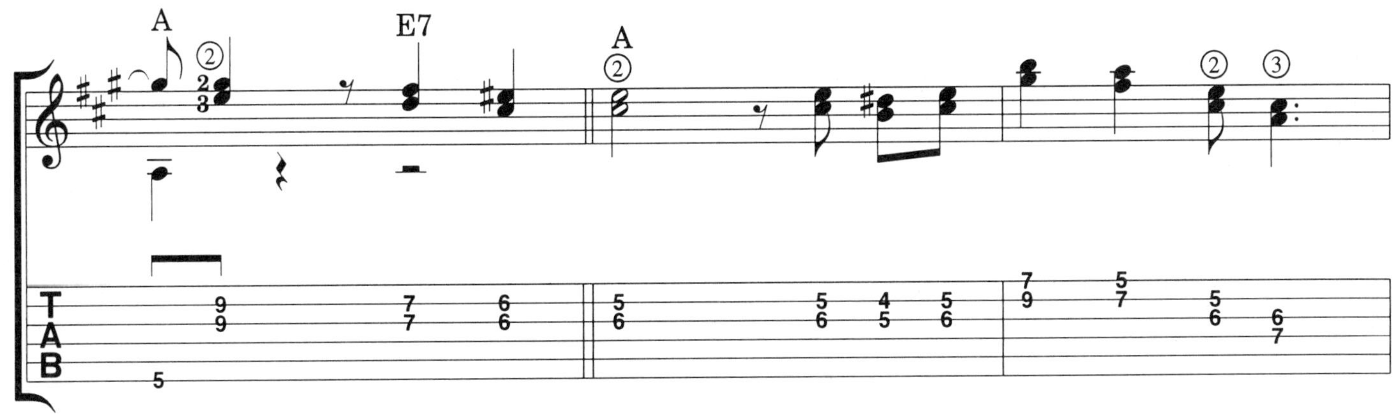
A
E7
A
TAB

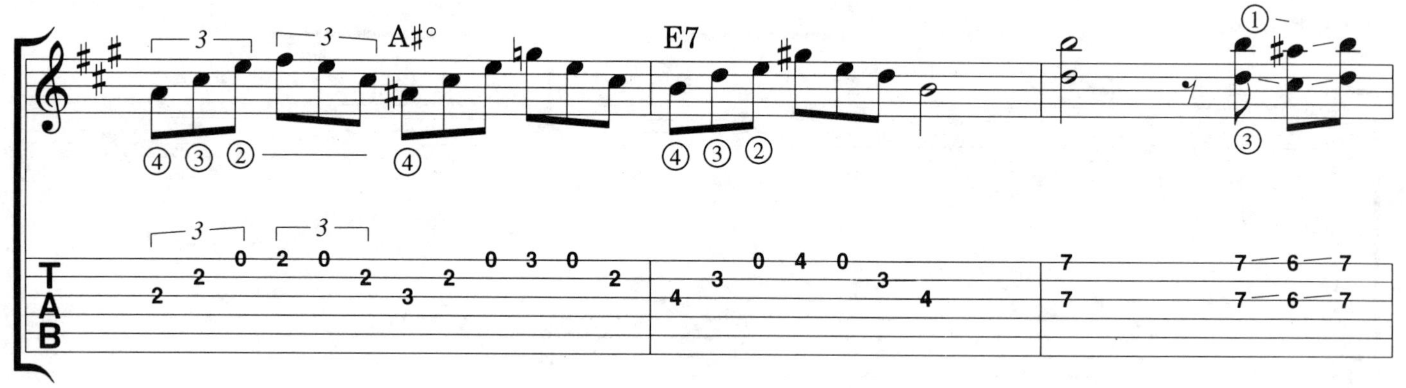
A♯°
E7

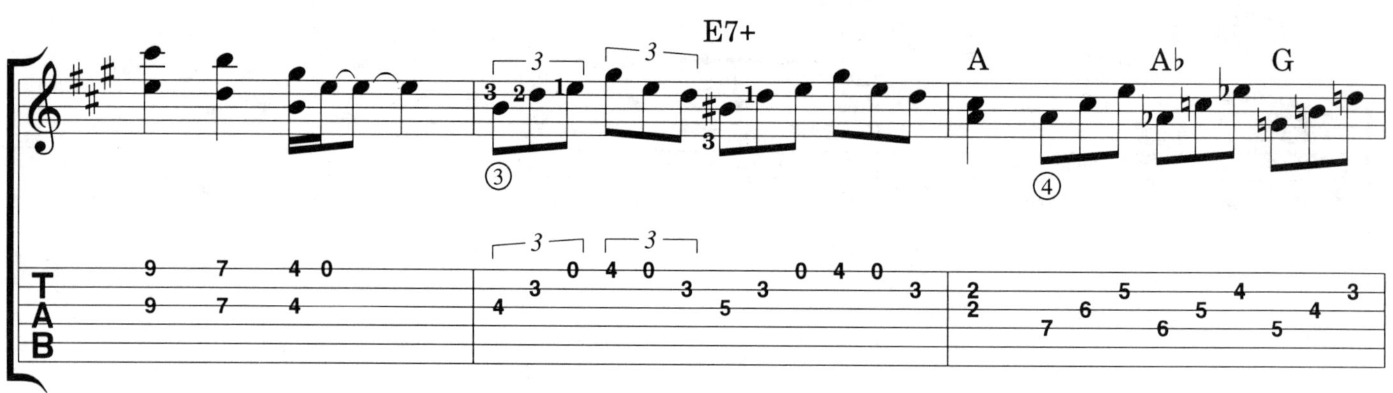
E7+
A
A♭
G

F♯
B9
E7

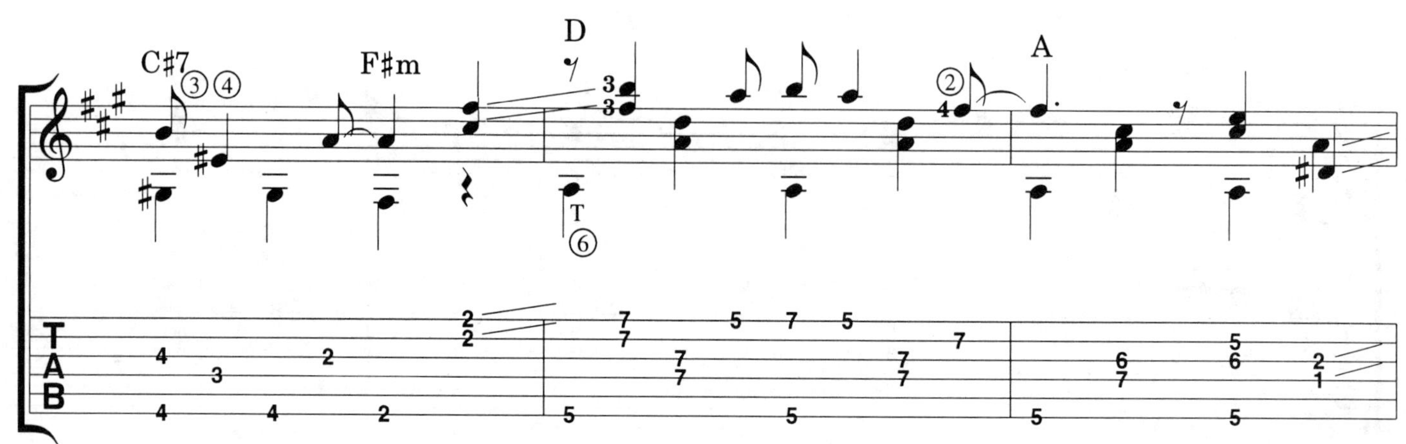
C♯7
F♯m
D
A

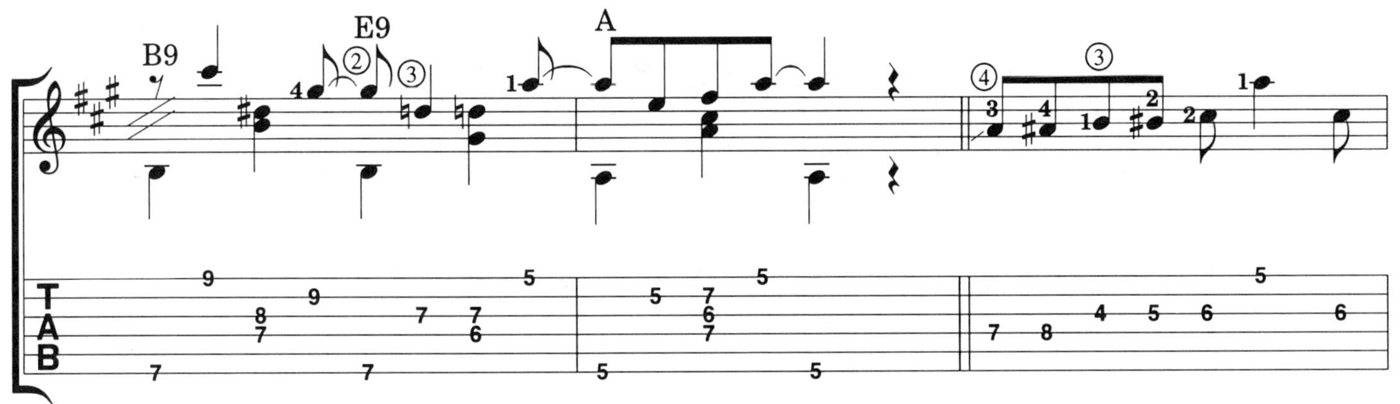
B9
E9
A

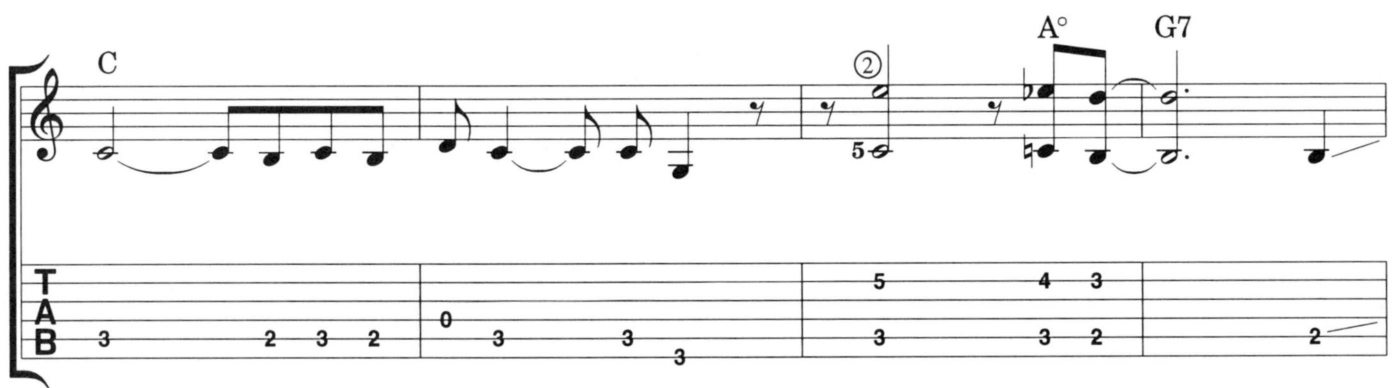
C
A°
G7

C
B
B♭

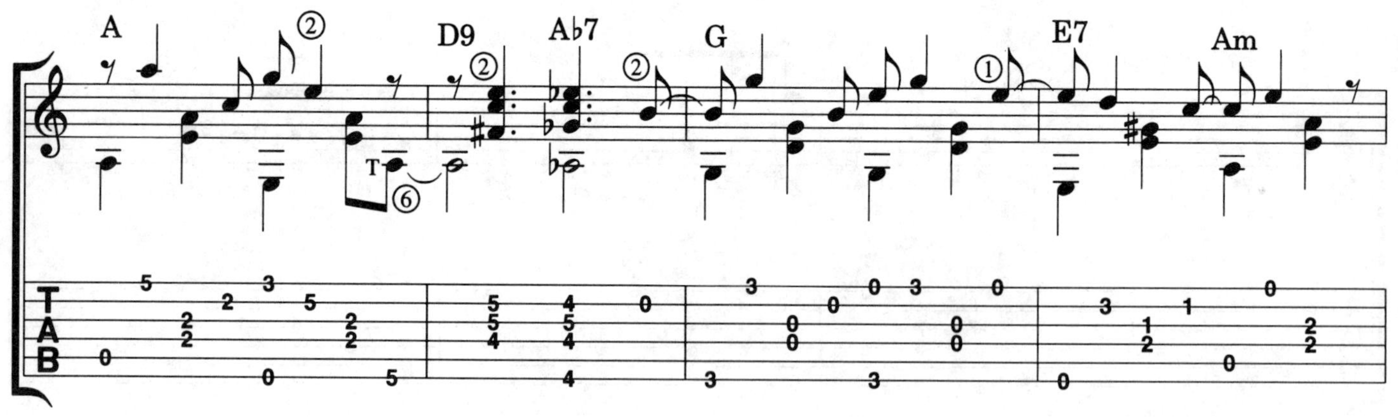
A
D9
A♭7
G
E7
Am

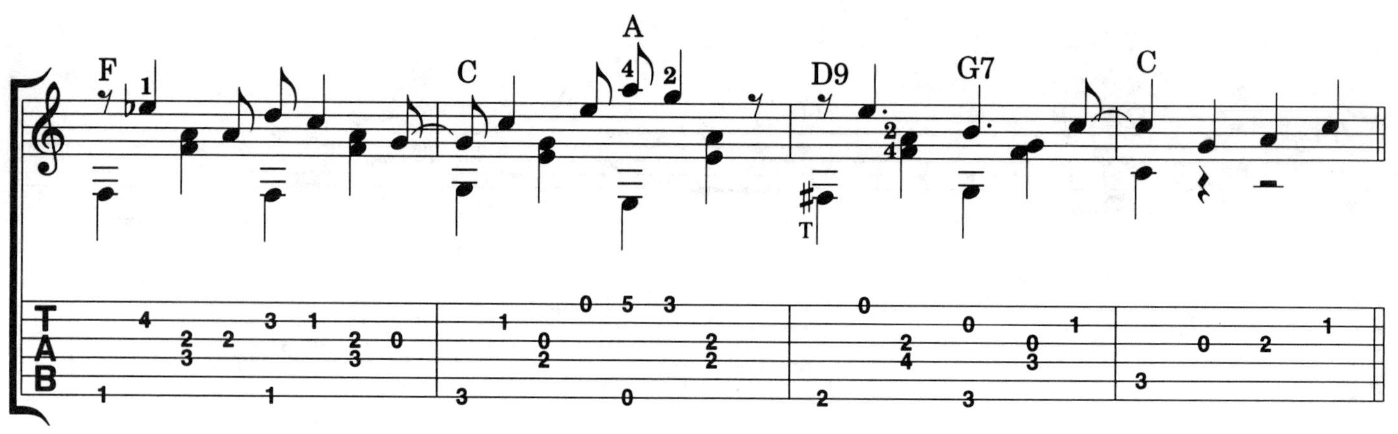
F
C
A
D9
G7
C

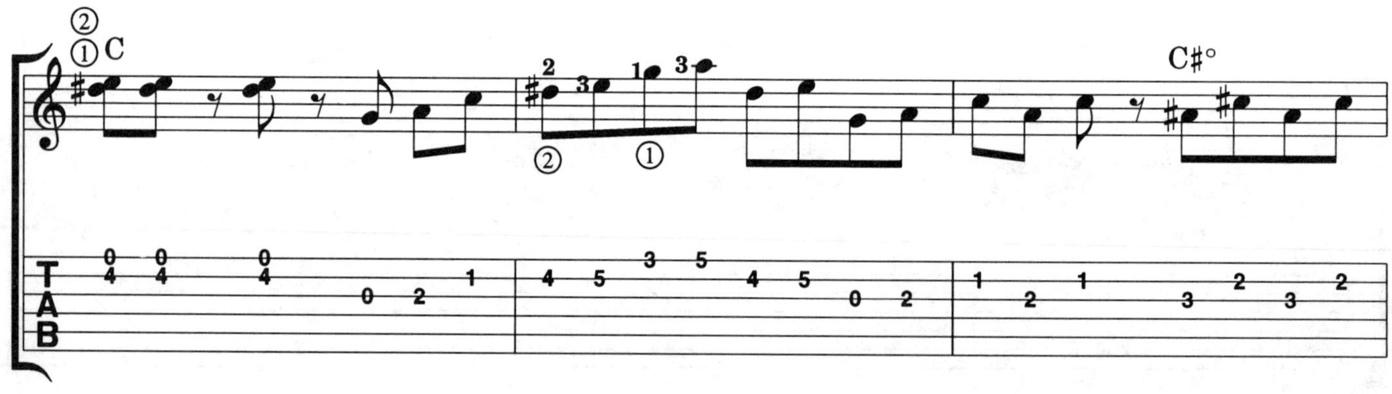
C
C♯°

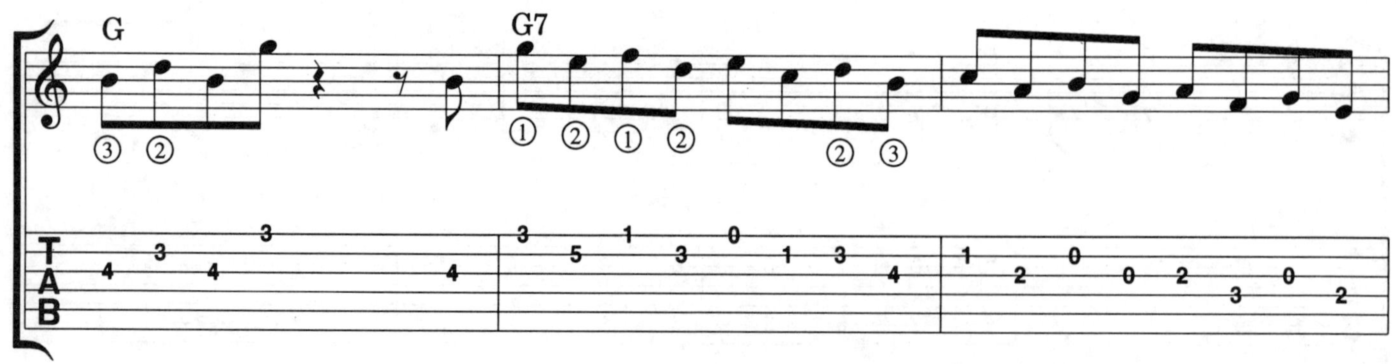
G
G7

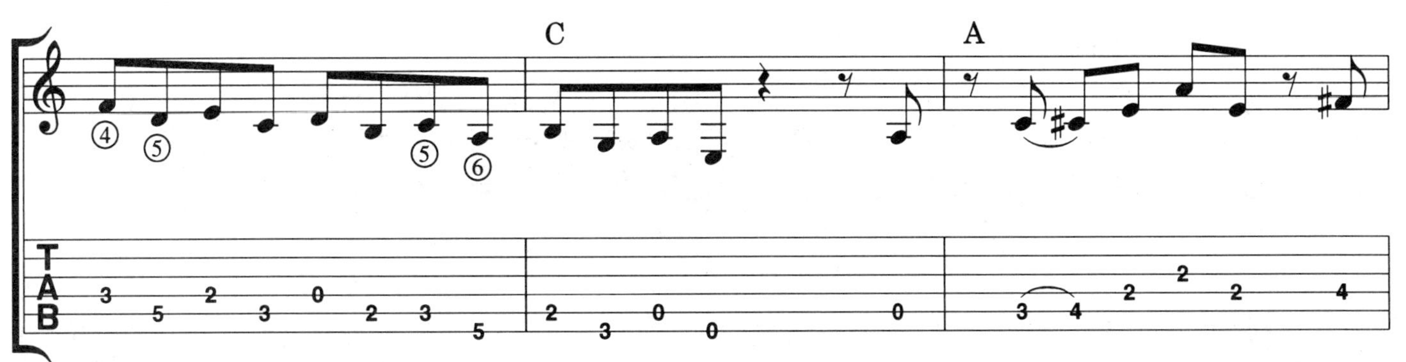
C
A
T
A
B

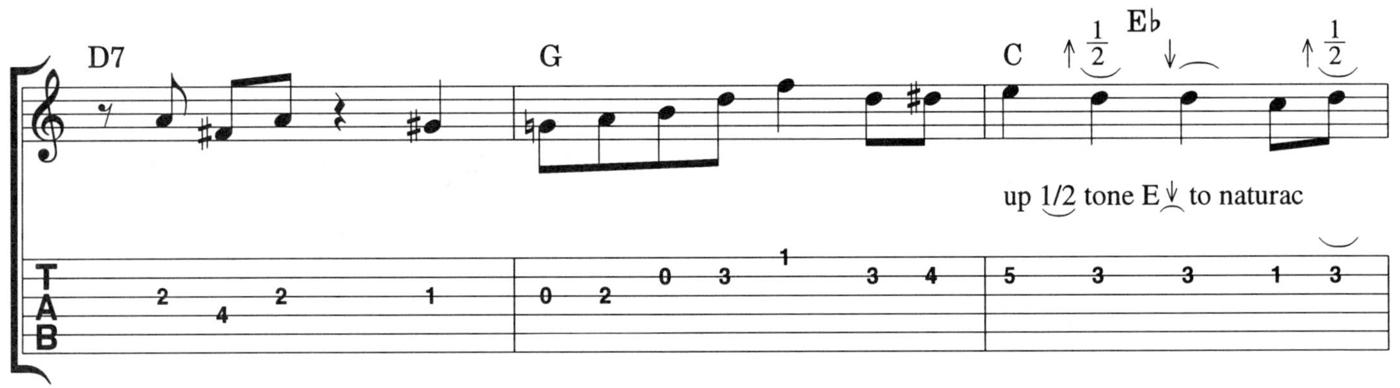
D7
G
C
Eb
up 1/2 tone E to naturac
T
A
B

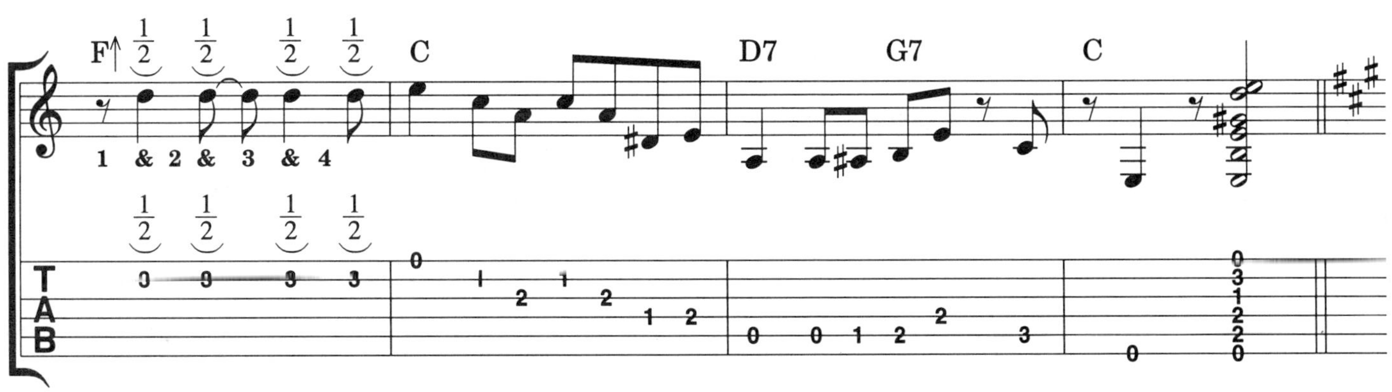
F
C
D7
G7
C
1 & 2 & 3 & 4
T
A
B

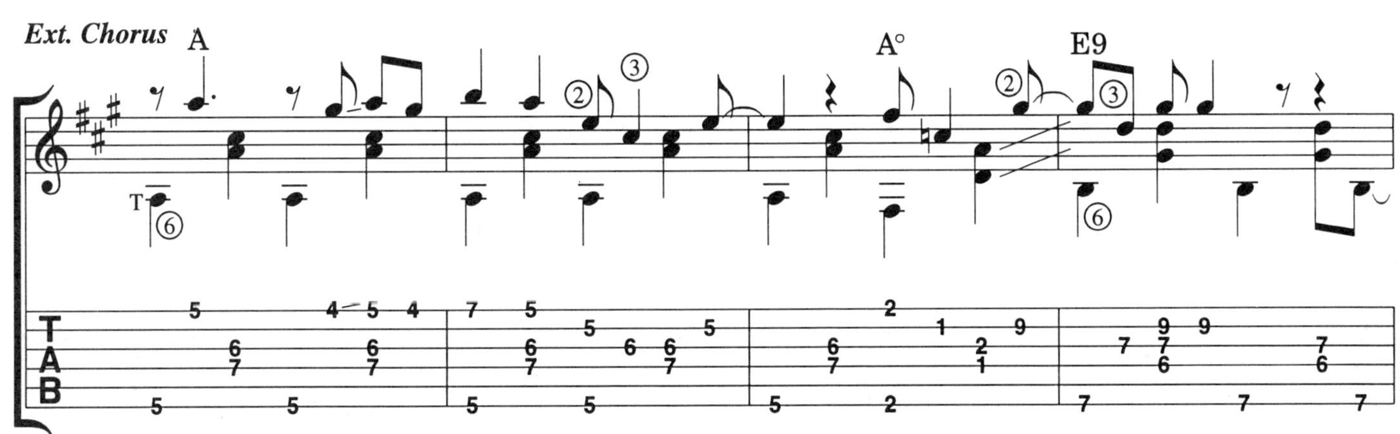
Ext. Chorus
A
A°
E9
T
A
B

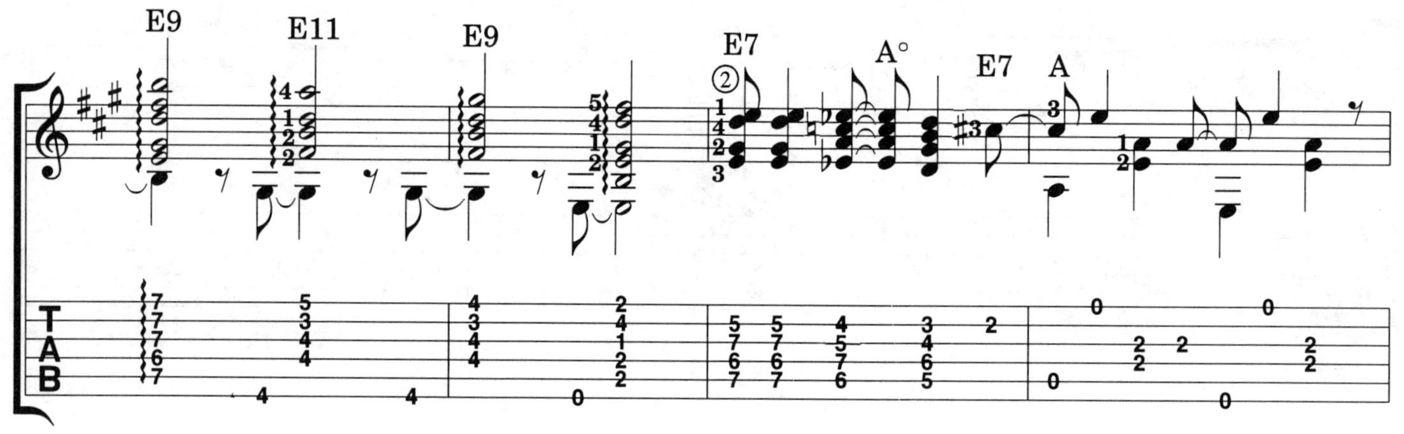
E9
E11
E9
E7
A°
E7
A
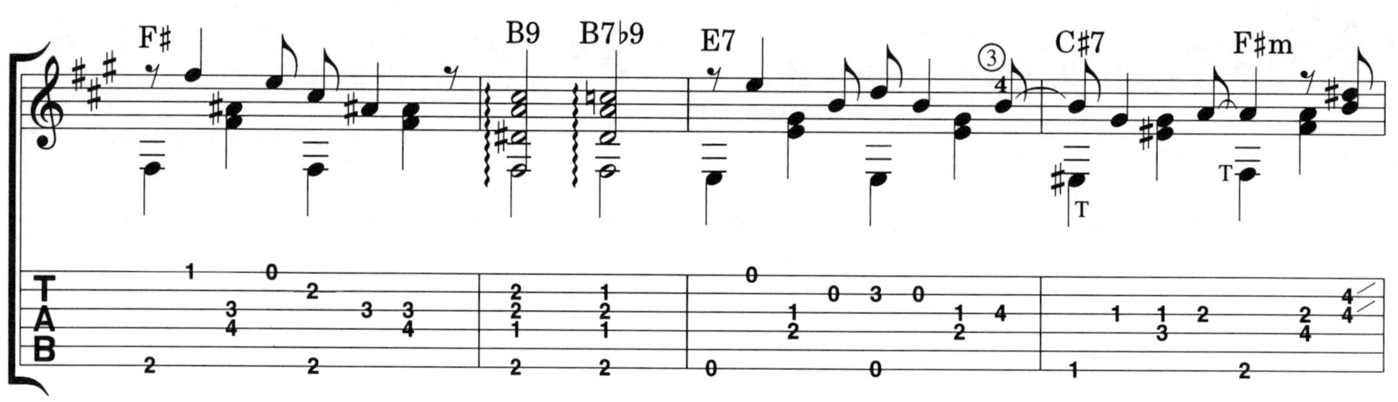
F♯
B9
B7♭9
E7
C♯7
F♯m
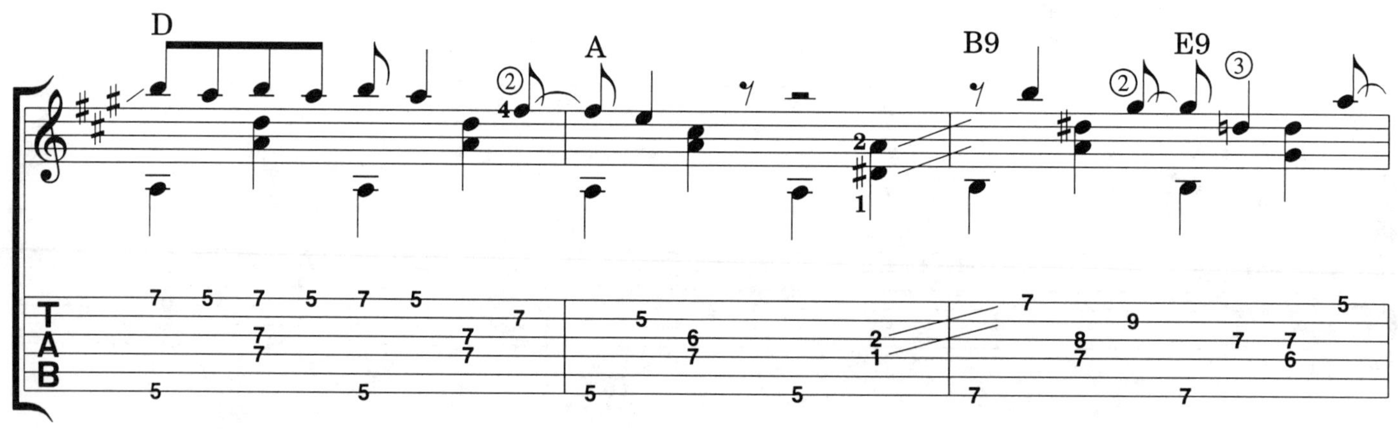
D
A
B9
E9
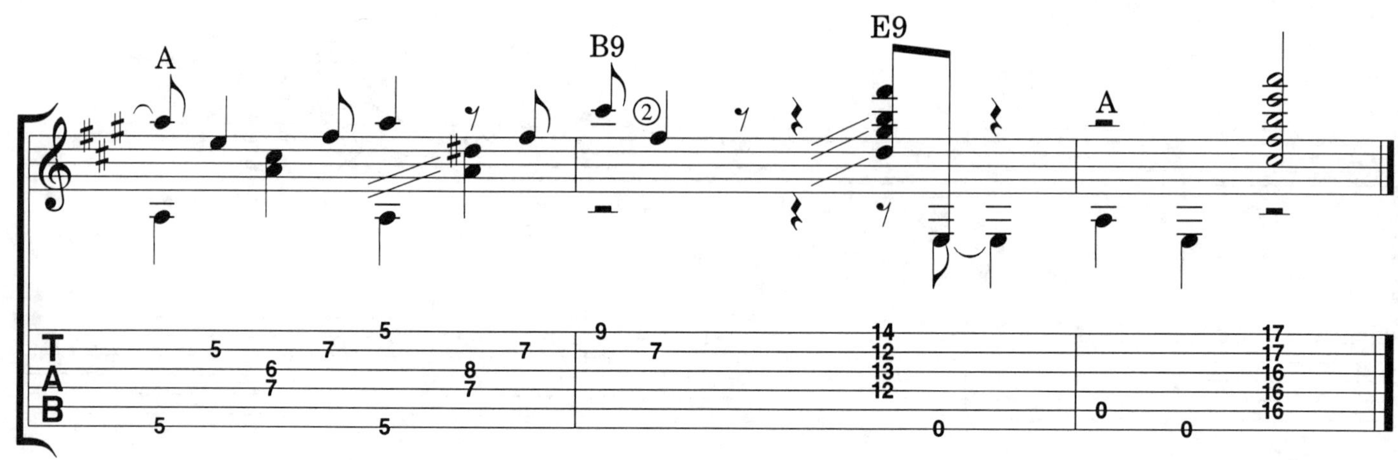
A
B9
E9
A

I'M THINKING TONIGHT OF MY BLUE EYES

Capo is on 5th fret.

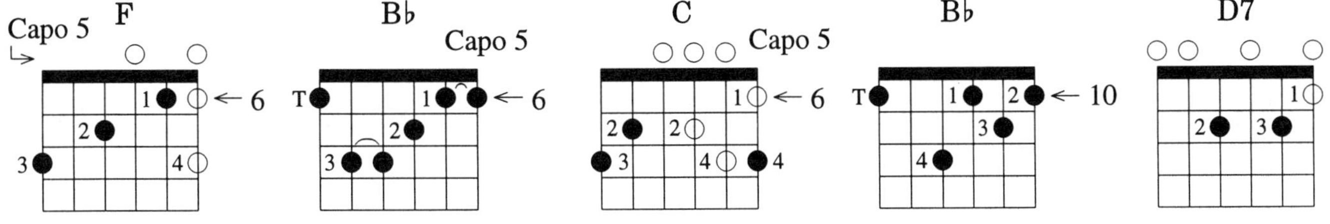

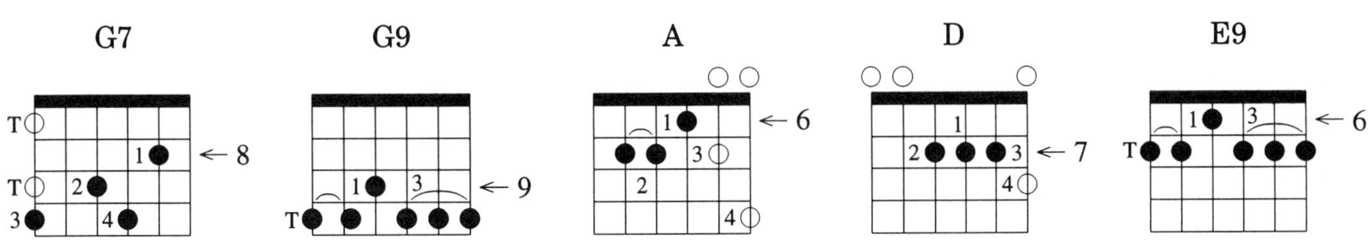

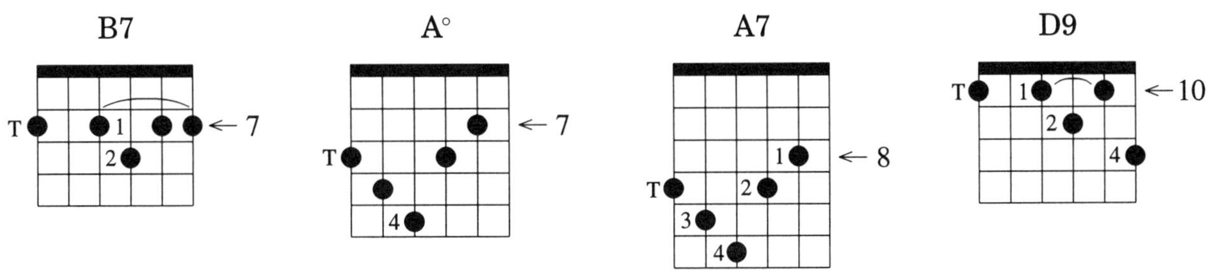

This arrangement of "I'm Thinking Tonight of My Blue Eyes" from the 1940's is an excellent example of Travis' use of chord substitution and improvisation. The first chorus is the straight melody in the I, IV and V progression. In the second chorus, he substitutes a VI7 and a II7 in the second, third and fourth measures. He modulates up a third to the key of A for the third chorus and this one is improvised. He also uses a II7 and a Idim. as passing tones.

I'M THINKING TONIGHT OF MY BLUE EYES

Capo on 5

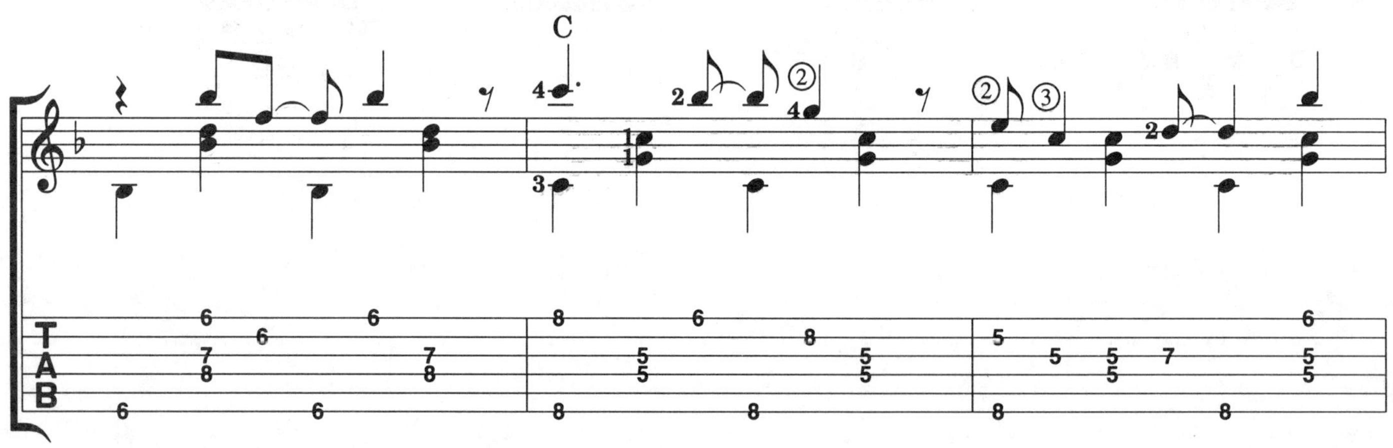

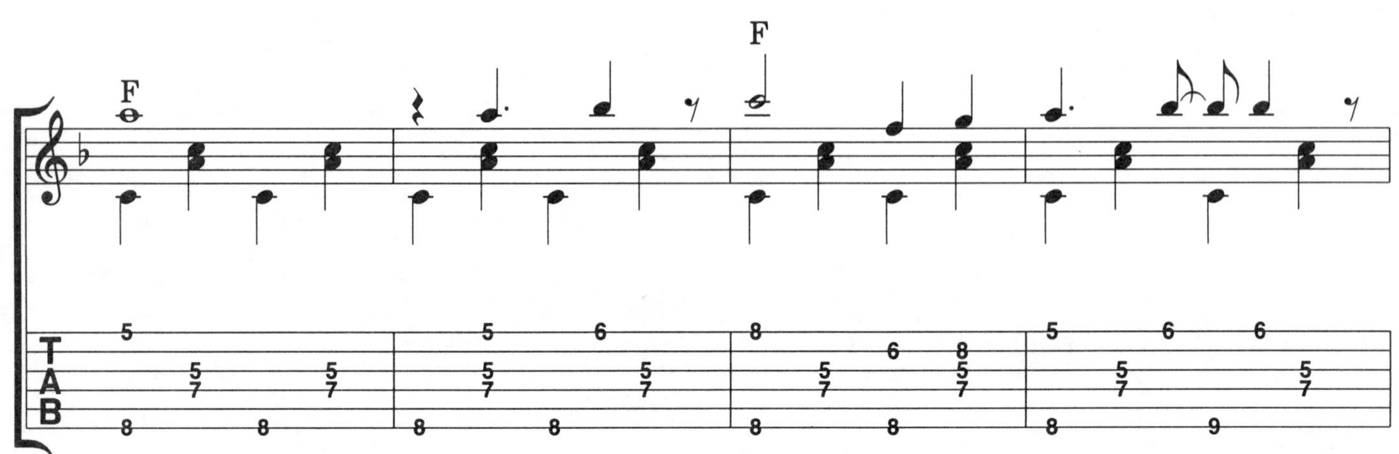

B♭
C
F
B♭
F
F
D7
G7
G7♭5
G7
C
T
A
B

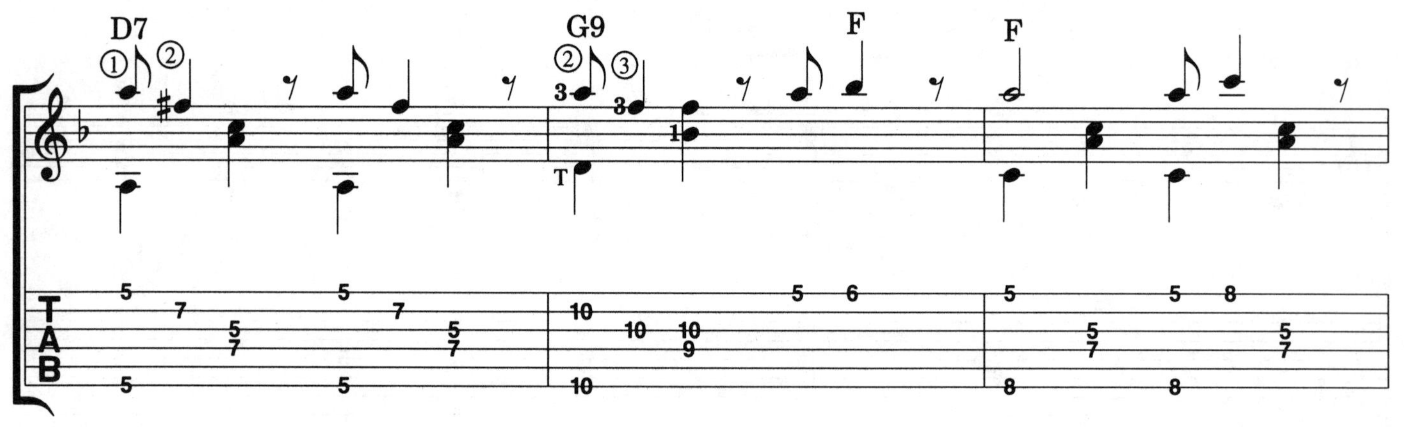
D7
G9
F
F

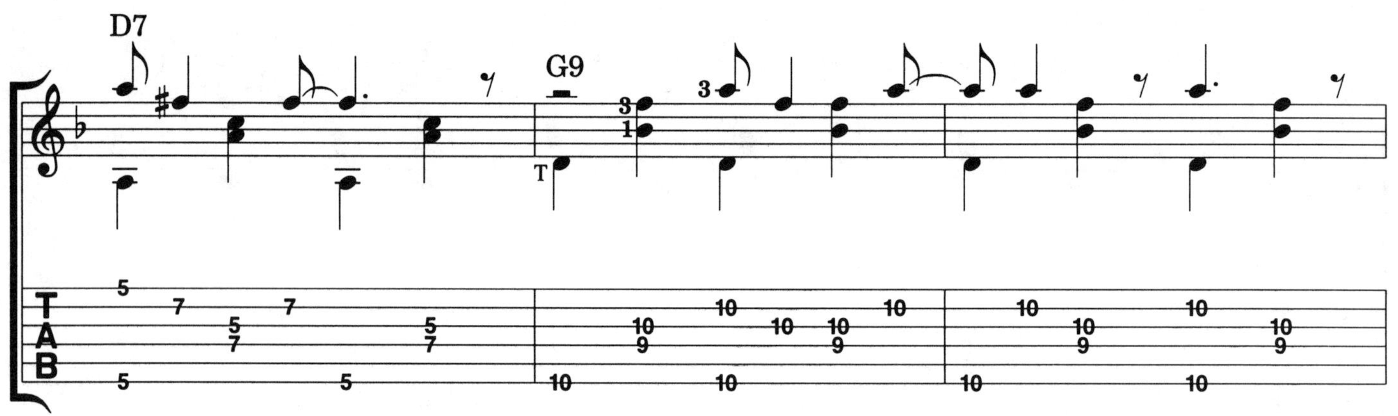
D7
G9

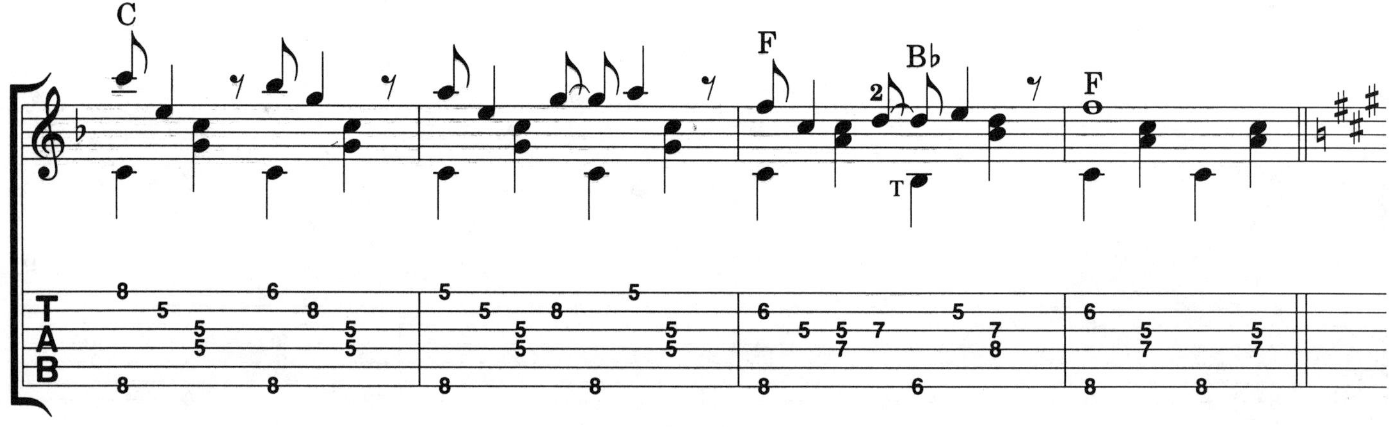
C
F
B♭
F

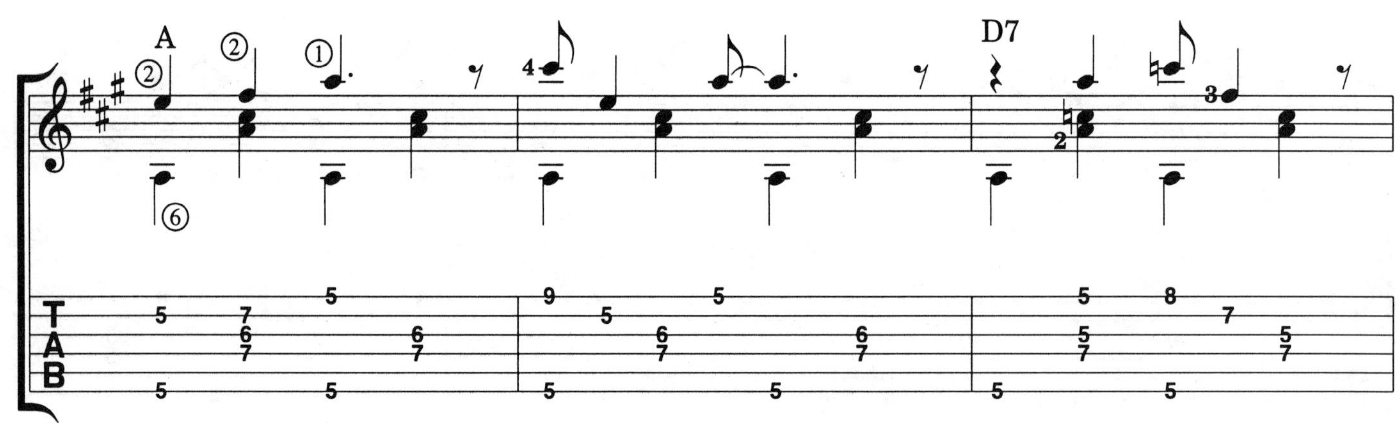
A
D7

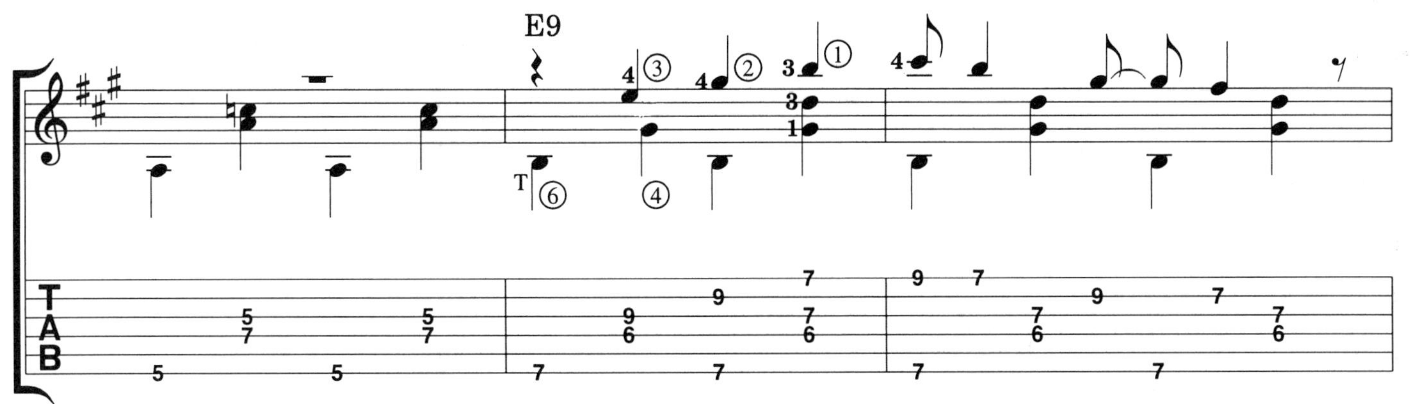
E9

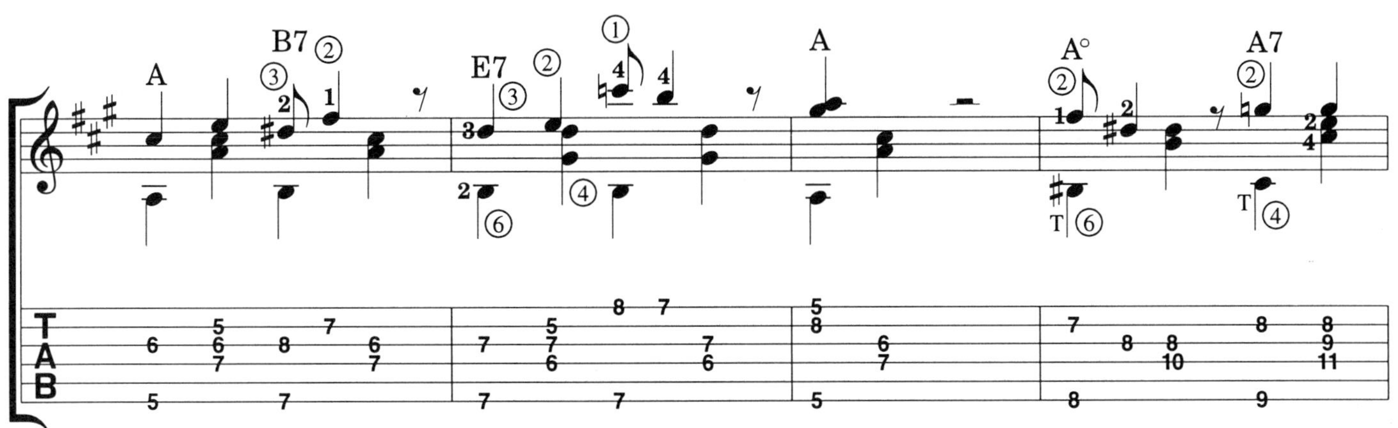
A
B7
E7
A
A°
A7

D9
E9

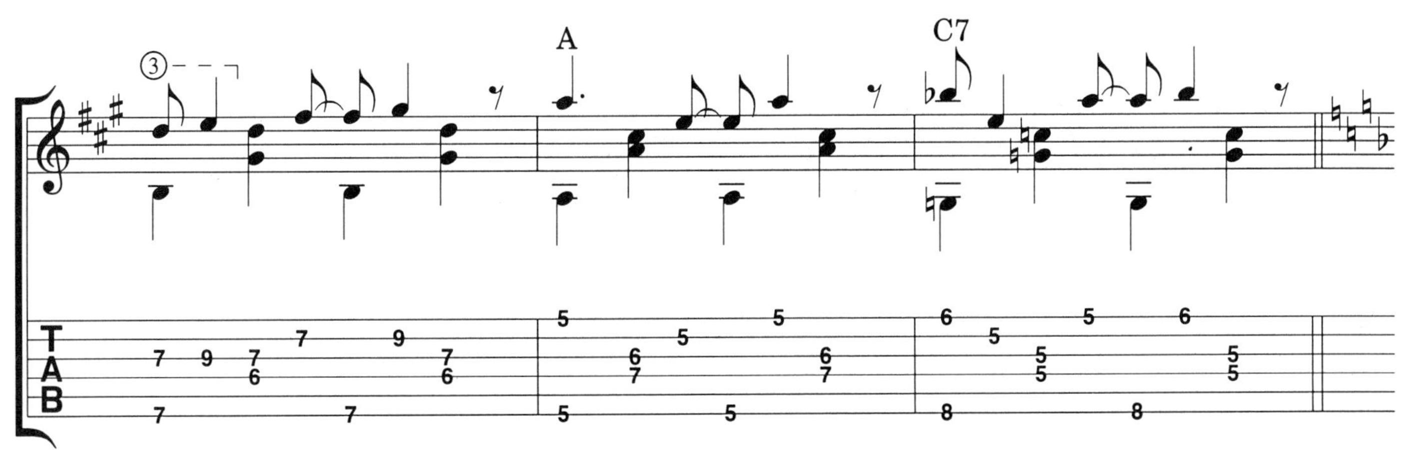
A
C7

F
B♭
TAB

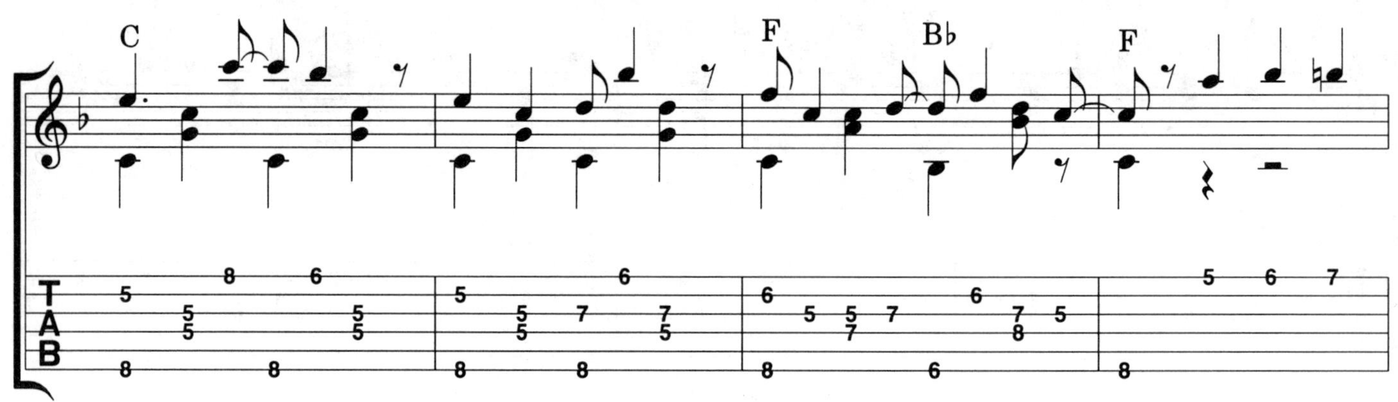
C
F
B♭
F
TAB

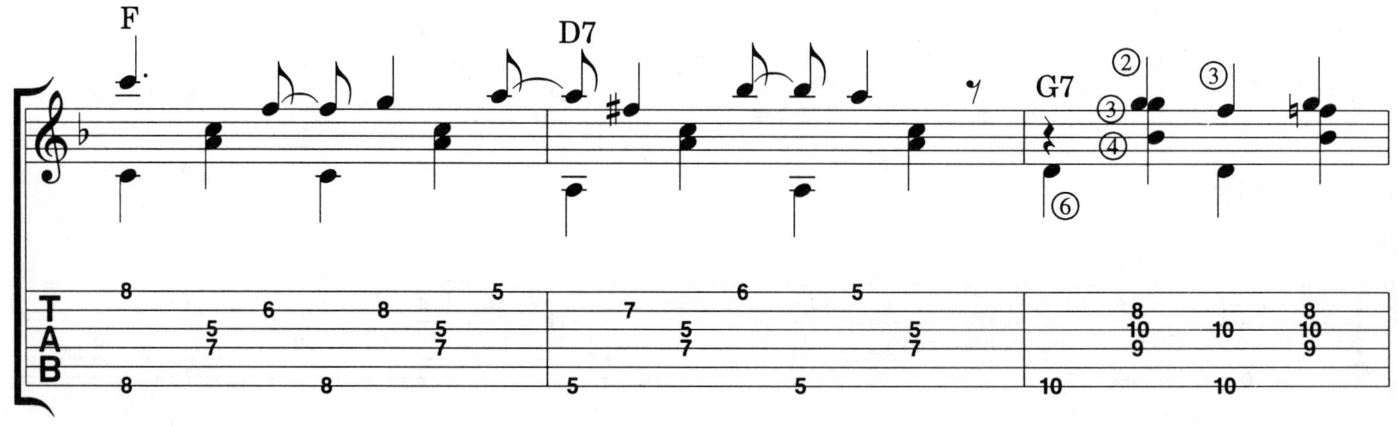
F
D7
G7
TAB

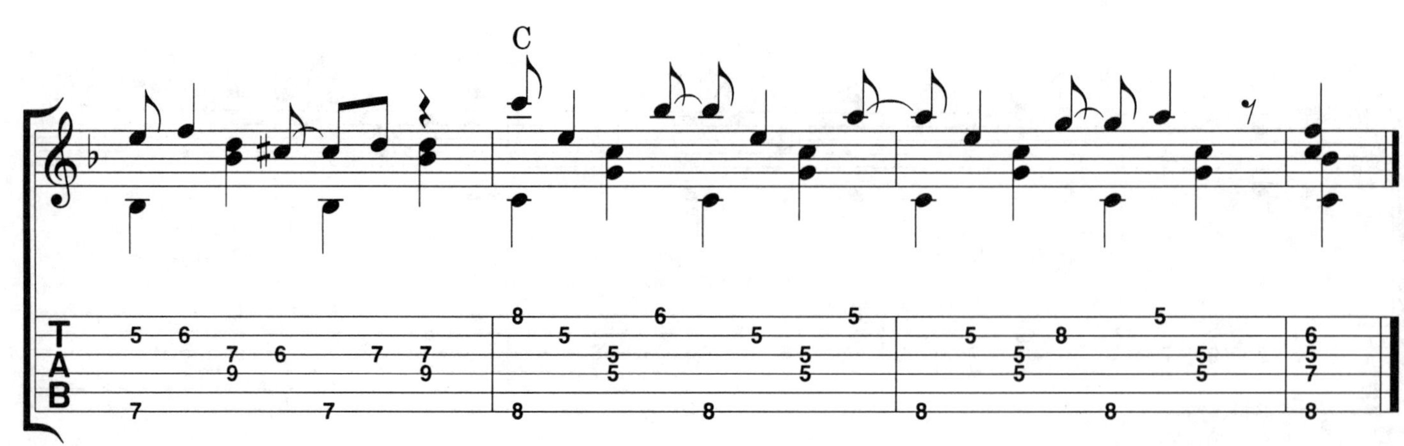
C
TAB

WAY DOWN YONDER IN NEW ORLEANS

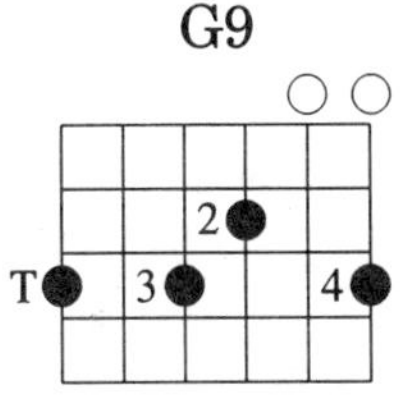

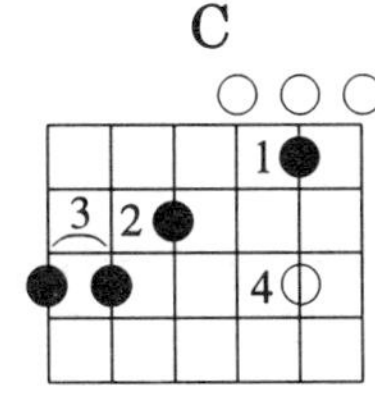

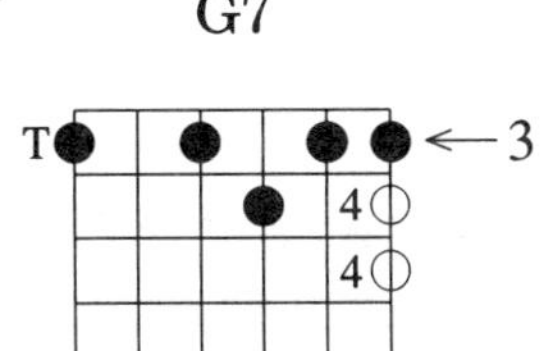

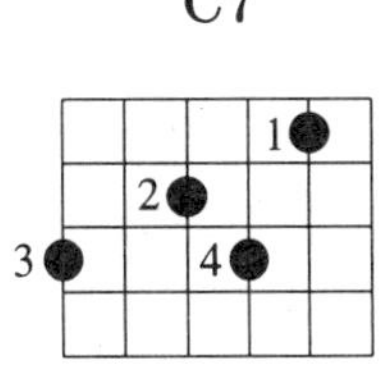

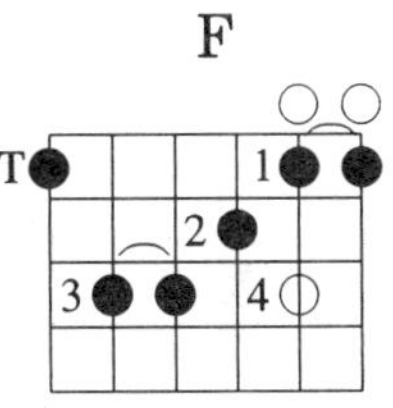

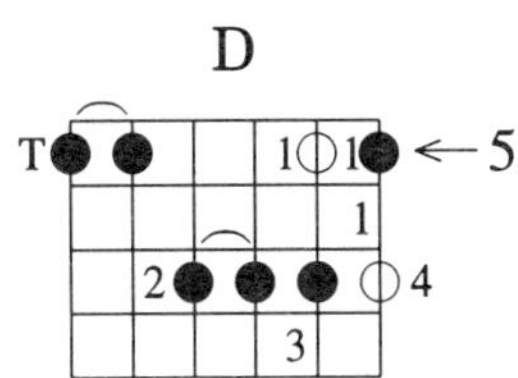

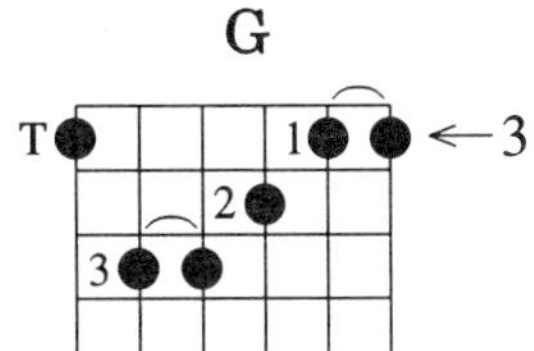

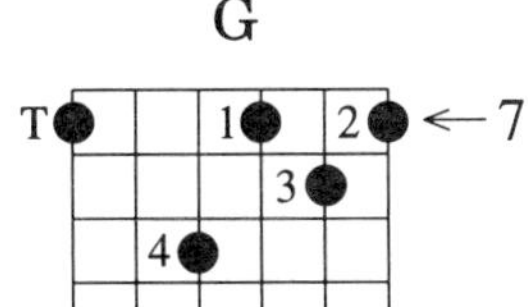

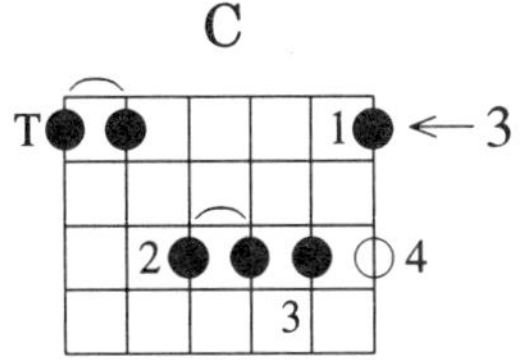

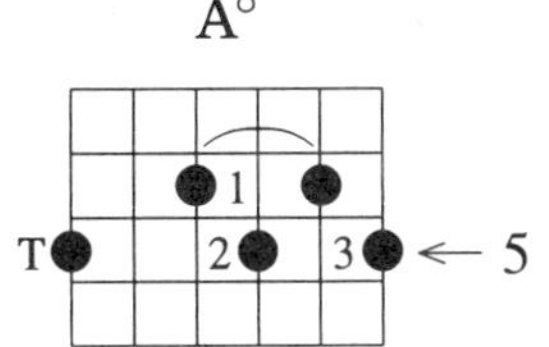

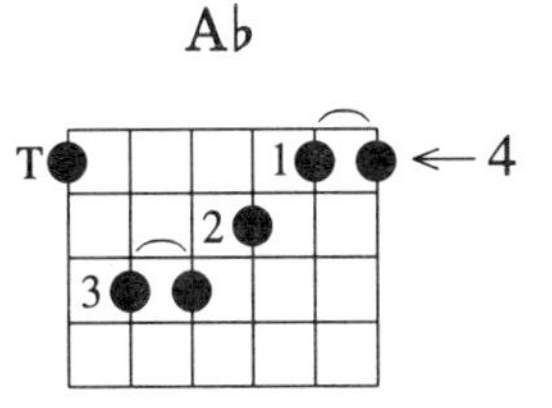

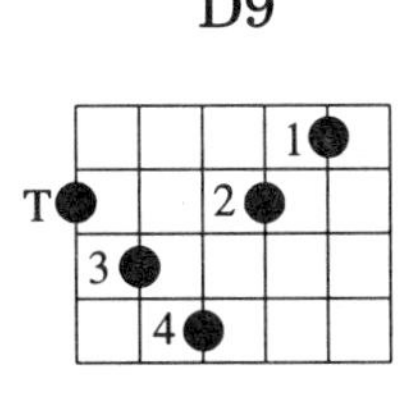

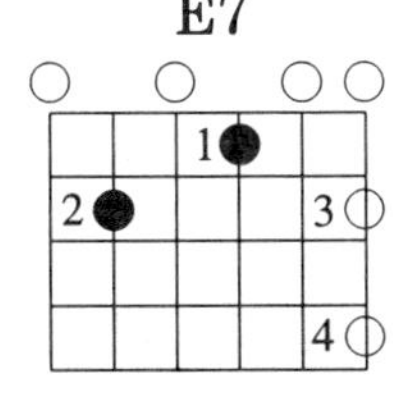

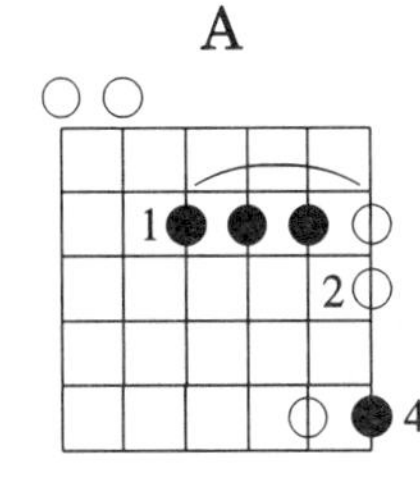

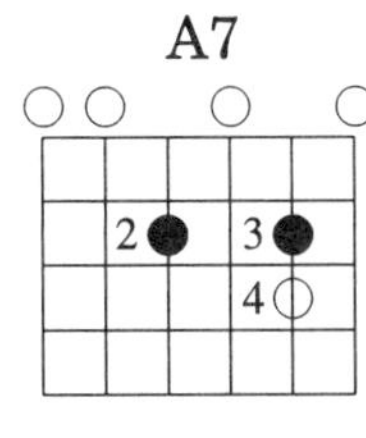

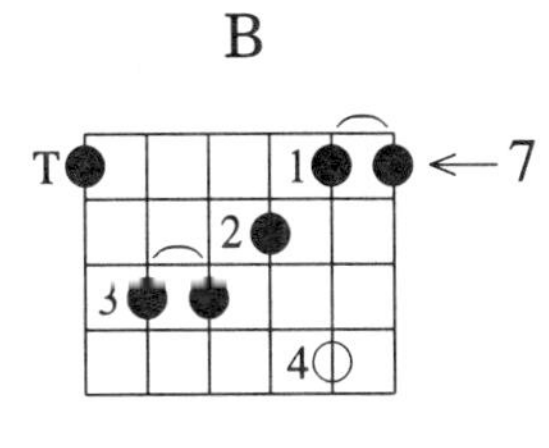

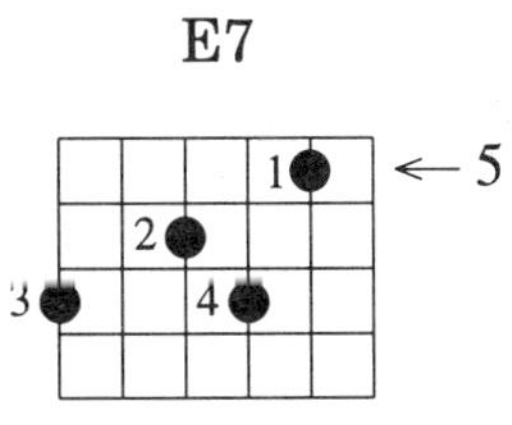

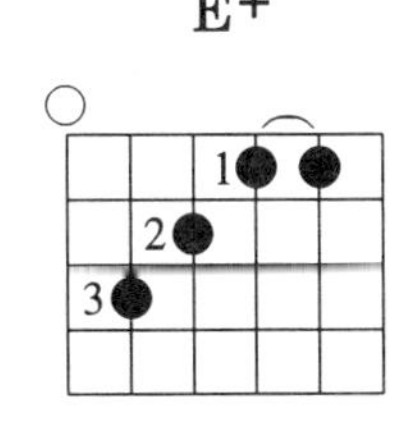

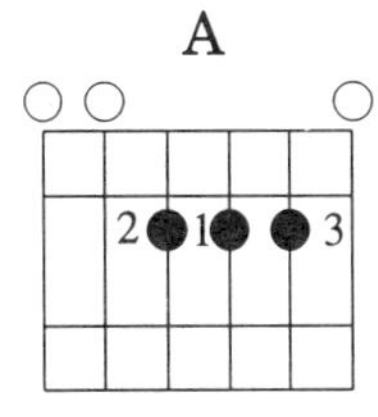

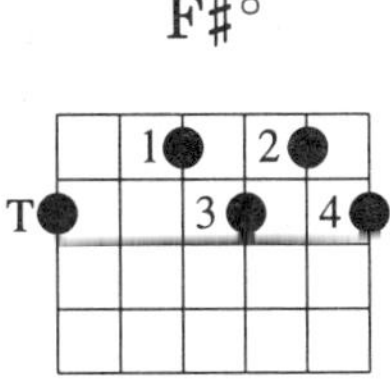

WAY DOWN YONDER IN NEW ORLEANS

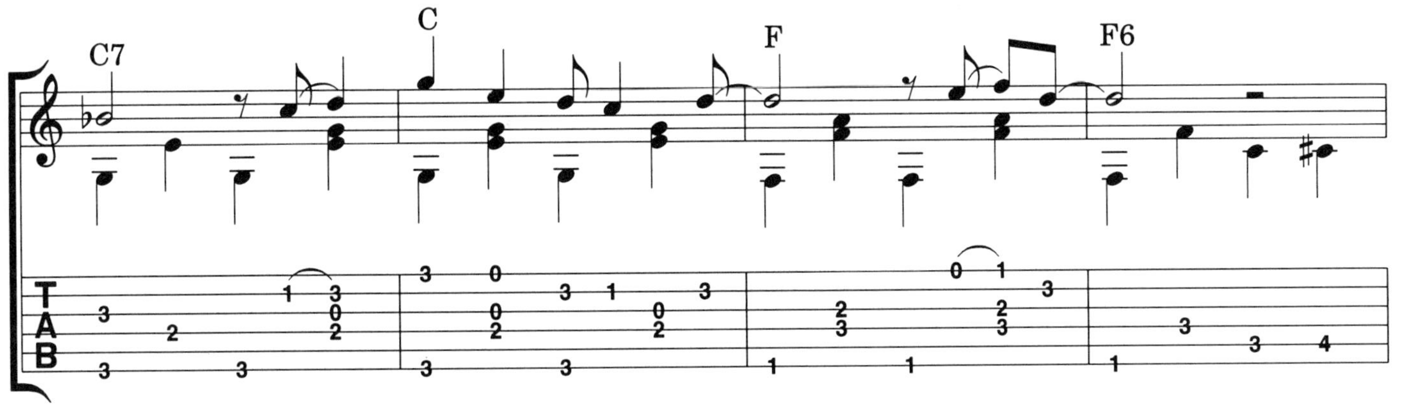
C7
C
F
F6

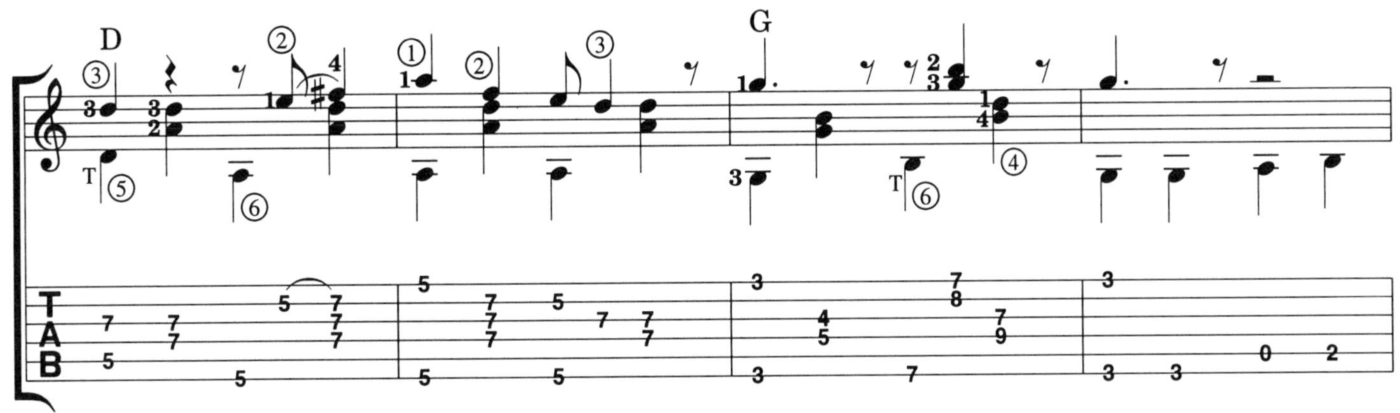
D
G

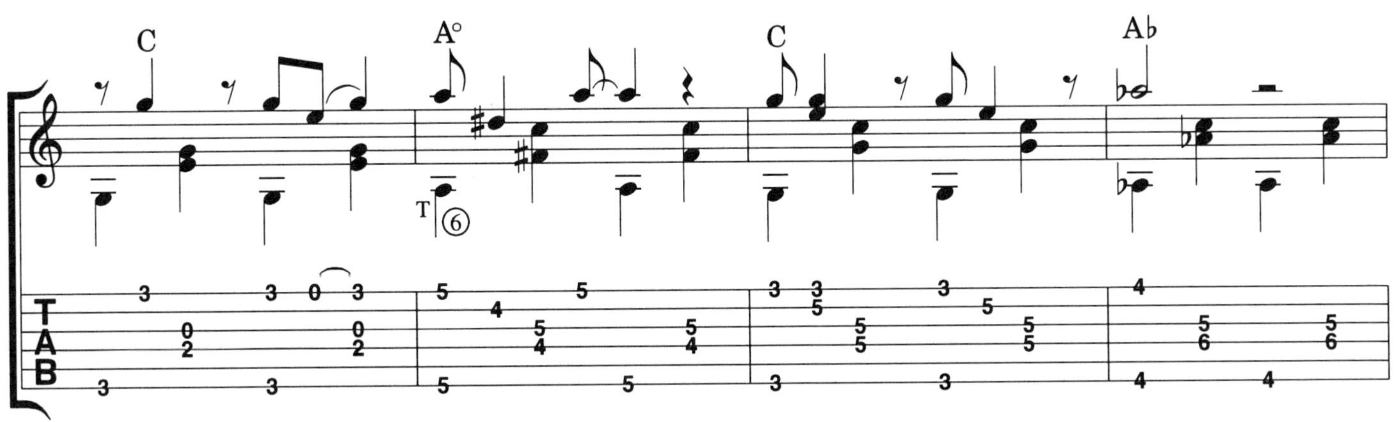
C
A°
C
A♭

C
D9
G9
C
F
C

Pluck strings near 14th frets.

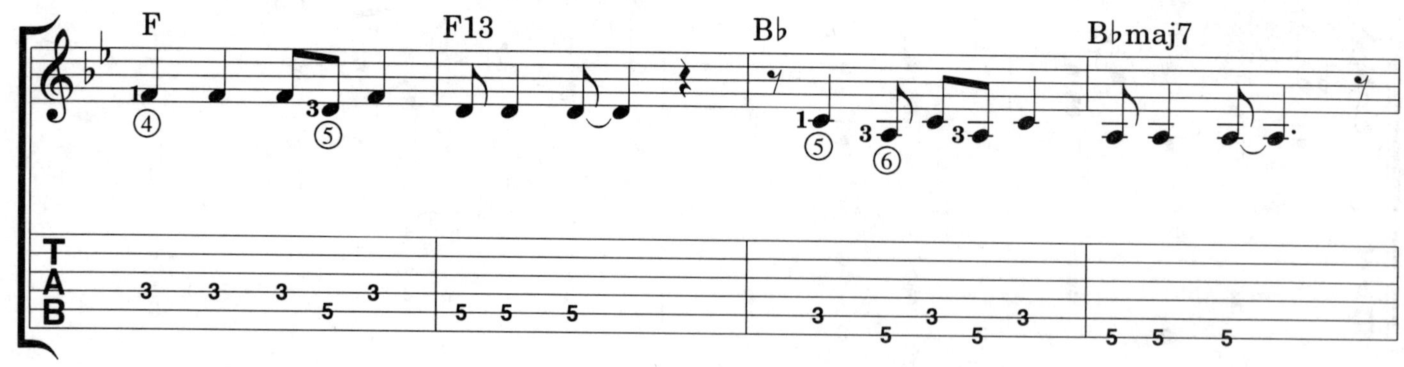

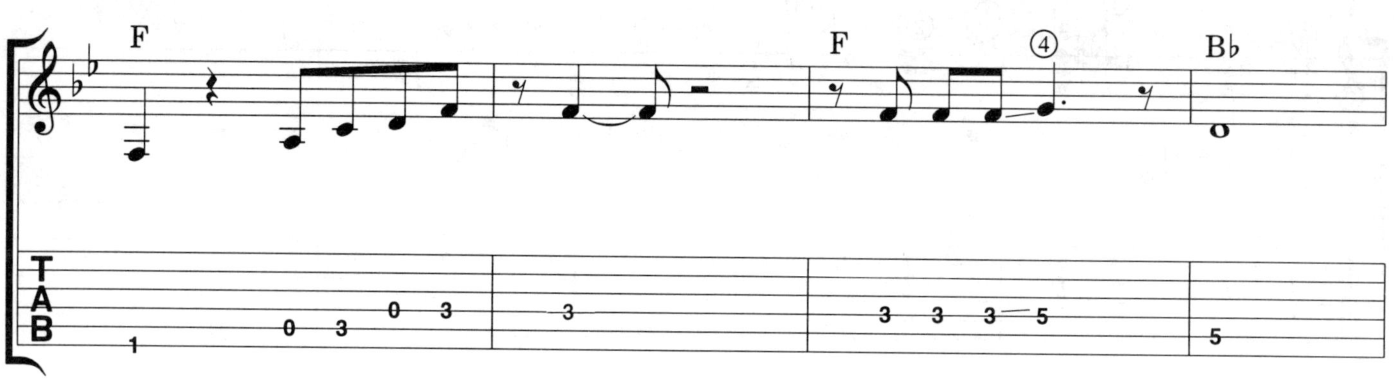

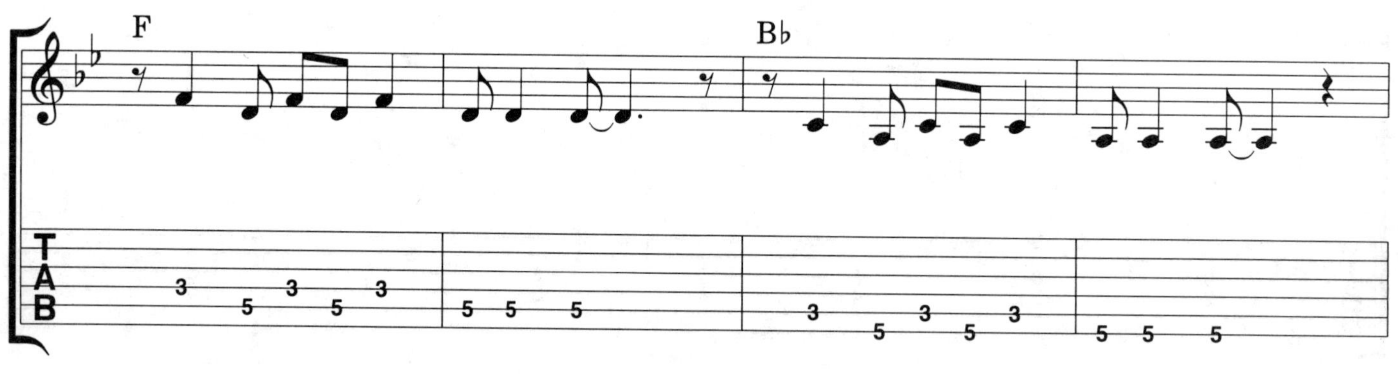

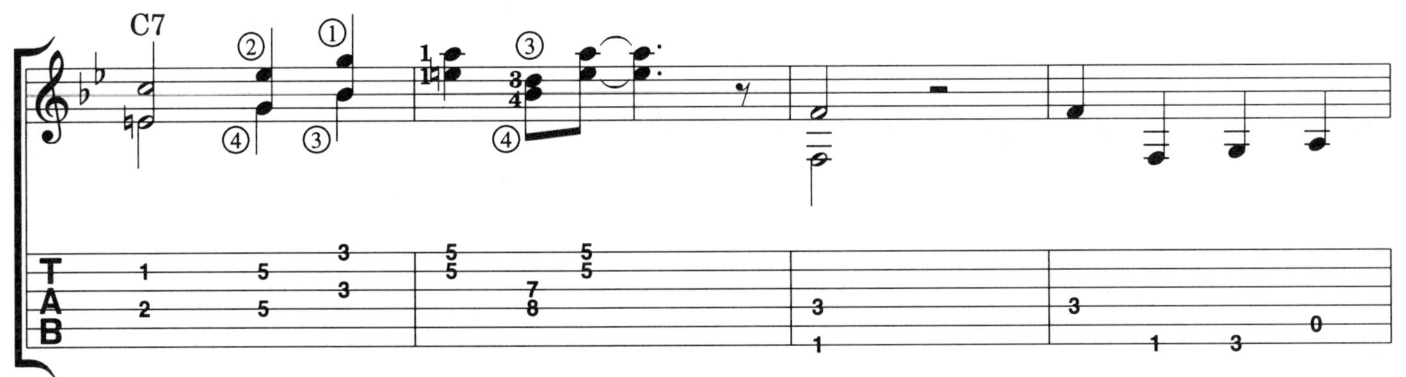
C7
1
2
5
5
3
3
5
5
7
8
5
5
3
1
3
1
3
0

B♭
G°
B♭
G♭
T
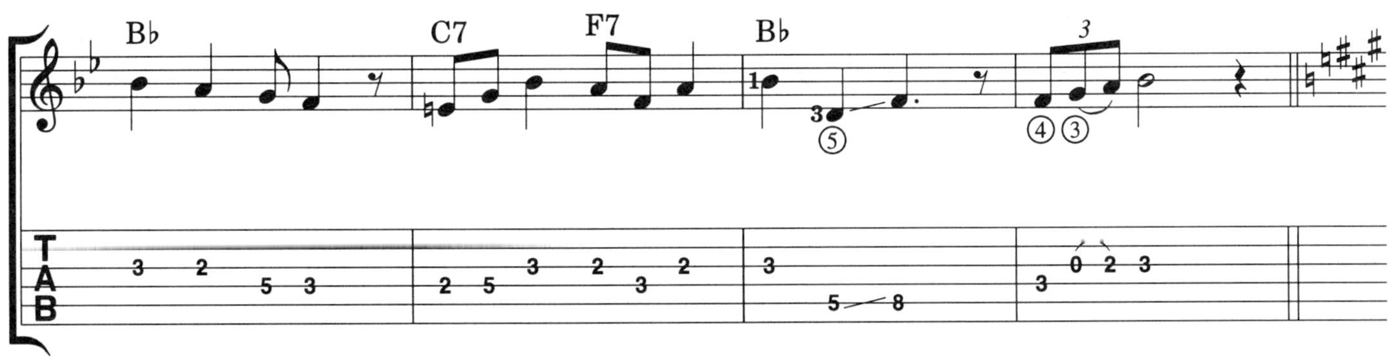
B♭
C7
F7
B♭
3

E7
A

E7

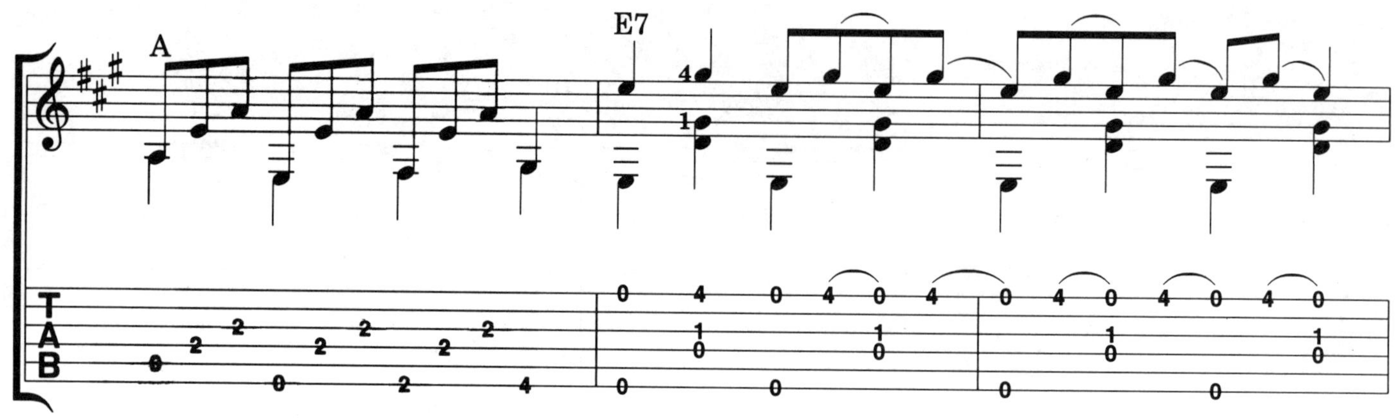
A
E7

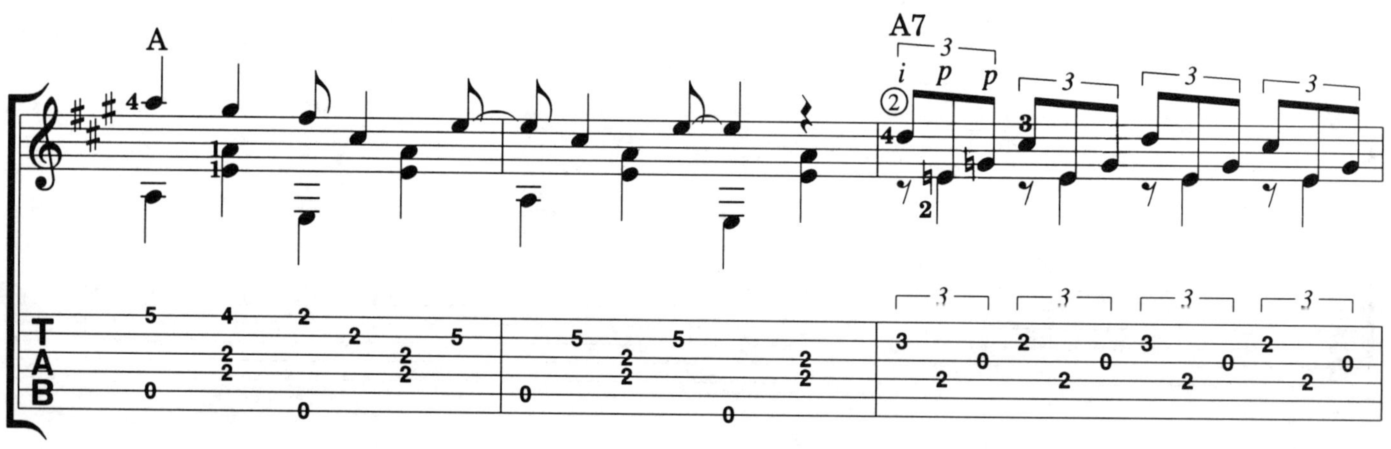
A
A7

D
Bend

B
E7

E+
A
F♯°

A
F
A

B9
E
A

G9
C
T
TAB
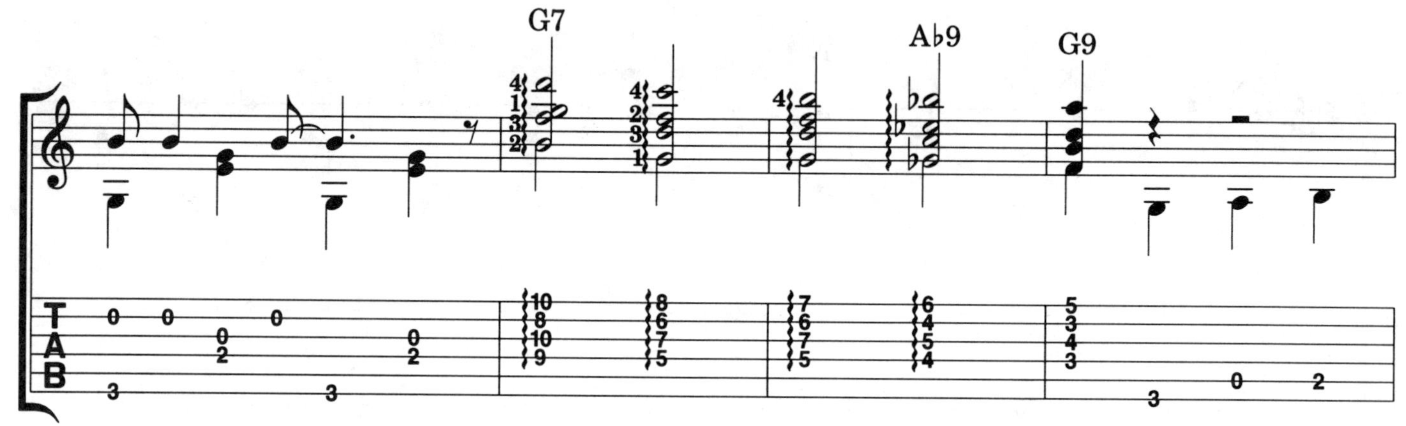
G7
A♭9
G9
TAB

C
G9
TAB

C
C7
TAB

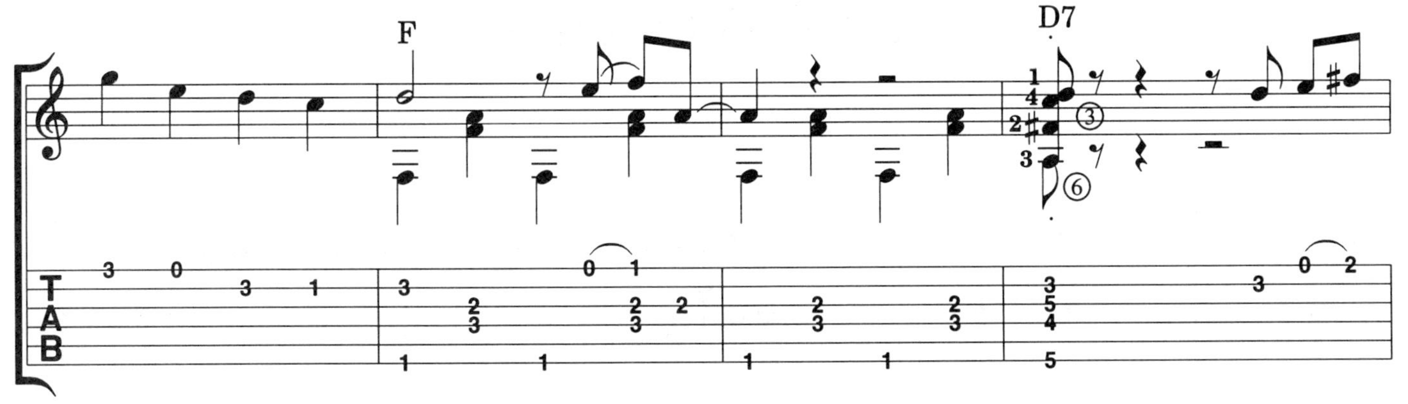
F
D7
TAB

G
C
TAB

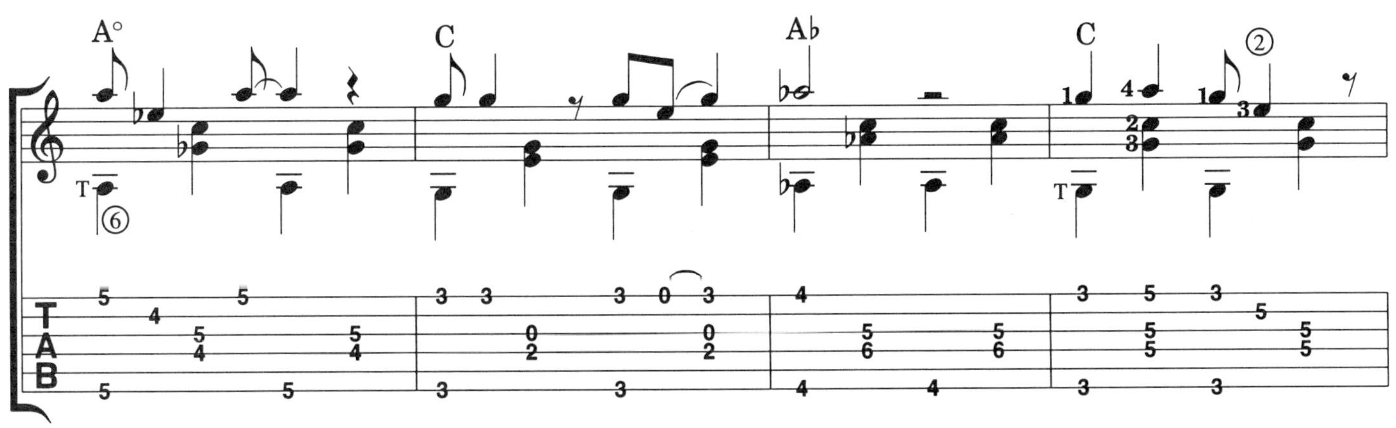
A°
C
A♭
C
TAB

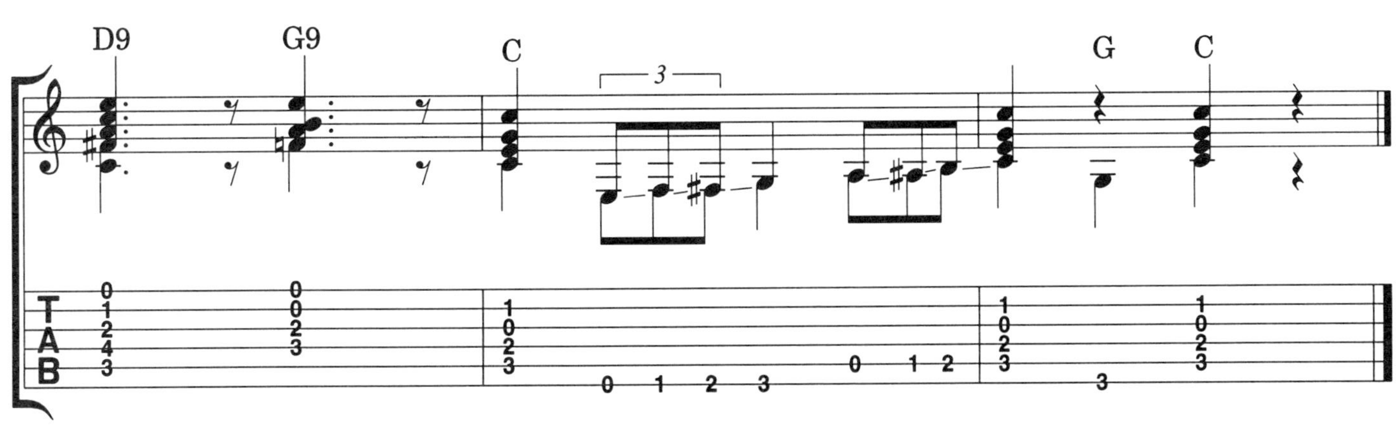
D9
G9
C
G
C
TAB

BAR B Q RAG

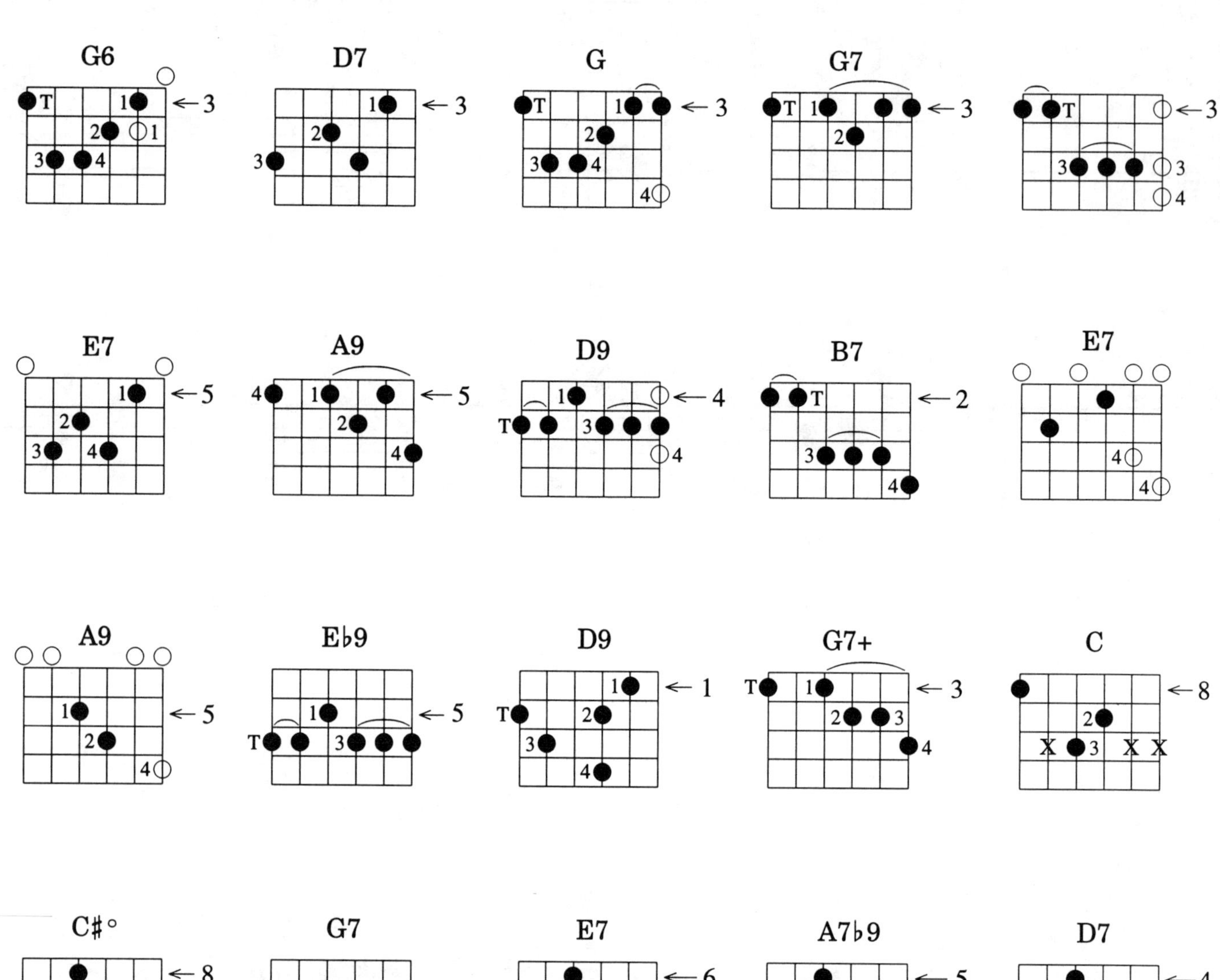

BAR B Q RAG

By Thom Bresh

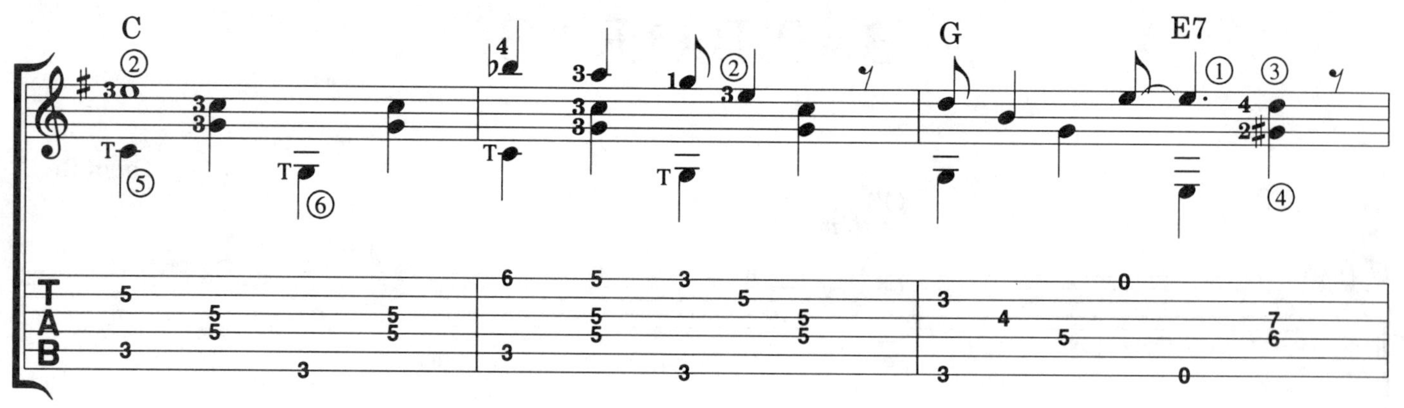
C
G
E7
TAB

A9
D9
G
G6
sl.
TAB

sl.
sl.
D7
TAB

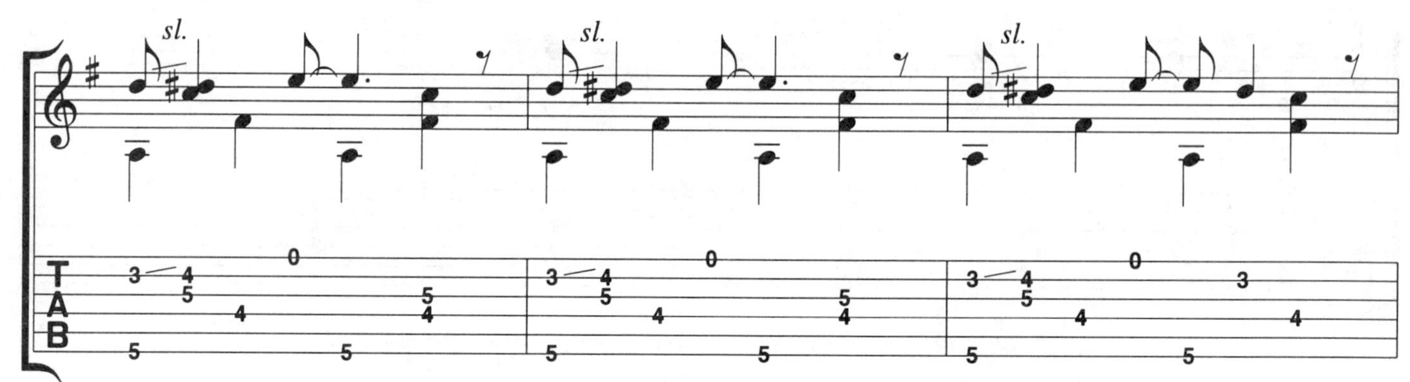
sl.
sl.
sl.
TAB

G
G6
sl.
sl.

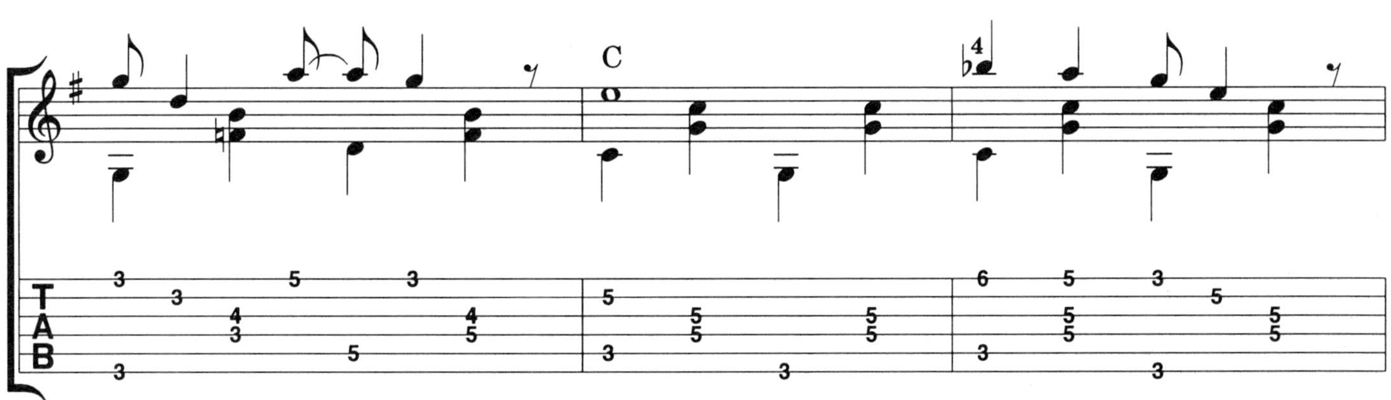
C

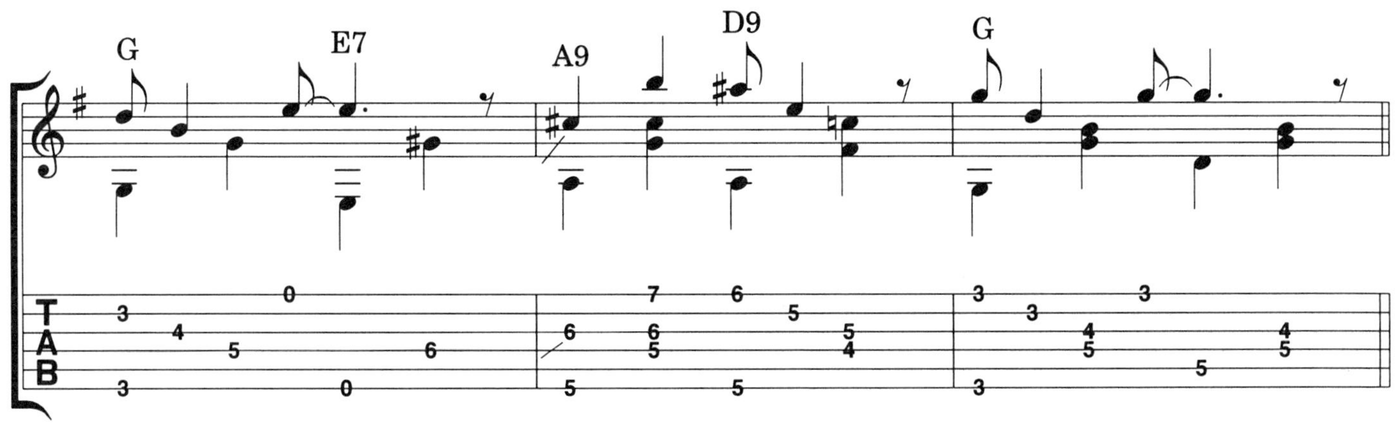
G
E7
A9
D9
G

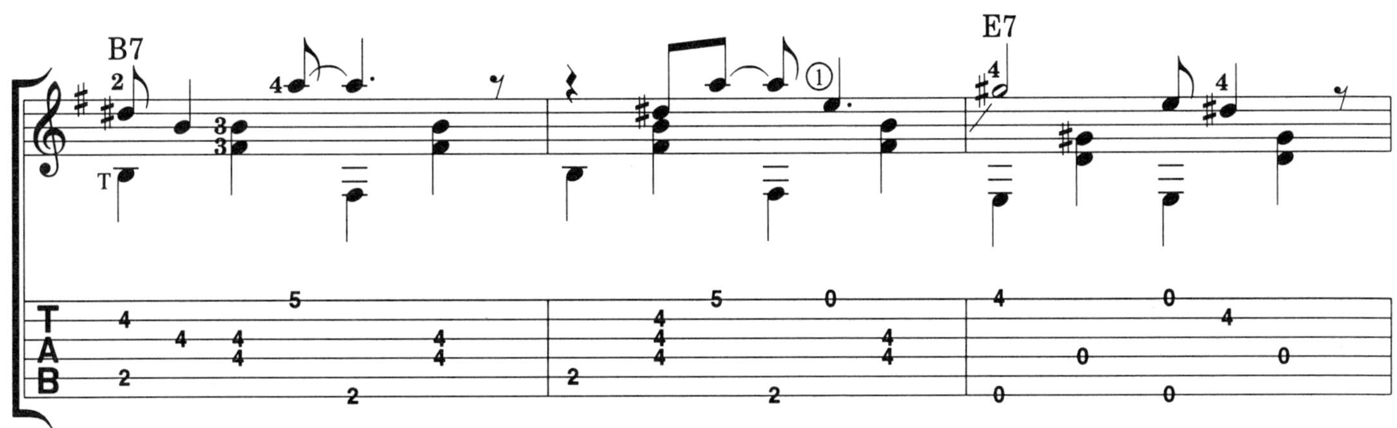
B7
E7

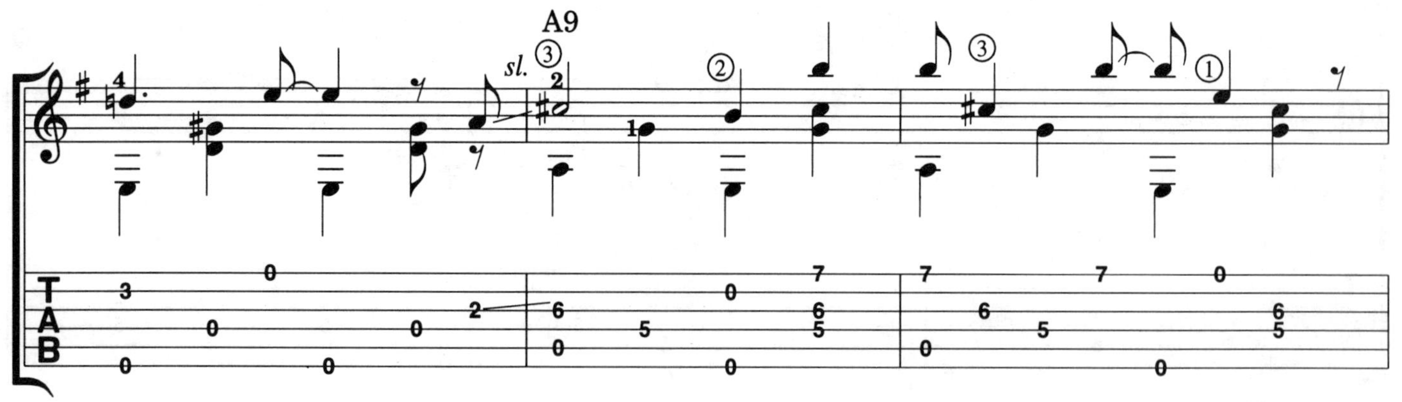
A9
sl.
TAB

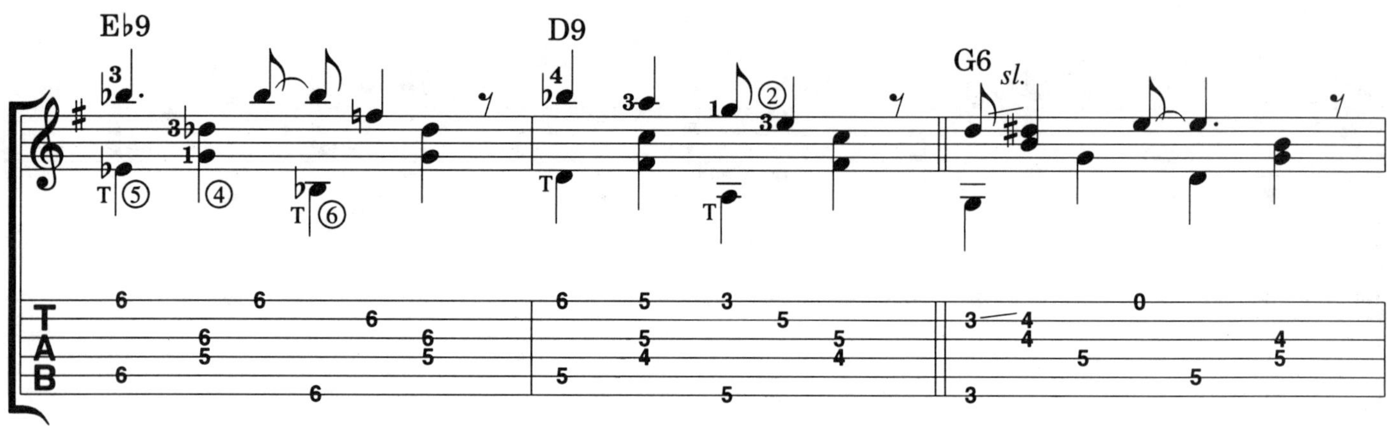
E♭9
D9
G6
sl.
TAB

sl.
sl.
D7
TAB

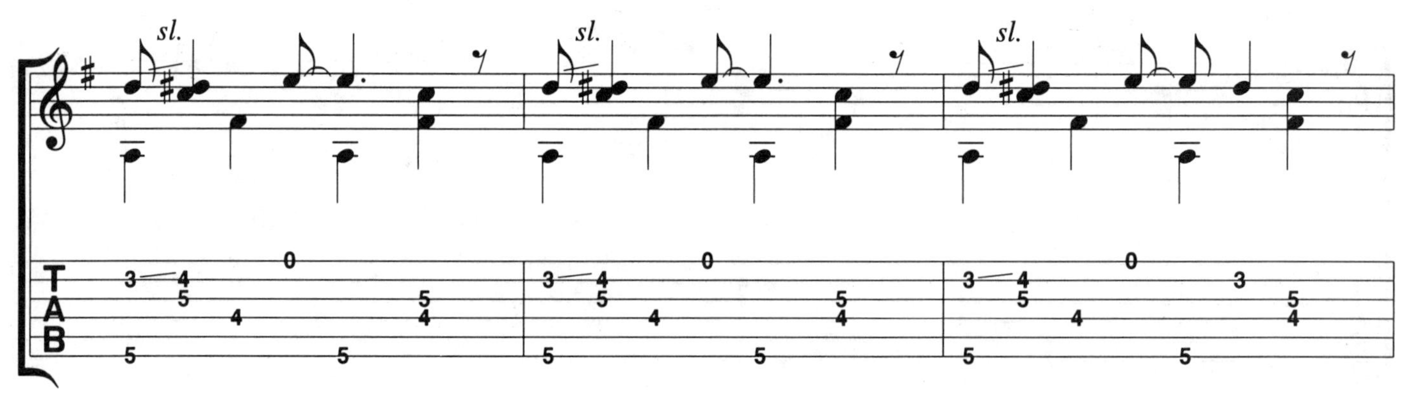
sl.
sl.
sl.
TAB

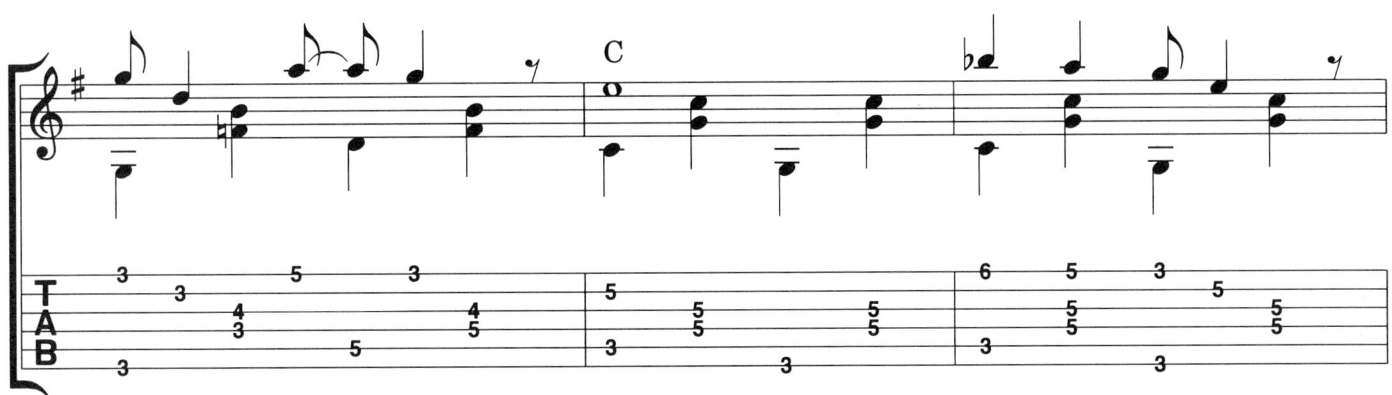

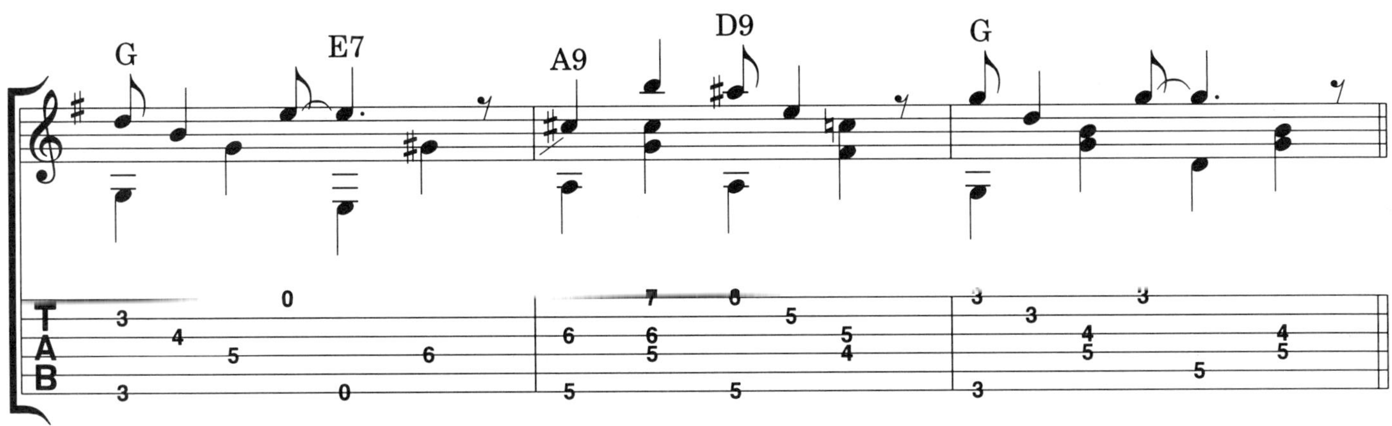

2nd Chorus

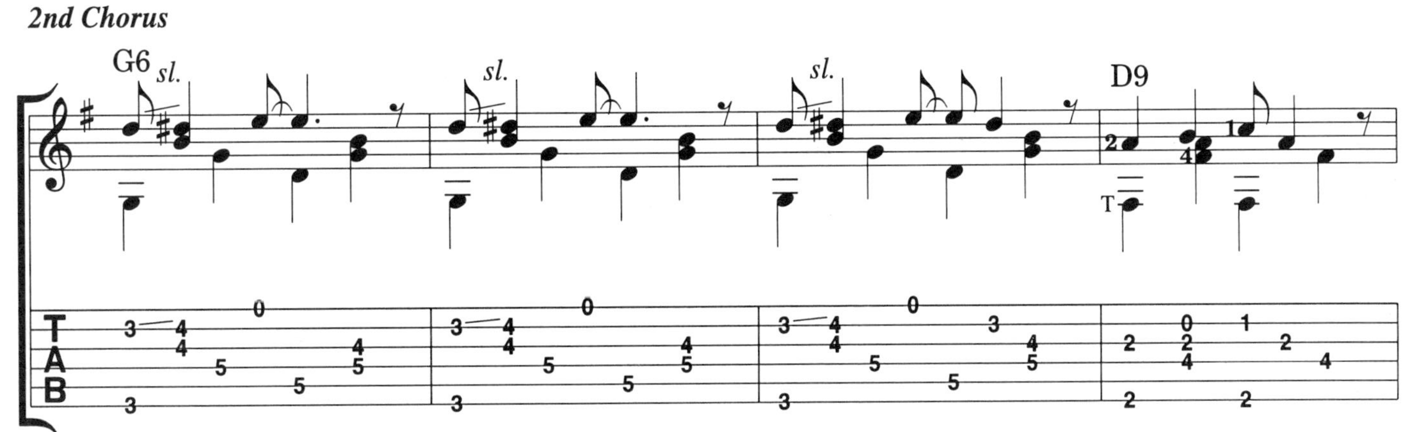

D7
sl.
sl.
D9

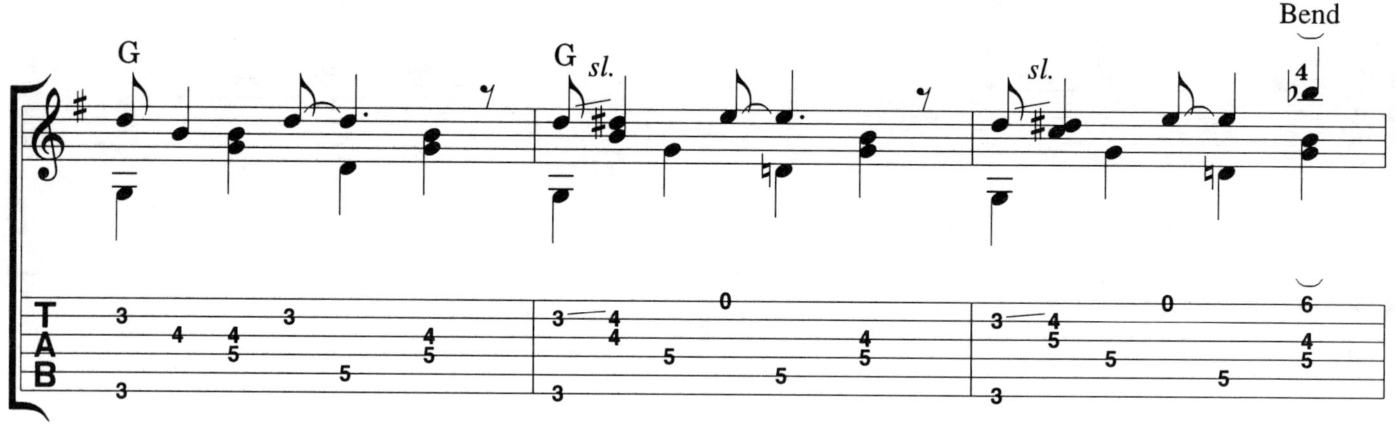
G
G
sl.
sl.
Bend

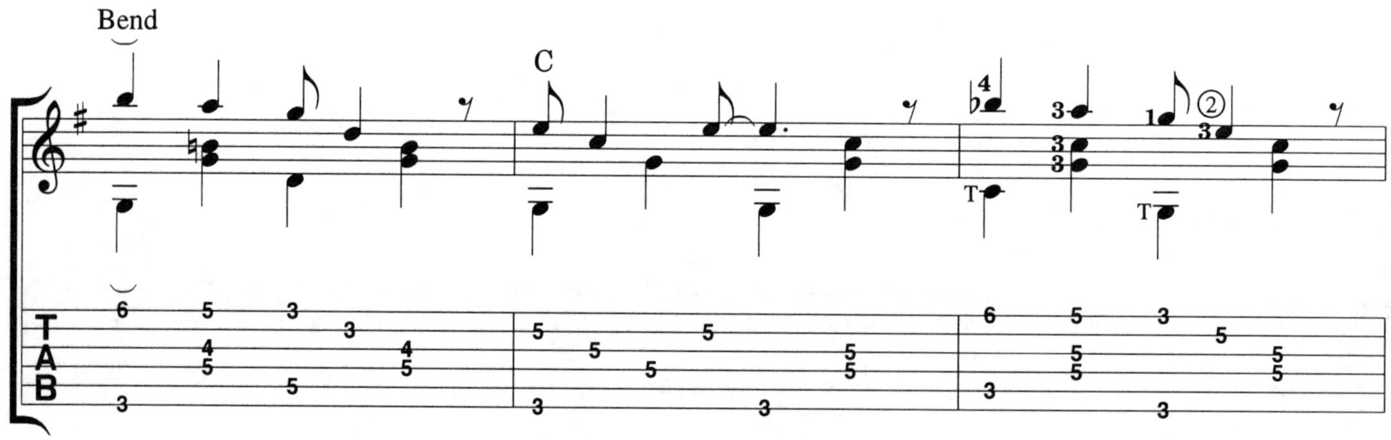
Bend
C

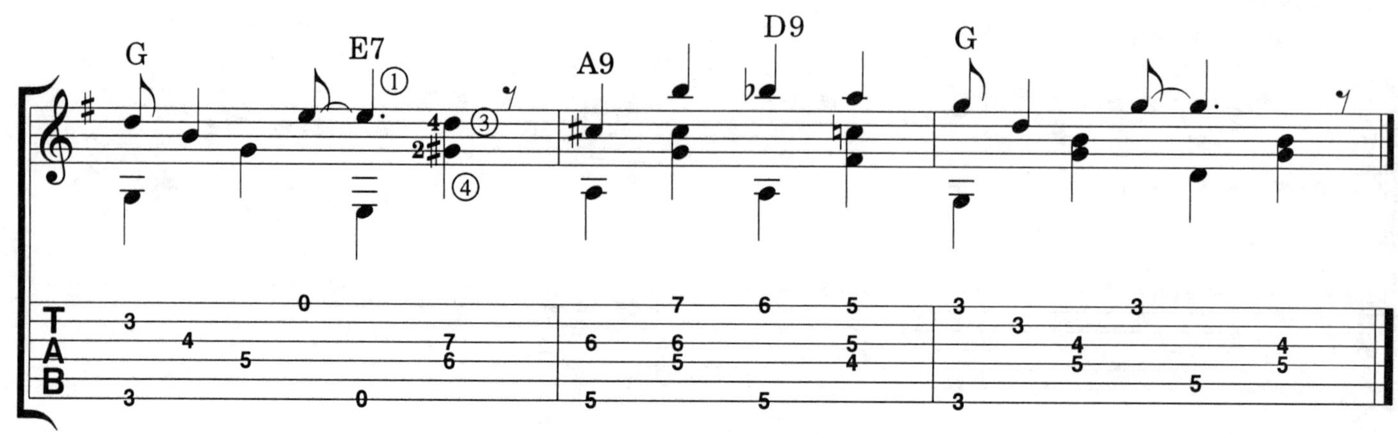
G
E7
A9
D9
G

B7
E7

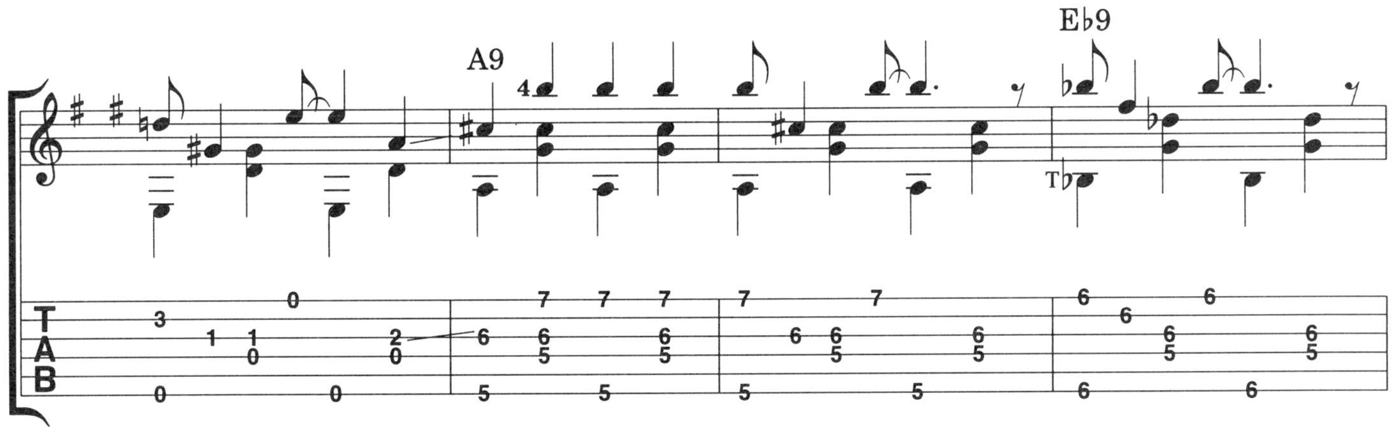
A9
E♭9

D9
G6
sl.
sl.
sl.

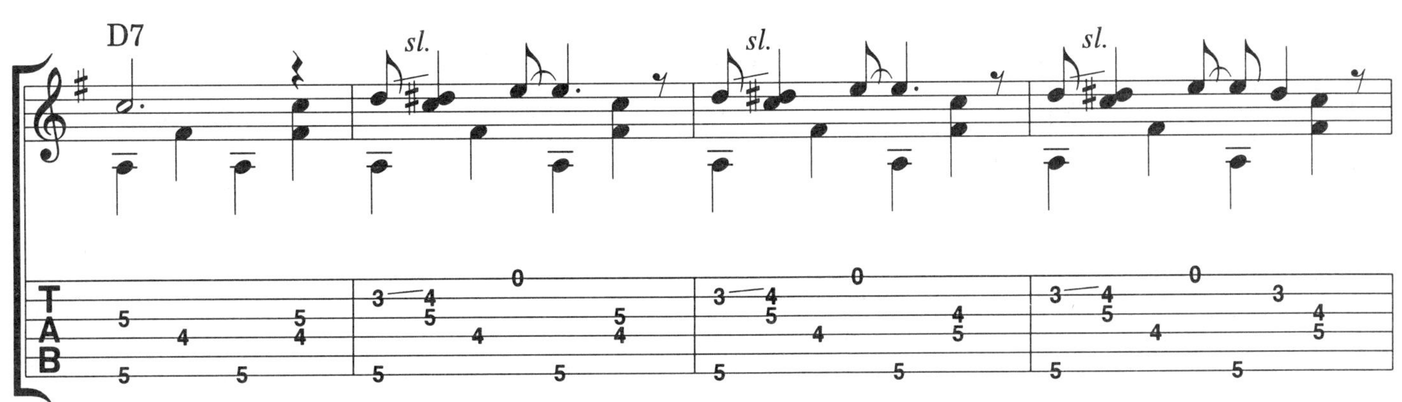
D7
sl.
sl.
sl.

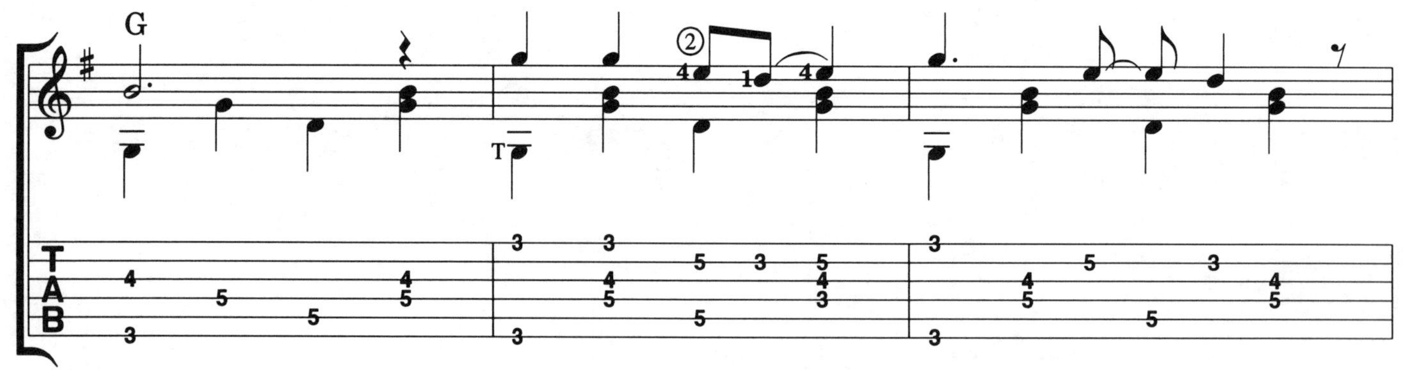
G
TAB

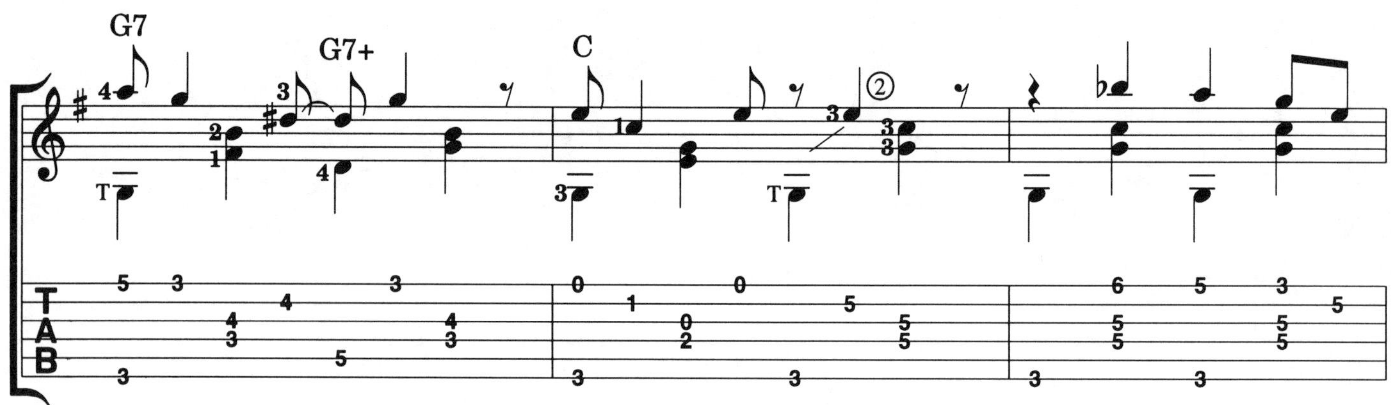
G7
G7+
C
TAB

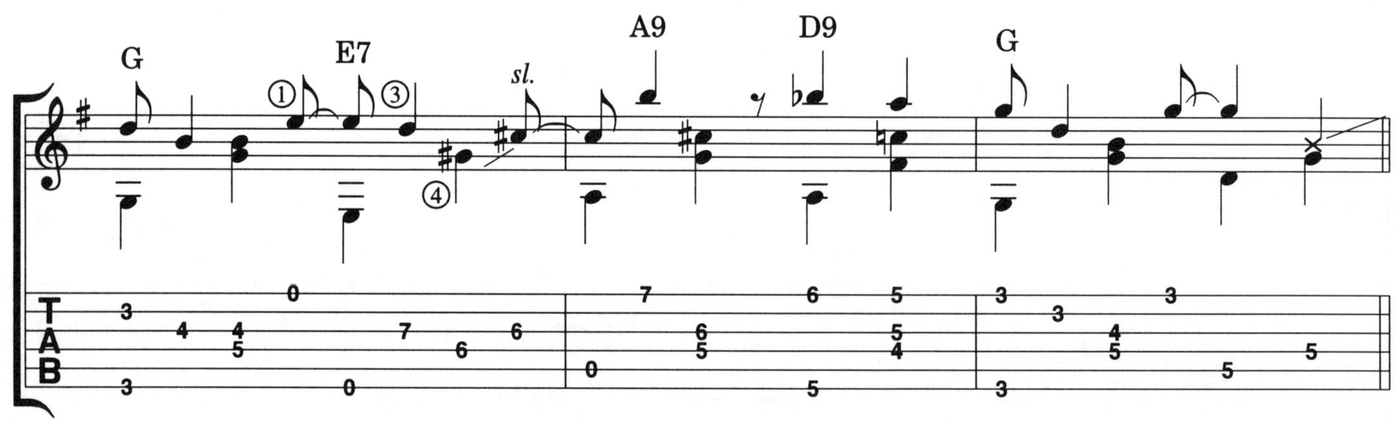
G
E7
sl.
A9
D9
G
TAB

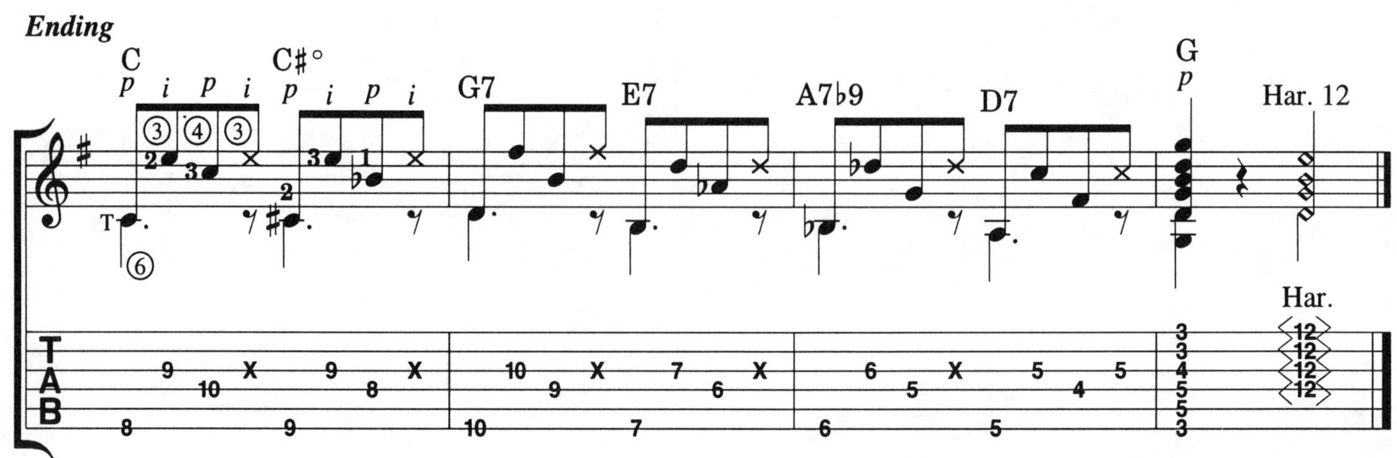
Ending
C
C♯°
G7
E7
A7♭9
D7
G
Har. 12
Har.
TAB

YOU TELL ME YOUR DREAMS I'LL TELL YOU MINE

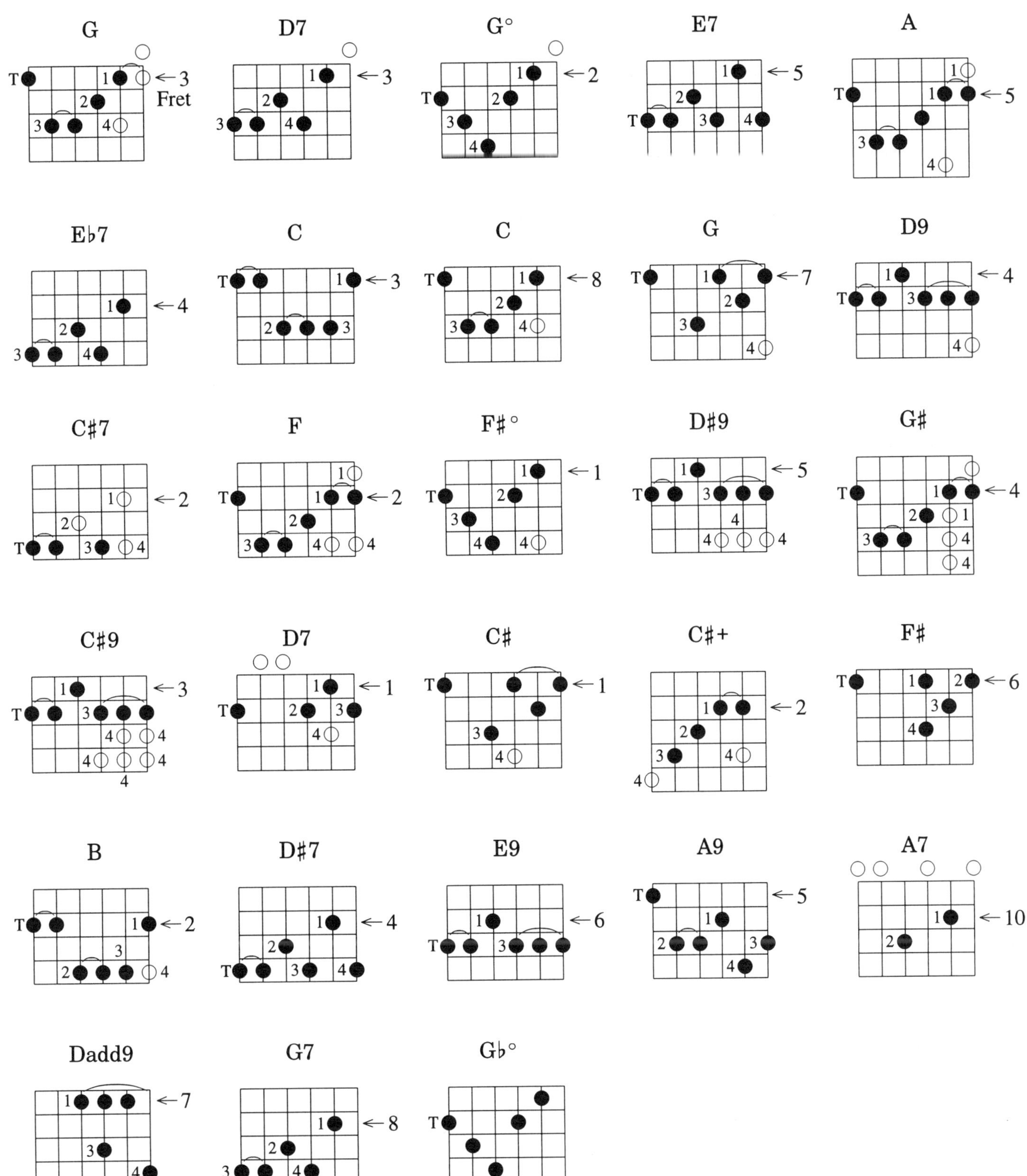

YOU TELL ME YOUR DREAMS, I'LL TELL YOU MINE

This Version Circa 1945

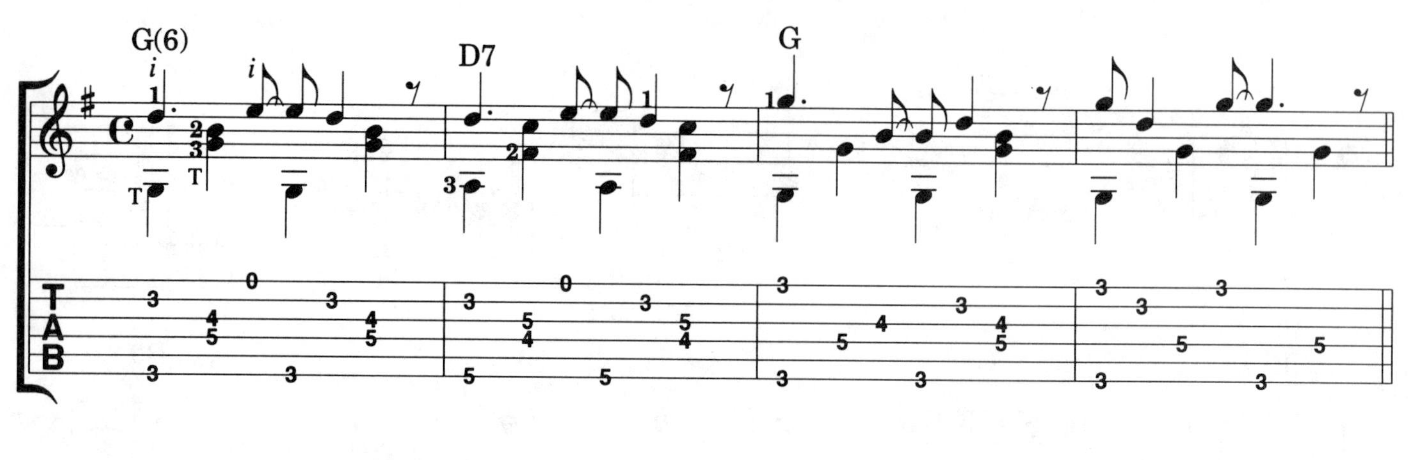

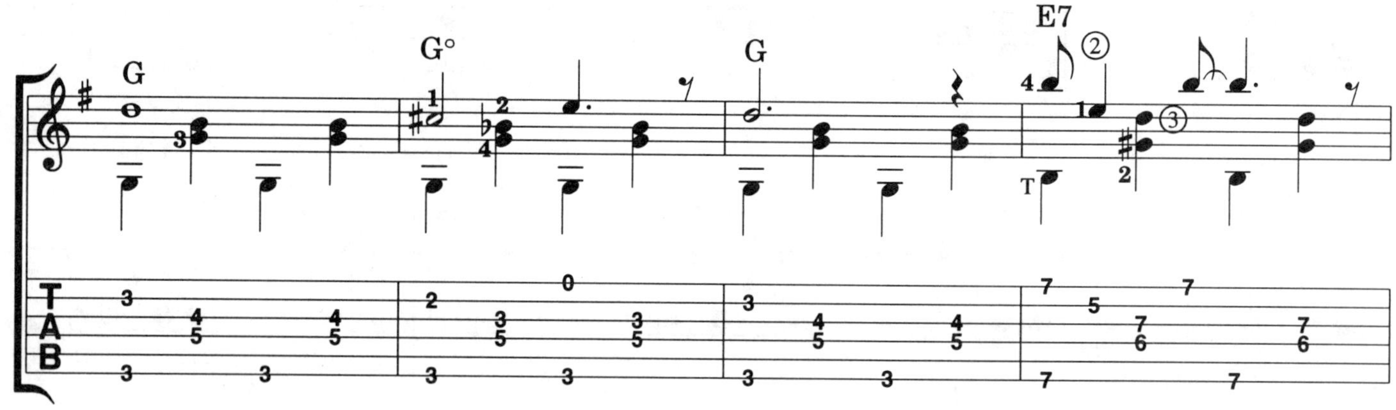

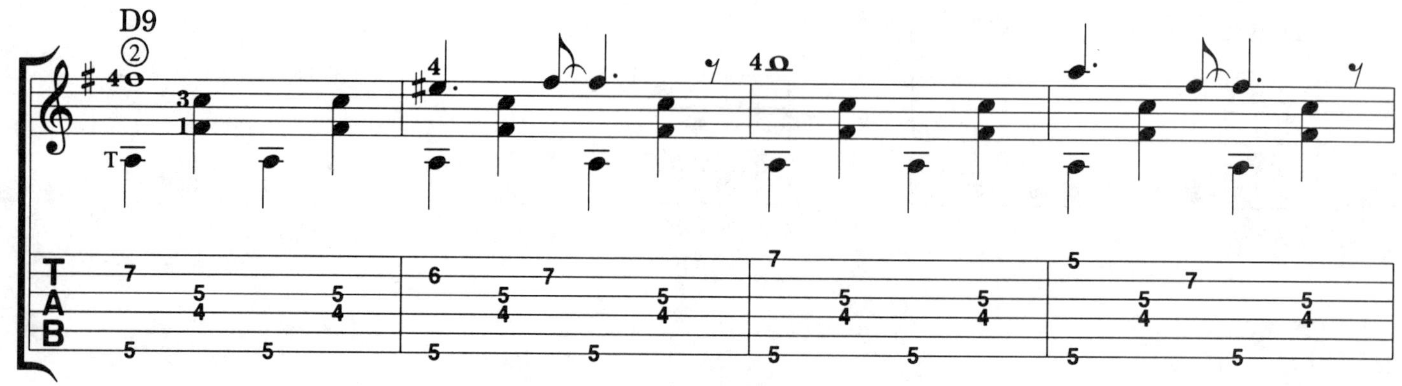

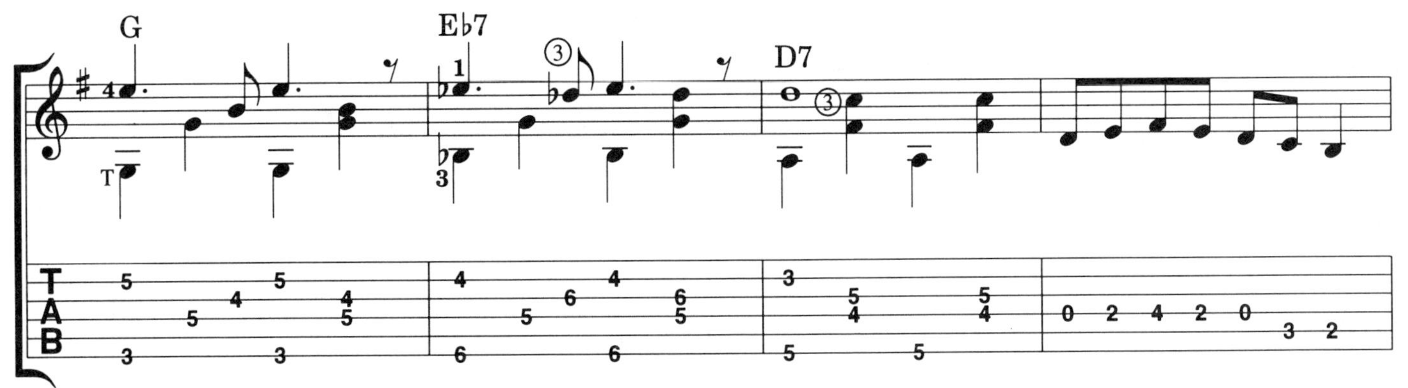
G
E♭7
D7
TAB
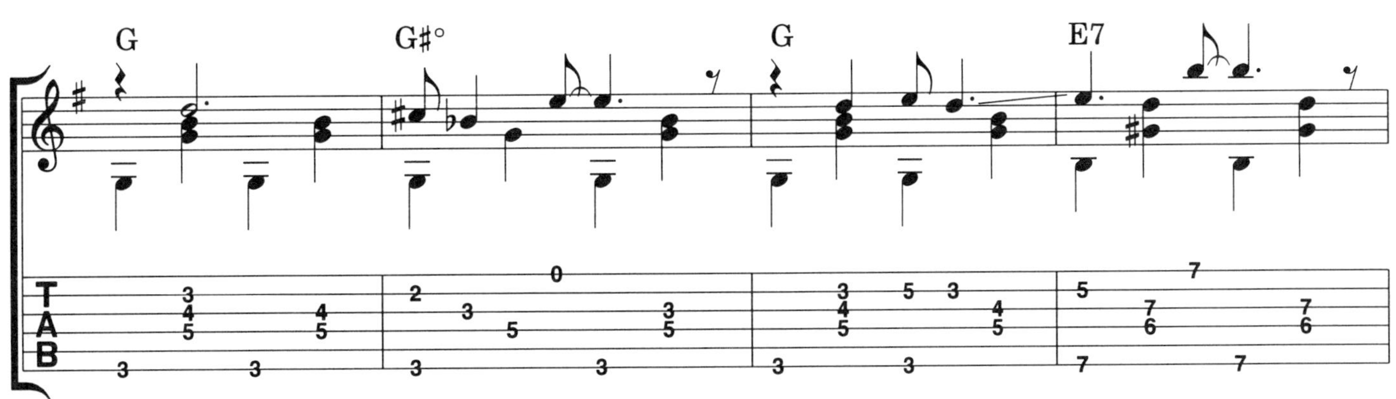
G
G♯°
G
E7
TAB

A
TAB
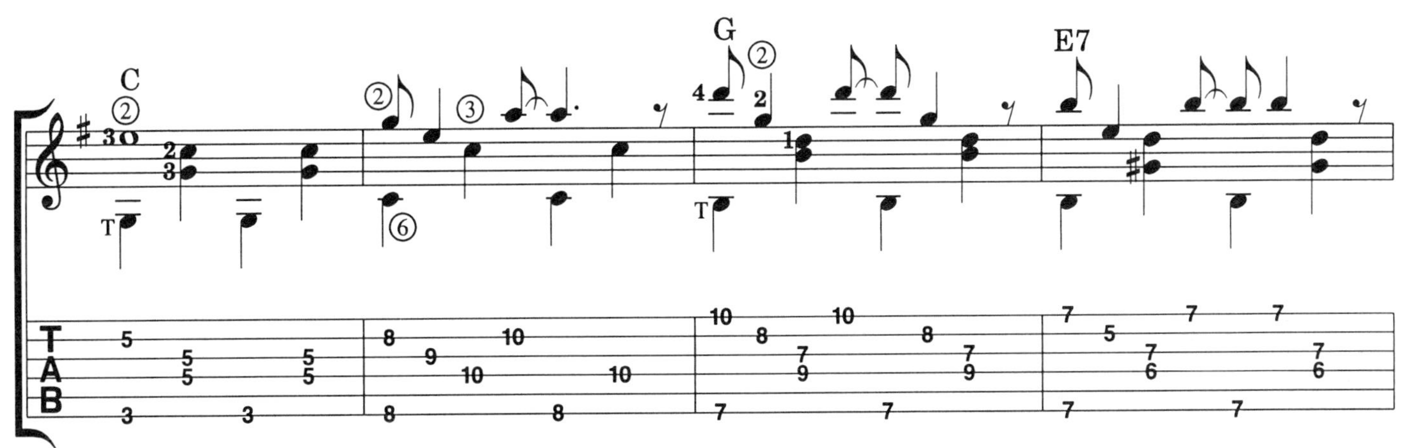
C
G
E7
TAB

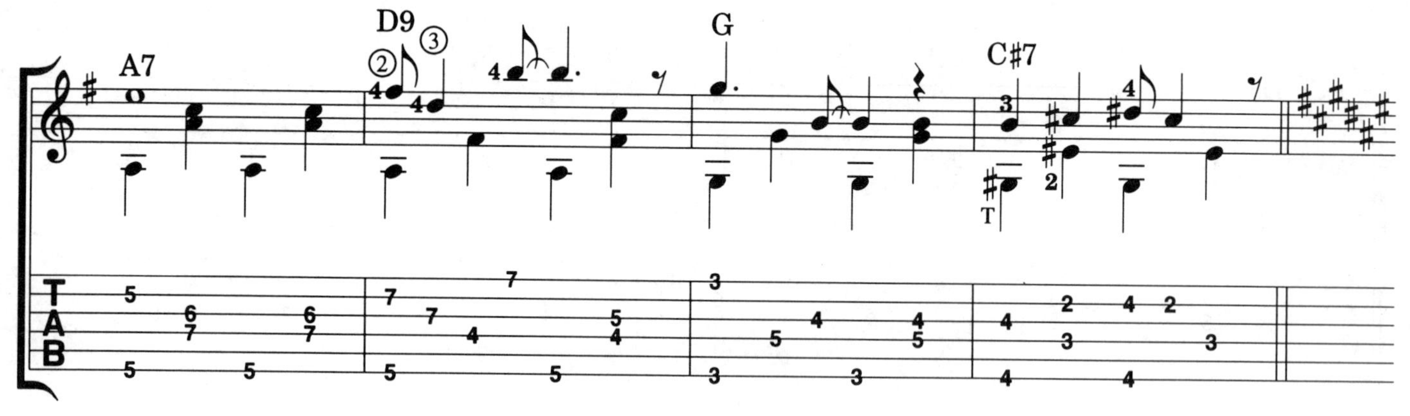
A7
D9
G
C♯7

F♯
F♯°
F♯

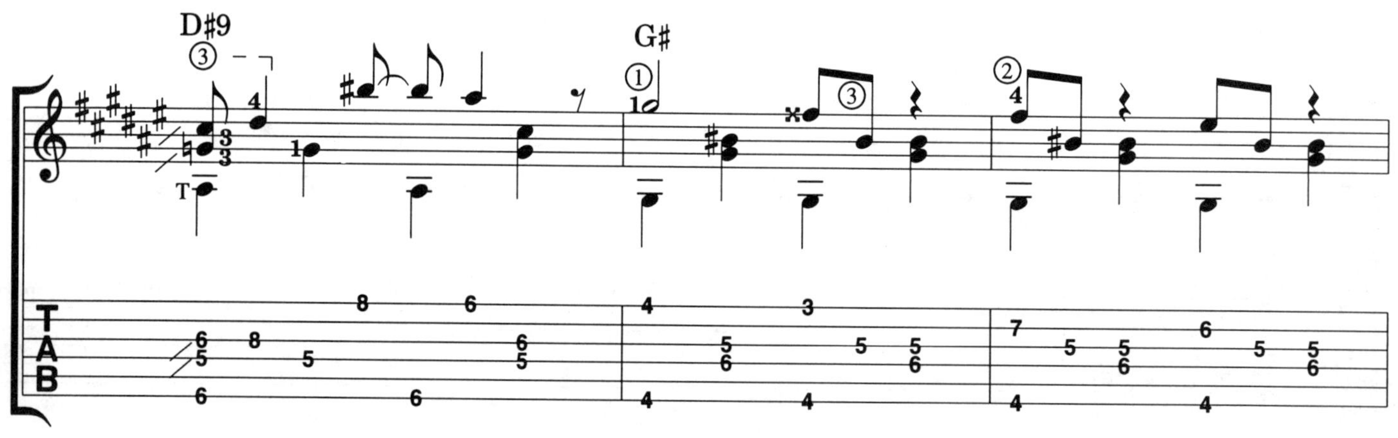
D♯9
G♯

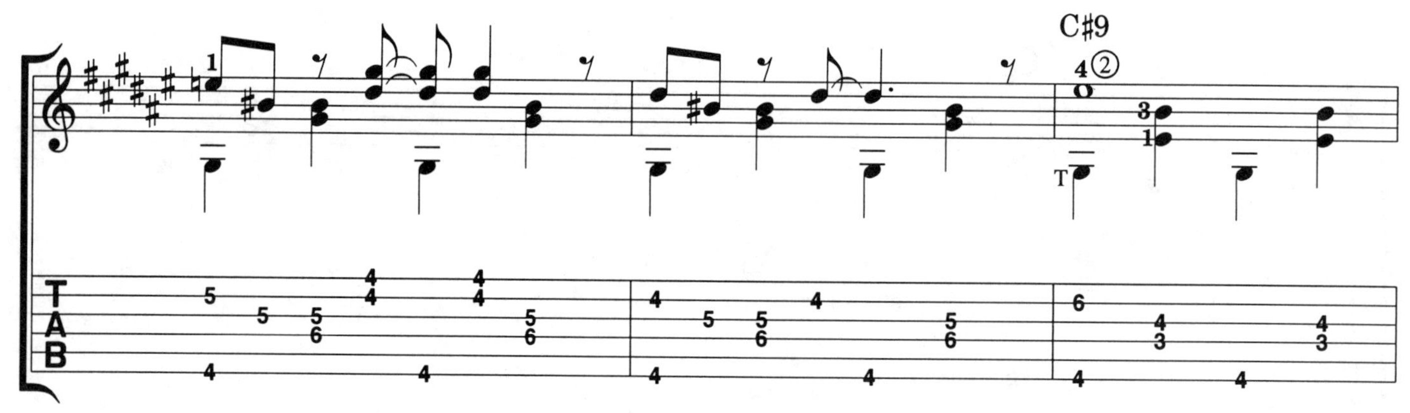
C♯9

F♯
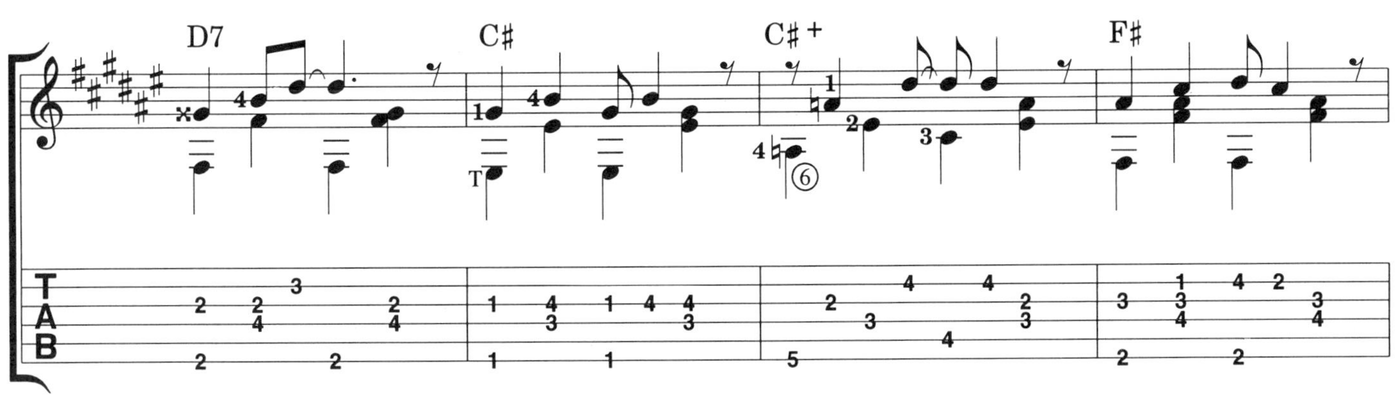
D7
C♯
C♯ +
F♯
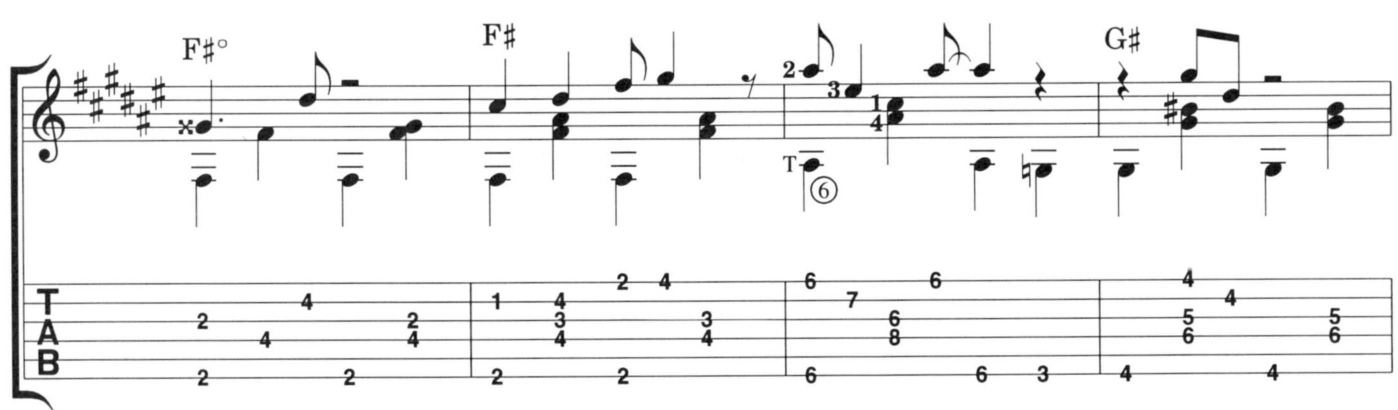
F♯°
F♯
G♯

B

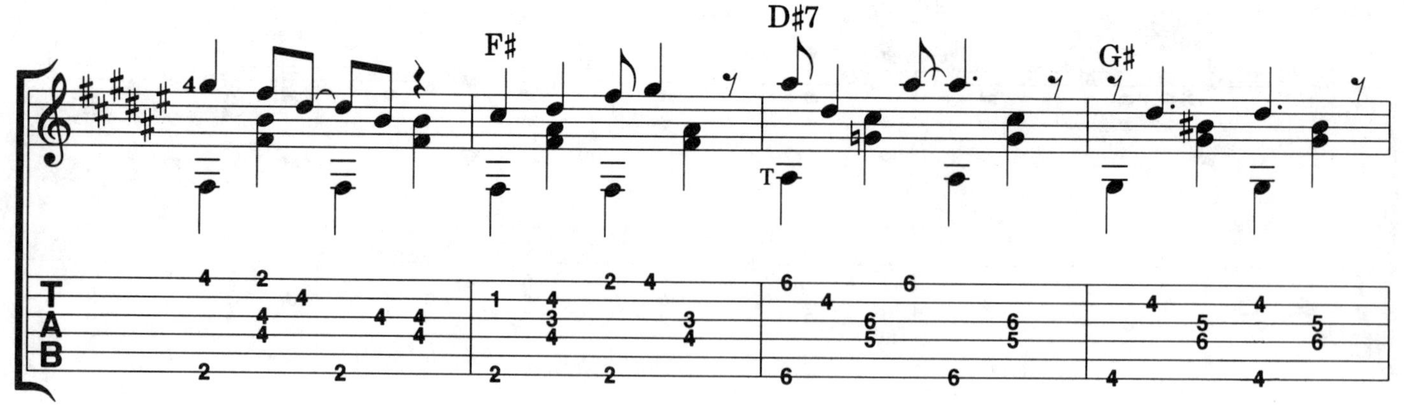
F#
D#7
G#
T
TAB

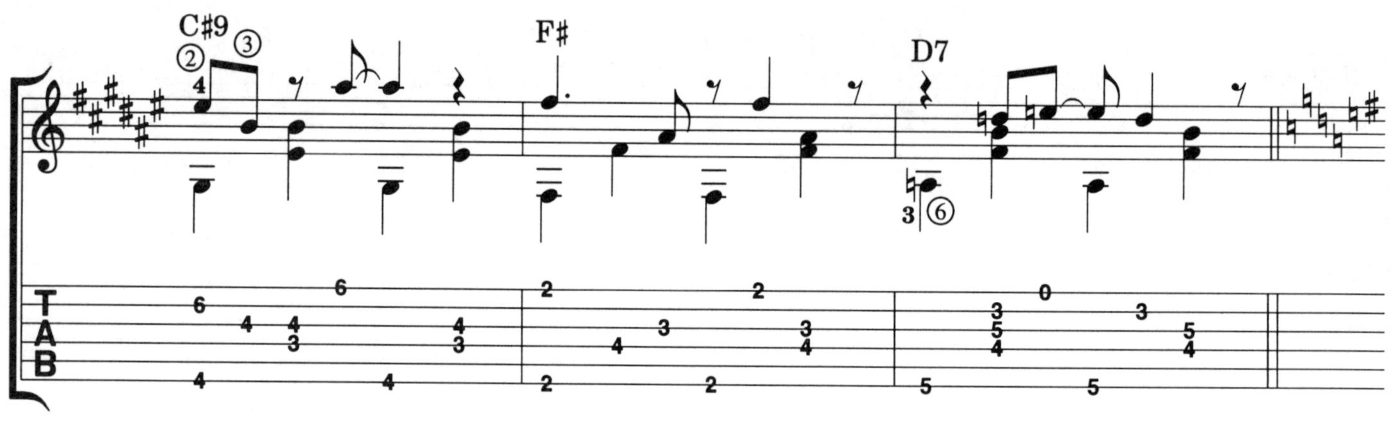
C#9
F#
D7
TAB

G
G°
G
TAB

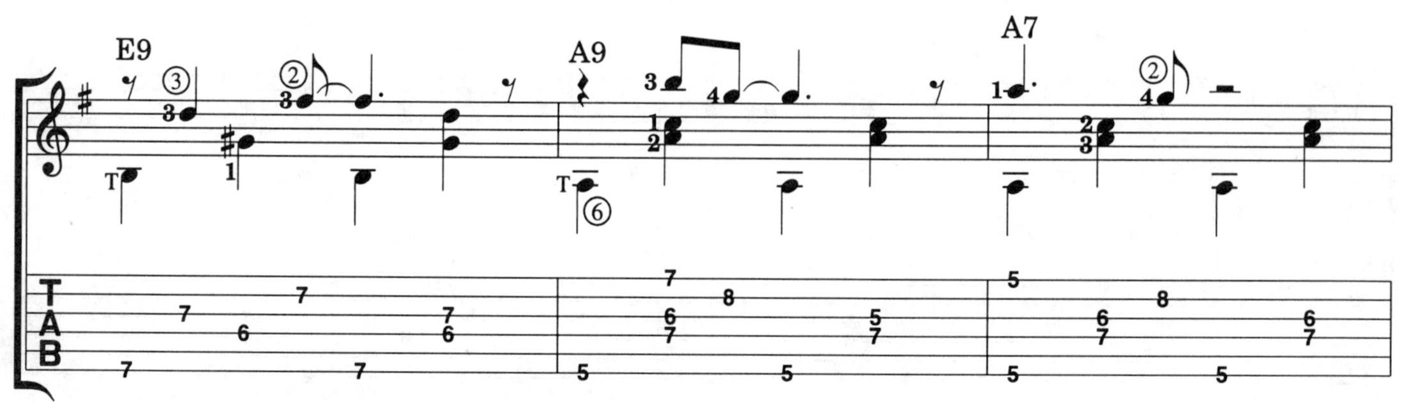
E9
A9
A7
T
T
TAB

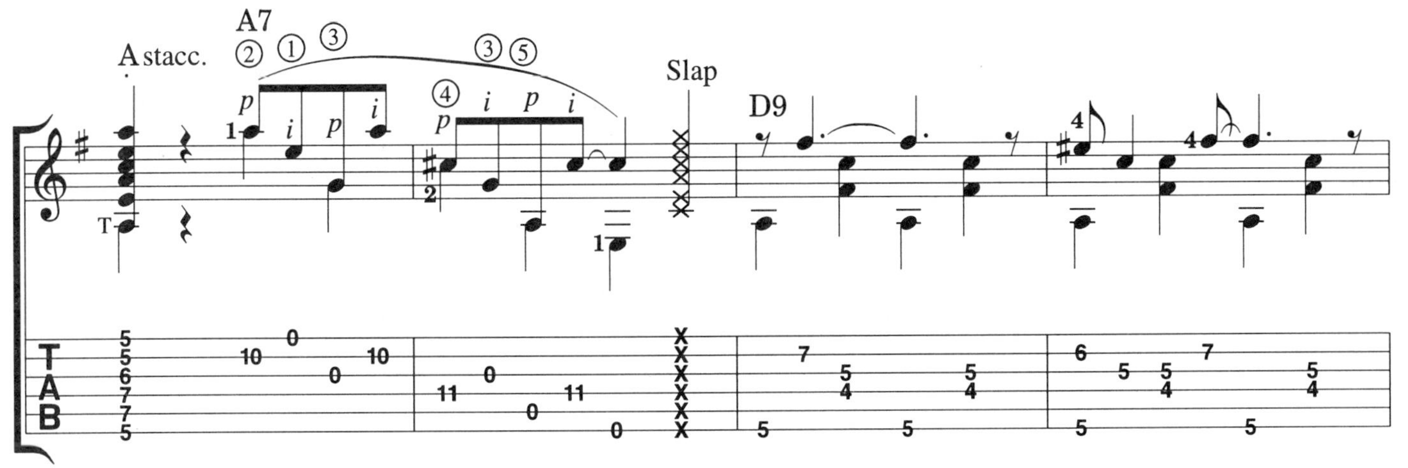
A stacc.
A7
Slap
D9

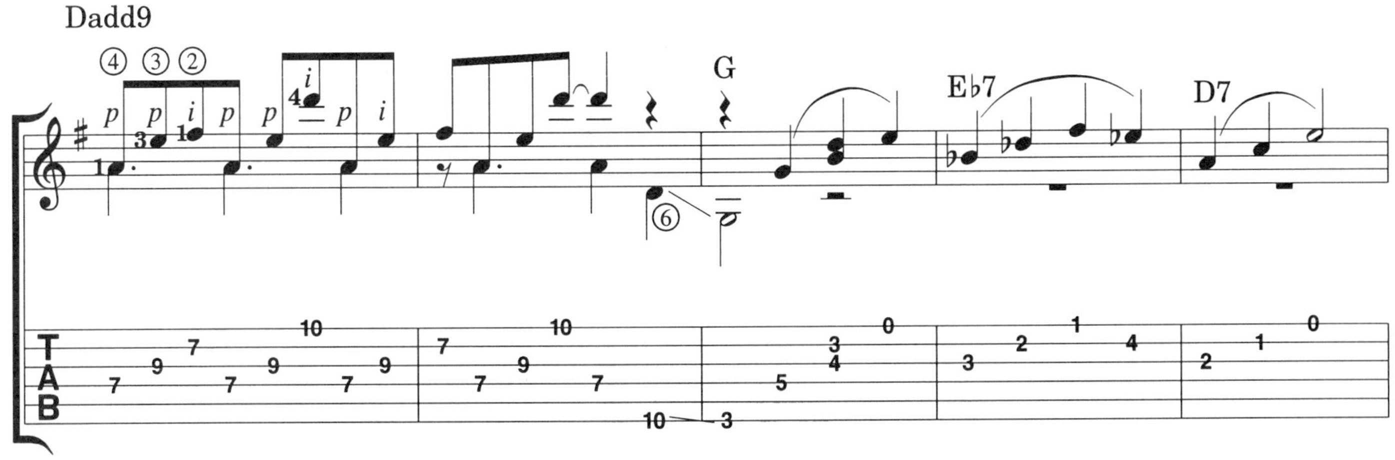
Dadd9
G
E♭7
D7

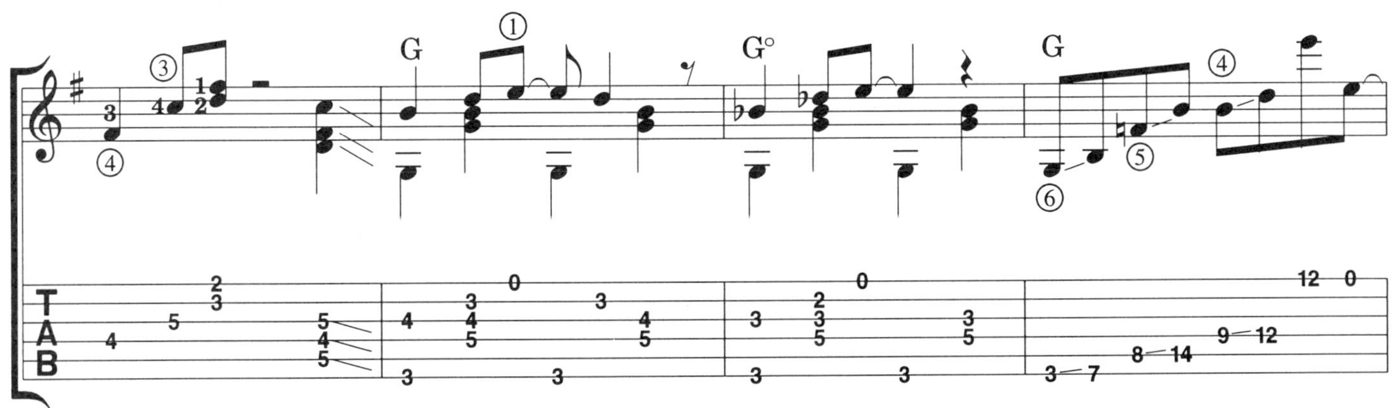
G
G°
G

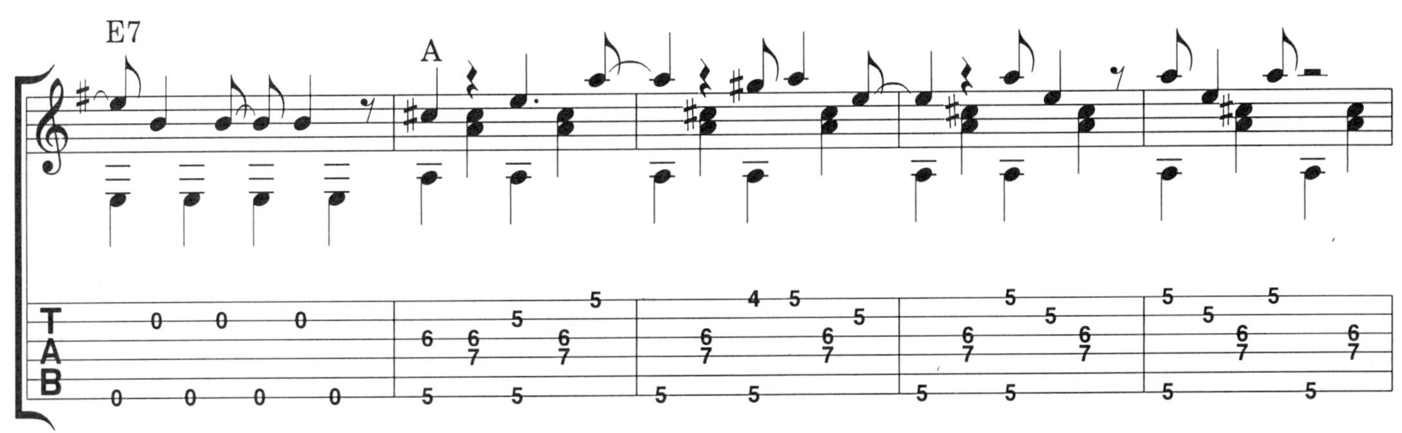
E7
A

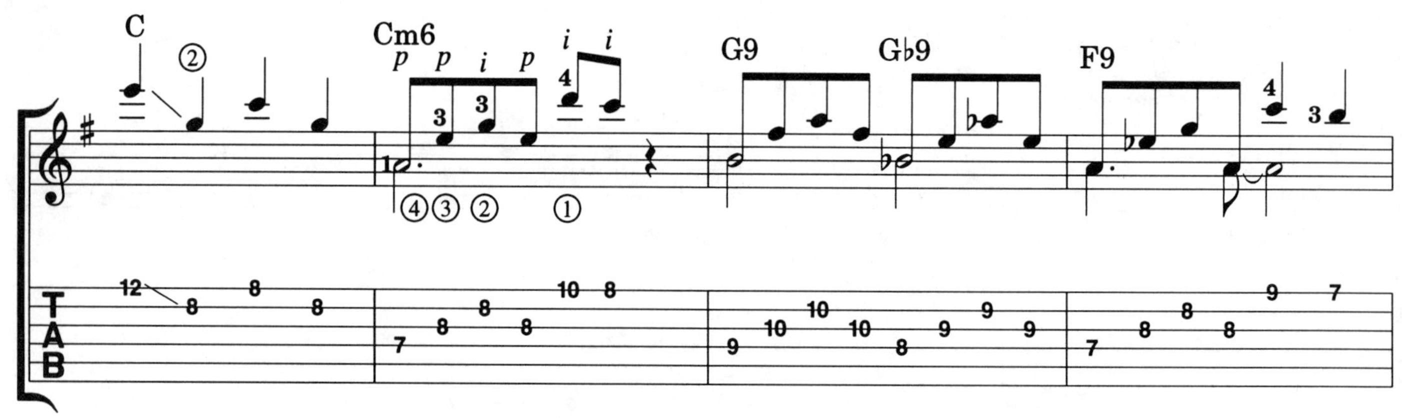
C
Cm6
G9
G♭9
F9

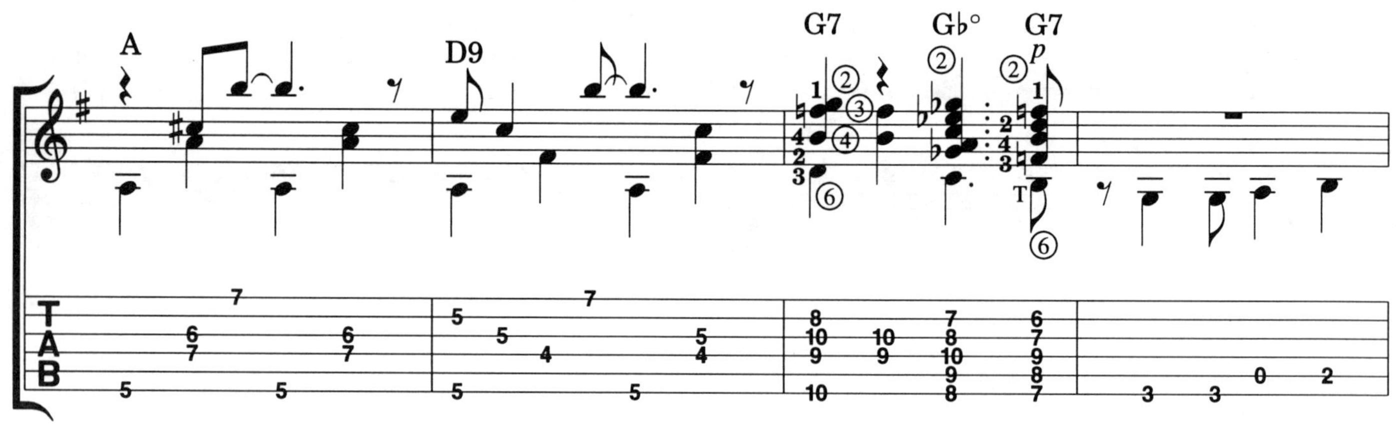
A
D9
G7
G♭°
G7

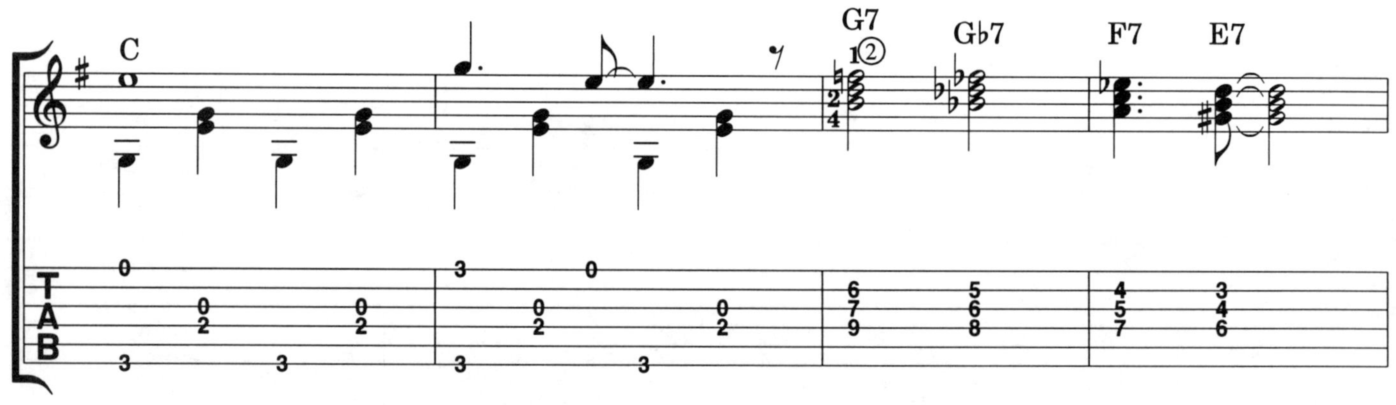
C
G7
G♭7
F7
E7

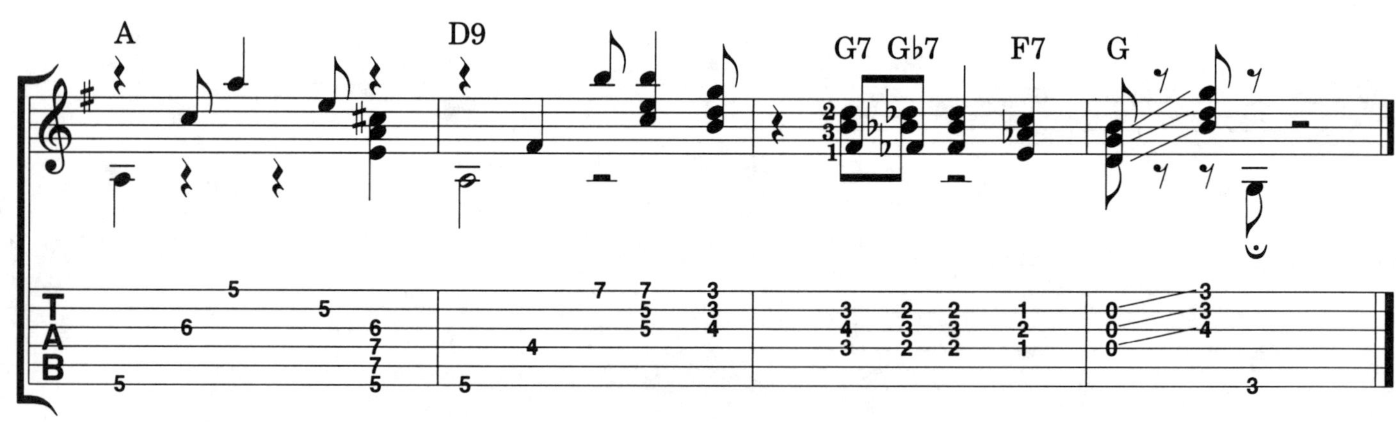
A
D9
G7
G♭7
F7
G

MEMPHIS BLUES

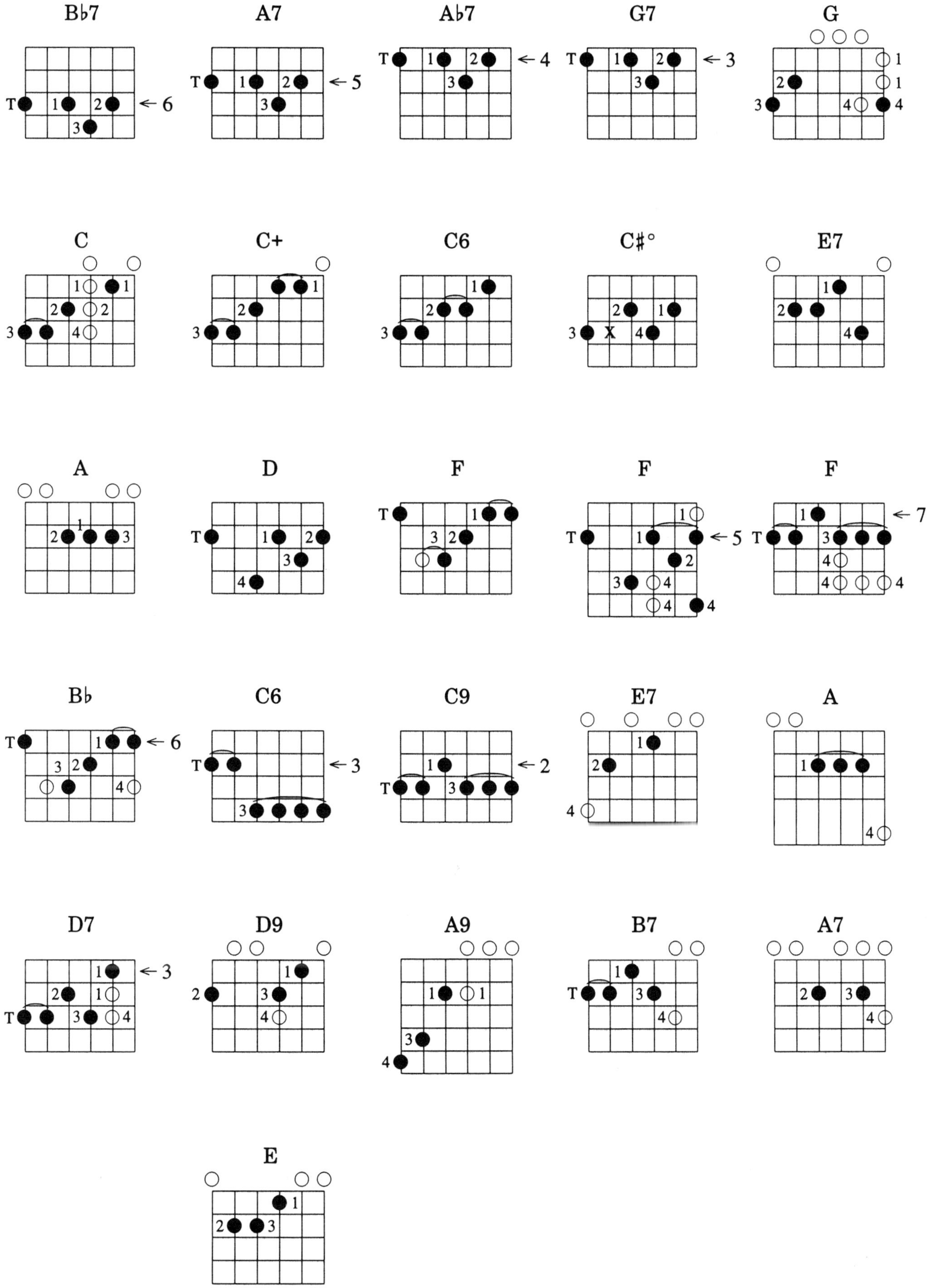

B♭7 A7 A♭7 G7 G

C C+ C6 C♯° E7

A D F F F

B♭ C6 C9 E7 A

D7 D9 A9 B7 A7

E

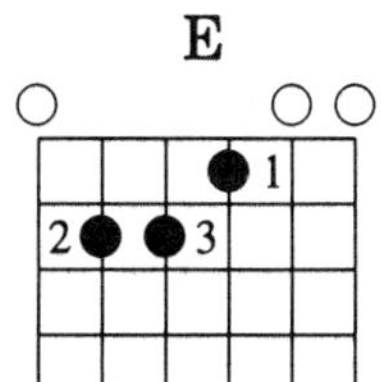

MEMPHIS BLUES

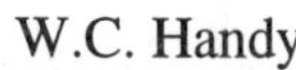

slap B♭7 A7

A♭7 G7 G

C C+ C6 C♯° G

C

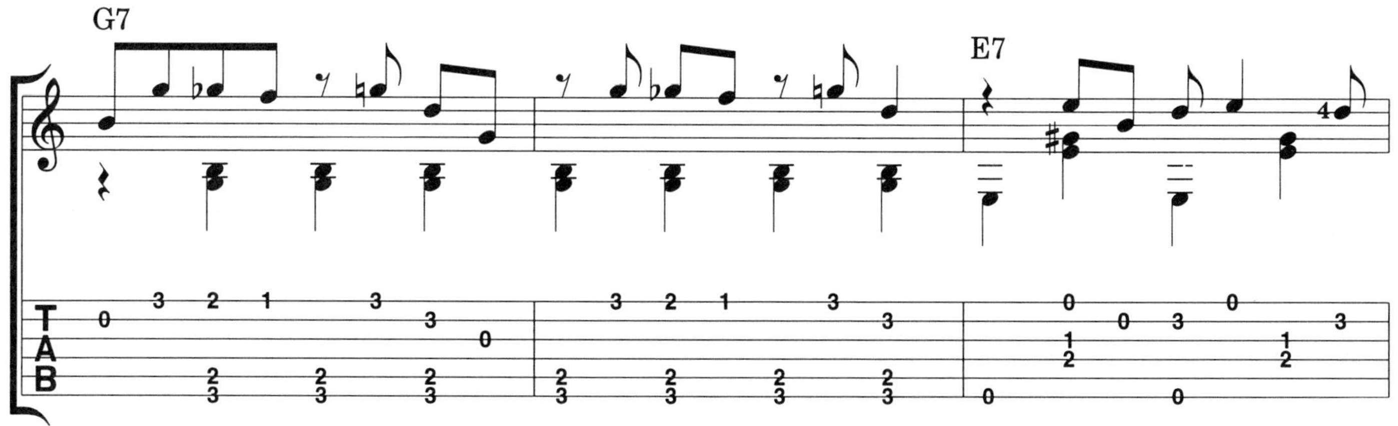
G7
E7
TAB

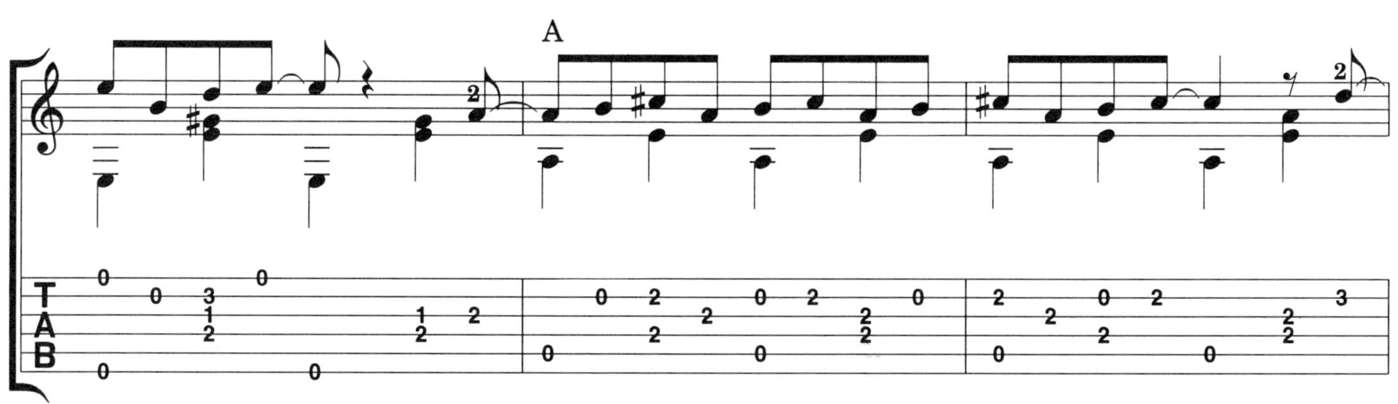
A
TAB

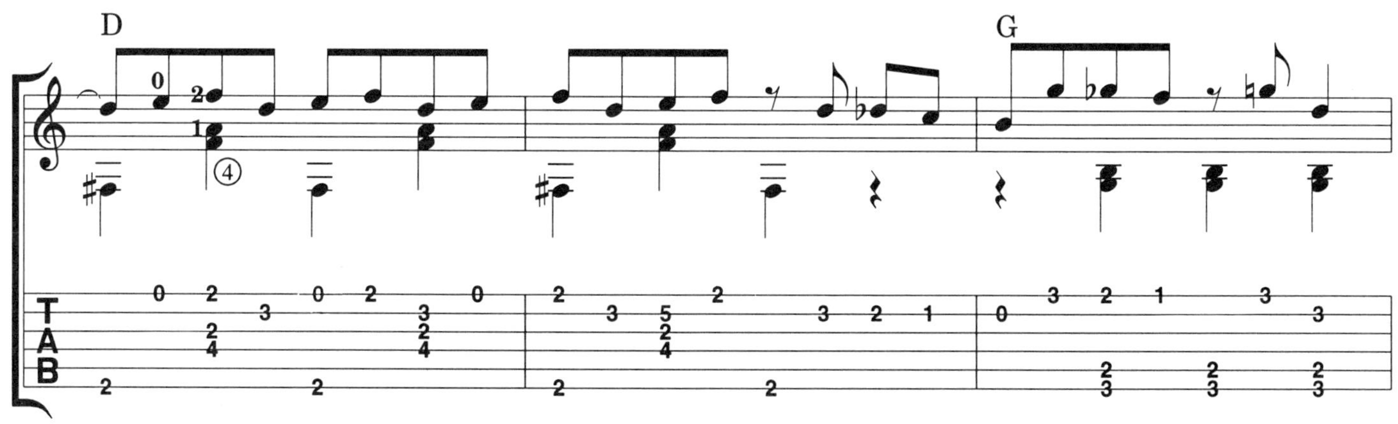
D
G
TAB

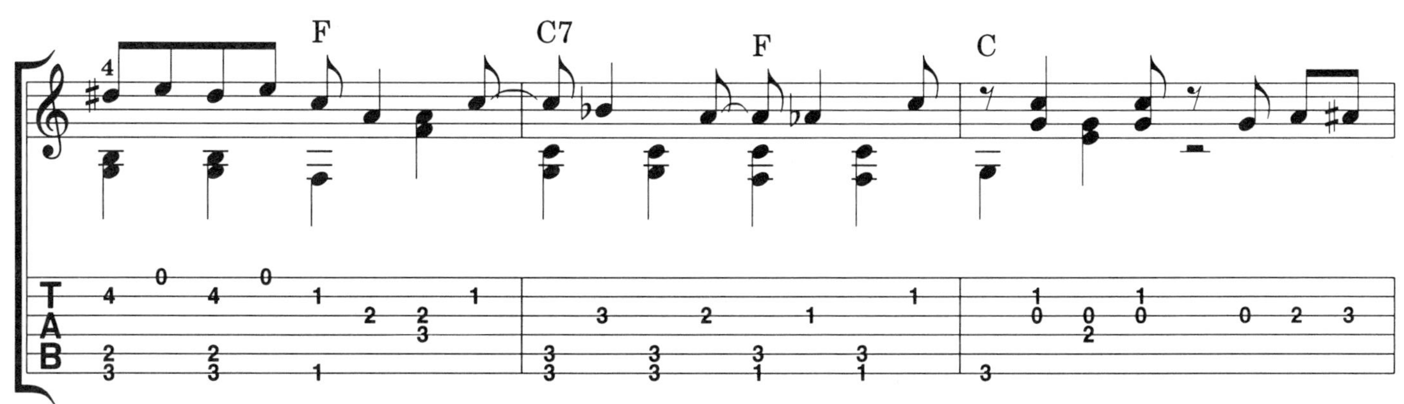
F
C7
F
C
TAB

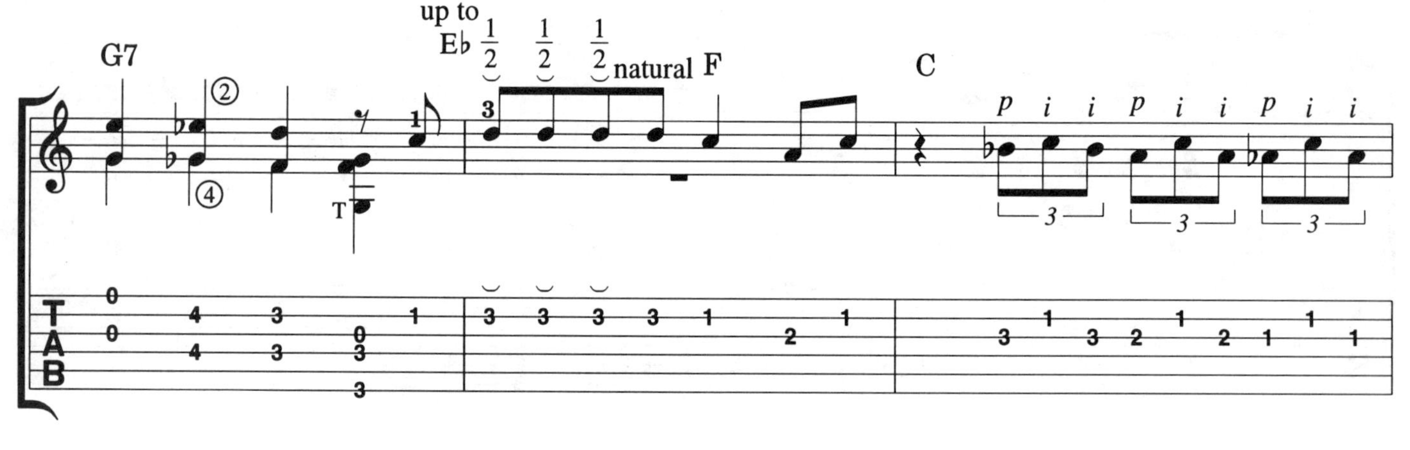
G7
up to
E♭
natural
F
C
p i i p i i p i i
T
A
B

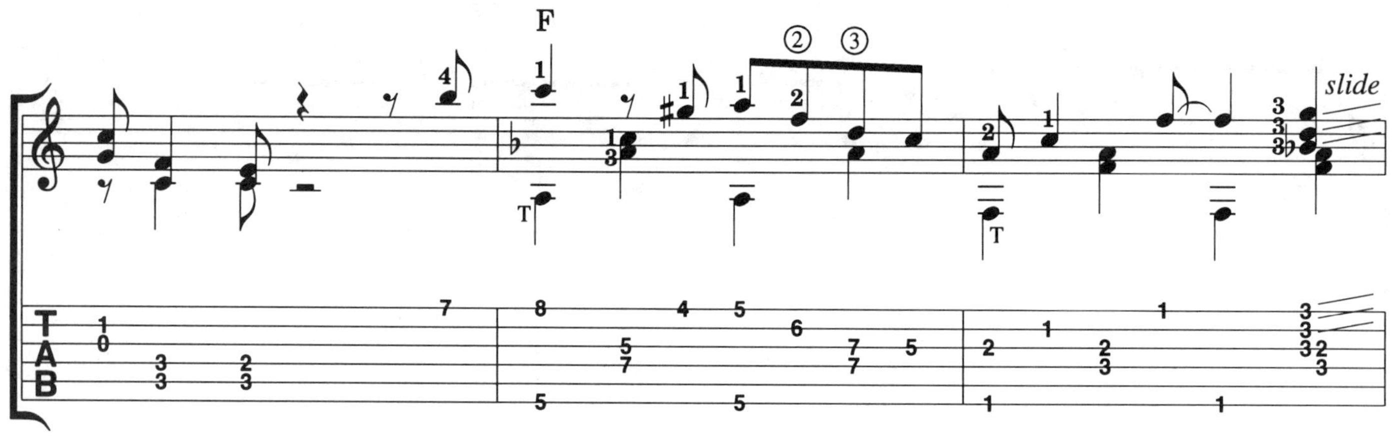
F
slide
T
A
B

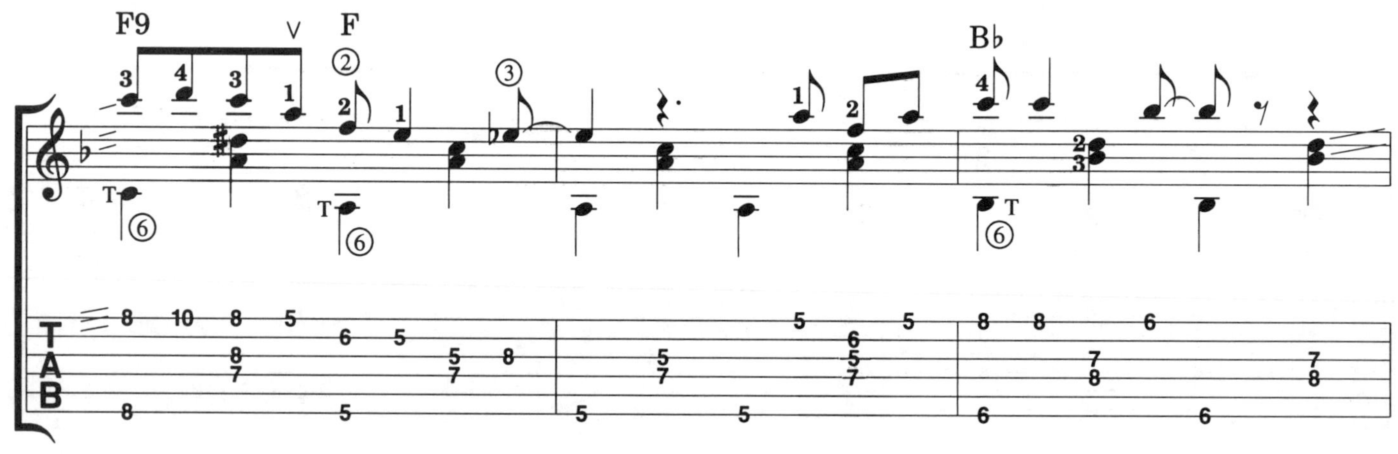
F9
F
B♭
T
A
B

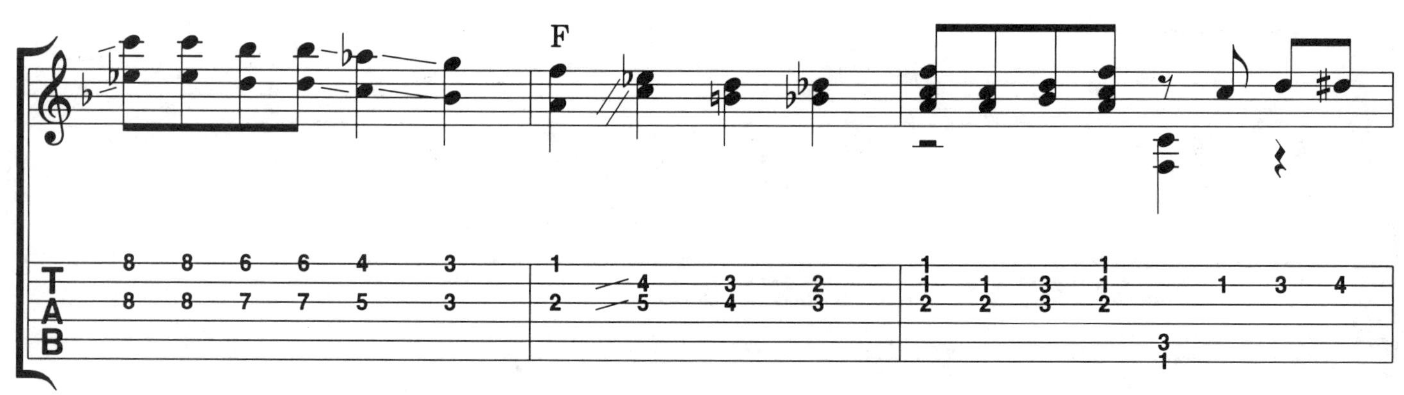
F
T
A
B

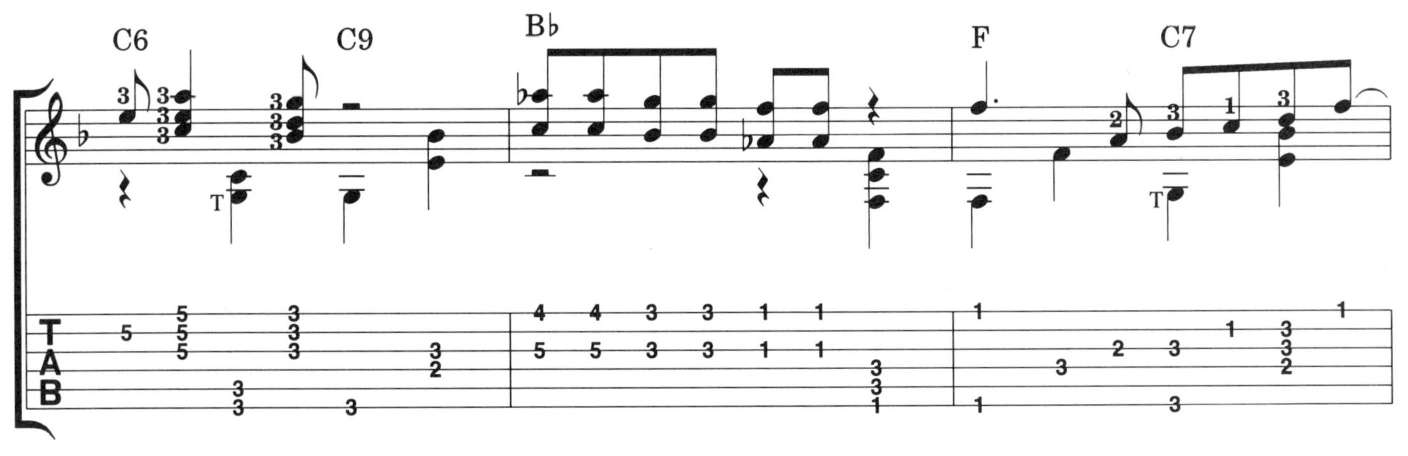
C6
C9
B♭
F
C7

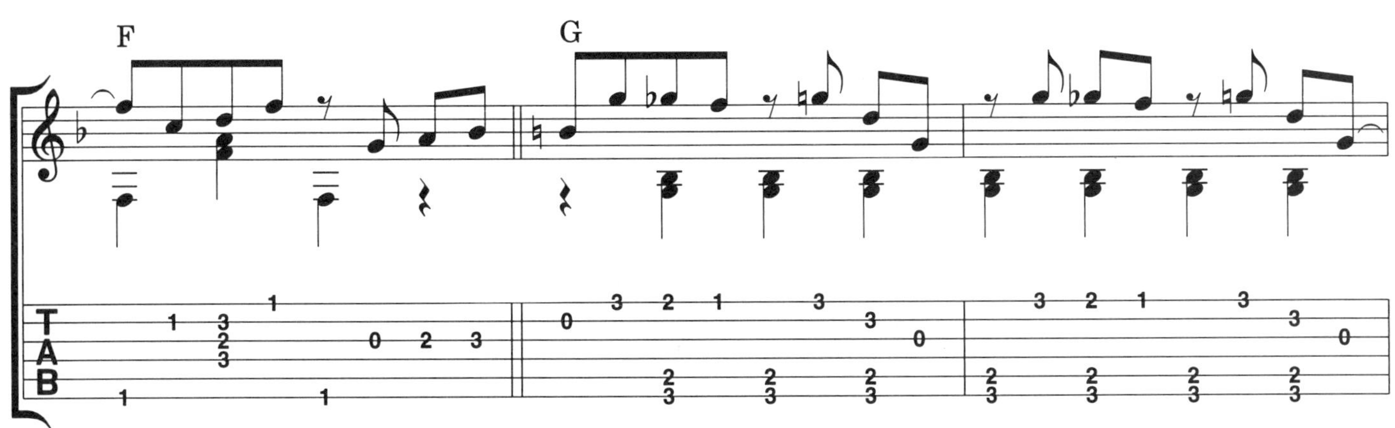
F
G

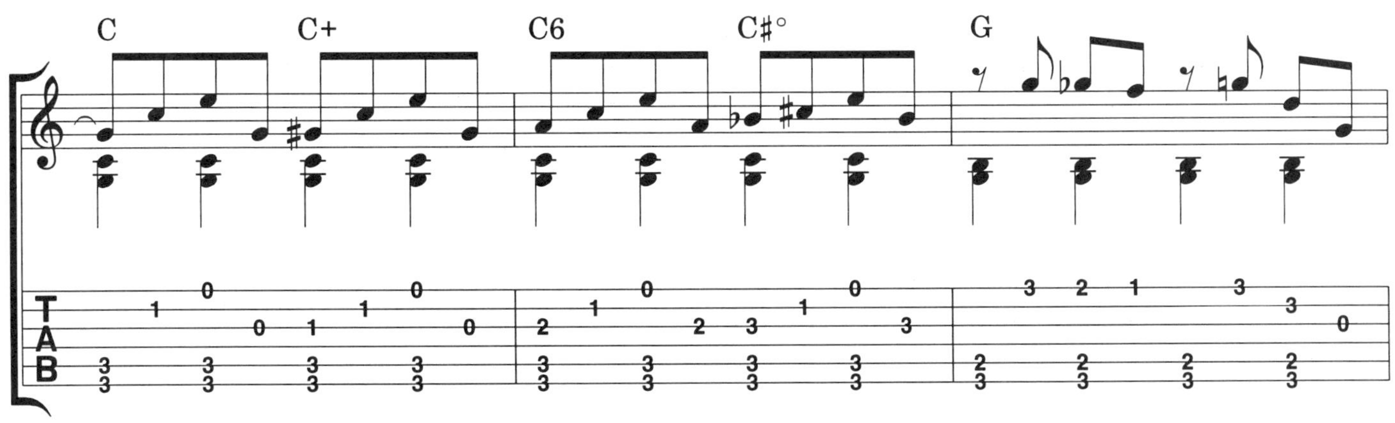
C
C+
C6
C♯°
G

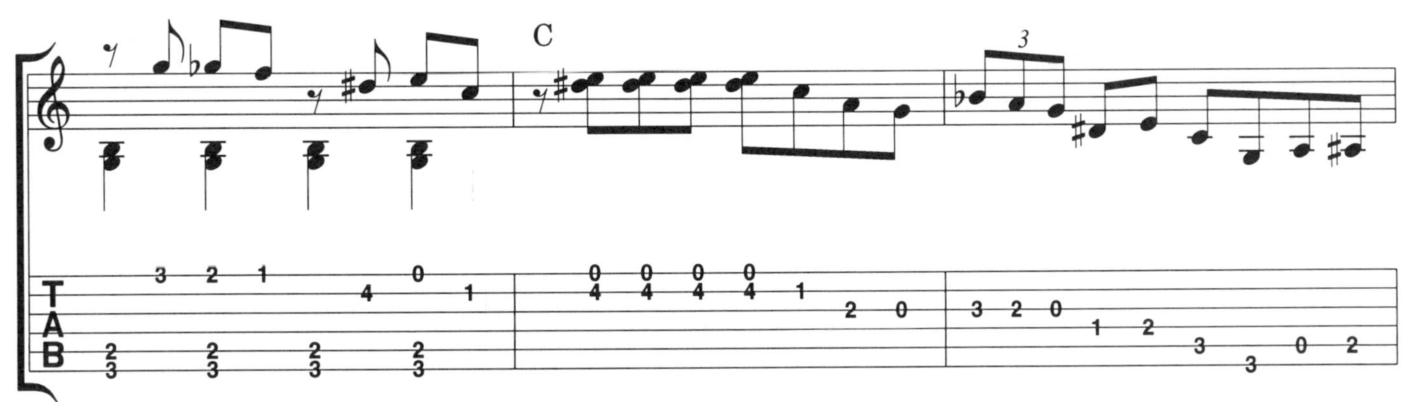
C

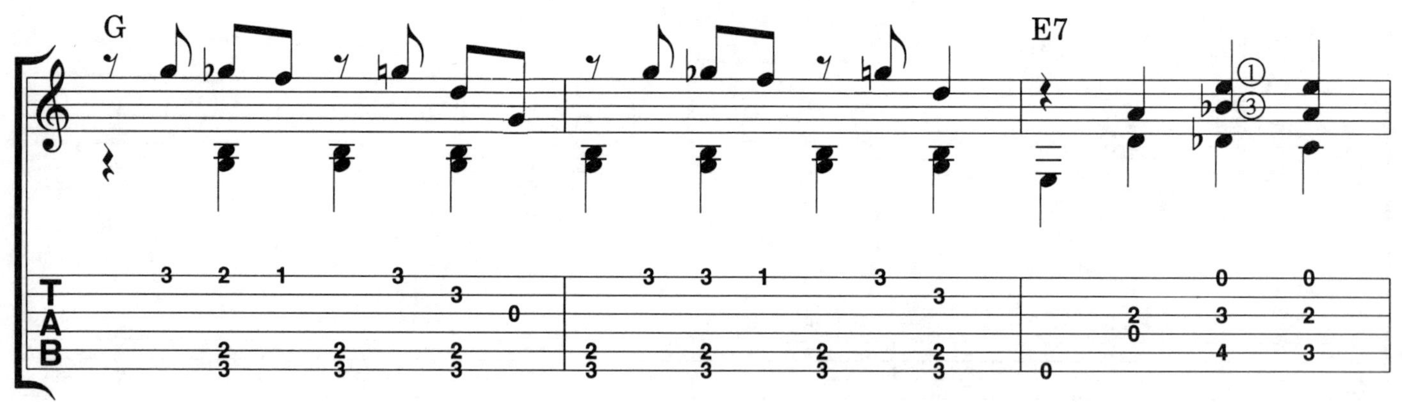
G
E7

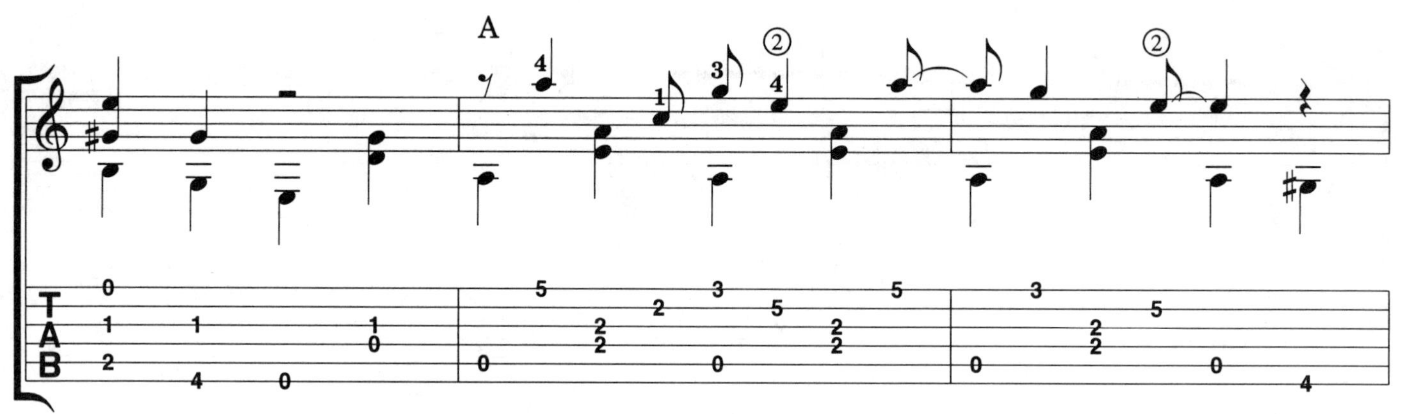
A

D7
G
dead chord

F
C
F
Fm
C

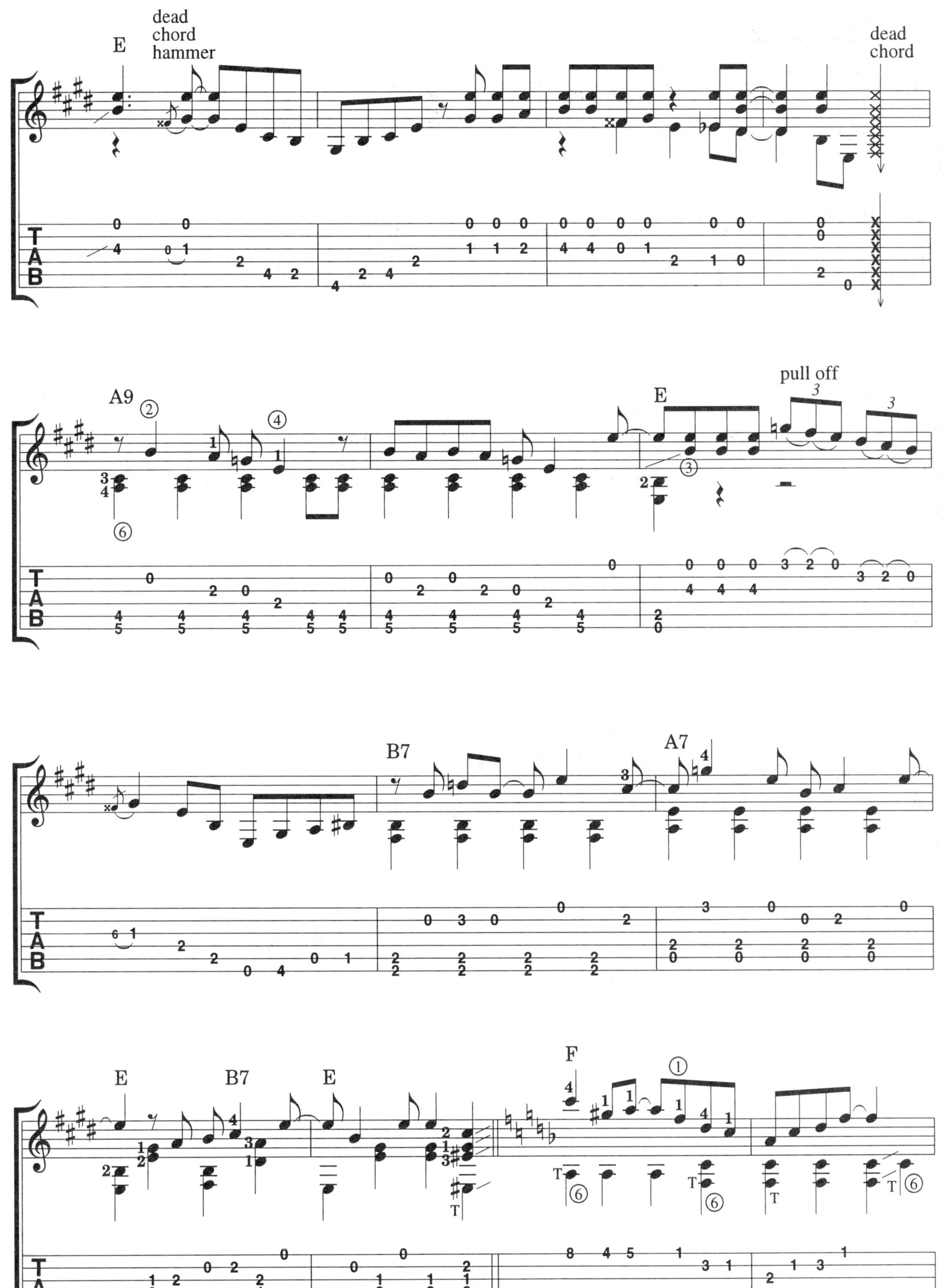

E
dead
chord
hammer
dead
chord
A9
pull off
E
B7
A7
E
B7
E
F

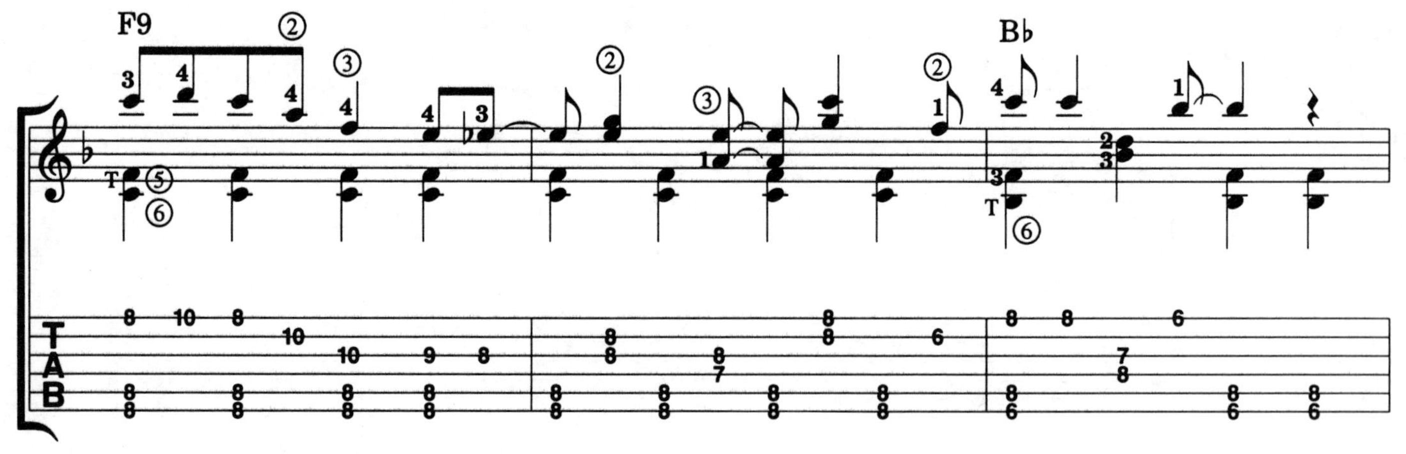
F9
B♭

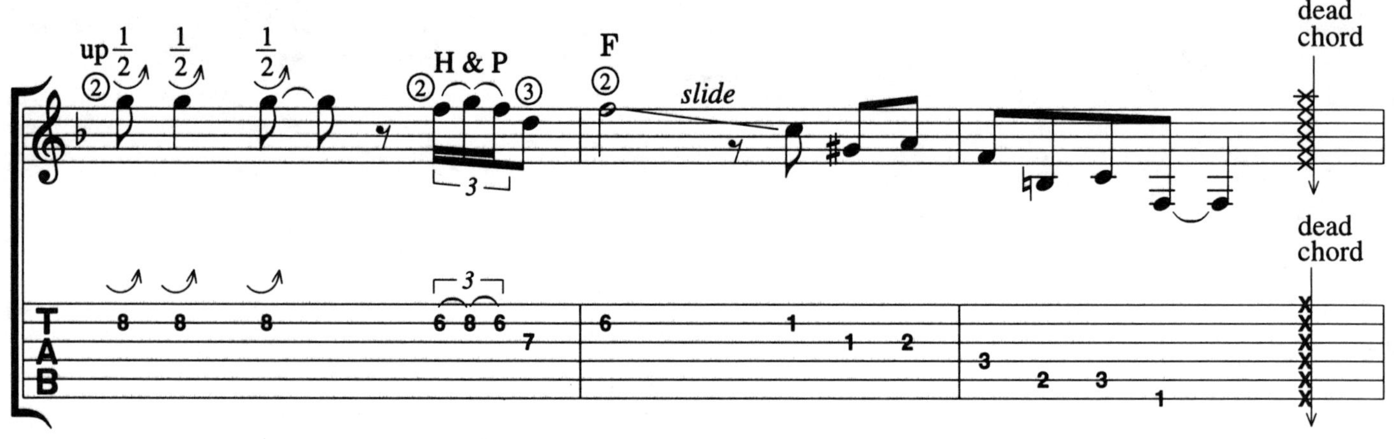
up
H & P
F
slide
dead chord
dead chord

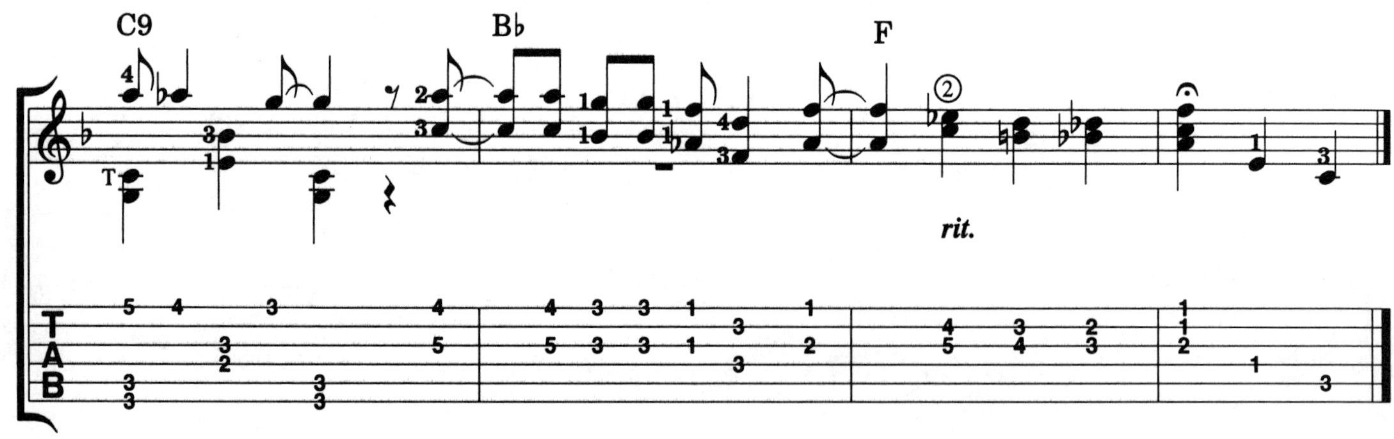
C9
B♭
F
rit.

MERLE'S BUCK DANCE

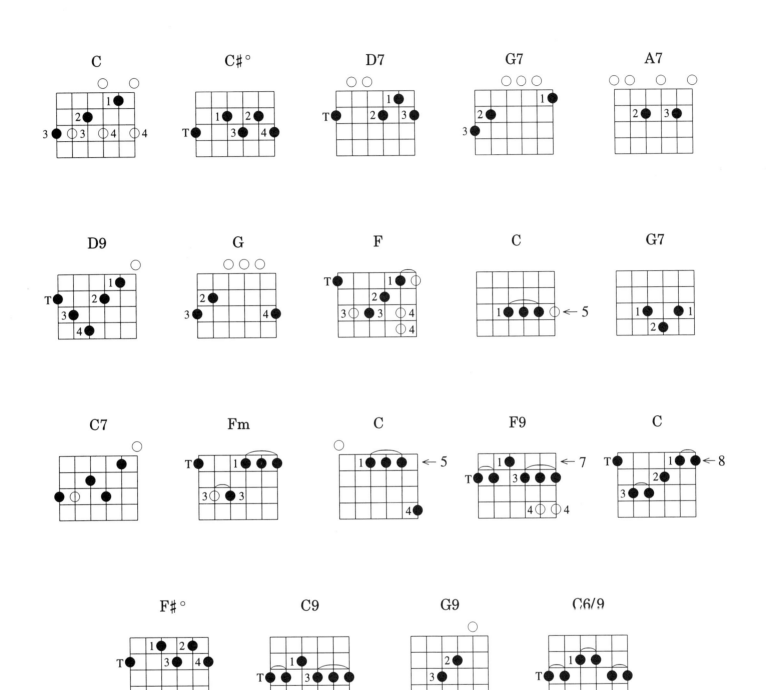

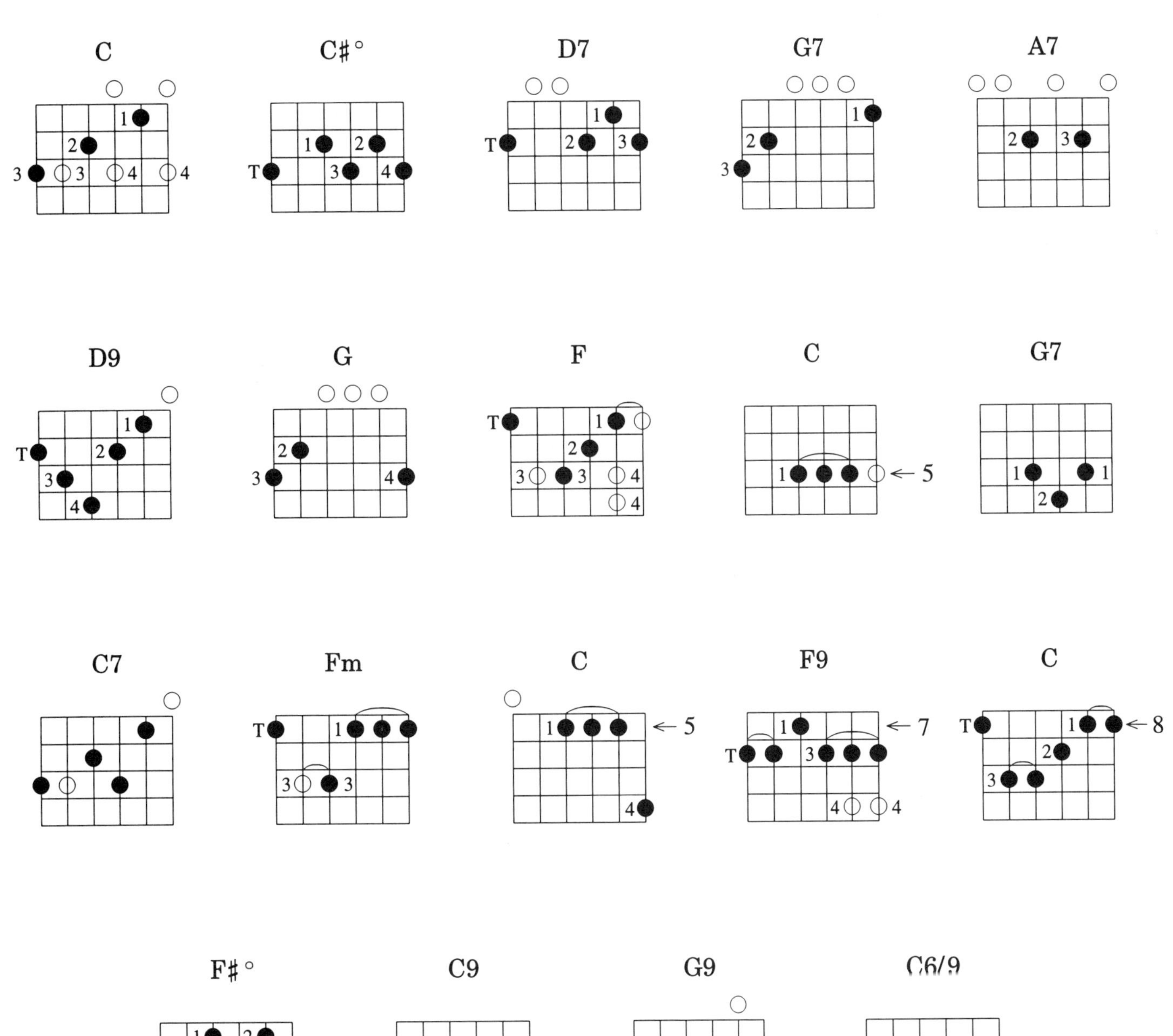

MERLE'S BUCK DANCE

Merle Travis

Words and music by Merle Travis.

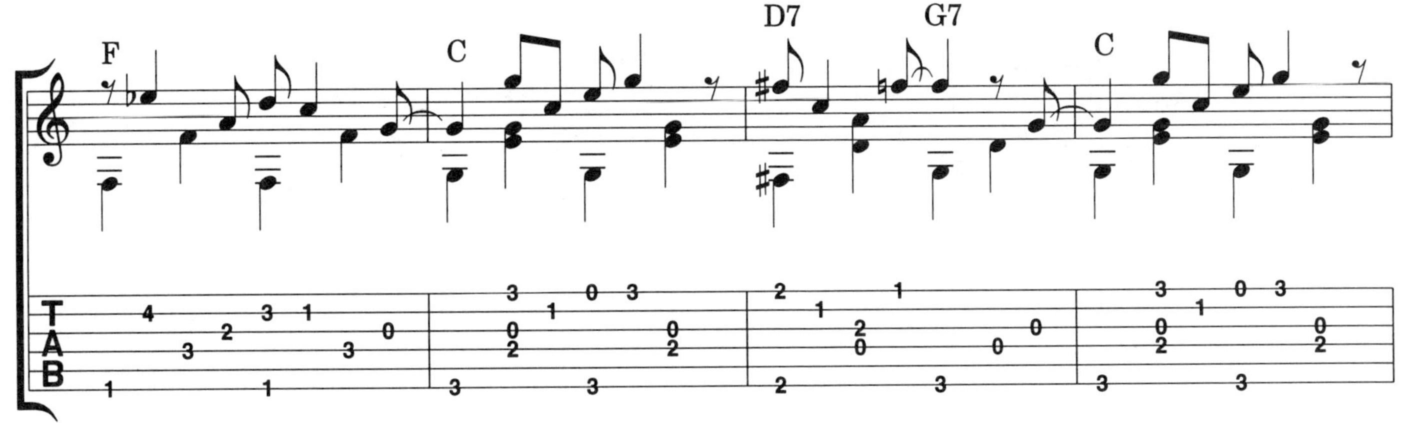
F
C
D7
G7
C

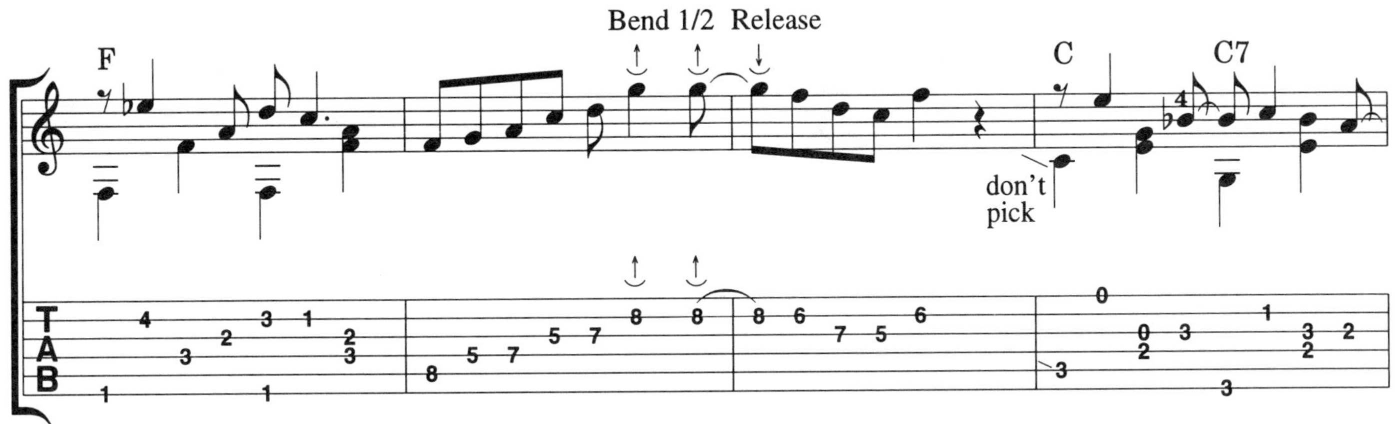
F
Bend 1/2
Release
C
C7
don't
pick

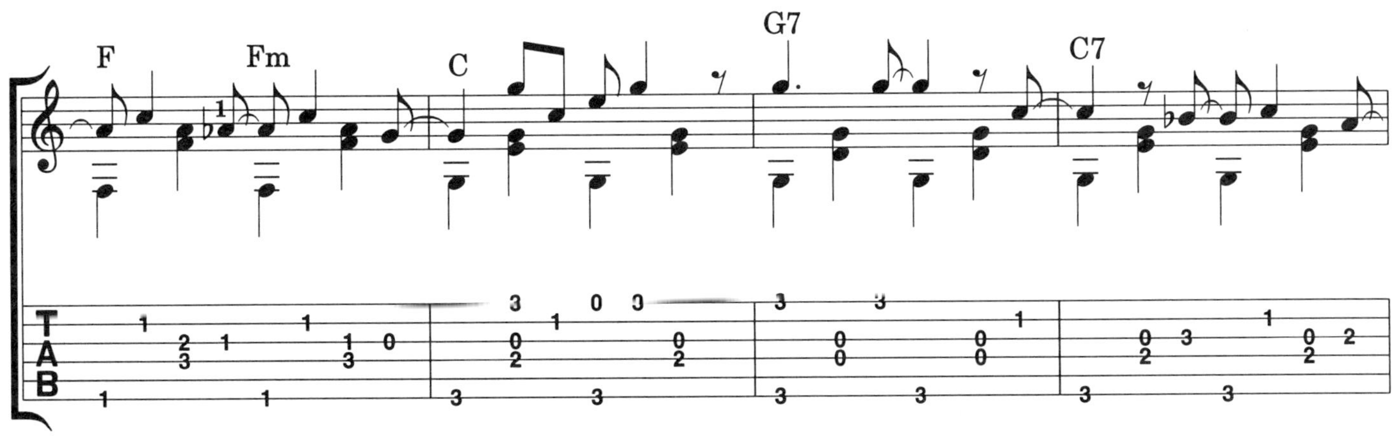
F
Fm
C
G7
C7

F
Fm
C
G
C
C

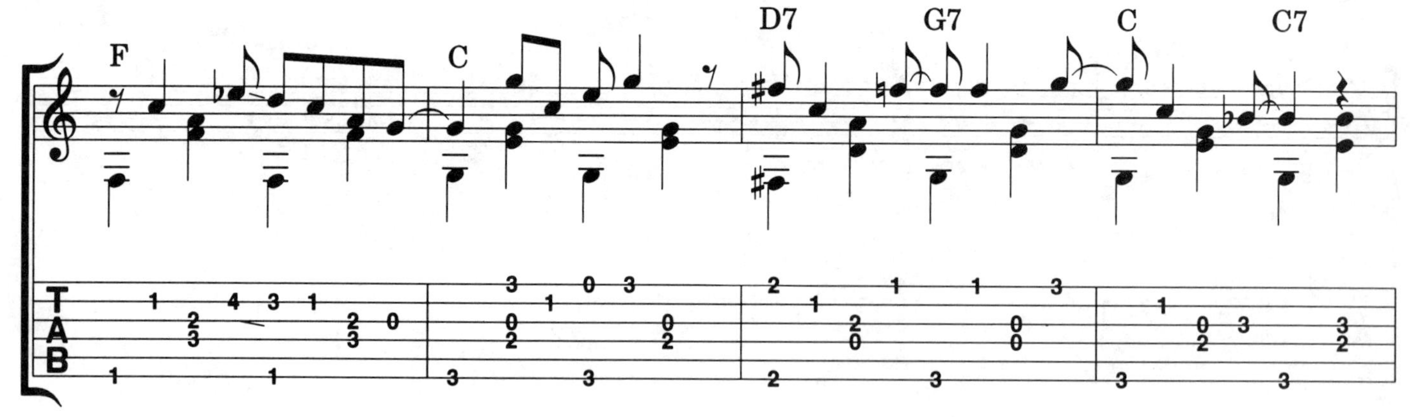
F
C
D7
G7
C
C7

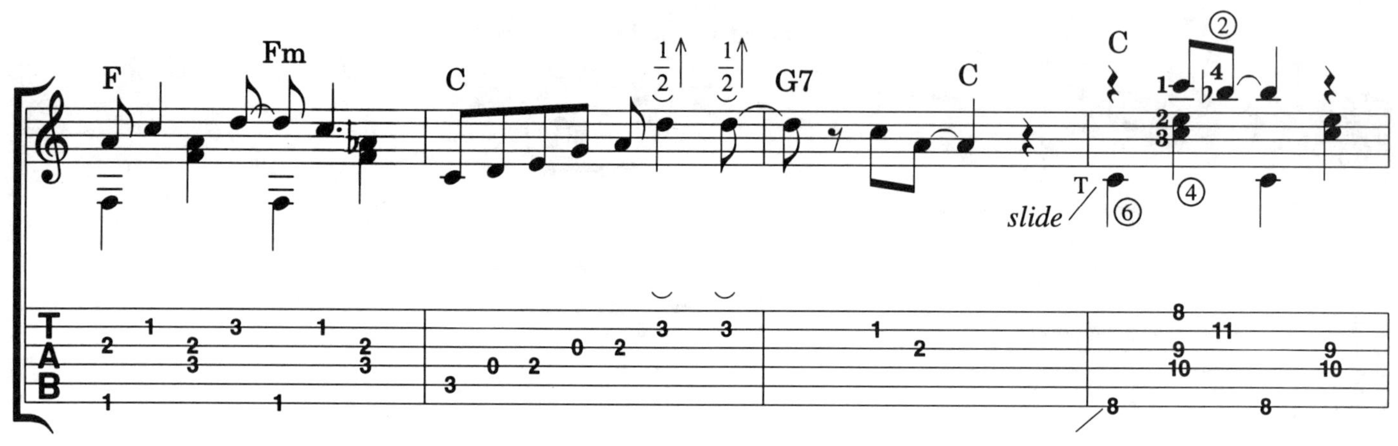
F
Fm
C
G7
C
C
slide

F9
C
D9
G

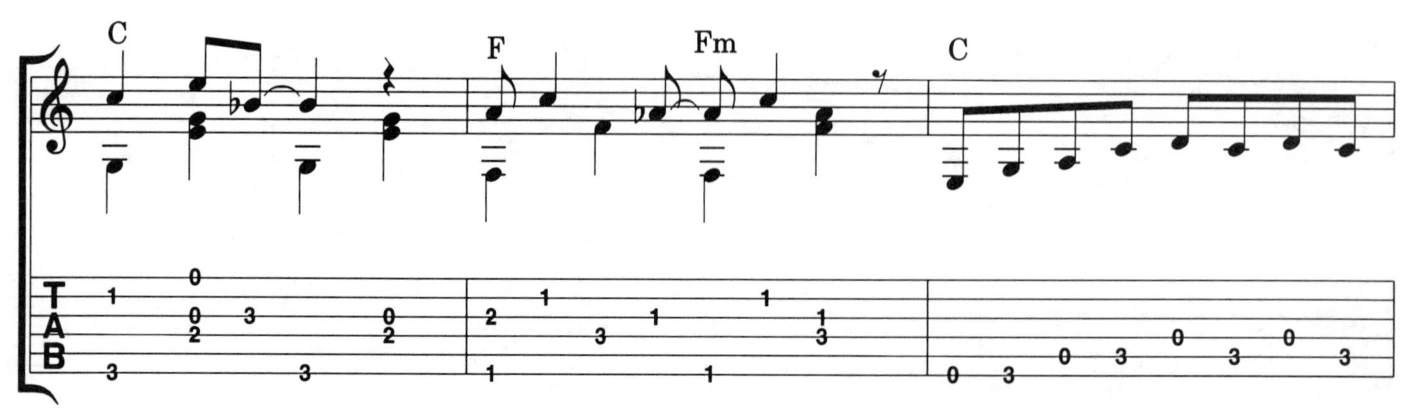
C
F
Fm
C

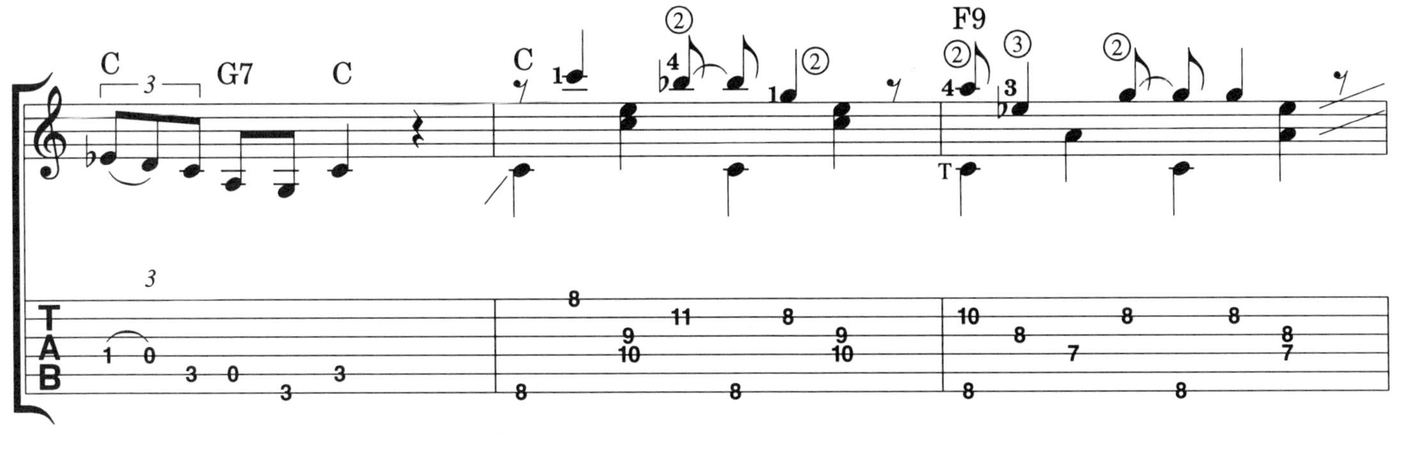
C
G7
C
C
F9
T
3
T
A
B

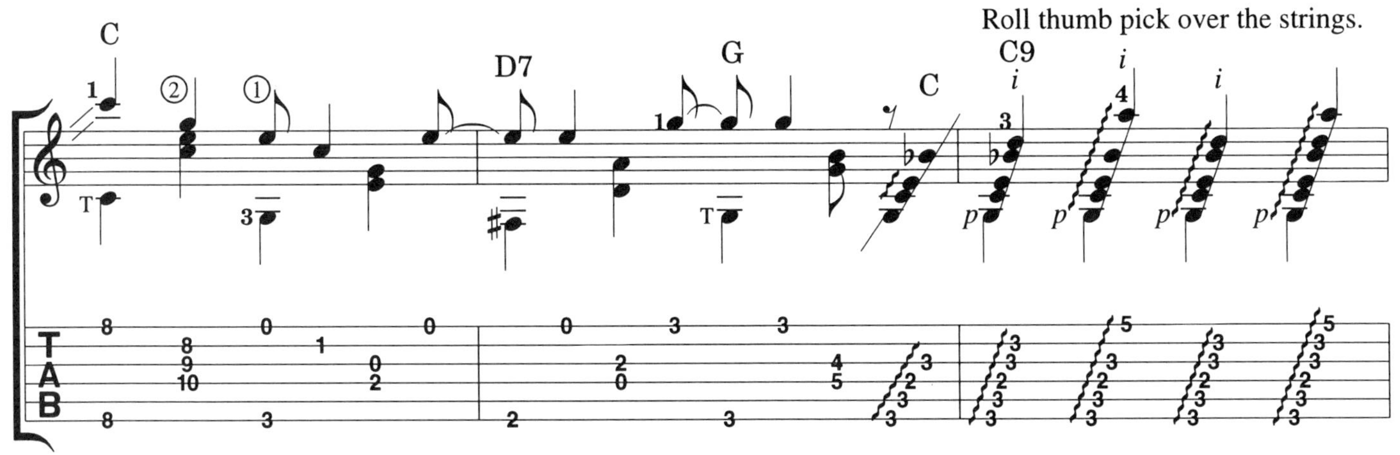
Roll thumb pick over the strings.
C
D7
G
C
C9
T
A
B

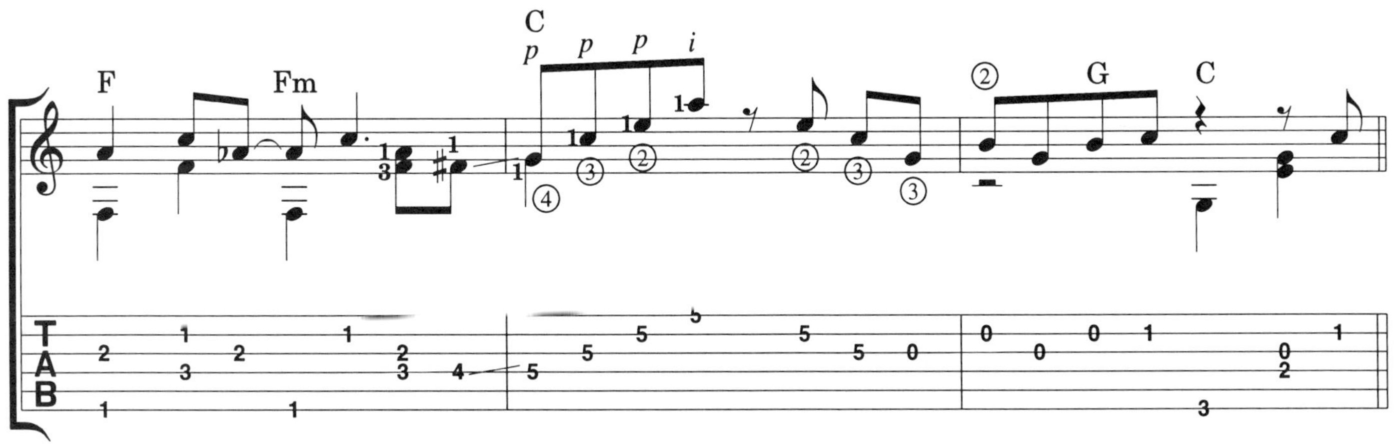
F
Fm
C
G
C
T
A
B

C
F
C
T
A
B

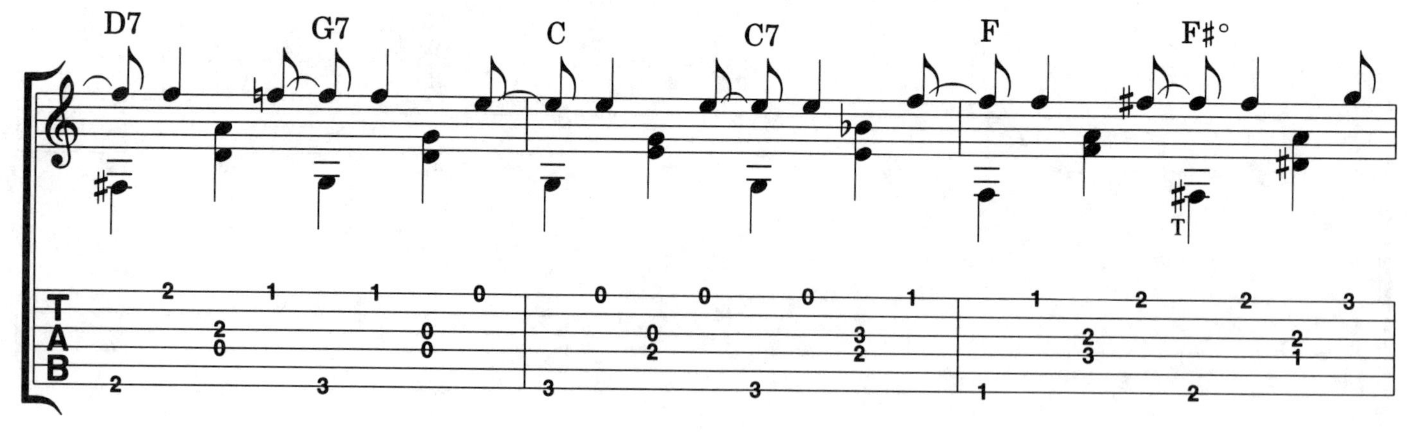
D7
G7
C
C7
F
F♯°
T
TAB

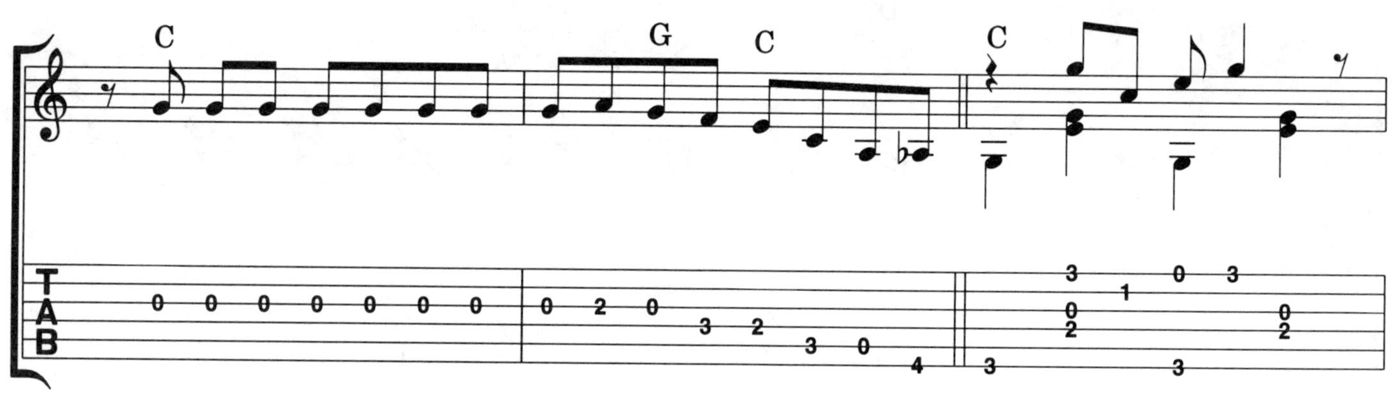
C
G
C
C
TAB

F
C
D7
G
TAB

C
F
Fm
C
TAB

F
Fm
C
F
G
C
TAB

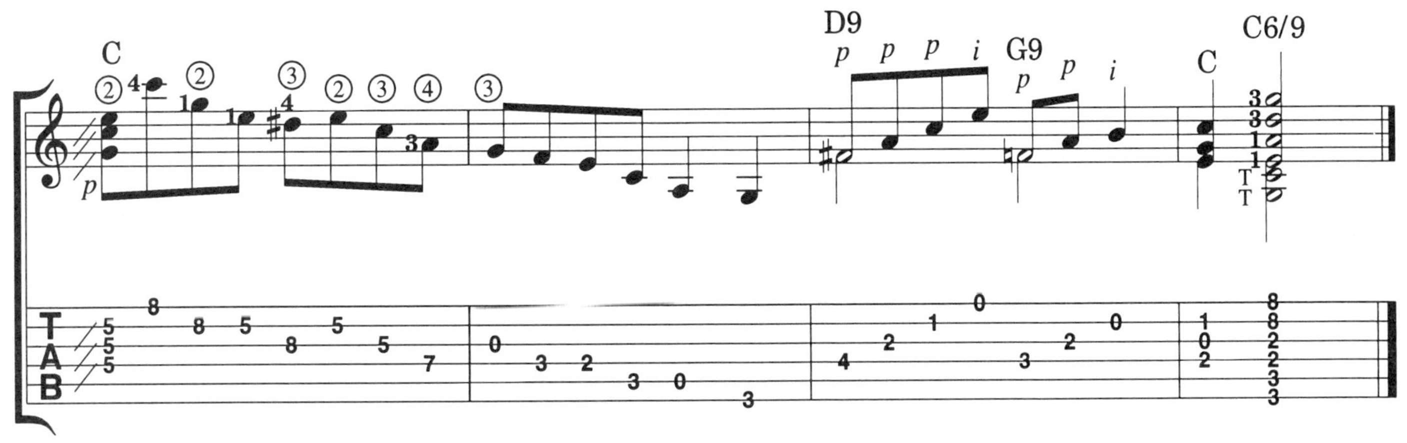
C
D9
G9
C
C6/9
TAB

DANCE OF THE GOLDENROD

I think "Dance of the Goldenrod" is one of the most beautiful melodies that Travis ever composed. I heard a Kentucky guitarist named Johnny Hammer play it on a local radio station, before I heard Travis play it. He announced that Merle had written it.

I believe the first time I heard Travis do it was on the recording of the vocal version which was released in the early fifties.

He recorded various versions of the tune, one of which is on the "Atkins Travis Traveling Show," which won a grammy.

The chords he used for this solo were somewhat unusual, such as the A9 using only one finger on the ④th string, eleventh fret, with the other five strings open. By leaving that finger in position and adding other notes on the ②nd string while picking the first four strings together, he played melody and harmony.

Merle said he wrote this tune when he was a young man.

I believe this melody, with the chord structure, form and technique illustrates how Travis was a forward thinker, ahead of his time.

DANCE OF THE GOLDENROD

By Merle Travis

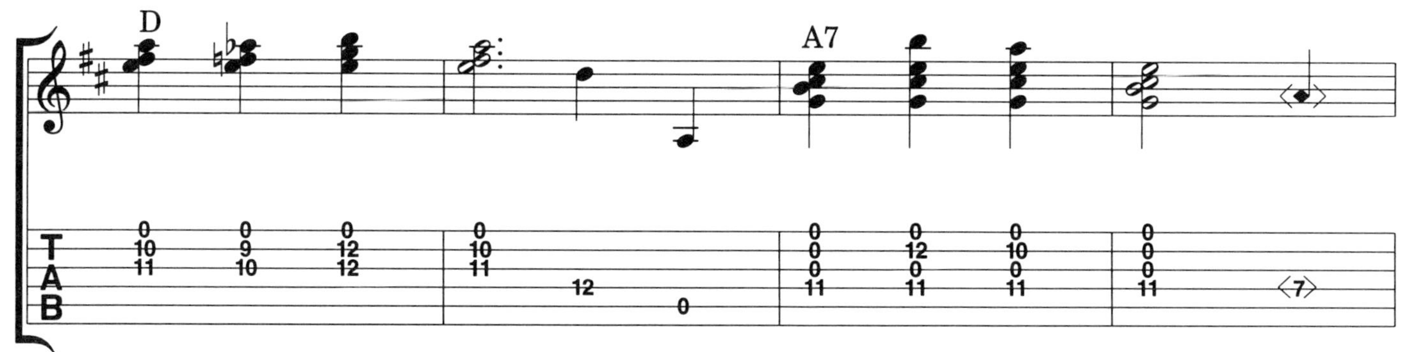
D
A7
T
A
B

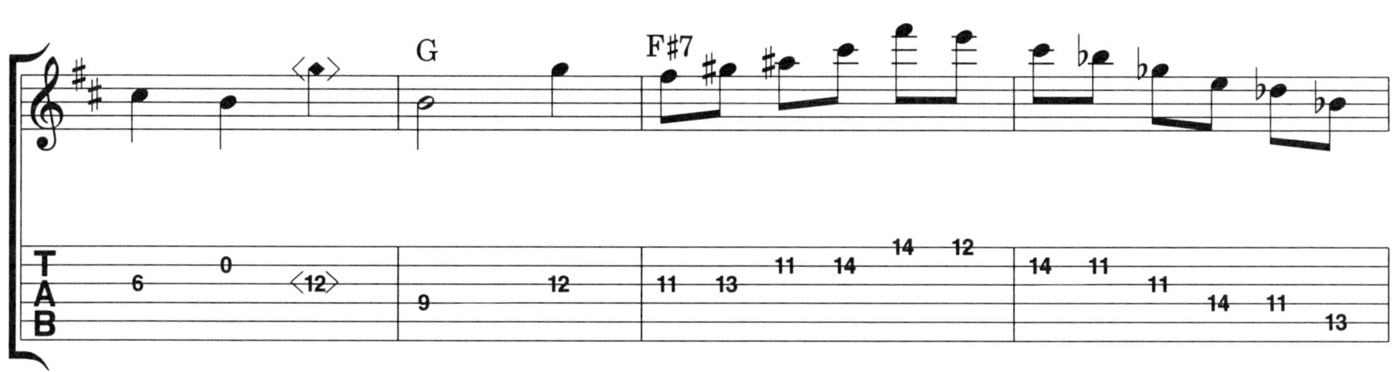
G
F♯7
T
A
B

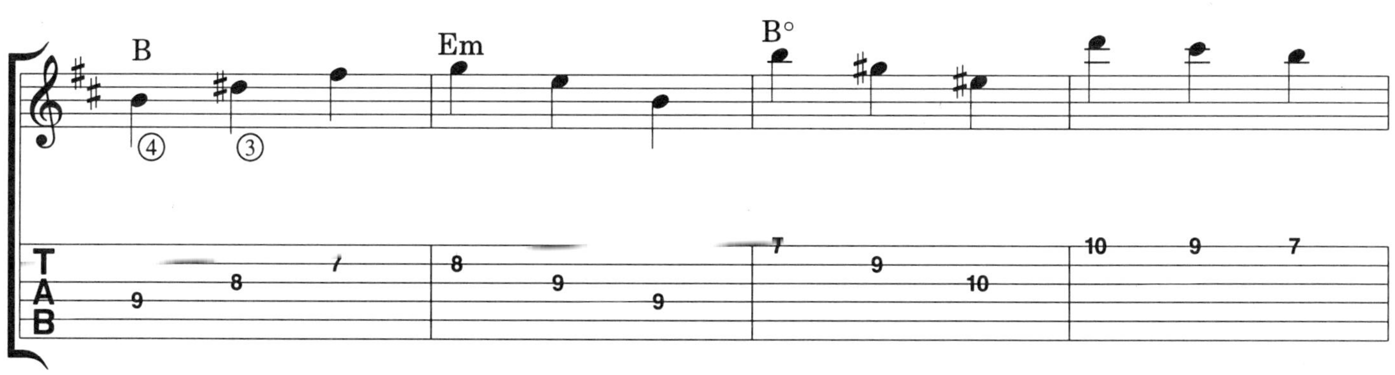
B
Em
B°
T
A
B

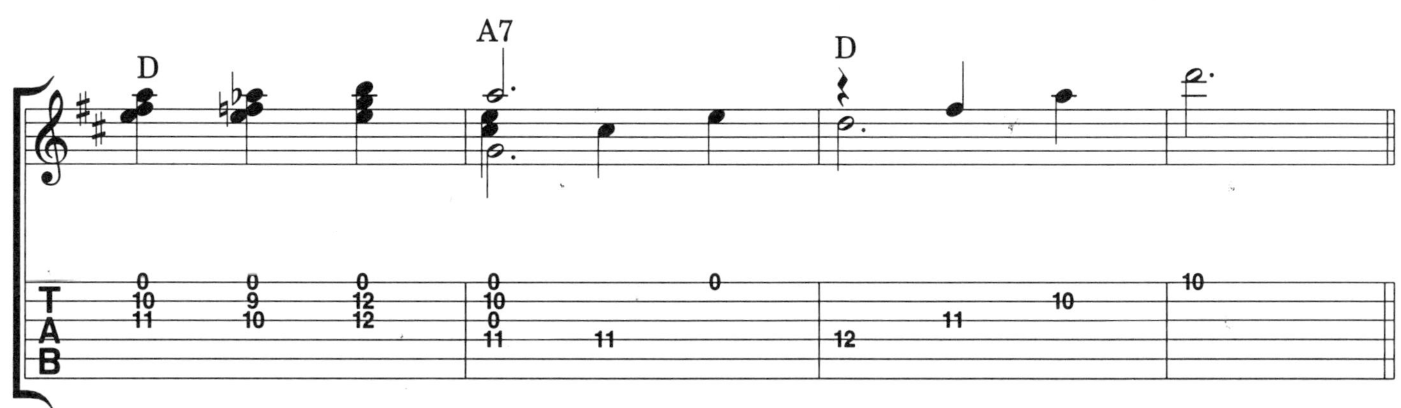
D
A7
D
T
A
B

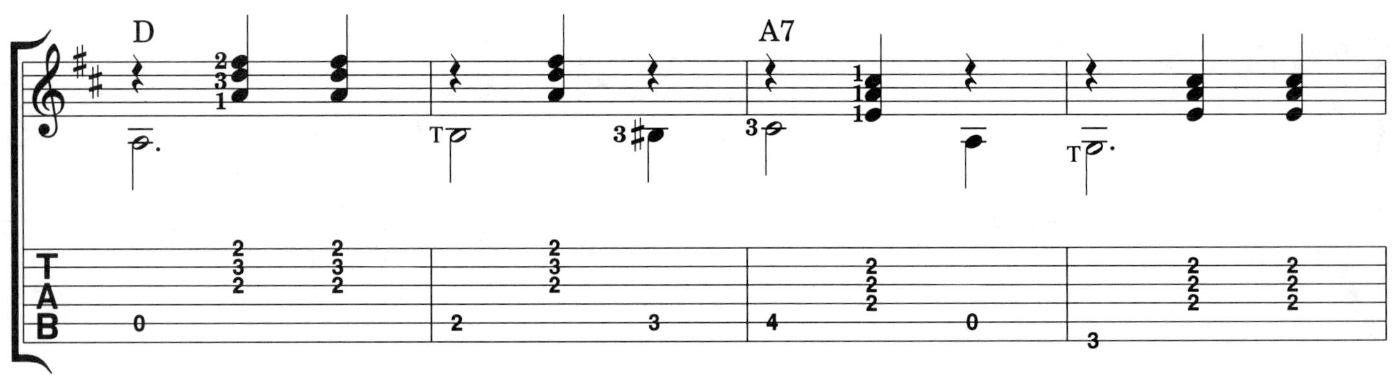
D
A7

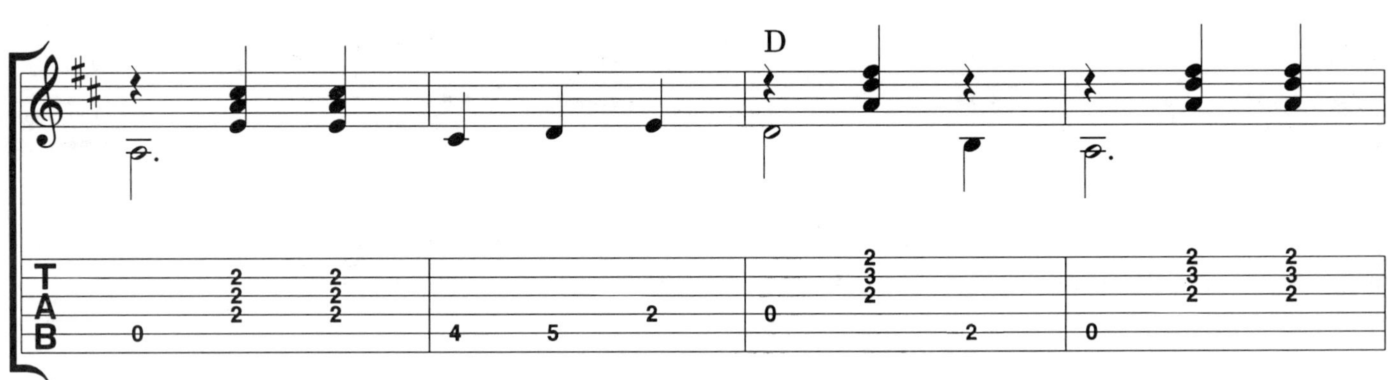
D

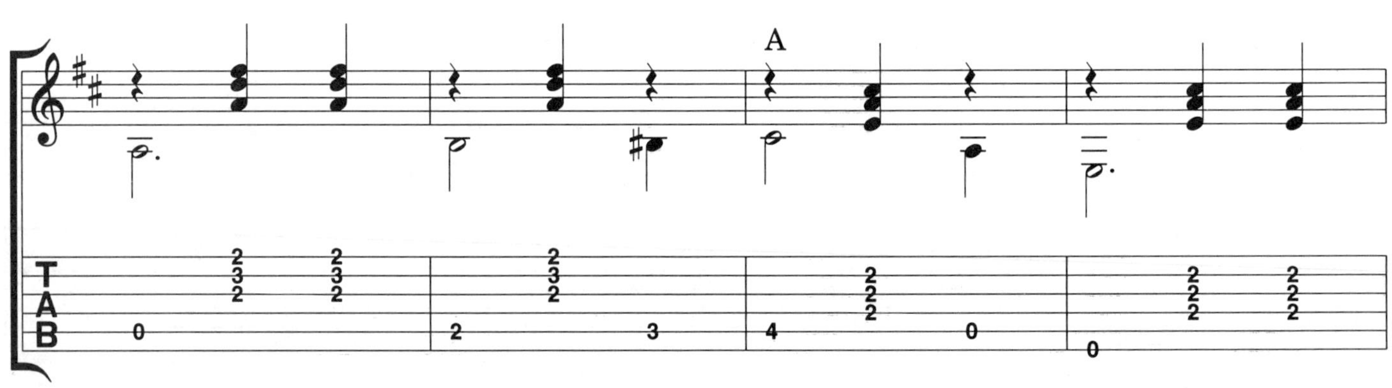
A

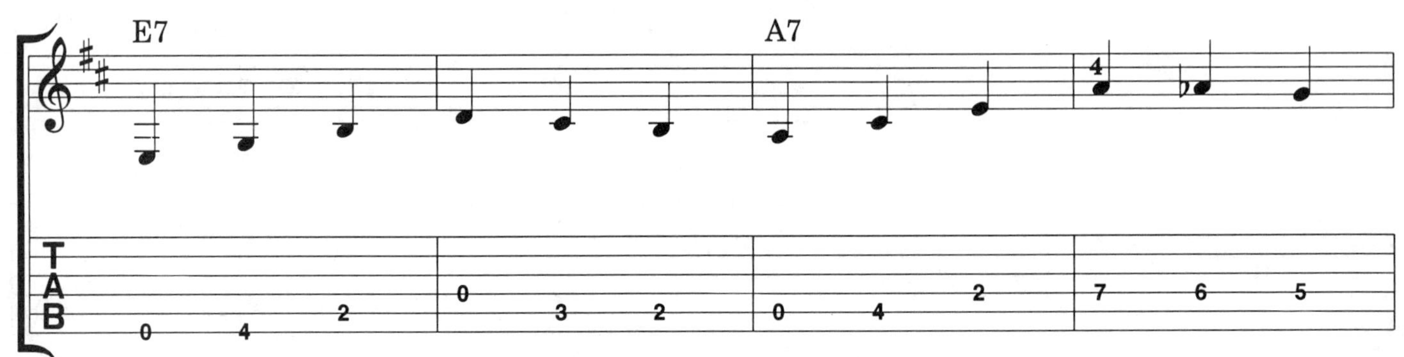
E7
A7

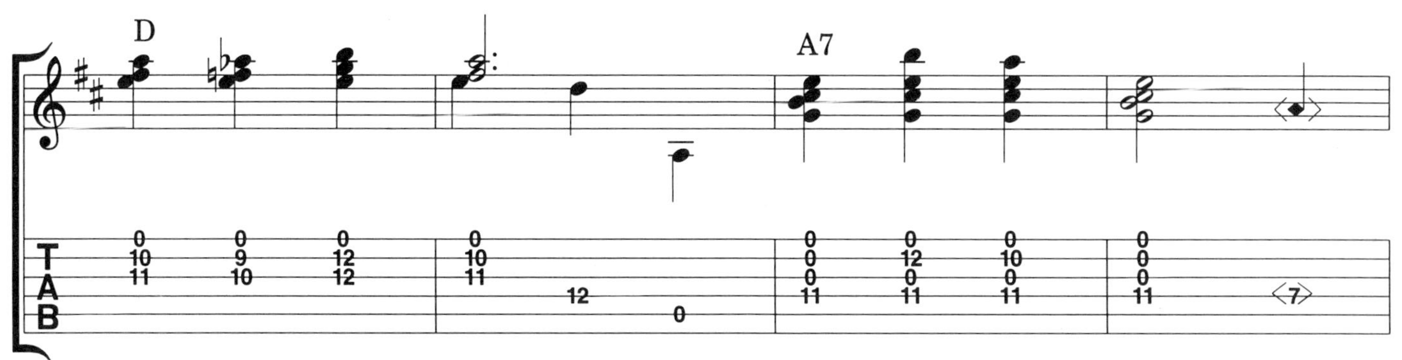
D
A7
T
A
B

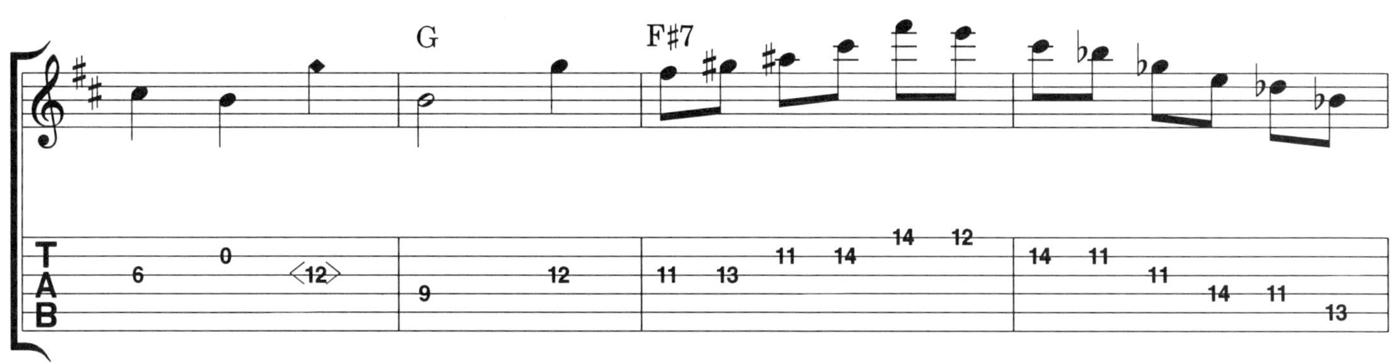
G
F#7
T
A
B

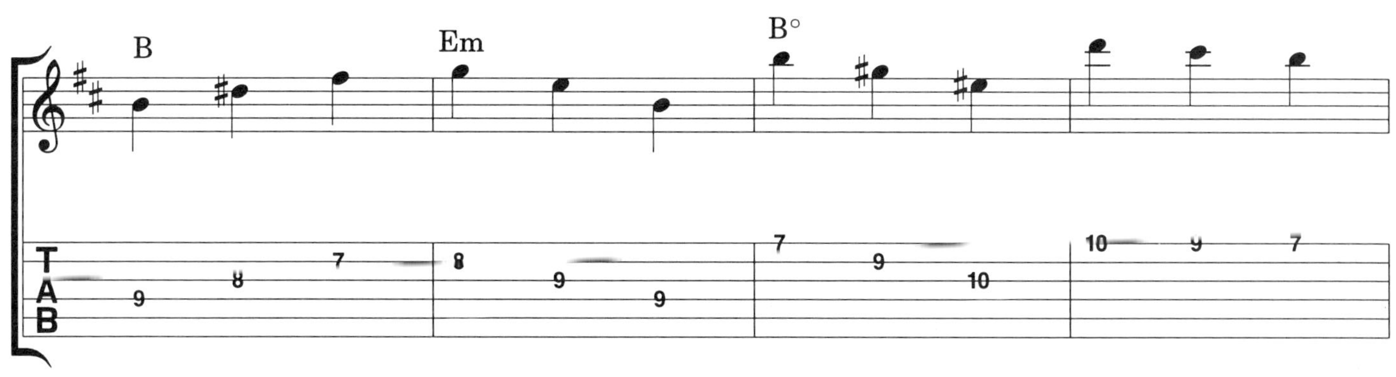
B
Em
B°
T
A
B

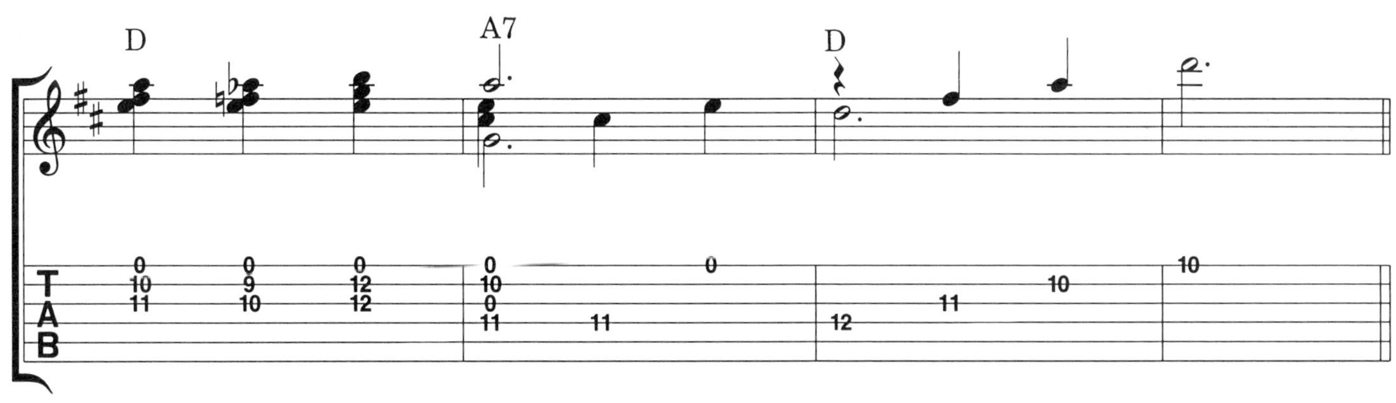
D
A7
D
T
A
B

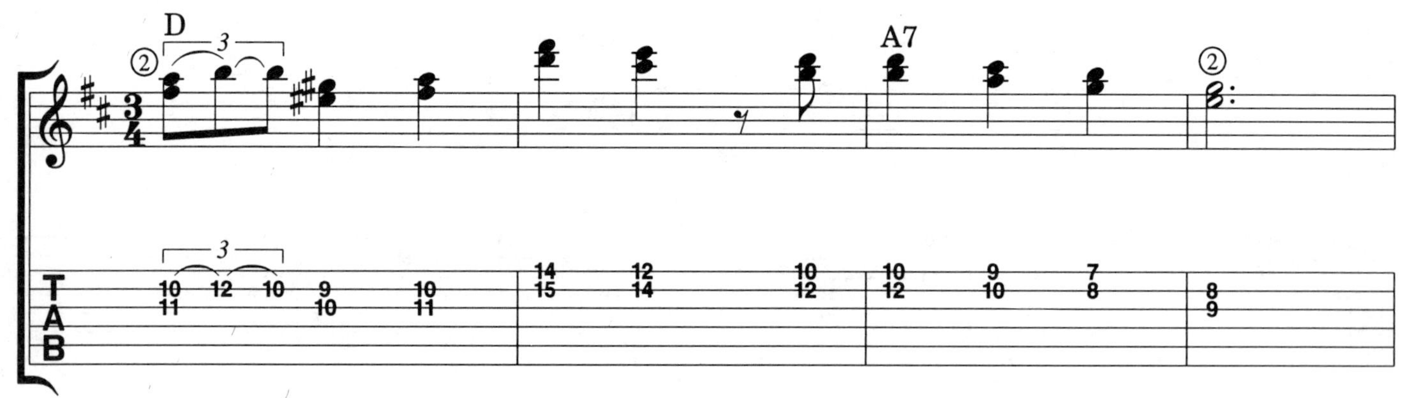
D
A7

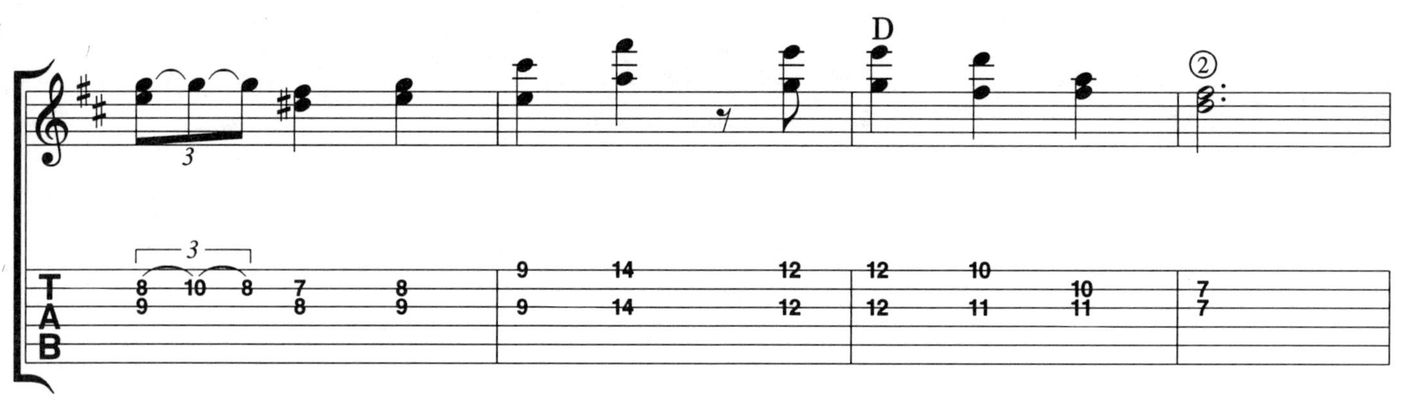
D

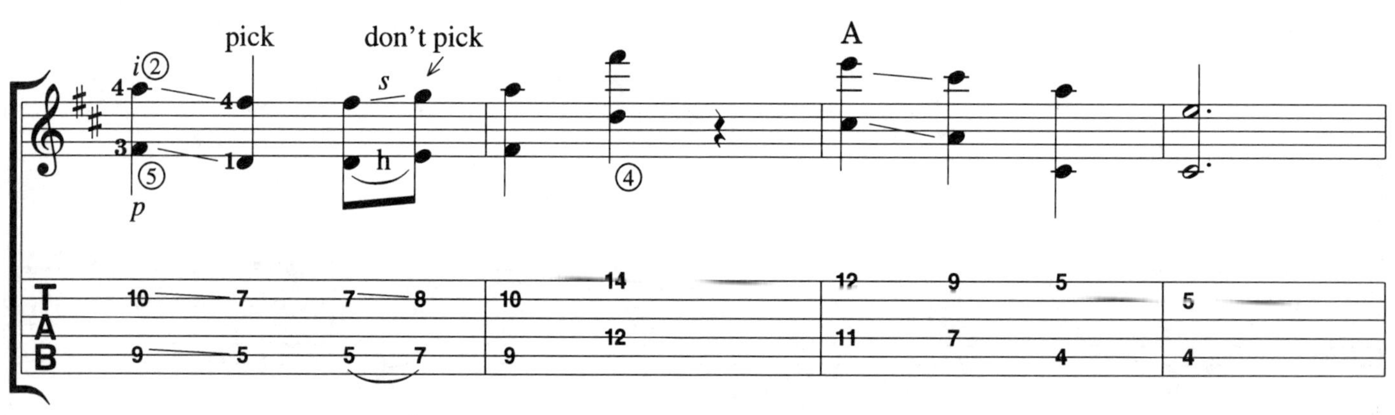
pick
don't pick
A

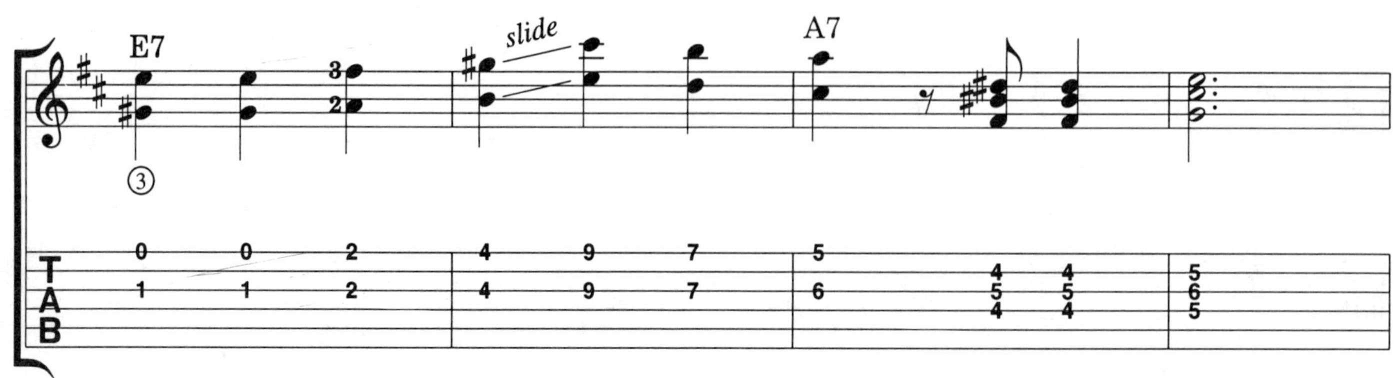
E7
slide
A7

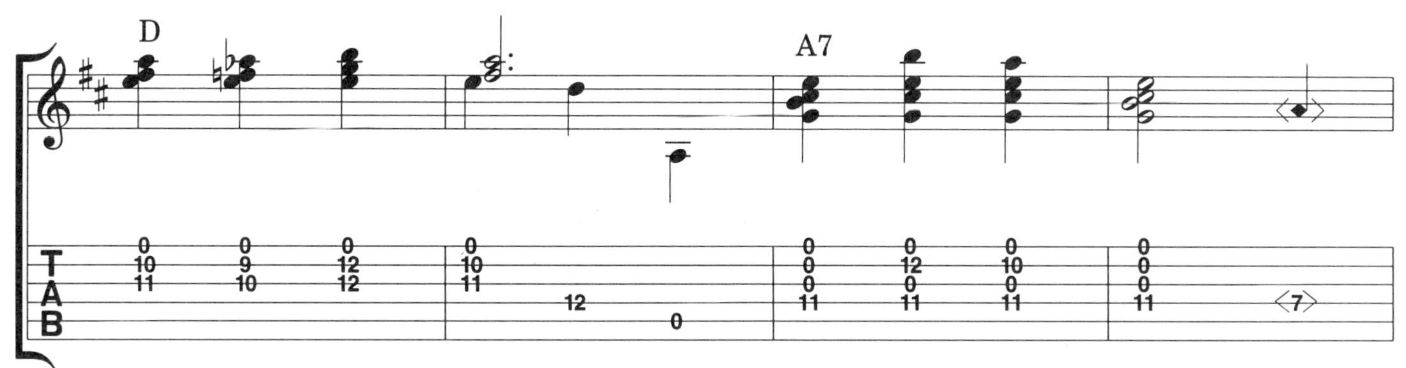
D
A7
TAB

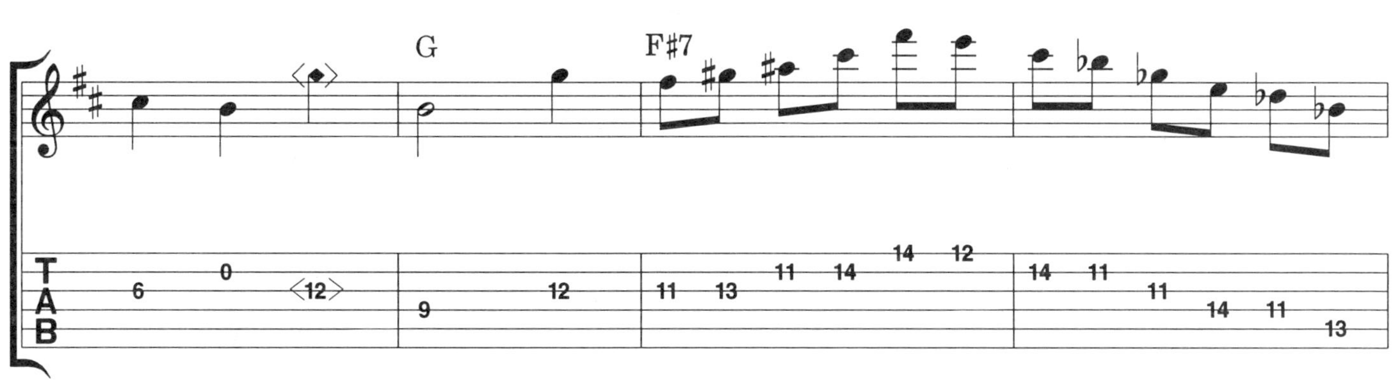
G
F#7
TAB

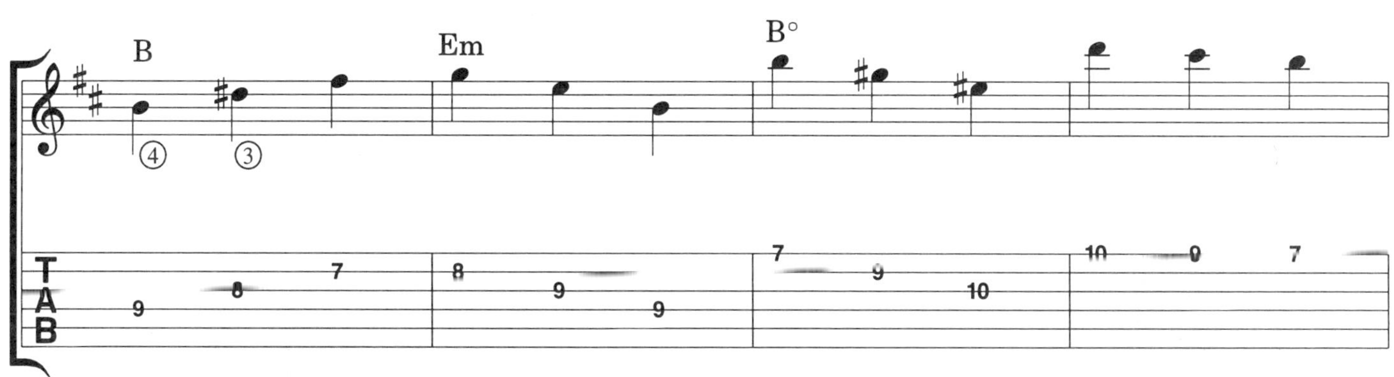
B
Em
B°
TAB

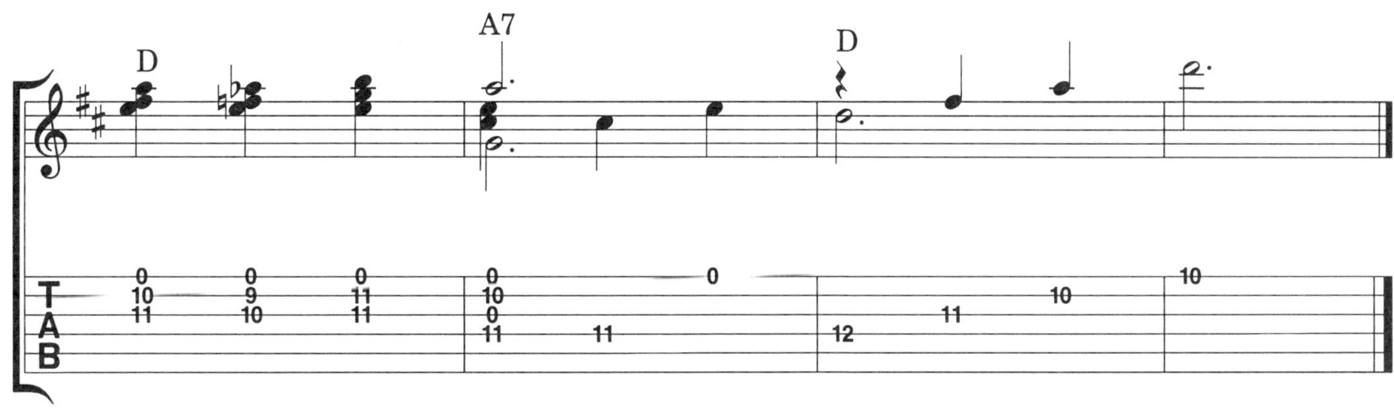
D
A7
D
TAB

CBS
CBS
AFRS
MERLE TRAVIS

DANCE OF THE GOLDENROD

Vocal Version

Merle Travis

On rare occasions, Travis would sing the words to Goldenrod. When this happened, he would modulate to the key of G for the bridge, then back to D for the last sixteen bars, as shown in the following arrangement.

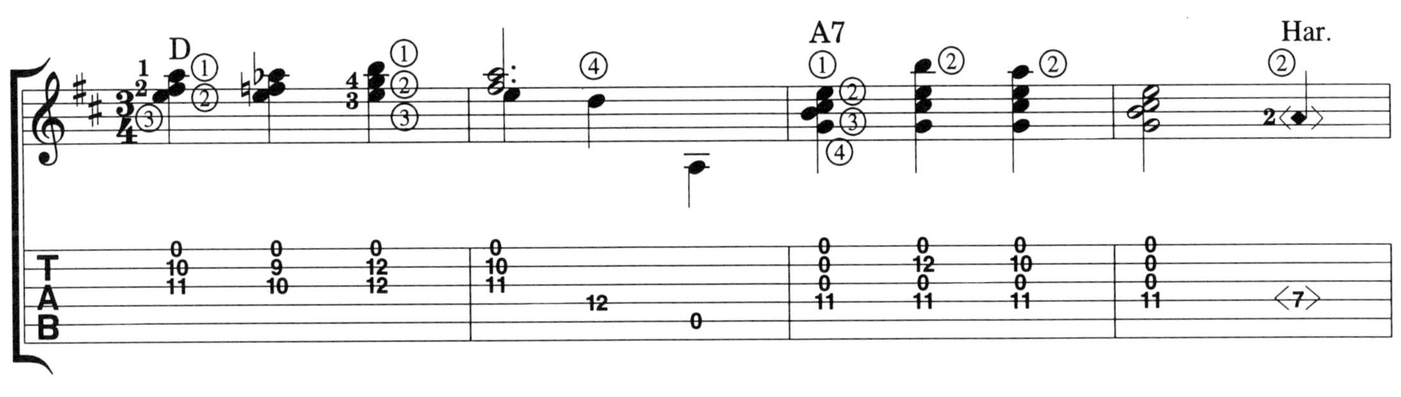

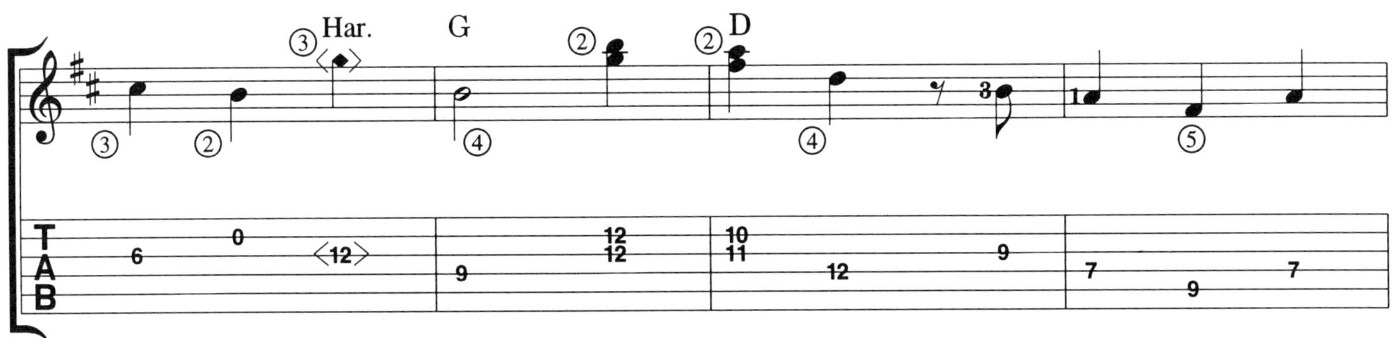

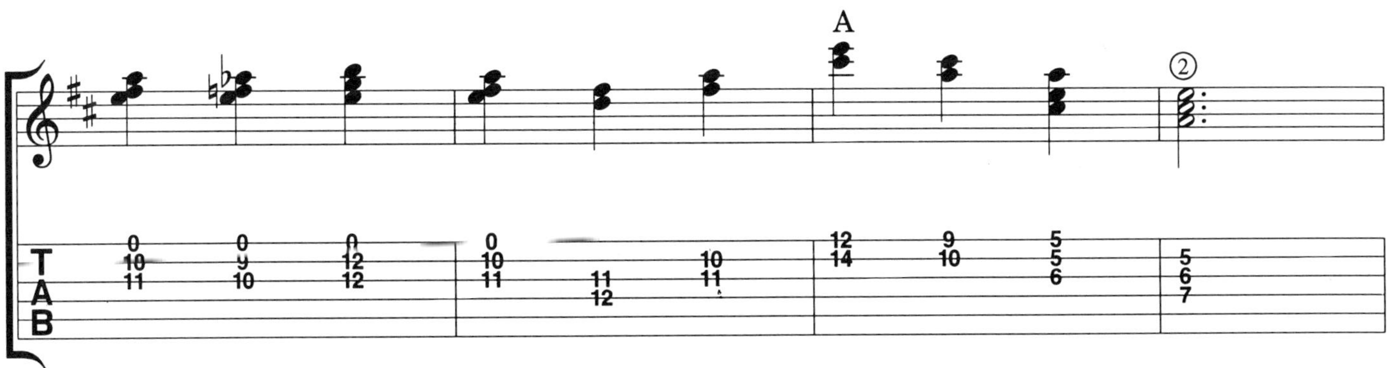

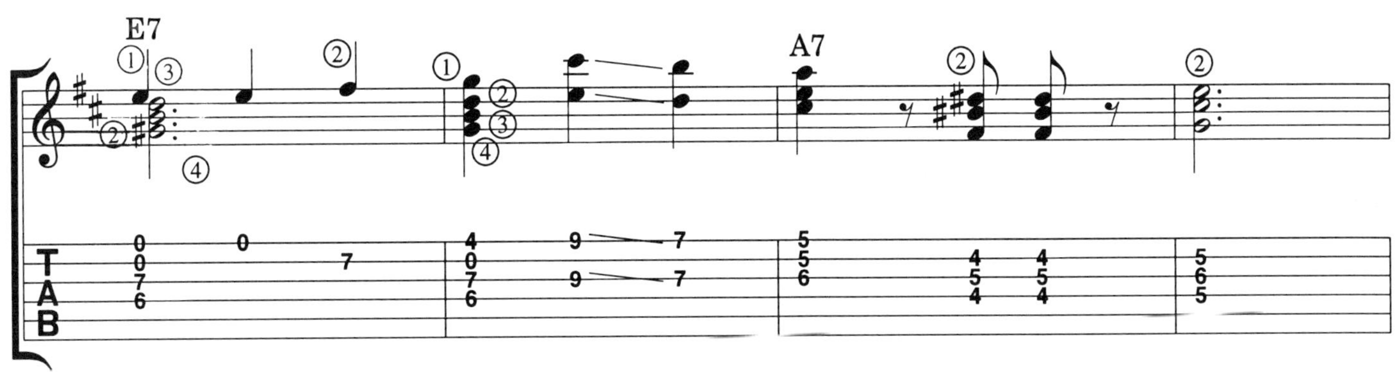

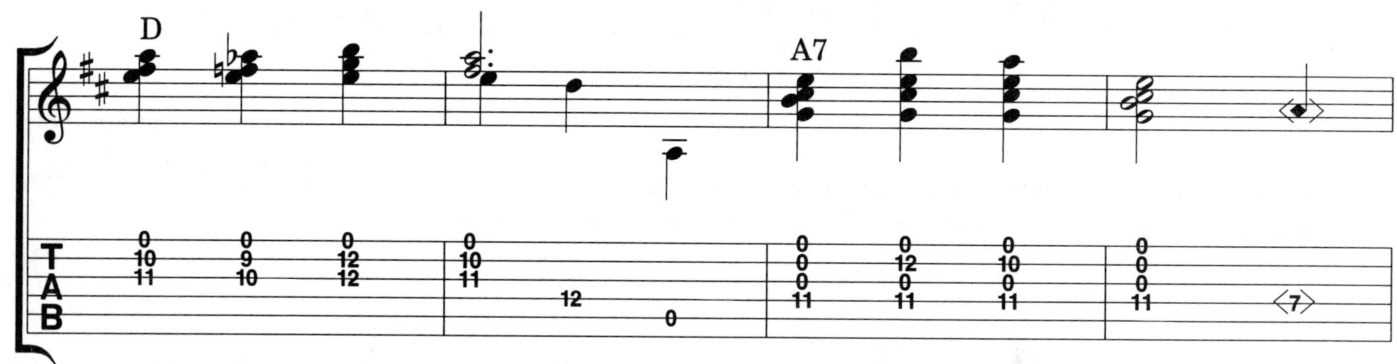
D
A7
TAB

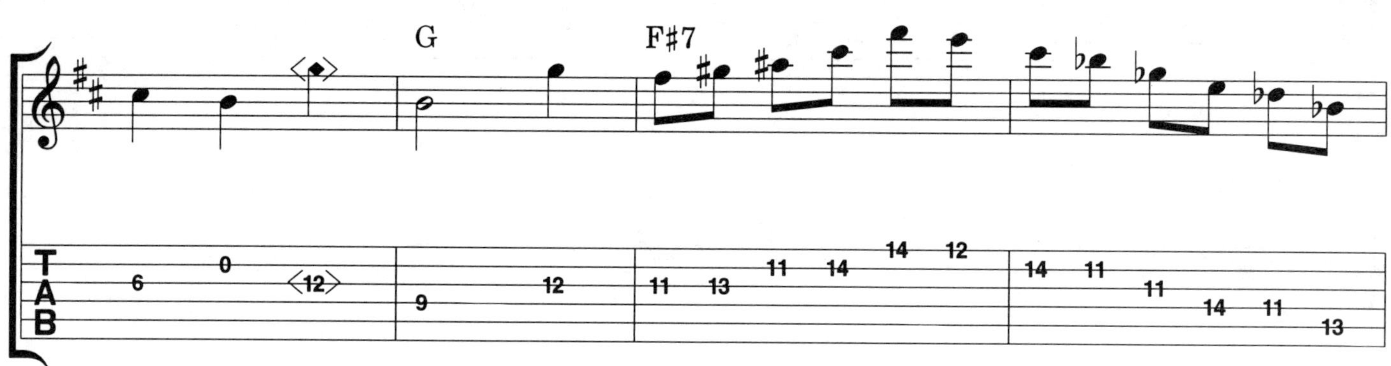
G
F#7
TAB

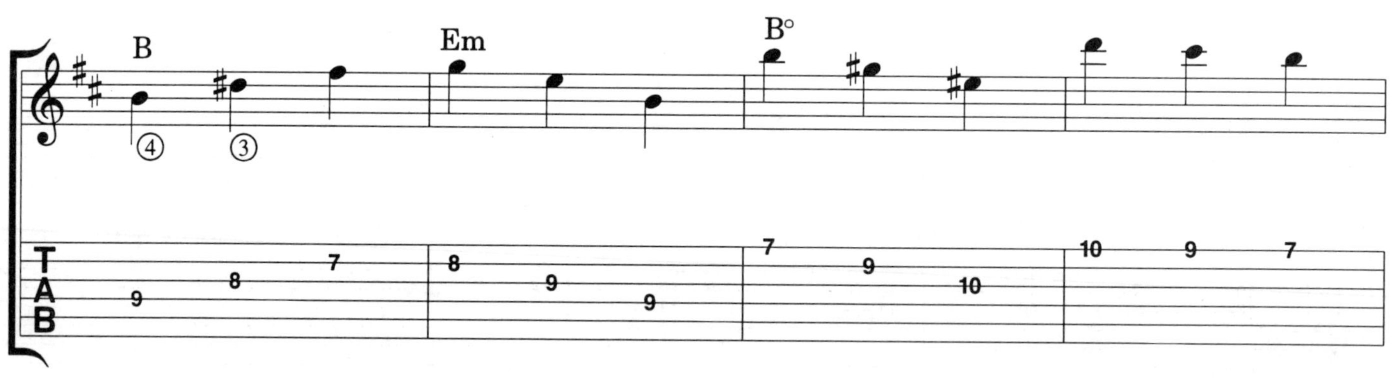
B
Em
B°
TAB

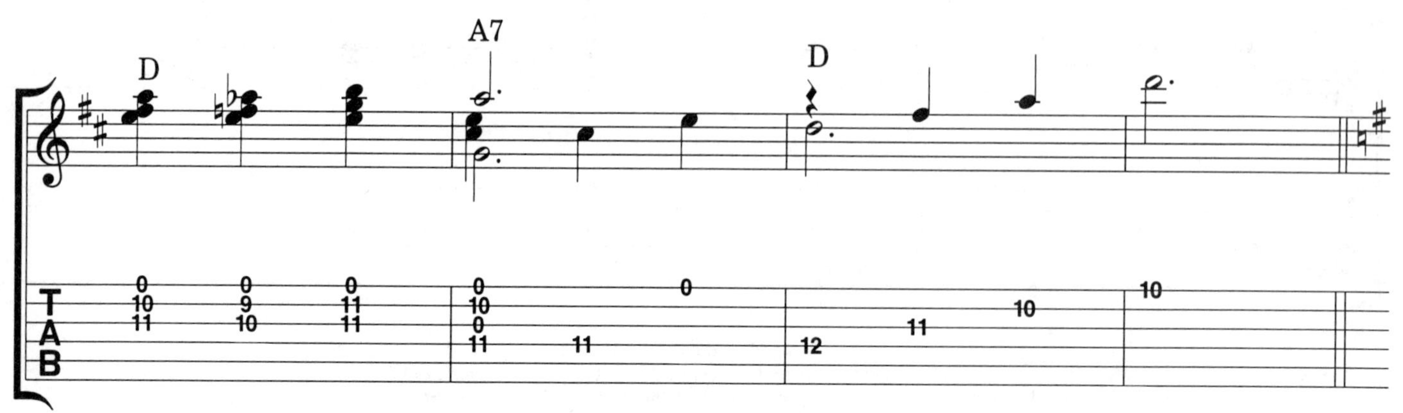
D
A7
D
TAB

Bridge

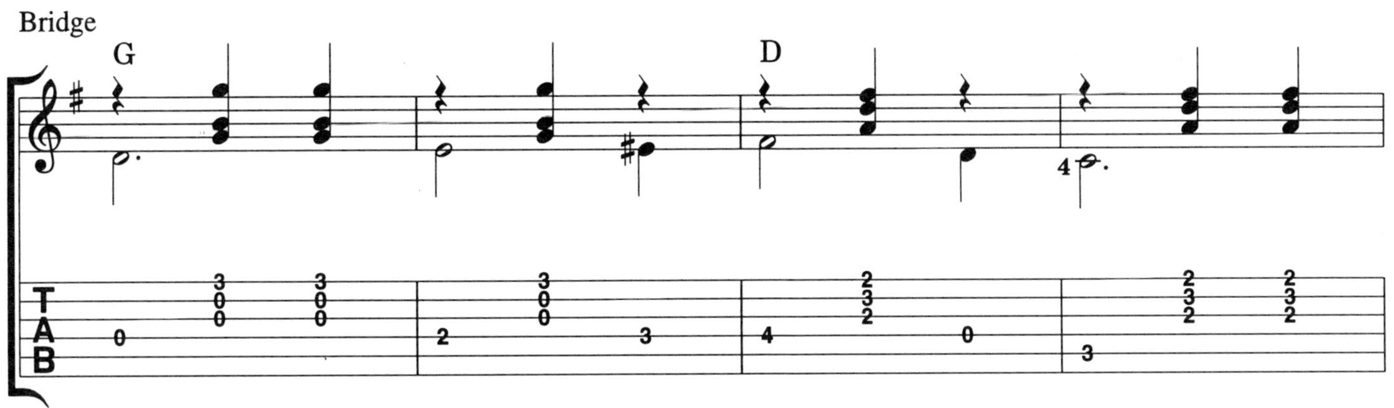

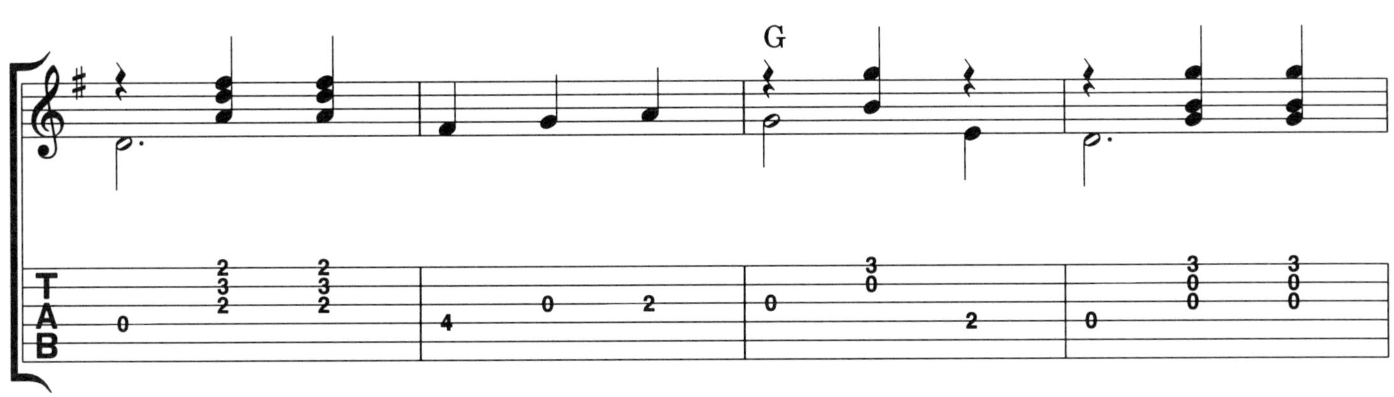

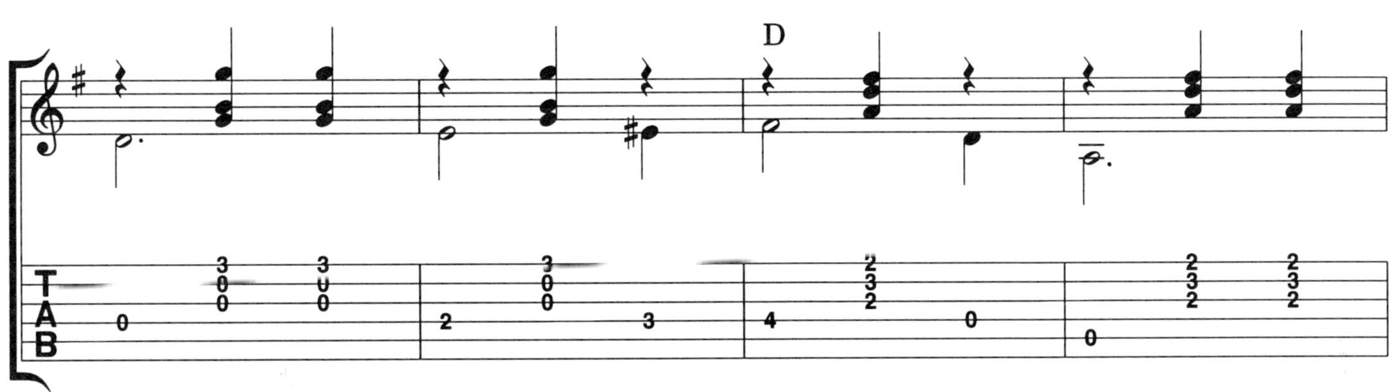

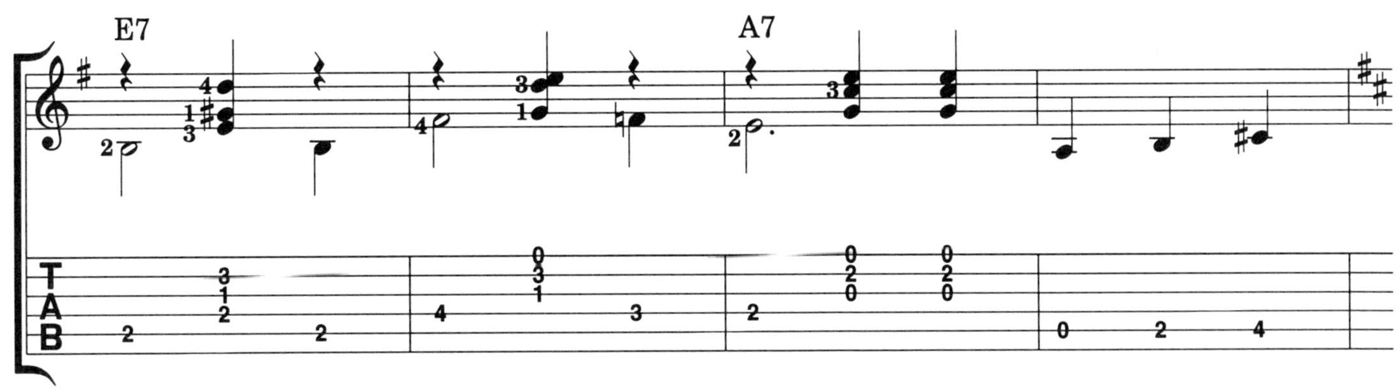

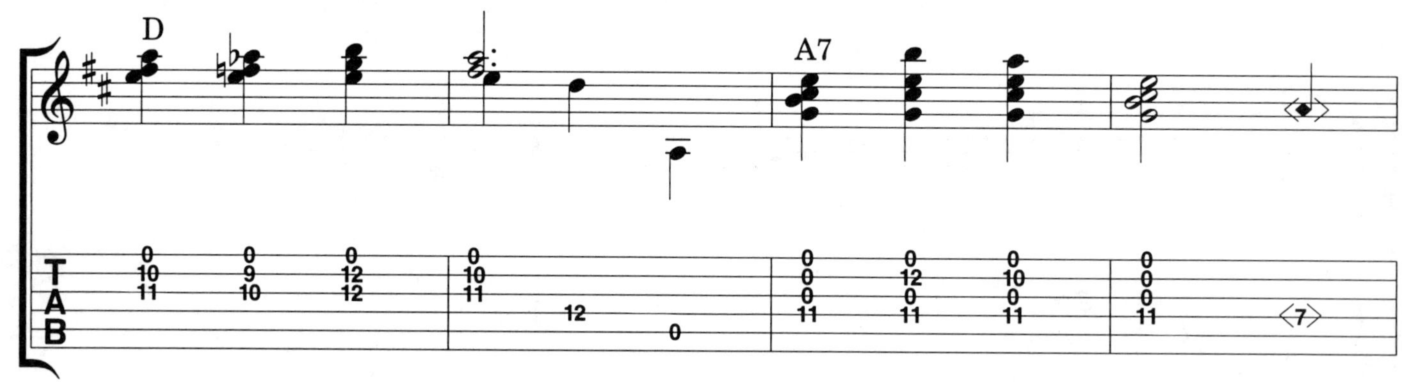
D
A7
TAB

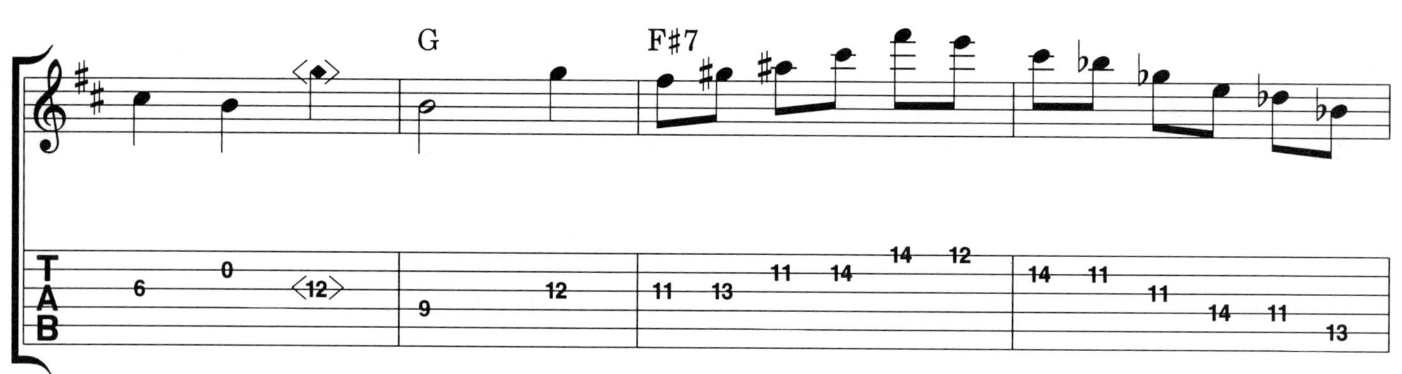
G
F#7
TAB

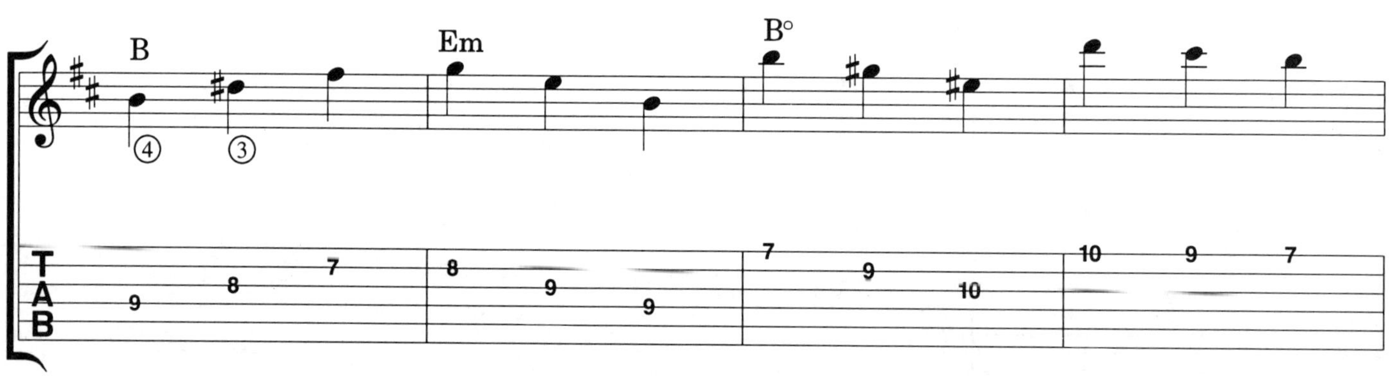
B
Em
B°
TAB

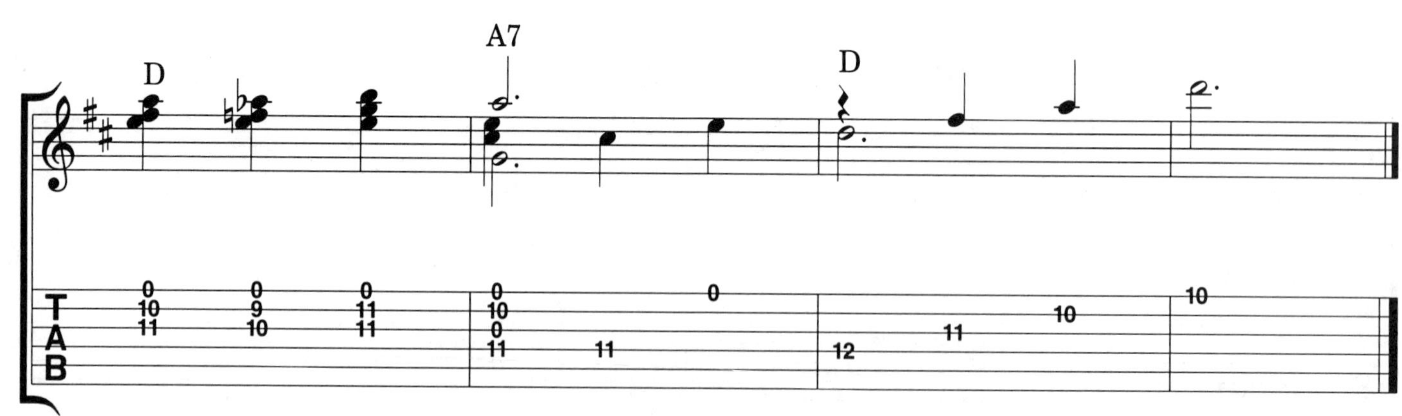
D
A7
D
TAB

DANCE OF THE GOLDENROD

Travis told me that he wrote "Dance of the Goldenrod" when he was a young man. I heard the instrumental version long before the vocal version on Capitol Records. The words appearing on this page are from a 45 RPM record that I believe was released in the early 1950's.

Dance of the Goldenrod

Merle Travis

```
D                              A7
 Darling they're playing that old melody,
                  G    D
 they played when I met you,
                              A
 One summer night, when I first held you tight,
E7                         A7
 Back when our love was new,
D                       A7
 You left the party to go stroll with me,
              G        F♯7
 As down the lane we trod,
B7             Em            E°           G♯°  B♭°
 We heard the sweet music steal through the trees,
    D               A7     D
 The Dance Of The Goldenrod - - - .


 Bridge

G                 D    D7
 Now I'm with you again,
                  G
 Old dreams are new again,
              D
 I'll never be blue again,
E7                     A7
 While you're by my side,
     D
 The dancing has ended,
         A7
 They've called it a day,
                 G          F♯7
 The band leader just gave a nod,
B7              Em           E°   G♯°   B♭°
 We'll keep on dancing as long as they play,
D                   A7    D
 The Dance Of The Goldenrod.
```

Words and music by Merle Travis.